SO-FJU-068

CELESTIAL FORECASTER ®

2008

EVERYONE'S
DAILY ASTROLOGY GUIDE

FEATURING:

- Daily forecasts based on planetary alignments
- Monthly overview of significant aspects
- NEW Lunar aspects guide
- Time zone adjustments chart
- Daily table of aspect influences
- Full year calendar, and
- Built-in ephemeris

Loon Feather Publications
Box 47031 Victoria, B.C.
V9B 5T2 Canada
www.metaphysical.ca/forecaster
email: loonfeather@metaphysical.ca

Acknowledgements:

Thanks to all of you for continuing to make the Celestial Forecaster
a success. Your enthusiasm is what keeps the Forecaster going.
Special thanks to Soror SSH for the great work editing,
to Frater 72 for production.

Printing and Binding: Data reproductions Corporation
Production & cover: Frater 72
Editing: Soror SSH
Inside Graphics: Merx Toledo International
ISBN: 0-9731518-5-4

4

TABLE OF CONTENTS

2008 calendar . . . . inside front
Time zone adjustment chart 5
Definition of terms 6
Glossary of symbols 7
How to use this book 7
Mercury retrograde periods 8
Overview – aspects at a glance 9
Table of aspect influences 18
Lunar aspects guide 22
Detailed forecasts 35
Ephemeris 234
Horoscope blank . . . . inside back

TIME ZONE ADJUSTMENTS

In the *Celestial Forecaster* we show Pacific Time and Eastern Time. Most poeple in North America are familiar with adjusting to one of those two zones. If you use **Central Time**, add two hours to Pacific Time. For **Rocky Mountain Time**, add one hour to Pacific Time. To get **Greenwich Mean Time**, add 8 hours to Pacific Time (PST) or seven hours to Pacific Daylight Time (PDT). If you live outside North America, you can refer to the Time Zone Map below.

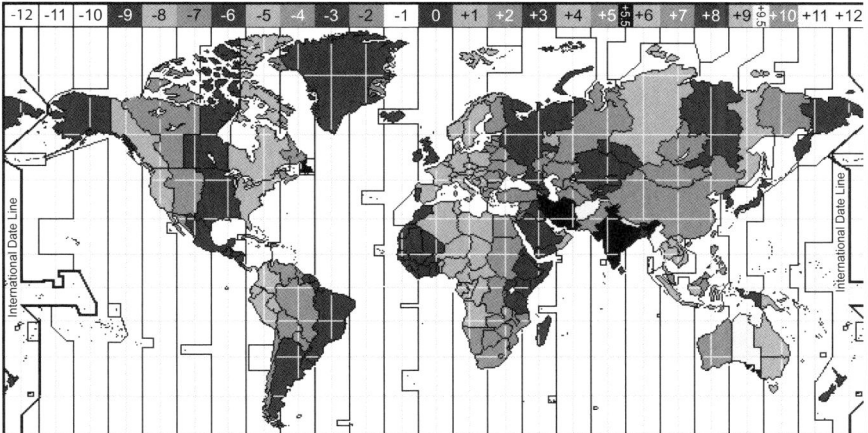

Definitions of Terms

Aspect: Planets are said to be "in aspect" with each other when their location in the sky forms particular angles with the earth which are deemed significant. The main aspects and angles used in this book are as follows:

✳ **Sextile (60°):** The sextile aspect is considered to be favorable, and opens up possibilities and opportunities to work energies out between the two planetary influences.

☐ **Square (90°):** The square aspect indicates a struggle or stress between two planetary influences. This aspect often brings obstacles, or difficulties in our ability to learn and understand. A positive way to address this aspect is to see it as a time when we need to work through our challenges. In these blocks or obstacles a great deal of energy is concentrated. If one acts with caution and care, the energy released by dealing with our challenges can be harnessed, and overcoming the obstacle becomes a personal triumph that leads to growth and the strengthening of character.

△ **Trine (120°):** The most advantageous and harmonious aspect. It is considered to bring the most positive effects. A trine aspect brings gifts, and talents are often realized and acted upon.

☍ **Opposition (180°):** The opposition is the furthest apart the two planets are able to be in their orbits. This aspect brings an acute awareness of the energies that two planetary influences have upon us. It can also bring an overwhelming effect, and handling the polarity often requires awareness and caution.

☌ **Conjunction (0°):** Conjunction is the act of joining, or the state of being joined. When two planets have reached the same degree in the sky this is called a conjunction. It represents the direct confrontation of these energies which will be positive or negative depending on the nature of the planets which are in conjunction.

The Orb: The orb is the area of influence before and after an exact aspect, measured in degrees. The smaller the orb, the closer we are to an exact aspect, and the more strongly we feel the planetary influences. Orbs are divided into two parts: applying and separating. **Applying** — the part of the orb when the planetary aspect is approaching the exact time of reaching its peak. **Separating** — the part of the orb when the planetary aspect is moving away from the peak point of the aspect. Orbs in this book have been calculated using an orb of 6° applying, and 3° separating for all aspects except the sextile, for which 4° applying and 2° separating have been used.

v/c **Void-of-course Moon:** As it travels through a zodiacal sign, the Moon is in aspect with a number of planets. The final major aspect it reaches in a sign marks the time when the Moon goes void-of-course (v/c), meaning it will undergo no further aspects while in that zodiac sign. The Moon will remain void-of-course until it enters the next zodiac sign. While the Moon is void-of-course is a time of less direction and more confusion, particularly on the emotional or mood level.

R **Retrograde:** This occurs when the orbit of a planet causes it to appear to move backward through the sky. It represents a time of moving back over old ground, and inverting influences. The section on Mercury retrograde (page 8) gives examples of how retrogrades work. The Sun and Moon, not being planets, do not go retrograde.

D **Direct:** After a period of retrograde motion, the planet ceases its backward motion and moves forward again through the zodiacal signs. It represents a time of release and forward movement, though the old ground that was just covered in retrograde fashion must be gone over again before any new progress can be made.

Glossary of Astrological Symbols

Aries	♈	Sun	☉	
Taurus	♉	Moon	☽	
Gemini	♊	Mercury	☿	
Cancer	♋	Venus	♀	
Leo	♌	Mars	♂	
Virgo	♍	Jupiter	♃	
Libra	♎	Saturn	♄	
Scorpio	♏	Neptune	♆	
Sagittarius	♐	Uranus	♅	
Capricorn	♑	Pluto	♇	
Aquarius	♒			
Pisces	♓			

How to Use this Book

To adjust for time zones other than Pacific or Eastern USA, use the *Time Zone Adjustments* table on page 5.

For planetary aspectarian and for the phases of the Moon: use the *Overview of Significant Aspects in 2006* found on pages 9 – 17.

For major daily influences at a glance: look at the *Table of Aspect Influences* on pages 18 - 21.

For exact zodiacal position of a planet: use the *Ephemeri*s on pages 248-254.

For daily commentary and analysis: see the main section pages 22-247, including:

Sun Signs: The glyph for the current sun sign is shown in the upper right margin on each page of the daily commentary.

Headers: The date headers at the top of each day show the date, the day of the week, and a selection of notable holidays.

Moon signs and void-of-course periods: Below the date header is the Moon's sign. The Moon's void-of-course period and entry to the next sign is shown chronologically with the day's planetary aspects. The numerous lunar aspects are included this year, and are interpreted in the new *Lunar aspects guide* on pages 22 - 34.

Aspects: Below the Moon's sign in the header is a list of the day's exact planetary and lunar aspects, together with their time of occurrence. Also listed are aspects whose orb of influence is just beginning, and the aspect's date of exact occurrence. Occasionally the aspect information is followed by quotes from famous people.

Mood Watch: Each day features a *Mood Watch* section. This commentary examines key lunar aspects of the day, and explains their likely influence on our moods. Like our moods, these lunar aspects are generally short-lived.

Aspect Analysis: Below the *Mood Watch* section are shown the day's main planetary aspects, the dates their orb of influence occurs, and an in-depth aspect analysis.

7

Mercury retrograde periods: 2008

BEGINS (Mercury goes retrograde)   **ENDS** (Mercury goes direct)

BEGINS (Mercury goes retrograde)	ENDS (Mercury goes direct)
January 28 in Aquarius	February 18 in Aquarius
May 26 in Gemini	June 19 in Gemini
September 24 in Libra	October 15 in Libra

Mercury Retrograde through the Air Signs

Mercury represents how we process information and communicate. Mercury retrograde is a term that describes the orbital shift as Mercury moves backwards through a sign. Technically, it only *appears* to move backwards through the degrees of the zodiac from our geocentric view. Astrologically, this is a time of communication related setbacks, reiterations, or inconsistencies; particularly the first days going into and out of the retrograde period. Mercury retrograde periods take place for an average of three weeks at a time, and will occur on the average of three times a year.

Mercury retrograde is a time of going back over various topics, and repeating or correcting, a lot of information. General misinformation is the most common Those who are not so adept at, or inclined towards paying attention to important details and communicating accurately, can be highly affected by Mercury retrograde, and in a more difficult way. Mercury retrograde periods affect business, media, and news casting. They also affect anyone who relies on the accuracy of information. While Mercury is retrograde, the professionals work hard to correct communication mistakes, no matter how thick the stratosphere is with misinformation.

This year Mercury will go retrograde in the three air signs of the zodiac; Aquarius, Gemini, and Libra. As Mercury goes retrograde through the air signs, communications of an intellectual nature are likely to be easily misinterpreted. It may be very difficult to accurately describe academic concepts, or to communicate technical information which requires logic. It is best not to underestimate the intellect of others when attempting to communicate during Mercury retrograde in the air signs. It will also be good to give some slack with regard to a myriad of simple mistakes which are bound to occur in the recording, printing, and relaying of information. In turn, expect to be confused at times, or perplexed by the intellectual rants of others while receiving messages.

While Mercury is retrograde in Aquarius, communication mistakes and mishaps will be apparent and highlighted in Aquarius related topics such as technology, science, inventions, experiments, and politics. While Mercury is retrograde in the Mercury-ruled sign, Gemini, be careful not to get caught up in gossip disputes and misunderstandings with others. Also, be on the look out for bouts of dyslexia - the switching around of numbers, thought forms, and words, and other communication mistakes in Gemini related activities such as writing, speaking, journalism, and overall communications. While Mercury is retrograde in Libra, miscommunications between friends and loved ones are likely to occur quite frequently, and there may be delays and re-scheduling occurring within the courts and various levels of the justice system.

8

Overview of Significant Aspects in 2008

January

		PST	EST	
2	Mars opposite Pluto	1:23 PM	4:23 PM	
6	Sun sextile Uranus	4:18 AM	7:18 AM	
	Venus square Saturn	5:38 AM	8:38 AM	
7	Mercury enters Aquarius	8:46 PM	11:46 PM	
8	**New Moon in Capricorn**	3:36 AM	6:36 AM	
12	Venus square Uranus	9:22 AM	12:22 PM	
15	**First QTR Moon in Aries**	11:44 AM	2:44 PM	
16	Venus sextile Neptune	11:35 AM	2:35 PM	
19	Venus opposite Mars	7:10 PM	10:10 PM	
20	Sun enters Aquarius	8:43 AM	11:43 AM	
21	Jupiter trine Saturn	1:14 AM	4:14 AM	
22	Full Moon in Leo	5:43 AM	8:43 AM	
	Mercury conjunct Neptune	5:16 PM	8:16 PM	
23	Venus conjunct Pluto	10:58 PM	1:58 AM	(Jan. 24)
24	Venus enters Capricorn	12:05 AM	3:05 AM	
25	PLUTO ENTERS CAPRICORN	6:38 PM	9:38 PM	
28	Mercury goes retrograde	12:31 PM	3:31 PM	
29	Venus trine Saturn	6:18 PM	9:18 PM	
	Last QTR Moon in Scorpio	9:03 PM	12:03 AM	(Jan. 30)
30	Mars goes direct	2:34 PM	5:34 PM	

February

		PST	EST	
1	Venus conjunct Jupiter	3:33 AM	6:33 AM	
2	Mercury conjunct Neptune	4:53 PM	7:53 PM	
	New Moon in Aquarius – solar eclipse	7:44 PM	10:44 PM	
6	Sun conjunct Mercury	10:18 AM	1:18 PM	
	Venus sextile Uranus	6:22 PM	9:22 PM	
10	Sun conjunct Neptune	6:02 PM	9:02 PM	
13	**First QTR Moon in Taurus**	7:33 PM	10:33 PM	
14	Sun trine Mars	8:38 AM	11:38 AM	
17	Venus enters Aquarius	8:22 AM	11:22 AM	
18	Mercury goes direct	6:58 PM	9:58 PM	
	Sun enters Pisces	10:49 PM	1:49 AM	(Feb. 19)
19	Sun sextile Pluto	2:47 PM	5:47 PM	
20	**Full Moon in Virgo - lunar eclipse**	7:30 PM	10:30 PM	

February (Cont'd)

		PST	EST
24	Sun opposite Saturn	1:47 AM	4:47 AM
26	Mercury conjunct Venus	9:56 AM	12:56 PM
28	**Last QTR Moon in Sagittarius**	6:18 PM	9:18 PM

March

		PST	EST
4	Mars enters Cancer	1:57 AM	4:57 AM
6	Sun sextile Jupiter	11:03 AM	2:03 PM
	Venus conjunct Neptune	4:02 PM	7:02 PM
7	Mars opposite Pluto	1:10 AM	4:10 AM
	New Moon in Pisces	9:13 AM	12:13 PM
8	Sun conjunct Uranus	12:19 PM	3:19 PM
9	Mercury conjunct Neptune	12:50 AM (PST)	2:50 AM (EDT)

		PDT	EDT
	DAYLIGHT SAVINGS TIME BEGINS		
	(Turn clocks ahead one hour)	2:00 AM	2:00 AM
12	Venus enters Pisces	3:51 PM	6:51 PM
13	Venus sextile Pluto	12:08 PM	3:08 PM
14	**First QTR Moon in Gemini**	3:46 AM	6:46 AM
	Mars sextile Saturn	2:28 PM	5:28 PM
	Mercury enters Pisces	3:44 PM	6:44 PM
15	Mercury sextile Pluto	10:09 AM	1:09 PM
	Venus opposite Saturn	1:16 PM	4:16 PM
16	Venus trine Mars	1:21 AM	4:21 AM
17	Mercury opposite Saturn	2:46 AM	5:46 AM
18	Mercury trine Mars	4:36 AM	7:36 AM
19	**Vernal Equinox**		
	Sun enters Aries	10:48 PM	1:48 AM (March 20)
21	Sun square Pluto	1:38 AM	4:38 AM
	Full Moon in Libra	11:40 AM	2:40 PM
24	Mercury conjunct Venus	6:23 AM	9:28 AM
27	Mercury sextile Jupiter	11:55 AM	2:55 PM
	Mercury conjunct Uranus	1:06 PM	4:06 PM
28	Venus sextile Jupiter	3:35 PM	6:35 PM
	Venus conjunct Uranus	3:58 PM	6:58 PM
	Jupiter sextile Uranus	5:17 PM	8:17 PM
29	**Last QTR Moon in Capricorn**	2:46 PM	5:46 PM
30	Sun square Mars	12:20 AM	3:20 AM

April

2	Pluto goes retrograde	2:24 AM	5:24 AM
	Mercury enters Aries	10:43 AM	1:43 PM

April (Cont'd)

		PDT	EDT	
3	Mercury square Pluto	1:53 AM	4:53 AM	
5	**New Moon in Aries**	8:54 PM	11:54 PM	
	Venus enters Aries	10:35 PM	1:35 AM	(Apr. 6)
6	Venus square Pluto	8:48 PM	11:48 PM	
10	Sun square Jupiter	7:10 AM	10:10 AM	
	Mercury square Mars	10:12 AM	1:12 PM	
12	**First QTR Moon in Cancer**	11:32 AM	2:32 PM	
13	Sun sextile Neptune	12:30 AM	3:30 AM	
	Mercury square Jupiter	10:48 AM	1:48 PM	
14	Mercury sextile Neptune	3:09 PM	6:09 PM	
16	Sun conjunct Mercury	12:23 AM	3:23 AM	
17	Mercury enters Taurus	2:06 PM	5:06 PM	
18	Mercury trine Pluto	2:21 AM	5:21 AM	
	Mercury trine Saturn	11:10 AM	2:10 PM	
19	Sun enters Taurus	9:51 AM	12:51 PM	
20	**Full Moon in Scorpio**	3:25 AM	6:25 AM	
	Sun trine Pluto	11:56 AM	2:56 PM	
21	Sun trine Saturn	6:04 AM	9:04 AM	
22	Mars trine Uranus	7:47 AM	10:47 AM	
23	Venus square Mars	11:07 AM	2:07 PM	
	Venus square Jupiter	6:35 PM	9:35 PM	
24	Mars opposite Jupiter	6:22 AM	9:22 AM	
25	Venus sextile Neptune	9:33 AM	12:33 PM	
27	Venus sextile Uranus	7:36 PM	10:36 PM	
28	Mercury trine Jupiter	6:40 AM	9:40 AM	
	Last QTR Moon in Aquarius	7:12 AM	10:12 AM	
29	Mercury square Neptune	6:10 AM	9:10 AM	
	Mercury sextile Mars	3:20 PM	6:20 PM	
30	Venus enters Taurus	6:34 AM	9:34 AM	

May

		PDT	EDT
1	**Beltane / May Day**		
	Venus trine Pluto	12:48 AM	3:48 AM
	Venus trine Saturn	3:20 PM	6:20 PM
2	Mercury enters Gemini	1:00 PM	4:00 PM
	Saturn goes direct	8:08 PM	11:08 PM
3	Mercury square Saturn	12:51 PM	3:51 PM
5	**New Moon in Taurus**	5:18 AM	8:18 AM
9	Jupiter goes retrograde	5:12 AM	8:12 AM
	Mars enters Leo	1:19 PM	4:19 PM

May (Cont'd)

		PDT	EDT	
11	**First QTR Moon in Leo**	8:47 PM	11:47 PM	
	Sun sextile Uranus	9:32 PM	12:32 PM	(May 12)
12	Sun trine Jupiter	10:28 AM	1:28 PM	
14	Sun square Neptune	8:50 AM	11:50 AM	
18	Venus sextile Uranus	4:22 AM	7:22 AM	
	Venus trine Jupiter	8:17 AM	11:17 AM	
19	**Full Moon in Scorpio**	7:11 PM	10:11 PM	
	Venus square Neptune	11:27 PM	2:27 AM	(May 20)
20	Sun enters Gemini	9:00 AM	12:00 PM	
21	Jupiter sextile Uranus	11:03 AM	2:03 PM	
22	Sun square Saturn	11:25 AM	2:25 PM	
24	Venus enters Gemini	3:51 PM	6:51 PM	
26	Mercury goes retrograde	8:48 AM	11:48 AM	
	Neptune goes retrograde	9:15 AM	12:15 PM	
	Venus square Saturn	10:10 AM	1:10 PM	
27	**Last QTR Moon in Pisces**	7:56 PM	10:56 PM	

June

		PDT	EDT	
3	**New Moon in Gemini**	12:22 PM	3:22 PM	
6	Venus sextile Mars	1:15 AM	4:15 AM	
7	Sun conjunct Mercury	8:26 AM	11:26 AM	
	Mercury conjunct Venus	2:03 PM	5:03 PM	
8	Mercury sextile Mars	11:28 AM	2:28 PM	
	Sun conjunct Venus	9:19 PM	12:19 AM	(June 9)
10	**First QTR Moon in Virgo**	8:04 AM	11:04 AM	
12	Venus square Uranus	12:38 AM	3:38 AM	
	Sun square Uranus	10:24 PM	1:24 AM	(June 13)
13	Venus trine Neptune	7:53 AM	10:53 AM	
	Pluto enters Sagittarius	10:12 PM	1:12 AM	(June 14)
14	Sun trine Neptune	2:01 PM	5:01 PM	
17	Venus opposite Pluto	11:45 PM	2:45 AM	(June 18)
18	Venus enters Cancer	1:48 AM	4:48 AM	
	Full Moon in Sagittarius	10:30 AM	1:30 PM	
19	Mercury goes direct	7:32 AM	10:32 AM	
	Sun opposite Pluto	12:42 PM	3:42 PM	
	Summer Solstice			
	Sun enters Cancer	4:59 PM	7:59 PM	

June (Cont'd)

		PDT	EDT	
21	Venus sextile Saturn	2:14 AM	5:14 AM	
	Mars opposite Neptune	8:31 AM	11:31 AM	
24	Sun sextile Saturn	10:00 PM	1:00 AM	(June 25)
26	**Last QTR Moon in Aries**	5:09 AM	8:09 AM	
	Uranus goes retrograde	5:01 PM	8:01 PM	
30	Mars trine Pluto	3:56 PM	6:56 PM	

July

		PDT	EDT	
1	Mars enters Virgo	9:21 AM	12:21 PM	
2	**New Moon in Cancer**	7:18 PM	10:18 PM	
	Venus opposite Jupiter	10:17 PM	1:17 AM	(July 3)
5	Mercury square Uranus	4:05 AM	7:05 AM	
6	Mercury trine Neptune	3:44 AM	6:44 AM	
	Venus trine Uranus	11:31 AM	2:31 PM	
9	Sun opposite Jupiter	12:39 AM	3:39 AM	
	First QTR Moon in Libra	9:35 PM	12:35 PM	(July 10)
10	Mercury opposite Pluto	2:48 AM	5:48 AM	
	Mars conjunct Saturn	11:11 AM	2:11 PM	
	Mercury enters Cancer	1:16 PM	4:16 PM	
12	Venus enters Leo	11:38 AM	2:38 PM	
14	Mercury sextile Saturn	1:34 AM	4:34 AM	
	Sun trine Uranus	8:03 AM	11:03 AM	
15	Mercury sextile Mars	2:09 PM	5:09 PM	
18	**Full Moon in Capricorn**	12:58 AM	3:58 AM	
19	Mercury opposite Jupiter	12:53 PM	3:53 PM	
22	Sun enters Leo	3:54 AM	6:54 AM	
	Mercury trine Uranus	2:09 PM	5:09 PM	
25	**Last QTR Moon in Taurus**	11:40 AM	2:40 PM	
26	Mars trine Jupiter	3:04 PM	6:04 PM	
29	Sun conjunct Mercury	1:04 PM	4:04 PM	
31	Venus opposite Neptune	9:29 AM	12:29 PM	

August

		PDT	EDT	
1	**Lammas / Lughnassad**			
	New Moon in Leo – total solar eclipse	3:13 AM	6:13 AM	
4	Venus trine Pluto	9:53 PM	12:53 AM	(Aug. 5)
5	Venus enters Virgo	9:19 PM	12:19 AM	(Aug. 6)

13

August (Cont'd)

		PDT	EDT	
6	Mars opposite Uranus	11:37 AM	2:37 PM	
	Mercury opposite Neptune	11:40 AM	2:40 PM	
8	**First QTR Moon in Scorpio**	1:20 PM	4:20 PM	
9	Mercury trine Pluto	11:18 AM	2:18 PM	
10	Mercury enters Virgo	3:53 AM	6:53 AM	
13	Venus conjunct Saturn	10:03 AM	1:03 PM	
15	Sun opposite Neptune	12:42 AM	3:42 AM	
	Mercury conjunct Saturn	1:00 PM	4:00 PM	
16	**Full Moon in Aquarius**	2:15 PM	5:15 PM	
	Venus trine Jupiter	5:15 PM	8:15 PM	
	Mars square Pluto	11:15 PM	2:15 AM	(Aug. 17)
17	Mercury trine Jupiter	6:23 PM	9:23 PM	
19	Mars enters Libra	3:03 AM	6:03 AM	
20	Sun trine Pluto	11:50 PM	2:50 AM	(Aug. 21)
21	Mercury conjunct Venus	8:45 AM	11:45 AM	
22	Sun enters Virgo	11:02 AM	2:02 PM	
	Mercury opposite Uranus	11:13 PM	2:13 AM	(Aug. 23)
23	Venus opposite Uranus	8:48 AM	11:48 AM	
	Last QTR Moon in Gemini	4:49 PM	7:49 PM	
27	Mercury square Pluto	6:37 PM	9:37 PM	
28	Mercury enters Libra	7:52 PM	10:52 PM	
29	Venus square Pluto	2:51 AM	5:51 AM	
30	Venus enters Libra	7:41 AM	10:41 AM	
	New Moon in Virgo	12:58 PM	3:58 PM	

September

3	Sun conjunct Saturn	6:59 PM	9:59 PM	
4	Sun trine Jupiter	10:41 AM	1:41 PM	
7	**First QTR Moon in Sagittarius**	7:04 AM	10:04 AM	
	Mars square Jupiter	2:05 PM	5:05 PM	
	Jupiter goes direct	9:17 PM	12:17 AM	(Sep. 8)
	Mercury square Jupiter	10:10 PM	1:10 AM	(Sep. 8)
8	Mercury conjunct Mars	10:47 AM	1:47 PM	
	Jupiter trine Saturn	4:18 PM	7:18 PM	
	Pluto goes direct	8:14 PM	11:14 PM	
9	Venus square Jupiter	1:12 PM	4:12 PM	
11	Venus conjunct Mars	7:05 PM	10:05 PM	

14

September (Cont'd)

		PDT	EDT	
12	Sun opposite Uranus	7:21 PM	10:21 PM	
14	Mercury conjunct Venus	6:35 PM	9:35 PM	
15	**Full Moon in Pisces**	2:12 AM	5:12 AM	
18	Venus trine Neptune	6:58 AM	9:58 AM	
19	Mercury trine Neptune	8:24 PM	11:24 PM	
20	Sun square Pluto	8:45 PM	11:45 PM	
21	Mars trine Neptune	7:56 PM	10:56 PM	
	Last QTR Moon in Gemini	10:04 PM	1:04 AM	(Sep. 22)
22	**Autumnal Equinox**			
	Sun Enters Libra	8:45 AM	11:45 AM	
	Venus sextile Pluto	3:24 PM	6:24 PM	
23	Mercury conjunct Mars	3:44 AM	6:44 AM	
24	Mercury goes retrograde	12:17 AM	3:17 AM	
28	Mercury trine Neptune	5:19 AM	8:19 AM	
29	**New Moon in Libra**	1:13 AM	4:13 AM	

October

1	Mars sextile Pluto	9:01 PM	12:01 AM	(Oct. 2)
3	Mars enters Scorpio	9:33 PM	12:33 AM	(Oct. 4)
5	Venus sextile Jupiter	1:22 AM	4:22 AM	
6	Sun square Jupiter	9:52 AM	12:52 PM	
	Sun conjunct Mercury	1:53 PM	4:53 PM	
	Mercury square Jupiter	4:46 PM	7:46 PM	
	Venus sextile Saturn	10:42 PM	1:42 AM	(Oct. 7)
7	**First QTR Moon in Capricorn**	2:03 AM	5:03 AM	
9	Venus trine Uranus	10:47 PM	1:47 AM	(Oct. 10)
11	Venus square Neptune	1:20 PM	4:20 PM	
14	Sun trine Neptune	6:18 AM	9:18 AM	
	Full Moon in Aries	1:01 PM	4:01 PM	
15	Mercury goes direct	1:06 PM	4:06 PM	
	Venus enters Sagittarius	11:30 AM	2:30 PM	
21	**Last QTR Moon in Cancer**	4:55 AM	7:55 AM	
	Sun sextile Pluto	5:23 PM	8:23 PM	
22	Sun enters Scorpio	6:08 PM	9:08 PM	
26	Mercury square Jupiter	5:13 AM	8:13 AM	
27	Mars sextile Jupiter	1:29 PM	4:29 PM	
28	**New Moon in Scorpio**	4:14 PM	7:14 PM	

October (Cont'd)

		PDT	EDT	
29	Mercury trine Neptune	11:10 PM	2:10 AM	
30	Mars sextile Saturn	8:51 PM	11:51 PM	
31	**All Hallows (Halloween) / Samhain / Witches' New Year**			
31	Mars trine Uranus	1:32 PM	4:32 PM	

November

		PDT	EDT	
1	Neptune goes direct	11:39 PM	2:39 AM	(Nov. 2)
2	**DAYLIGHT SAVINGS TIME ENDS**	**PST**	**EST**	
	(Turn clocks back one hour at 2:00 a.m.)	2:00 AM	2:00 AM	
3	Venus square Saturn	12:41 AM	3:41 AM	
	Venus square Uranus	3:18 AM	6:18 AM	
	Mercury sextile Pluto	9:31 PM	12:31 AM	(Nov. 4)
	Mars square Neptune	11:44 PM	2:44 AM	(Nov. 4)
4	Saturn opposite Uranus	5:35 AM	8:35 AM	
	Mercury enters Scorpio	7:59 AM	10:59 AM	
5	Venus sextile Neptune	4:56 AM	7:56 AM	
	First QTR Moon in Aquarius	8:02 PM	11:02 PM	
10	Sun sextile Jupiter	12:54 AM	3:54 AM	
	Sun trine Uranus	1:21 PM	4:21 PM	
11	Sun sextile Saturn	6:24 AM	9:24 AM	
	Venus conjunct Pluto	9:54 PM	12:54 AM	(Nov. 12)
12	Venus enters Capricorn	7:24 AM	10:24 AM	
	Jupiter sextile Uranus	9:39 PM	12:39 AM	(Nov. 13)
	Full Moon in Taurus	10:16 PM	1:16 AM	(Nov. 13)
13	Sun square Neptune	4:31 AM	7:31 AM	
15	Mercury trine Uranus	10:36 PM	1:36 AM	(Nov. 16)
16	Mars enters Sagittarius	12:26 AM	3:26 AM	
	Mercury sextile Jupiter	8:00 AM	11:00 AM	
	Mercury sextile Saturn	4:27 PM	7:27 PM	
17	Mercury square Neptune	3:30 PM	6:30 PM	
19	**Last QTR Moon in Leo**	1:31 PM	4:31 PM	
21	Jupiter trine Saturn	4:12 AM	7:12 AM	
	Sun enters Sagittarius	3:44 PM	6:44 PM	
22	Mercury enters Sagittarius	11:09 PM	2:09 AM	(Nov. 23)
25	Sun conjunct Mercury	8:52 AM	11:52 AM	
26	Pluto enters Capricorn	5:02 PM	8:02 PM	

November (Cont'd)

		PST	EST	
27	Uranus goes direct	8:09 AM	11:09 AM	
	New Moon in Sagittarius	8:54 AM	11:54 AM	
28	Venus sextile Uranus	1:20 AM	4:20 AM	
	Mercury conjunct Mars	7:39 PM	10:39 PM	
29	Venus trine Saturn	8:36 PM	11:36 PM	

December

		PST	EST	
1	Venus conjunct Jupiter	12:44 AM	3:44 AM	
4	Mercury square Uranus	9:52 PM	12:52 PM	
5	**First QTR Moon in Pisces**	1:24 PM	4:24 PM	
	Sun conjunct Mars	2:03 PM	5:03 PM	
6	Mercury square Saturn	11:13 AM	2:13 PM	
	Mercury sextile Neptune	8:37 PM	11:37 PM	
7	Venus enters Aquarius	3:36 PM	6:36 PM	
10	Sun square Uranus	4:03 AM	7:03 AM	
11	Mars square Uranus	10:50 PM	1:50 AM	(Nov. 12)
12	**Full Moon in Gemini**	8:37 AM	11:38 AM	
	Mercury enters Capricorn	2:12 AM	5:12 AM	
	Mercury conjunct Pluto	10:42 AM	1:42 PM	
	Sun square Saturn	6:19 PM	9:19 PM	
13	Sun sextile Neptune	6:05 AM	9:05 AM	
15	Mars square Saturn	2:46 PM	5:46 PM	
16	Mars sextile Neptune	6:15 AM	9:15 AM	
19	**Last QTR Moon in Virgo**	2:30 AM	5:30 AM	
21	**Winter Solstice**			
	Sun enters Capricorn	4:03 AM	7:03 AM	
22	Sun conjunct Pluto	1:23 AM	4:23 AM	
24	**Christmas Eve**			
	Mercury sextile Uranus	8:33 AM	11:33 AM	
26	Mercury trine Saturn	3:38 AM	6:38 AM	
	Mars enters Capricorn	11:30 PM	2:30 AM	(Nov. 27)
27	**New Moon in Capricorn**	4:22 AM	7:22 AM	
	Venus conjunct Neptune	4:28 AM	7:28 AM	
28	Mars conjunct Pluto	12:01 PM	3:01 PM	
31	**New Year's Eve**			
	Mercury conjunct Jupiter	3:41 AM	6:41 AM	
	Saturn goes retrograde	10:08 AM	1:08 PM	

TABLE OF ASPECT INFLUENCES

JANUARY 2008

1	2	3	4	5	6	7	8	9	10	11	12	13	14	15	16	17	18	19	20	21	22	23	24	25	26	27	28	29	30	31

Aspects:
- ♂☍♀
- ♃△♄
- ♀□♄   ♀☍♂   ♂△♇
- ♀✶♇   ♀☌♀   ♀☌♃
- ♀□♅   ♀△♄
- ☉△♄   ☿△♂
- ☉✶♅   ☿☌♆
- ☉☌♃

FEBRUARY 2008

1	2	3	4	5	6	7	8	9	10	11	12	13	14	15	16	17	18	19	20	21	22	23	24	25	26	27	28

Aspects:
- ♂△♇   ♂☍♀
- ♀☌♃
- ☿△♂   ♀✶♅   ♀☌♀
- ☿☌♆   ☉△♂
- ☉☌♀   ☉✶♀
- ☉☌♆   ☉☍♄

MARCH 2008

1	2	3	4	5	6	7	8	9	10	11	12	13	14	15	16	17	18	19	20	21	22	23	24	25	26	27	28	29	30	31

Aspects:
- ♄△♀
- ♃✶♅
- ♂☍♀   ♀✶♃
- ♂✶♄   ♀☌♅
- ♀☌♆   ♀△♂   ☿✶♃
- ♀✶♃
- ☿☌♆   ♀☍♄   ♂☌♅
- ☉✶♃   ☿△♂   ☉□♂
- ☿✶♀
- ☉☌♅   ♀☍♄
- ☿☌♀
- ☉□♀

TABLE OF ASPECT INFLUENCES

APRIL 2008

<table>
<tr><td>1</td><td>2</td><td>3</td><td>4</td><td>5</td><td>6</td><td>7</td><td>8</td><td>9</td><td>10</td><td>11</td><td>12</td><td>13</td><td>14</td><td>15</td><td>16</td><td>17</td><td>18</td><td>19</td><td>20</td><td>21</td><td>22</td><td>23</td><td>24</td><td>25</td><td>26</td><td>27</td><td>28</td><td>29</td><td>30</td></tr>
<tr><td colspan="30">♄△♇</td></tr>
<tr><td colspan="30">♃✶♅</td></tr>
<tr><td colspan="3"></td><td colspan="6">♀□♇</td><td colspan="7"></td><td colspan="14">♂☍♃</td></tr>
<tr><td colspan="14"></td><td colspan="14">♂△♅</td><td colspan="2"></td></tr>
<tr><td colspan="10"></td><td colspan="4">☿□♃</td><td colspan="6"></td><td colspan="6">♀□♃</td><td colspan="1"></td><td colspan="3">♀△♇</td></tr>
<tr><td colspan="4">☿□♇</td><td colspan="3"></td><td colspan="5">☿□♂</td><td colspan="6"></td><td colspan="9">♀□♂</td><td colspan="3"></td></tr>
<tr><td colspan="12"></td><td colspan="3">☿✶♆</td><td colspan="1"></td><td colspan="3">☿△♄</td><td colspan="3"></td><td colspan="5">♀✶♆</td><td colspan="1"></td><td colspan="2">♀△♄</td></tr>
<tr><td colspan="5"></td><td colspan="8">☉□♃</td><td colspan="2"></td><td colspan="4">☿△♇</td><td colspan="6"></td><td colspan="4">☿△♃</td><td colspan="1"></td></tr>
<tr><td colspan="12"></td><td colspan="6">☉☌☿</td><td colspan="9"></td><td colspan="3">☿✶♂</td></tr>
<tr><td colspan="9"></td><td colspan="6">☉✶♆</td><td colspan="1"></td><td colspan="7">☉△♇</td><td colspan="3"></td><td colspan="4">☿□♆</td></tr>
<tr><td colspan="25"></td><td colspan="3">☿✶♅</td><td colspan="2"></td></tr>
<tr><td colspan="17"></td><td colspan="7">☉△♄</td><td colspan="6"></td></tr>
</table>

MAY 2008

<table>
<tr><td>1</td><td>2</td><td>3</td><td>4</td><td>5</td><td>6</td><td>7</td><td>8</td><td>9</td><td>10</td><td>11</td><td>12</td><td>13</td><td>14</td><td>15</td><td>16</td><td>17</td><td>18</td><td>19</td><td>20</td><td>21</td><td>22</td><td>23</td><td>24</td><td>25</td><td>26</td><td>27</td><td>28</td><td>29</td><td>30</td><td>31</td></tr>
<tr><td colspan="31">♄△♇</td></tr>
<tr><td colspan="31">♃✶♅</td></tr>
<tr><td colspan="3">♀△♇</td><td colspan="11"></td><td colspan="6">♀△♃</td><td colspan="11"></td></tr>
<tr><td colspan="4">♀△♄</td><td colspan="12"></td><td colspan="6">♀□♆</td><td colspan="9"></td></tr>
<tr><td colspan="5">☿□♄</td><td colspan="10"></td><td colspan="4">♀✶♅</td><td colspan="3"></td><td colspan="6">♀□♄</td><td colspan="3"></td></tr>
<tr><td colspan="8"></td><td colspan="7">☉△♃</td><td colspan="7"></td><td colspan="7">☿△♆</td><td colspan="2"></td></tr>
<tr><td colspan="17"></td><td colspan="14">☿□♅</td></tr>
<tr><td colspan="10"></td><td colspan="7">☉□♆</td><td colspan="1"></td><td colspan="7">☉□♄</td><td colspan="3"></td><td colspan="3">☉✶♂</td></tr>
<tr><td colspan="8"></td><td colspan="6">☉✶♅</td><td colspan="13"></td><td colspan="4">☉☌♀</td></tr>
</table>

JUNE 2008

<table>
<tr><td>1</td><td>2</td><td>3</td><td>4</td><td>5</td><td>6</td><td>7</td><td>8</td><td>9</td><td>10</td><td>11</td><td>12</td><td>13</td><td>14</td><td>15</td><td>16</td><td>17</td><td>18</td><td>19</td><td>20</td><td>21</td><td>22</td><td>23</td><td>24</td><td>25</td><td>26</td><td>27</td><td>28</td><td>29</td><td>30</td></tr>
<tr><td colspan="11">♄△♇</td><td colspan="4"></td><td colspan="11">♂☍♆</td><td colspan="4"></td></tr>
<tr><td colspan="12">♃✶♅</td><td colspan="2"></td><td colspan="6">♀☍♇</td><td colspan="4"></td><td colspan="6">♂△♇</td></tr>
<tr><td colspan="1"></td><td colspan="8">♀✶♂</td><td colspan="6">♀△♆</td><td colspan="3"></td><td colspan="4">♀✶♄</td><td colspan="8"></td></tr>
<tr><td colspan="8"></td><td colspan="6">♀□♅</td><td colspan="16"></td></tr>
<tr><td colspan="5"></td><td colspan="5">☿✶♂</td><td colspan="20"></td></tr>
<tr><td colspan="3">☿□♅</td><td colspan="1"></td><td colspan="5">☿☌♀</td><td colspan="7"></td><td colspan="7">☉☍♇</td><td colspan="7"></td></tr>
<tr><td colspan="9">☉✶♂</td><td colspan="1"></td><td colspan="7">☉△♆</td><td colspan="4"></td><td colspan="6">☉✶♄</td><td colspan="3"></td></tr>
<tr><td colspan="4"></td><td colspan="5">☉☌☿</td><td colspan="21"></td></tr>
<tr><td colspan="8"></td><td colspan="8">☉□♅</td><td colspan="14"></td></tr>
<tr><td colspan="19">☉☌♀</td><td colspan="11"></td></tr>
</table>

TABLE OF ASPECT INFLUENCES

JULY 2008

<table>
<tr><td>1</td><td>2</td><td>3</td><td>4</td><td>5</td><td>6</td><td>7</td><td>8</td><td>9</td><td>10</td><td>11</td><td>12</td><td>13</td><td>14</td><td>15</td><td>16</td><td>17</td><td>18</td><td>19</td><td>20</td><td>21</td><td>22</td><td>23</td><td>24</td><td>25</td><td>26</td><td>27</td><td>28</td><td>29</td><td>30</td><td>31</td></tr>
<tr><td colspan="5">♂△♇</td><td></td><td></td><td></td><td></td><td></td><td></td><td></td><td></td><td></td><td></td><td></td><td></td><td></td><td></td><td></td><td></td><td colspan="9">♂△♃</td><td></td></tr>
<tr><td colspan="5">♀☍♃</td><td></td><td></td><td></td><td></td><td></td><td></td><td></td><td colspan="5">☿✶♂</td><td></td><td></td><td></td><td></td><td></td><td></td><td></td><td></td><td></td><td></td><td colspan="4">♀☍♆</td></tr>
<tr><td></td><td></td><td></td><td colspan="5">♀△♅</td><td></td><td></td><td></td><td></td><td></td><td></td><td></td><td></td><td></td><td colspan="3">☿☍♃</td><td></td><td></td><td></td><td></td><td></td><td></td><td></td><td></td><td></td><td></td><td></td></tr>
<tr><td></td><td></td><td colspan="6">☿△♆</td><td></td><td></td><td></td><td colspan="4">☿✶♄</td><td></td><td></td><td></td><td></td><td></td><td colspan="3">☿△♅</td><td></td><td></td><td></td><td></td><td></td><td></td><td></td><td></td></tr>
<tr><td></td><td colspan="6">☿□♅</td><td colspan="4">☿☍♇</td><td></td><td></td><td></td><td></td><td></td><td></td><td></td><td></td><td></td><td></td><td></td><td></td><td></td><td></td><td colspan="6">☉☌☿</td></tr>
<tr><td></td><td></td><td></td><td></td><td></td><td colspan="6">☉☍♃</td><td></td><td></td><td></td><td></td><td></td><td></td><td></td><td></td><td></td><td></td><td></td><td></td><td></td><td></td><td></td><td></td><td></td><td></td><td></td><td></td></tr>
<tr><td></td><td></td><td></td><td></td><td></td><td></td><td></td><td></td><td></td><td></td><td colspan="7">☉△♅</td><td></td><td></td><td></td><td></td><td></td><td></td><td></td><td></td><td></td><td></td><td></td><td></td><td></td><td></td></tr>
</table>

AUGUST 2008

<table>
<tr><td>1</td><td>2</td><td>3</td><td>4</td><td>5</td><td>6</td><td>7</td><td>8</td><td>9</td><td>10</td><td>11</td><td>12</td><td>13</td><td>14</td><td>15</td><td>16</td><td>17</td><td>18</td><td>19</td><td>20</td><td>21</td><td>22</td><td>23</td><td>24</td><td>25</td><td>26</td><td>27</td><td>28</td><td>29</td><td>30</td><td>31</td></tr>
<tr><td colspan="11">♂☍♅</td><td></td><td></td><td></td><td></td><td></td><td></td><td></td><td></td><td colspan="12">♃△♄</td></tr>
<tr><td colspan="2">♀☍♆</td><td></td><td></td><td></td><td></td><td></td><td></td><td></td><td></td><td></td><td colspan="10">♂□♇</td><td></td><td></td><td></td><td></td><td></td><td></td><td></td><td></td><td></td><td></td></tr>
<tr><td></td><td colspan="6">♀△♇</td><td></td><td></td><td></td><td></td><td></td><td></td><td colspan="5">♀△♃</td><td></td><td></td><td></td><td></td><td></td><td></td><td></td><td colspan="6">♀□♇</td></tr>
<tr><td></td><td></td><td></td><td colspan="4">☿☍♆</td><td></td><td></td><td colspan="7">♀☌♄</td><td></td><td></td><td></td><td colspan="6">♀☍♅</td><td></td><td></td><td></td><td></td><td></td><td></td></tr>
<tr><td></td><td></td><td></td><td></td><td></td><td></td><td colspan="5">☿△♇</td><td></td><td></td><td></td><td colspan="5">☿△♃</td><td></td><td></td><td></td><td></td><td></td><td colspan="5">☿□♇</td><td></td><td></td></tr>
<tr><td></td><td></td><td></td><td></td><td></td><td></td><td></td><td></td><td></td><td></td><td></td><td></td><td colspan="5">☿☌♄</td><td></td><td></td><td></td><td colspan="4">☿☍♅</td><td></td><td></td><td></td><td></td><td></td><td></td><td></td></tr>
<tr><td></td><td></td><td></td><td></td><td></td><td></td><td></td><td></td><td></td><td></td><td></td><td></td><td></td><td colspan="18">☿☌♀</td></tr>
<tr><td></td><td></td><td></td><td></td><td></td><td></td><td></td><td></td><td></td><td></td><td colspan="8">☉☍♆</td><td></td><td></td><td></td><td></td><td></td><td></td><td></td><td></td><td></td><td></td><td></td><td></td><td></td></tr>
<tr><td></td><td></td><td></td><td></td><td></td><td></td><td></td><td></td><td></td><td></td><td></td><td></td><td></td><td></td><td></td><td></td><td colspan="8">☉△♇</td><td></td><td></td><td></td><td></td><td></td><td></td><td></td></tr>
</table>

SEPTEMBER 2008

<table>
<tr><td>1</td><td>2</td><td>3</td><td>4</td><td>5</td><td>6</td><td>7</td><td>8</td><td>9</td><td>10</td><td>11</td><td>12</td><td>13</td><td>14</td><td>15</td><td>16</td><td>17</td><td>18</td><td>19</td><td>20</td><td>21</td><td>22</td><td>23</td><td>24</td><td>25</td><td>26</td><td>27</td><td>28</td><td>29</td><td>30</td></tr>
<tr><td colspan="30">♃△♄</td></tr>
<tr><td></td><td colspan="11">♂□♃</td><td></td><td></td><td></td><td></td><td colspan="10">♂△♆</td><td></td><td colspan="3">♂✶♇</td></tr>
<tr><td></td><td></td><td></td><td></td><td></td><td></td><td colspan="5">♀□♃</td><td></td><td colspan="6">♀△♆</td><td></td><td></td><td></td><td></td><td></td><td></td><td></td><td></td><td></td><td></td><td></td><td></td></tr>
<tr><td></td><td></td><td></td><td></td><td></td><td colspan="12">♀☌♂</td><td></td><td></td><td colspan="5">♀✶♇</td><td></td><td></td><td></td><td></td><td></td><td></td></tr>
<tr><td></td><td></td><td></td><td></td><td colspan="6">☿□♃</td><td></td><td></td><td></td><td></td><td></td><td></td><td></td><td></td><td></td><td></td><td></td><td></td><td></td><td></td><td></td><td></td><td></td><td></td><td></td><td></td></tr>
<tr><td></td><td colspan="25">☿☌♂</td><td></td><td></td><td></td><td></td></tr>
<tr><td></td><td></td><td></td><td></td><td></td><td></td><td></td><td></td><td></td><td></td><td></td><td></td><td></td><td colspan="17">☿△♆</td></tr>
<tr><td colspan="19">☿☌♀</td><td></td><td></td><td></td><td></td><td></td><td></td><td></td><td></td><td></td><td></td><td></td></tr>
<tr><td colspan="7">☉△♃</td><td></td><td colspan="7">☉☍♅</td><td></td><td colspan="7">☉□♇</td><td></td><td></td><td></td><td></td><td></td><td></td><td></td></tr>
<tr><td colspan="7">☉☌♄</td><td></td><td></td><td></td><td></td><td></td><td></td><td></td><td></td><td></td><td></td><td></td><td></td><td></td><td></td><td></td><td></td><td></td><td></td><td></td><td></td><td></td><td></td><td></td></tr>
</table>

TABLE OF ASPECT INFLUENCES

OCTOBER 2008

<table>
<tr><td>1</td><td>2</td><td>3</td><td>4</td><td>5</td><td>6</td><td>7</td><td>8</td><td>9</td><td>10</td><td>11</td><td>12</td><td>13</td><td>14</td><td>15</td><td>16</td><td>17</td><td>18</td><td>19</td><td>20</td><td>21</td><td>22</td><td>23</td><td>24</td><td>25</td><td>26</td><td>27</td><td>28</td><td>29</td><td>30</td><td>31</td></tr>
<tr><td colspan="4">♂∗♇</td><td colspan="7"></td><td colspan="20">♄☍♅</td></tr>
<tr><td colspan="31">♃△♄</td></tr>
<tr><td colspan="2"></td><td colspan="4">♀∗♃</td><td colspan="2"></td><td colspan="5">♀□♆</td><td colspan="10"></td><td colspan="8">♂∗♃</td></tr>
<tr><td colspan="4"></td><td colspan="4">♀∗♄</td><td colspan="18"></td><td colspan="5">♂∗♄</td></tr>
<tr><td colspan="2">☿△♆</td><td colspan="4"></td><td colspan="6">♀△♅</td><td colspan="14"></td><td colspan="5">♂△♅</td></tr>
<tr><td colspan="3"></td><td colspan="6">☿□♃</td><td colspan="14"></td><td colspan="6">☿□♃</td><td colspan="2"></td></tr>
<tr><td colspan="2"></td><td colspan="7">☉□♃</td><td></td><td colspan="7">☉△♆</td><td></td><td colspan="5">☉∗♇</td><td colspan="3"></td><td colspan="5">☿△♆</td></tr>
<tr><td colspan="4"></td><td colspan="3">☉☌☿</td><td colspan="24"></td></tr>
</table>

NOVEMBER 2008

<table>
<tr><td>1</td><td>2</td><td>3</td><td>4</td><td>5</td><td>6</td><td>7</td><td>8</td><td>9</td><td>10</td><td>11</td><td>12</td><td>13</td><td>14</td><td>15</td><td>16</td><td>17</td><td>18</td><td>19</td><td>20</td><td>21</td><td>22</td><td>23</td><td>24</td><td>25</td><td>26</td><td>27</td><td>28</td><td>29</td><td>30</td></tr>
<tr><td colspan="30">♄☍♅</td></tr>
<tr><td colspan="30">♃△♄</td></tr>
<tr><td colspan="23">♃∗♅</td><td colspan="3"></td><td colspan="4">♀☌♃</td></tr>
<tr><td colspan="8">♂□♆</td><td colspan="6"></td><td colspan="3">☿∗♄</td><td colspan="9"></td><td colspan="4">♀△♄</td></tr>
<tr><td colspan="3">♂∗♄</td><td colspan="5"></td><td colspan="6">♀☌♇</td><td colspan="11"></td><td colspan="4">♀∗♅</td><td></td></tr>
<tr><td colspan="4">♂△♅</td><td colspan="9"></td><td colspan="4">☿∗♃</td><td colspan="7"></td><td colspan="6">☿☌♂</td></tr>
<tr><td colspan="2"></td><td colspan="4">♀∗♆</td><td colspan="8"></td><td colspan="5">☿□♆</td><td colspan="11"></td></tr>
<tr><td colspan="5">♀□♄</td><td colspan="8"></td><td colspan="4">☿△♅</td><td colspan="7"></td><td colspan="6">☉☌♂</td></tr>
<tr><td colspan="5">♀□♅</td><td></td><td colspan="6">☉∗♃</td><td colspan="7"></td><td colspan="11">☉☌☿</td></tr>
<tr><td></td><td colspan="4">☿∗♇</td><td colspan="4"></td><td colspan="7">☉□♆</td><td colspan="14"></td></tr>
<tr><td colspan="8"></td><td colspan="4">☉∗♄</td><td colspan="18"></td></tr>
<tr><td colspan="6"></td><td colspan="7">☉△♅</td><td colspan="17"></td></tr>
</table>

DECEMBER 2008

<table>
<tr><td>1</td><td>2</td><td>3</td><td>4</td><td>5</td><td>6</td><td>7</td><td>8</td><td>9</td><td>10</td><td>11</td><td>12</td><td>13</td><td>14</td><td>15</td><td>16</td><td>17</td><td>18</td><td>19</td><td>20</td><td>21</td><td>22</td><td>23</td><td>24</td><td>25</td><td>26</td><td>27</td><td>28</td><td>29</td><td>30</td><td>31</td></tr>
<tr><td colspan="31">♄☍♅</td></tr>
<tr><td colspan="11">♃△♄</td><td></td><td colspan="7">♂∗♆</td><td colspan="4"></td><td colspan="8">♂☌♇</td></tr>
<tr><td colspan="10"></td><td colspan="9">♂□♄</td><td colspan="4"></td><td colspan="6">♀☌♆</td><td colspan="2"></td></tr>
<tr><td colspan="4">♀☌♃</td><td colspan="2"></td><td colspan="10">♂□♅</td><td colspan="11"></td><td colspan="4">☿☌♃</td></tr>
<tr><td colspan="2">♀△♄</td><td colspan="2"></td><td colspan="4">☿∗♆</td><td></td><td colspan="5">☿☌♇</td><td colspan="9"></td><td colspan="5">☿△♄</td><td colspan="3"></td></tr>
<tr><td colspan="2">☿☌♂</td><td></td><td colspan="5">☿□♄</td><td colspan="14"></td><td colspan="3">☿∗♅</td><td colspan="6"></td></tr>
<tr><td></td><td colspan="5">☿□♅</td><td colspan="4"></td><td colspan="5">☉∗♆</td><td colspan="3"></td><td colspan="7">☉☌♇</td><td colspan="6"></td></tr>
<tr><td colspan="16">☉☌♂</td><td colspan="15"></td></tr>
<tr><td colspan="7"></td><td colspan="8">☉□♄</td><td colspan="16"></td></tr>
<tr><td colspan="6"></td><td colspan="7">☉□♅</td><td colspan="18"></td></tr>
</table>

LUNAR ASPECTS GUIDE

MOON TO SUN ASPECTS

In general, the Moon aspects to the Sun bring us a greater awareness of our feelings with regard to the season through which we are passing.

Moon sextile Sun

Moon sextile Sun brings optimism, or a brighter spirit, towards whatever seasonal activities are occurring and our moods are more likely to be encouraged by the endearing qualities of the season. This aspect helps our moods to accept and be at peace with the relevant seasonal factors, getting in tune with the seasonal pace. It assists us in making the shift from the early stage of emotional experience to the next stage of emotional development. In general, Moon sextile Sun brings positive vibrations, and acts as a catalyst in the ebb and flow of the emotions. It brings the promising potential for acceptance and reassurance and, where such moods are absent, there is the driving hope to reach a happy medium. Moon sextile Sun brings inspiration to our dreams and gives us a sense of where we are going next.

Moon square Sun (First and Last Quarter Moons)

Moon square Sun represents the First and Last Quarter stages of the Moon. It is the middle road, the half-way mark between the waxing and waning process of the Moon. It is the pinnacle of the in-between stage, and it represents the crux of what we hope to establish in our emotional process as it is affected by the Moon. The square aspect represents struggle or challenge; this tends to be the point where we exercise our emotions with diligent effort. The square of the Moon to the Sun is a time when we tend to make extra adjustments with our emotional process, and we take extra steps towards the place we have determined that our emotions are headed. This is characterized by the sign the Moon is in, and how we respond, individually, with the qualities of that sign. Moon square Sun summons some very lively and busy emotional responses in the course of our dreams.

First Quarter Moon (Waxing Quarter Moon) Halfway in between the New and Full Moon, the First Quarter Moon has built up some momentum in our emotional process. This is a positive, upbeat, anticipatory time. The sign that the Moon is in will denote the types of focuses and themes that will preoccupy us, and these are the things we will be building up and strengthening in our emotional core. As the waxing Moon reaches this First Quarter mark, this is a good time for maintaining and nurturing positive emotional vibrations.

Last Quarter Moon (Waning Quarter Moon) Halfway in between the Full and New Moon, the Last Quarter Moon breaks down the emotional momentum that was built up during the Full Moon period of the previous week. This is a time of letting go, of finishing or completing certain aspects of the emotional process. The waning Moon allows us to process and let go of emotionally taxing sensations, and from there we begin to be less weighted down by our feelings. When we struggle with letting go, it is highlighted through this stage of lunar development. As the waning Moon reaches this Last Quarter mark, this is a good time for weeding out and cleaning up emotional negativity, and for letting go of unnecessary emotional baggage.

Moon trine Sun

Overall, Moon trine Sun brings good vibes; it allows us to create or to access congenial, hopeful, and positive moods. Moon trine Sun always reminds us of the aspects of the current season that are inspiring and uplifting. Whenever the trine aspect occurs, the Moon and Sun will both (usually) be in the same element together: a fire, water, air, or earth sign. This brings synchronization and focuses the energy of our moods on positive and cohesive emotional responses. Moon trine Sun brings beautiful harmony to the mood of the day. In general, this aspect brings sunny, cheerful moods, and a positive outlook on life. Moon trine Sun influences dreams with positive vibrations, and it brings sparkling delights and gifts of happiness.

Moon opposite Sun (Full Moon)

The Full Moon represents the fruition of our emotional process. Moon opposite Sun magnifies the emotional or spiritual qualities of the season. This is a time when we access and harness a great deal of emotional energy. It's a great time to establish positive affirmations, and to celebrate the bountiful fullness of the season. Often, the Full Moon time brings a whirlwind of activity, and this represents the crescendo or climax of our emotional process as it is affected by the Moon. This climax of the Moon's luminous reflections of the Sun brings the greatest amount of light to our emotional experience, and this is a very good time to count your blessings and enjoy the wonders of your life. Moon opposite Sun brings astonishing images and rich, fulfilling, experiences to the dream world.

Moon conjunct Sun (New Moon)

The New Moon represents the beginning; a starting point, where our feelings begin their development, and where our pre-established feelings are renewed, confirmed, or re-established. This is a dark time of night, as the Moon joins forces with the daytime Sun. Through this time, our emotional process is often internalized, where it is replenished with a sense of newness. Here, newer feelings may emerge with a certain affirmation or assurance. It is here that we muster new hope, new faith, and there is a subtle – but certain – expression of re-birth in our emotional understanding. This is the time to tap into the wiser parts of the soul, to allow our older feelings to be recycled and renewed, and to open up to, and give room for, new feelings as they begin to emerge. It is also important to remember to rest, to let emotions just be, without adding complexity to them. Moon conjunct Sun brings insightful, regenerative, and profound images to the dream world.

MOON TO MERCURY ASPECTS

Moon sextile Mercury

Moon sextile Mercury brings the potential for inspiring news and communications. This lunar aspect brings clear and succinct communications which will assist us to keep business running along smoothly. It's a good time to reiterate plans, schedules, and messages and to handle communications very thoroughly. Moon sextile Mercury inspires our moods with informative talk and information but, when Mercury is retrograde, it would be wise to follow up any new information with careful research. This time brings the potential for inspiration through thoughts and ideas, and all this is possible despite the travails of Mercury retrograde periods. Moon sextile Mercury brings the potential for some intelligent brainstorming between people, and this will be a very good time to run your ideas by others. It brings intellectually stimulating dreams and reveals a lot about your thoughts and ideas.

Moon square Mercury

Moon square Mercury often brings a challenging time for communications. This may be a time when it is difficult to reassure others, and moods may be challenged by intellectual debates and discussions. It may be difficult to get the message across in the way it was intended. It may also bring uncommunicative moods, or we may find that it is difficult to describe our moods. This lunar aspect is the least ideal aspect for communications under the influence of Mercury retrograde. Moon square Mercury tends to bring moods or emotional responses which are thwarted by complex communications and difficult subjects, and defensive moods may become argumentative. This is a good time to use caution with our words and to consider the impact that harsh statements may have on others. Moon square Mercury adds mental nervousness to the course of our dreams, and may contribute to nightmarish feelings and thoughts about our dreams.

Moon trine Mercury

Moon trine Mercury brings moods in harmony with communications. This is an excellent time to talk, relay thoughts, and communicate with greater ease. Moon trine Mercury brings the gift of thoughtfulness, making communications very harmonious. This aspect brings pleasantly talkative and mindful moods, leading to discussions that may clarify misinterpreted facts. It will assist us to communicate more clearly during Mercury retrograde periods. Moon trine Mercury brings a superb time for us to communicate amicably and effectively. As a general rule, this is the time to promote positive thoughts. As the day closes, Moon trine Mercury brings a helpful time to rest the mind, but for those who are awake, this may seem like an excellent time to think matters through more easily. Moon trine Mercury brings positive thoughts to our dreams.

Moon opposite Mercury

Moon opposite Mercury brings a deeper sense of awareness – or curiosity – while we are communicating. This lunar aspect inspires a surge of thoughts and discussion, and it may be necessary to comprehend a lot of things at once. This is a time when we tend to be overwhelmed or overloaded by communications or the communication process. Our feelings are more readily challenged by our thoughts. Sometimes this lunar aspect gives us the feeling that there is a great deal more to be communicated. Beware of exhausting arguments. Moon opposite Mercury brings an intense need to communicate, to reiterate on complex messages, and to set the record straight when Mercury retrograde periods have brought havoc to our communications. Moon opposite Mercury brings complex nervous responses and complex thoughts with regard to what we are feeling or sensing. As for dreams, this aspect brings very nervous or restless kinds of dreams which may seem overwhelming and possibly loaded with too much information.

Moon conjunct Mercury

Moon conjunct Mercury brings mental clarity and acuity, inspiring thoughtful and communicative moods – this is a great time to catch up on journals, research, and correspondence. Moon conjunct Mercury brings a pensive time, and our moods will be as clearly succinct as our thinking. It engages us in mindful and resourceful planning. Moon conjunct Mercury invites us to take some time to explain various matters very carefully, especially when Mercury is retrograde. This aspect reminds us of our need to pay attention to what is being communicated, and to stay on top of communications. It allows us to drop nervous tension in our sleep, and lets those who can't sleep think clearly and relevantly through their mental processes. Moon conjunct Mercury affects our dreams and moods with the desire to connect to brilliance and intelligent ideas.

MOON TO VENUS ASPECTS

Moon sextile Venus

Moon sextile Venus brings moods inspired by beauty and there are opportunities for our moods to tune into the power of love and affection. This aspect brings moods inspired by kind and attractive feminine influences, finding us easily captivated by the law of attraction. Moon sextile Venus brings the potential for very pleasurable, affectionate, and beautiful feelings to occur. It holds the potential to bring moods that will be responsive to love, affection and gentle kindness. It also brings the potential for positive vibes between loved ones, but a definite effort to create those positive vibes will have to be made. Moon sextile Venus brings pleasant dreams touched by infinite beauty.

Moon square Venus

Moon square Venus brings moods challenged by matters of love and attraction. It's also bound to bring some challenging weather between loved ones, and this may be a good time to avoid making idealistic promises that could possibly go unfulfilled. Our moods are likely to be strained by the effort to maintain beauty and comfort. Moon square Venus tests our affections and our ability to feel and express love, and may cause unpleasant moods due to a lack of kindness or love wherever it is needed. This lunar aspect may be a difficult time for us to find the kind of affections we need, but it's best to patiently persevere through love related challenges. Moon square Venus brings dreams that may seem particularly unpleasant, and dreams that may leave us feeling abandoned, torn asunder, or separate from the things to which we are attached.

Moon trine Venus

Moon trine Venus is the most receptive and advantageous time to spread loving energy. This lunar aspect generally brings moods which will be pleasant and easily prone to affection. Moon trine Venus brings gentle, beautiful, and harmonious moods and vibrations. It often blesses our moods with kindness, and increases our fondness and appreciation for beauty. Moon trine Venus brings the strong urge for love, and loving energy won't be too hard to find. This lunar aspect helps to smooth over chaotic energies with loving and kind moods. Moon trine Venus puts us in the mood for love and for all those things that bring us comfort, inspiring especially beautiful, alluring, and relaxing dreams.

Moon opposite Venus

Moon opposite Venus brings moods that will make us acutely aware of our affections – both the giving of, and the desire for, all kinds of affection. This aspect will draw relationships and love related situations into focus, and it may be especially difficult to try to please everyone, especially our loved ones. Moon opposite Venus may bring overwhelming or obsessive desires for beauty and pleasure. This aspect implies that our moods may be dominated by feminine expression or demands. Lady Justice is blind, but that doesn't mean that her logic is not sound. Sometimes, Moon opposite Venus brings obsessive or agitating moods with regard to love. Here, we often find that our affections have been spread too thin. We may feel overwhelmed by compelling attractions. This lunar aspect brings dramatic moods and dreams about our needs for affection and beauty.

Moon conjunct Venus

Moon conjunct Venus brings gentleness, kindness, and love to our moods. It puts us directly in touch with those things we are attracted to. This lunar aspect can bring deeply affectionate and sometimes very intense loving moods. Different levels and expressions of affection occur, depending on the sign in which the Moon and Venus are conjunct. Moon conjunct Venus brings moods that will be instantly drawn to beauty and love wherever it exists. This is a good time to seek pleasure and to appreciate beauty to the fullest. Moon conjunct Venus brings dazzling beauty and pleasure to the scope of our dreams.

MOON TO MARS ASPECTS

Moon sextile Mars

Moon sextile Mars tends to bring energetic moods which are motivated by force and activity, and inspired by high energy levels. Incisive action and the affirmation of will infuse our moods. Moon sextile Mars brings moods that may point to the need to take action, but this inclination is not always acted upon. Generally, Moon sextile Mars brings positive energy, strength and courage to our moods. It brings strong impulses and urges, and our dreams will seem triumphant, although somewhat martial and headstrong in attitude.

Moon square Mars

Moon square Mars suggests our moods will be challenged by invasive forcefulness, our patience levels will be tested, and it may be difficult to get amicably motivated. This aspect brings offensive and maddening challenges to our moods where abrupt energies and unbalanced temperaments will seem like bullying martial forces. Moon square Mars – this is a recipe for accidents, fights, headaches – and many people will find that they are being especially defensive as well as impatient. This lunar aspect may lead to difficulty or conflict when one is attempting to take initiative to do things, and it often tests our temper, strength, and willpower. Moon square Mars usually brings challenging moods with regard to masculine energies. While we sleep, cruelty or mad aggression may be evident in our dreams.

Moon trine Mars

Moon trine Mars brings moods that will be gifted with lots of vibrant, positive energy and our moods are often in harmony with masculine energies and courageous activities. This aspect invites optimism that inspires action. For some, this aspect brings vibrant emotional and physical energy, positive strength and might. It's an advantageous time to build on our strength, get motivated, and to get things rolling. Moon trine Mars harmoniously energizes our dreams, often making us stronger than we ever imagined.

Moon opposite Mars

Moon opposite Mars brings moods which are opposed to offensive kinds of pressures. Some may find that they are opposed to, or overwhelmed by, masculine force. In general, it brings moods at odds with some disharmonizing force. Forcefulness and brazen activity are highlighted, and Moon opposite Mars brings exceedingly energetic and feisty moods which are sometimes offensive. A surge of emotional heat may lead to anger for some. This lunar aspect is known for its extreme force, and may stimulate alarming kinds of offensive and defensive behavior. Some folks may be overwhelmed or affronted by the activities and actions occurring around them. Without a doubt, Moon opposite Mars motivates us, and brings a sharp awareness of martial forces and masculine energies. Some folks may appear to be obsessed by or preoccupied with aggressive forces. This may also be an accident prone time. Moon opposite Mars may bring pushy, impatient, or overly defensive moods, and it can bring bloody battles to the forefront of our dream world.

Moon conjunct Mars

The sign where the Moon and Mars are conjunct will have a strong bearing on the type of energy conjured by this lunar conjunction. Moon conjunct Mars activates our moods with a feeling of get-up-and-go, stirring our moods with energy and adrenaline that may seem refreshingly positive for some and overly aggressive for others. While Moon conjunct Mars occurs, our moods are active, hot, and eager to take action. Energized moods may lead to incredulous force. Moon conjunct Mars may bring moods activated by complex and reactionary kinds of aggression. Sometimes, this conjunction puts us in touch with our anger issues. Moon conjunct Mars impresses our moods with the need to take action on some level, and to get in touch with our true will. It's bound to stir up raw energy and action in our dreams.

MOON TO JUPITER ASPECTS

Moon sextile Jupiter

Moon sextile Jupiter brings the potential for our moods to be inspired by a sense of joviality, prosperity, travel, and adventure. It also brings moods inspired by opportunity, generosity, and extravagance. This lunar aspect invites moods which are generally hopeful and optimistic, inspired by promising prospects and propositions. It brings the potential for a warm and generous spirit, and sets the tone of the day with the potential for positive, upbeat feelings, and a sense of wellbeing and prosperity. Moon sextile Jupiter brings adventurous dreams.

Moon square Jupiter

Moon square Jupiter may cause our moods to be less generous than usual. We may find we are less willing to extend ourselves beyond our limits. Moon square Jupiter often brings moods challenged by matters of expenses and wealth. This lunar aspect may bring some apprehension with regard to the need to prosper, and this often leads to prudent or unreceptive moods. Jupiter's influence represents joy, and some folks may be prone to depression as they struggle with their ability to find joy or to express it. Many people may be irritated by rising costs or hidden expenses. We may find difficulty in handling large productions. Sometimes, our moods are challenged by travel related expenses, inconveniences, and delays. Our dreams may appear like a gambler's losing streak. Moon square Jupiter brings moods that are challenged by overextension — or perhaps, overexertion — especially in the dream world. The events in our dreams are often reflected by the fear of loss.

Moon trine Jupiter

Moon trine Jupiter brings moods that will be very generous, joyous, and gregarious, and it tops our experience with optimistic and prosperous moods. This aspect is an excellent time to appreciate good fortune, and to enjoy parties, fund raisers, and social affairs. Good luck, happiness, and positive vibes, often ensure a sense of wellbeing, bringing a healthy desire to prosper. Moon trine Jupiter harmonizes our moods with an outgoing spirit and an enthusiastic sense of adventure. Generally speaking, this aspect brings especially pleasant moods, and our dreams are bound to lead us into a pot of gold.

Moon opposite Jupiter

Moon opposite Jupiter brings moods that may be overwhelmed by abundance and rapid growth. People may be put off by, or suspicious of, extreme generosity. Moon opposite Jupiter brings deeply involved moods, especially with regard to our livelihoods, our fortunes, and our sense of wellbeing. This aspect brings an acute awareness of the need to excel and to prosper, and there may be something very tempting calling out to us at this time. Our moods could seem overwhelmed by overextension, either on a financial or a psychological level. Moon opposite Jupiter brings a bit of a roller coaster ride on the collective wheel of fortune, which in turn brings a lot of excitement with regard to our expenditures and our sense of wellbeing. Beware of a tendency towards compulsive gambling. In some cases, this lunar aspect puts us in touch with the feeling of greed, as Jupiter brings the compulsory need to gain, profit, and get ahead of all the financial commotion. Moon opposite Jupiter brings a tendency to overindulge, and there may be a lot of defensiveness over expenditures. In the dream world, we may get lost, or find that we have gone too far out on a limb, leaving us with the feeling of overextension.

Moon conjunct Jupiter

For those who are willing to tap into it, this lunar aspect impresses our moods with rich and prosperous feelings. Moon conjunct Jupiter brings abundant enthusiasm. Moods are especially extravagant and optimistic, connecting us with a sense of joy, wealth, joviality, prosperity, and wellbeing. This is a good time to count your blessings. Moon conjunct Jupiter puts us in touch with our visions and our hopes. It's a great time to enjoy feasts and epicurean delights. This is also an excellent time to exercise, travel, and to explore new territory. With this lunar conjunction, our dreams are often gratifyingly joyous and prosperous in nature.

MOON TO SATURN ASPECTS

Moon sextile Saturn

Moon sextile Saturn opens up our moods to employment opportunities. This is a great time to instill discipline and a sense of duty, to teach, and to work. Moon sextile Saturn inspires discipline and focus, but this usually only starts to occur when some effort towards work is made. In other words, just do the work, and the inspiration to carry on will follow. Our moods tend to be expressed a little more seriously, or with greater expectation towards seeing results. Here, seeing others apply discipline can often inspire us to do the same, making this a great time to set an example, and to focus on getting things done rather than putting them off. The Moon sets the tone of the mood, the sextile aspect brings raw potential and opportunity, and the influence of Saturn gets things done. Moon sextile Saturn brings serious dreams that inspire a sense of duty and discipline.

Moon square Saturn

Moon square Saturn brings moods which are tested by deadlines, responsibilities, and limitations. It often causes challenges with our ability to concentrate, stay focused and handle pending deadlines. Sometimes, Moon square Saturn infringes on the comfort zones of our moods which may seem overshadowed by a foreboding kind of seriousness. Moon square Saturn brings another dimension to our moods, as many folks will be troubled by the burdensome responsibility of difficult work, adding a feeling of being restricted. Moon square Saturn sometimes brings moods challenged by authority. Sometimes, time is warped, or we may find ourselves wishing that time would go by a little faster. While we sleep, Moon square Saturn slips into the night and into our dreams, bringing moods often irritated by the need for discipline; with any luck, this is a time to rest and not to worry. Moon square Saturn may bring troublesome dreams about our struggles over having control, or not having it. Sleeplessness is usually filled by obsessions over career challenges, troublesome work, or burdensome responsibilities. Hang in there – stay on course with your efforts.

Moon trine Saturn

Moon trine Saturn often inspires an amicable work mood. It is a superb time to practice disciplines and to work on things that require perfect timing, allowing for a greater sense of control, precision, and focus. Moon trine Saturn brings harmonious moods with regard to our approach to discipline, or to work in general, and this usually results in more effective teamwork. It also brings moods that are likely to be in harmony with our responsibilities and, as a result, basic duties and tasks may be carried out much more smoothly than expected. This favorable aspect assures us that time is the healer. Moon trine Saturn brings dreams that allow us to feel in control, and to go beyond our limitations, possibly accomplishing the impossible.

Moon opposite Saturn

Moon opposite Saturn is a very challenging time for our moods to stay the course of our work, and it may seem tedious to fulfill our responsibilities. These are times when we may feel overworked. Moon opposite Saturn brings moods which may appear opposed to — or overwhelmed by — restrictions and limitations. This will be a good time to keep work schedules light and to anticipate serious or reluctant moods with regard to work tasks. This is usually not an easy time to hold people's attention for very long, or to get them to perform tasks beyond their usual pace. Difficult jobs will seem that much harder and may take longer than usual to do. Moon opposite Saturn brings a serious tone to our dreams and we may tend to over-extend ourselves, even in the dream world. In general, this aspect puts us in touch with our limitations and reminds us of the mortal side of ourselves.

Moon conjunct Saturn

Moon conjunct Saturn brings serious moods in general, and there is often a strong sense of determination present. We also tend to be guarded, cautious, and work oriented. This conjunction occurs once a month, and it is therefore a good time to reiterate on personal goals and achievements. Moon conjunct Saturn brings moods that will be inclined towards discipline and responsibility, and will appeal to our protective instincts as well. It brings moods that awaken us to the awareness of our limitations. The act of completion is an important part of the Moon/Saturn conjunction, and this is a good time to recognize what level of completion has been achieved in the various stages of our lives. It's also a good time to count blessings as well as setting goals.

MOON TO NEPTUNE ASPECTS

Moon sextile Neptune

Moon sextile Neptune brings peaceful moods, responsive to spiritual expression. It can bring a calmness that allows us to pace ourselves comfortably, and our moods will be pleasant for the most part. This aspect brings moods inspired by spiritual perspectives. This time holds the potential for us to experience more accepting and flexible kinds of moods. Here, forgiveness is possible. Whenever it's convenient, this is a good lunar aspect to seek the comfort of a sanctuary and to enjoy some tranquility. Moon sextile Neptune brings moods that are influenced strongly by our beliefs. It inclines our moods towards simplicity or the path of least resistance. People tend to respond more intuitively to many situations. Moon sextile Neptune brings spiritual hope and reassuring beliefs. It assists us by bringing peaceful rest and calming dreams.

Moon square Neptune

Moon square Neptune brings struggles with regard to our beliefs and in spiritual matters. Our moods may be challenged by passivity, resignation, or perhaps even laziness, and they are often nebulous or vague. Moon square Neptune brings difficult spiritual forces into the picture, challenged by inactivity and passiveness. Moon square Neptune brings moods which may seem troubled by a lack of spiritual harmony, or possibly by addictions, temptations, and a lack of resistance. This aspect brings less tolerance of the beliefs of others and quite a bit of spiritual doubt. People may be questioning the burdening imposition or inconvenience of some beliefs. This is a time when people may be more susceptible to illusion. In general, Moon square Neptune brings disquieting moods, and many folks may have an insatiable urge to find a peaceful sanctuary away from the complexities of emotional clamor. This lunar aspect brings spiritually disturbing moods and dreams, and it may haunt our dreams with deceptive misconceptions.

Moon trine Neptune

Moon trine Neptune blesses our moods with spiritually uplifting vibrations. It settles our moods with a calm, cool acceptance of the way things are and brings the blessing of peacefulness. Moon trine Neptune brings our moods into perfect harmony with the spiritual energies around us, bringing tranquil and passive energy that is positive in nature. People will be inclined to kick back, relax and to accept their beliefs as they stand. This aspect adds calmness to the astrological atmosphere, and helps to smooth over the sting of any conflicting aspects that are simultaneously occurring. It also brings positive inspiration to our moods and is a superb time to apply, or enjoy, artistic expression. This is a great lunar aspect to share in spiritual ceremonies and customs with others. Moon trine Neptune brings relaxing and enchanting dreams filled with blessed tranquility and divine pleasures.

Moon opposite Neptune

Moon opposite Neptune brings moods that will be strongly stimulated by spiritual encounters and experiences, often challenging, and overwhelmed by doubt. This lunar aspect invites weakness with regard to our addictive tendencies. Moon opposite Neptune brings an especially strong awareness of our spiritual needs, but our feelings tend to be at odds with our beliefs. This lunar aspect brings moods that may be opposed to, or overwhelmed by, spiritualism. Moon opposite Neptune brings a strong and compelling awareness of the art, poetry, music, and spiritual beliefs that shape and form who and what we are in spirit and at heart. This lunar aspect awakens our spiritual nature and impresses upon us the need to apply our faith. It could be challenging for some folks to feel comfortable or spiritually in tune with others. Moon opposite Neptune may bring escapist tendencies and the potential for overindulgent moods, and we may be more easily susceptible to life's little deceptions. This aspect brings remarkable and impressionable subliminal images to our dreams.

Moon conjunct Neptune

Moon conjunct Neptune connects our moods with our beliefs and our spirituality. It brings a stronger spiritual awareness of life and there is the general feeling of connectedness among people. Moon conjunct Neptune brings moods that will be responsive to the need for tranquility and peacefulness, and our moods are able to merge easily with spiritual awareness. It brings us closer to a sense of spiritual oneness with the universe, and the common bonds that connect us are felt beyond the physical realms. This lunar conjunction brings peaceful and comforting dreams.

MOON TO URANUS ASPECTS

Moon sextile Uranus

Moon sextile Uranus brings lively and outgoing expressions of mood as well as the potential for wild and disorderly moods. As a general rule, it inspires us to let loose and feel free. When Moon sextile Uranus rolls around, our moods are more prone towards, or sympathetic to, reckless activity or behavior. It helps us to embrace the unusual and to find freedom from the mundane. Moon sextile Uranus brings freedom-loving rebelliousness and our dreams are likely to be explosive and colorful, reflecting a feeling of liberation.

Moon square Uranus

Moon square Uranus is often very challenging, as unexpected outbursts and radical surprises create chaotic moods complicated by explosive conflict. This aspect often brings disruptive disorder; moods may be intensified by undisciplined forces and by radical attitudes. During this time, many people tend to be less forgiving, particularly around unusual behavior and unconventional tones of expression. Moon square Uranus brings chaos – the kind of chaos which requires extra clean up work. It also brings confused and difficult dreams. To some folks, these dreams may seem more like explosive nightmares.

Moon trine Uranus

Moon trine Uranus brings crazy, fun-loving, and unusual kinds of moods and focuses. There's a feeling of wild and reckless abandon, and all is in harmony with the forces of chaos. Moon trine Uranus brings a sense of freedom and our moods will be carefree, or blithely reckless, but not with malicious intent. This lunar aspect can also inspire brilliance and spontaneous inventiveness. Moon trine Uranus brings very exciting and liberating dreams often in harmony with chaos and disorder.

Moon opposite Uranus

Moon opposite Uranus brings discordant sounds, disruptive energies, and explosive distractions. This lunar aspect ignites a strong urge for freedom from oppression, and makes us acutely aware of – and sensitive to – disruption of any kind. Our moods are agitated with an overwhelming feeling of chaos and disorder. Explosively contradictory moods shaken up by extreme or disruptive actions and expressions of thought are common. Moon opposite Uranus brings alarming dreams and unsettled feelings.

Moon conjunct Uranus

Moon conjunct Uranus brings moods that may seem out of the ordinary. It aligns us with the need for freedom, and we may find ourselves being somewhat coun-terproductive.   Beware of the tendency towards irrational or unusual behavior; rules may be broken. Moon conjunct Uranus may bring a feeling of acceptance for disorder, or it may inspire us to tackle disorder with unabashed determination. Either way, chaotic fortitude will be the energy of our mood. This lunar aspect animates our moods and our dreams with turbulent emotions.

MOON TO PLUTO ASPECTS

Moon sextile Pluto

Moon sextile Pluto brings moods inspired by vigilant efforts in the face of intensity and strife often affected by life's unchangeable circumstances. Our moods may be preoccupied with the need for trouble-shooting and problem solving. Moon sextile Pluto brings moods inspired by the opportunities that are shaped by fate and intensi-fied by powerful and variable situations. This aspect allows us to be receptive to the inevitable factors of life, and many folks will feel as though they can tolerate just about anything. Moon sextile Pluto brings moods that are influenced by the deeds of superpowers, and gives us the incentive to look for solutions to the troubles they generate. It also brings positive moods geared towards the necessity to find ways to change our apparent destiny. Moon sextile Pluto brings dreams that are open to helping us work out our individual struggles.

Moon square Pluto

Moon square Pluto brings moods challenged by the unforeseeable factors of life, by matters of fate and by perplexing transformations. This may be a difficult time to collaborate with people of another generation or those of a different cultural background. Our moods may be challenged by our hidden fears, particularly with regard to those irreversible processes of life. We may find that our moods are oppressed by dramatic losses, hopelessness, and troublesome realities. Moon square Pluto brings dramatic complexity to our moods, which very often ends up affecting everyone. It can bring troublesome and sometimes fearful moods and dreams.

Moon trine Pluto

Moon trine Pluto brings moods that will be inspired by transformation and permanent change. It gives us the strong incentive to tackle problems and find solutions and brings harmonious and therapeutic strength to our moods, especially with regard to matters of fate and the unchangeable factors of life. It also brings moods that will be attuned to the influences of superpowers. This lunar aspect promotes accordance among generations, and those with difficult realities will feel more in tune with the sympathies of others. Moon trine Pluto brings moods enriched with the acceptance of hardships and allows us to confront hardship with a lot less difficulty. This lunar aspect helps the process of healing wounds, and it brings moods that will lean amicably towards therapeutic methods of easing pain. Moon trine Pluto inspires a profound sense of renewed hope and brings a cathartic, as well as therapeutic, breakthrough in our dreams.

Moon opposite Pluto

Moon opposite Pluto makes us conscious of the troubles and the transformations occurring in our lives, especially those likely to be opposed by the influences of superpowers. This aspect causes moods which will be strongly affected by the generation gaps or the cultural gaps that exist between different folks. It also may be the cause of relentless kinds of obsessions, bringing moods that will inspire awareness of life's more intense qualities and hardships. There's a potential for dramatic, rocky moods. Moon opposite Pluto may be the cause of some sleepless energy for various folks, and there may be some overwhelming intensity to the scope of our dreams.

Moon conjunct Pluto

Moon conjunct Pluto brings intensity and extraordinary perspectives to our moods. It leads to an awareness of the influence of superpowers and how these forces affect everyone. Moon conjunct Pluto also brings moods which will be at one with a sense of acceptance of those things which we cannot change. It puts us in touch with world events, and our moods may be surprised by the peculiar ways in which destiny evolves. Moon conjunct Pluto puts our moods and dreams in tune with the relevance and importance of world events, which are busily shaping our individual lives and our lifestyles forever.

CAPRICORN

Key Phrase: "I USE"
Cardinal Earth Sign
Symbol : The Goat
December 21st, 2007
through January 20th, 2008

January 1st Tuesday

New Year's Day
Moon in Libra/ Scorpio

	PST	EST
Moon sextile Pluto	3:51 PM	6:51 PM
Moon trine Mars goes v/c	4:32 PM	7:32 PM
Moon enters Scorpio	5:33 PM	8:33 PM

Mood Watch: HAPPY NEW YEAR! With the passing of 2007, the final hours of this past weekend's Last Quarter Libra Moon put an emphasis on the need to make amends with others and unite peacefully. The waning Moon is a time to work on the process of releasing unwanted emotional patterns. Hope springs eternal as this New Year will bring a whole new level of energy and awareness in our evolutionary process. This year, a new generation of thought will unfold as Pluto, the outermost planet of our solar system which represents fate, transformation, and great change, will enter Capricorn *(see Jan. 25 and Nov. 26).* It is fitting that the first aspect of the year involves Pluto. Moon sextile Pluto brings moods that are triggered by the results of catastrophic events. These lunar aspects of Pluto are there to remind us to overcome fear with the mastery of the self. Later, as the Moon enters Scorpio, a greater perception of life enhances our moods.

January 2nd Wednesday

Moon in Scorpio

	PST	EST
Moon sextile Jupiter	12:15 AM	3:15 AM
Moon sextile Saturn	10:31 AM	1:31 PM
Mars opposite Pluto	1:23 PM	4:23 PM
Moon sextile Sun	5:56 PM	8:56 PM

Mood Watch: This Scorpio Moon day brings a bold determination to our moods, while Scorpio Moon always reminds us of the subtle pressures and underlying urgencies of life and the ever present need to live it to the fullest despite emotional pitfalls.

Mars opposite Pluto (occurring Dec. 26, 2007 – Jan. 11, 2008) For the final time this century, Mars in Gemini opposes Pluto in Sagittarius. This aspect will reoccur

February 25 – March 15, reaching another exact aspect on March 7 – only by then, Mars will be in Cancer. In fact, over the course of the next quarter century, Pluto in Capricorn (*see Jan. 25*), will henceforth be opposing Mars every time that Mars traverses through Cancer. Currently, Mars in Gemini ensures that our battles will be thought provoking and fraught with ironies and complexity. Pluto in Sagittarius opens our eyes widely to global struggles which are reflected locally, and it helps us to understand dramatically shifting trends. This long winded aspect will open up clear visions of the future and will force us to take actions with regard to matters of fate. What will we be battling? Typically, we'll be battling the symptoms of war, disease, decay, fear, prejudice, hate, global warming, and hopelessness. How do we battle these things? Don't focus on these things directly; instead, by focusing on solutions that are the diametric opposites: peace, health, regeneration, confidence, a sense of oneness with humanity, love, energy conservation, and hope. That's a tall order, but oppositions of this nature have a strong impact. This aspect reminds us we can neither ignore nor become used to the destructive trends occurring on the planet.

January 3ʳᵈ Thursday

Moon in Scorpio

	PST	EST	
Moon trine Uranus	12:49 AM	3:49 AM	
Moon square Neptune	10:44 AM	1:44 PM	
Moon sextile Mercury goes v/c	4:30 PM	7:30 PM	
Venus square Saturn begins (see January 6)			

Mood Watch: The waning Scorpio Moon is a good time to meditate on personal passions and to nourish simple desires and needs. Tonight's void-of-course Moon is likely to bring disappointment to those who hold nothing but high expectations. The waning void-of-course Scorpio Moon is a good time to focus on healing, resting, and easing restless tensions. It is also a time to be cautious, to watch for crime, and to be on guard. This evening, count your blessings. Out of this spirit of appreciation, pleasant surprises will pick up the quality of the mood. Where intensity has been difficult, quiet meditation calls to us.

January 4ᵗʰ Friday

Moon in Scorpio / Sagittarius

	PST	EST	
Moon enters Sagittarius	6:14 AM	9:14 AM	
Moon conjunct Venus	7:19 PM	10:19 PM	
Moon square Saturn	10:52 PM	1:52 AM	(January 5)
Sun sextile Uranus begins (see January 6)			

Mood Watch: Overnight, the waning Scorpio Moon brings imaginative and therapeutic dreams. Early this morning, the waning Moon enters Sagittarius, and our moods begin to explore inner space. An imaginative, curious, philosophical spirit gives glimpses of how the recent memories of 2007 will help to set the course of the newer visions of 2008. In our journey through Capricorn winter, day or night, through storm or slumber, Sagittarius Moon gives the impetus "to see" intuitively.

January 5th Saturday

Moon in Sagittarius

	PST	EST	
Moon square Uranus	1:13 PM	4:13 PM	
Moon sextile Neptune	10:54 PM	1:54 AM	(January 6)

Mood Watch: The winter days of Capricorn make us strong and focused, while the visionary guidance of the Sagittarius Moon points the way. The Sagittarius Moon brings explorative moods, and as the Moon wanes, much of this exploration is also reflected internally. This is a good time to venture beyond the usual bounds and to make discoveries. The mutable fire sign, Sagittarius, brings the need to satisfy curiosities and to interact with others with enthusiasm and appreciation.

January 6th Sunday

Moon in Sagittarius / Capricorn

	PST	EST
Sun sextile Uranus	4:18 AM	7:18 AM
Venus square Saturn	5:38 AM	8:38 AM
Moon opposite Mars	1:34 PM	4:34 PM
Moon conjunct Pluto goes v/c	4:27 PM	7:27 PM
Moon enters Capricorn	5:44 PM	8:44 PM

Mood Watch: The waning Sagittarius Moon brings contemplative moods. Later today, Moon conjunct Pluto brings intensity to our moods as the Moon also goes void-of-course. For a little over an hour, too many distractions sometimes lead to forgetfulness or hastiness. Tonight, when the Moon enters Capricorn, our moods enter a phase of determination. Moon in Capricorn brings serious moods, particularly now that it is waning on the dark side. Keep the focuses light and inspiring and the results will be good.

Sun sextile Uranus (occurring January 4 – 8) This occurrence of Sun sextile Uranus particularly affects those Capricorn folks celebrating birthdays January 4 – 8. These birthday people are being given an opportunity to blow off some chaotic steam and to reach for qualities of freedom that may have been absent in their recent past. This will be your time to make radical breakthroughs, birthday Capricorn; your natal Sun is currently sextile Uranus for a good reason – to find a liberating balance in the midst of the chaos. Once you've done this, you'll be ready to take the next step. Right now, there is no holding back, so go for it; discover your freedom. The victory of creative change will bring a more optimistic outlook on life. This aspect will repeat on May 11, affecting the lives of Taurus people whose birthdays fall between May 9 – 14.

Venus square Saturn (occurring January 3 – 8) Venus in Sagittarius is square to the retrograde Saturn in Virgo. It may be difficult to engage in romance, particularly when traveling, as it might seem that something is always getting in the way of basic pleasures. Perhaps it is best not to get bent out of shape over some people's need to create restrictions in order to protect their own sense of security while love related troubles are being worked out. No matter how much one prioritizes a focus on love, it is still likely to be misinterpreted on some level during Venus square Saturn. Love related dramas may be taken too seriously. The basic expression of love will flow more easily without the limitations of expectations or demands, though this advice may not work so well when it comes to making excuses. Give it your best, keep singing the praises of love and applying the law of attraction, but expect some challenges nonetheless. This aspect will reoccur May 23 - 28, reaching its exact aspect on May 26.

January 7th Monday

Moon in Capricorn

	PST	EST	
Moon conjunct Jupiter	2:25 AM	5:25 AM	
Moon trine Saturn	9:41 AM	12:41 PM	
Mercury enters Aquarius	8:46 PM	11:46 PM	
Moon sextile Uranus	11:53 PM	2:53 AM	(January 8)

Mood Watch: The darkly waning Capricorn Moon may bring the feeling that our sense of perseverance is being tested. The early part of today brings favorable working conditions with the Capricorn Moon trine Saturn. This is a good time to focus on goals and to make plans for achieving success.

Mercury enters Aquarius (Mercury in Aquarius: January 7 – March 14) Mercury in Aquarius is a time when we explore the power of knowledge through our communications. Mercury is the planet that represents the thought processes, as well as the means by which we communicate the message we are sending out into the world. Today, Mercury enters Aquarius, the *fixed air* sign of the zodiac, which represents humanity's knowledge. As the force of communication (Mercury) travels through the constellation of fixed thought and meditation (Aquarius), there are great opportunities for us to share and to empower each other through our knowledge. This is a splendid time to communicate ideas and investigate the latest in technology, science, and the world of invention. Mercury in Aquarius is also a special time to speak out on humanitarian issues and the rights of freedom. Eccentric talk and unusual subjects will fill the airwaves while Mercury is in Aquarius.

January 8th Tuesday

NEW MOON in CAPRICORN

	PST	EST
Moon conjunct Sun goes v/c	3:36 AM	6:36 AM

Mood Watch: **New Moon in Capricorn** (Moon conjunct Sun) brings down-to-earth determination to our moods. New beginnings occur on the physical plane with the Moon and the Sun in Capricorn. New Moon in Capricorn urges us to create fresh goals and to set new heights for ourselves. Unfortunately, the Moon will be void-of-course for the entire day and evening. There may be a tendency to feel melancholy or lonely, which makes this an opportune day to cheer people up with an open and positive attitude. Be sure to dream big when it comes to setting goals and finding ways to break the patterns of negative feelings. Expect services to run slowly, and co-workers may appear lazy. Beware of the tendency for employers and leaders to expect too much, or to be disappointed in the way business goes today. No matter what, be positive!

January 9ᵗʰ Wednesday

♑

Moon in Capricorn / Aquarius

	PST	EST
Moon enters Aquarius	3:14 AM	6:14 AM
Moon conjunct Mercury	7:37 AM	10:37 AM
Venus square Uranus begins (see January 12)		
Jupiter trine Saturn begins (see January 21)		

Mood Watch: Early, the newly waxing Moon enters Aquarius. Today will feel like a brand new day for our moods. Yesterday, we reached the first New Moon of the year; we are beginning to recover from the disruption of holiday mayhem, and a young Aquarius Moon shows the way to develop a science of thought leading to freedom from oppression. Aquarius Moon invites our moods to experiment with our knowledge and to learn from and teach the people around us. Aquarius Moon conjunct Mercury begins the day with all the fortification we will need, inspiring intelligent thought and communication. Whatever thoughts you have as the day begins will be sure to set the tone for the course of the day. Anyone can have knowledge – *apply* knowledge and wisdom will follow.

January 10ᵗʰ Thursday

Moon in Aquarius

	PST	EST
Moon sextile Venus	3:34 AM	6:34 AM
Moon conjunct Neptune	5:30 PM	8:30 PM

Mood Watch: The season of winter commences the return of light, but it is still much too early in winter for the light to awaken us. Capricorn sun days teach us how to sustain ourselves, while the newly waxing light of the Aquarius Moon entices us to break through the doldrums of daily conservative maintenance, and to enliven our moods with inspiring and useful knowledge. Our moods will be receptive to trying new methods of living more boldly and freely. Aquarius Moon encourages us to face problems with a confidence in what we know. There is a courageous quality about this time that compels us to seek knowledge.

January 11ᵗʰ Friday

Moon in Aquarius/ Pisces

	PST	EST
Moon trine Mars	4:28 AM	7:28 AM
Moon sextile Pluto goes v/c	9:51 AM	12:51 PM
Moon enters Pisces	10:45 AM	1:45 PM
Moon sextile Jupiter	8:48 PM	11:48 PM

Mood Watch: Early this morning, the Aquarius Moon trine Mars brings favorable incentives to become active. Moon sextile Pluto emphasizes the need to overcome trying situations. For a short time, the void-of-course Moon causes minor glitches and oversights. As the Moon enters Pisces, our moods become finely attuned to the feeling that exists in each place we go, and we are receptive to a wide range of emotions. Intuitive awareness abounds. Later, Moon sextile Jupiter brings opportunity and hope to our moods. The Capricorn Sun says, "act responsibly," and the Pisces Moon is saying "dream big!" This is a good time to engage in both.

January 12ᵗʰ Saturday

Moon in Pisces

	PST	EST
Moon opposite Saturn	1:18 AM	4:18 AM
Venus square Uranus	9:22 AM	12:22 PM
Moon conjunct Uranus	3:11 PM	6:11 PM
Moon square Venus	3:45 PM	6:45 PM

Mood Watch: Pisces Moon is the time to use the imagination and focus on artistic and creative endeavors. Late in the day, Moon conjunct Uranus brings a rebellious or explosive tone to the quality of our moods. Then, Moon square Venus challenges our moods to defend what we love, and to overcome the fear of losing what we are most attracted to. Pisces says "I believe;" the Pisces Moon requires belief in what we are doing, and it allows us to direct emotional energies in a way that brings the heart's desire to its fruition. Believe!

Venus square Uranus (occurring Jan. 9 – 14) Venus in Sagittarius square Uranus in Pisces notoriously stirs restless hearts to make radical decisions with regard to love. Rebellious kinds of love pursuits will be tested by chaos. Travel plans may be caused by – or thwarted by – unusual encounters. This aspect tends to put obstacles between love and freedom. Be careful not to become too personally affronted by explosive or extreme love matters. Be assured in self-love, and empower affection with personal integrity and a strong loving vision. People are changing at a rapid rate and it is essential to let love take its course when it concerns issues of personal freedom. This aspect will reoccur on two more occasions this year. The first is from June 9 – 14, reaching its exact peak on June 12. The second occurrence is from October 31 – November 5, reaching its exact square position on November 3.

January 13ᵗʰ Sunday

Moon in Pisces / Aries

	PST	EST
Moon sextile Sun	3:23 AM	6:23 PM
Moon square Mars	9:23 AM	12:23 PM
Moon square Pluto goes v/c	3:40 PM	6:40 PM
Moon enters Aries	4:24 PM	7:24 PM

Mood Watch: The Pisces Moon draws our attraction to art and music as well as to escapism and dreamy distractions. Pisces Moon, now waxing, creates the need for many to access an internal part of their own being, and to empower the spiritual side of the self. Moon square Mars will challenge and inspire our moods to overcome harsh aggression, particularly those things which challenge our strength. Pisces Moon puts us in touch with our belief systems and the trials we must endure individually concerning our own particular beliefs. For some there is a creative process unfolding; for others there is a battle going on with addictive behavior or the need to escape. For most, the dreamlike quality of this time drifts in a timeless fashion. Later on, there may be tendencies towards spacey and inattentive behavior. By the time the Moon enters Aries, our moods will be highly attuned to getting the kind of attention and action that inspires ambition and confidence.

40

January 14th Monday

Moon in Aries

	PST	EST
Moon square Jupiter	3:00 AM	6:00 AM
Moon sextile Mercury	10:32 AM	1:32 PM
Venus sextile Neptune begins (see January 16)		

Mood Watch: For many folks, Moon square Jupiter brings a reluctance to venture out of bed and explore, or there may be some unexpected detours in the course of our dreams. Fortunately, the waxing Aries Moon works its spirit into our conscience, inspiring us to take charge and to head off into the day with gusto. Moon sextile Mercury brings talkative and communicative moods. This is a good time to communicate boldly, with a message that possesses authority, confidence, and clear instructions. The spirit of the Aries Moon reminds us that hesitation brings the potential for loss, but that also, hastiness brings the potential for regret. Clarity of purpose will lead to positive personal breakthroughs. Aries Moon gives us the incentive to act on our volition with perfect intent.

January 15th Tuesday

Moon in Aries / Taurus – FIRST QUARTER MOON in ARIES

	PST	EST
Moon trine Venus	1:28 AM	4:28 AM
Moon sextile Neptune	4:23 AM	7:23 AM
Moon square Sun	11:44 AM	2:44 PM
Moon sextile Mars	12:39 PM	3:39 PM
Moon trine Pluto goes v/c	7:39 PM	10:39 PM
Moon enters Taurus	8:13 PM	11:13 PM

Mood Watch: As early morning commences, Moon sextile Neptune opens the day with calm and tranquil moods. **First Quarter Moon in Aries** (Moon square Sun) energizes our moods, and inspires an upbeat, outgoing, and forward manner. This is the time to get in tune with your own personal levels of energy, strength and vitality. There is a *self-starter* energy in the air and the active ones among us are on the prowl. Aries Moon brings on an expression of courageous vigor, as well as a sense of bold adventure. As a general rule, moods are marked by confidence and the drive to make a lasting impression. Moon in Aries squaring to the Sun in Capricorn is a good time to apply diligence and inspired ability to your work. This is especially true while Moon sextile Mars brings a burst of energy to our moods. Later, Moon trine Pluto brings positive healing energy, and while the Moon is void-of-course, people may seem easily distracted. As the Moon enters Taurus, many folks will gravitate towards simple luxuries and comforting pleasures.

January 16th Wednesday

Moon in Taurus

	PST	EST	
Moon trine Jupiter	7:18 AM	10:18 AM	
Moon trine Saturn	9:29 AM	12:29 PM	
Venus sextile Neptune	11:35 AM	2:35 PM	
Moon square Mercury	7:39 PM	10:39 PM	
Moon sextile Uranus	11:06 PM	2:06 AM	(January 17)

Mood Watch: The Taurus Moon focuses our moods on the need to align ourselves with good fortune. This is a good time to enjoy the art of earning, having, spending, saving, and using money. Taurus says, "I have," and the waxing Taurus Moon entices us to invite those things into our lives that give us the greatest sense of having something. This phenomenon doesn't always mean money, but of course, money is a fantastic example of how the feeling of having works. Tonight, Moon square Mercury may be a challenging time to communicate thoughts, while Moon sextile Uranus brings a tendency towards radical feelings or erratic kinds of energies. Use Taurus Moon's grounding and practical spirit to find relaxation and peace in chaotic spaces.

Venus sextile Neptune (occurring Jan. 14 – 18) Venus in Sagittarius sextile Neptune in Aquarius brings inspirational and creative love to the art of spirituality. The sextile of Venus to Neptune brings the opportunity for us to find spiritual enhancement in the adventure of love, and to spread its healing power around for all to share. This serves as an excellent time to reach out spiritually to those we love as well as to our spirit guides. This aspect will re-occur April 23 – 27, reaching its exact aspect on April 25. It will also reoccur on November 3 – 6, reaching its exact aspect on November 5.

January 17th Thursday

Moon in Taurus / Gemini	PST	EST	
Moon square Neptune	7:12 AM	10:12 AM	
Moon trine Sun goes v/c	7:05 PM	10:05 PM	
Moon enters Gemini	10:30 PM	1:30 AM	(January 18)
Venus opposite Mars begins (see January 19)			

Mood Watch: The waxing winter Moon in Taurus brings out the need for quality, security, and comfort. To start the day, try to take some extra time to meditate, or to empower positive reinforcement. Moon square Neptune brings a tendency for many to feel as if the morning's tranquility has been snapped away all too quickly. People may seem distant, as they may have missed their quiet time. Sun in Capricorn and Moon in Taurus brings an earthy determination to our step. There is a strong need to overcome financial burdens and concerns by acknowledging them. The physical world needs to be dealt with and today is a good time to do it. Tonight, Moon trine Sun brings good vibrations while at the same time, the void-of-course Moon brings a few hours of laziness, stubbornness, and a tendency for physical projects to require more patience. A positive attitude will prevail and, by the time the Moon enters Gemini, thoughtful reflection will pave the way for a better understanding of the best approach for tomorrow.

January 18th Friday

Moon in Gemini	PST	EST
Moon square Saturn	11:19 AM	2:19 PM

Mood Watch: Today's only lunar aspect, Moon square Saturn, is just another reminder that greater concentration is required. Some things will take a little extra time, and for some, time is of the essence on this busy Friday morning. The waxing Moon in Gemini tends to bring a nervous air to our moods, or perhaps a naïve sort of impatience occurs. Talkative moods bring bustling chatter. The more our thoughts stir the pot of the general mood, the thicker this gumbo stew of busy thoughts becomes. The mutable air sign of Gemini engages us in the need to communicate. There is a strong need to satiate our curiosities, and to indulge in our need to bounce our ideas off someone else. That's what the twin does, isn't it? One twin complements the other.

January 19th Saturday

Moon in Gemini

	PST	EST	
Moon square Uranus	1:01 AM	4:01 AM	
Moon trine Mercury	2:34 AM	5:34 AM	
Moon trine Neptune	9:00 AM	12:00 PM	
Moon opposite Venus	3:12 PM	6:12 PM	
Moon conjunct Mars	3:35 PM	10:10 PM	
Moon opposite Pluto goes v/c	11:46 PM	2:46 AM	(January 20)
Mercury conjunct Neptune begins (see January 22)			

Mood Watch: Gemini Moon days are filled with details. Through our dreams, Moon square Uranus brings complex, but liberating, breakthroughs. Moon trine Mercury harmonizes the nervous system and, as the morning blooms, Moon trine Neptune brings spiritually uplifted moods – a great time to nourish the higher aspirations. Later, Moon opposite Venus awakens our emotional sensitivities to the types of things we have been attracting to us. Attraction acts like a magnet. That's why it is commonly said, "be careful what you wish for," Moon conjunct Mars in Gemini activates our moods with emotional force which is backed by a strong, curious, drive. Much later, Moon opposite Pluto shifts the entire mood altogether, and there is a dynamic feeling that occurs with the differences that set us apart from the various generations and cultures around us. The Moon is also void-of-course; it's an excellent time to go to sleep and to rest deeply.

Venus opposite Mars (occurring Jan. 17 – 22) Venus in Sagittarius is opposing the retrograde Mars in Gemini. Women and men who are affected by this aspect are often crazed by the need to understand or accept the phenomenon of their dynamic differences coupled with their extreme attractions. The opposition of these planets can attract and repel at the same time, and there is a constant need to give and take with the act of compromise. If you are among those somehow caught up in this battle of the sexes, it is important to realize that losses can occur around attempts at moderation just as easily as with extremes. Venus in Sagittarius creates a particularly hot, fiery, and adventurous expression of love and attraction. Mars in Gemini brings out a driving curiosity and a very thought provoking form of martial (or masculine) energy. This may bring a particularly challenging time for loved ones to travel together, and it may be best to allow for some flexibility in the travel schedule. It is wisest to observe and learn as much as possible. By all means, go easy on your loved ones during this period of Venus opposite Mars.

AQUARIUS
Key Phrase: "I KNOW"
Fixed Air Sign
Symbol : The Water Bearer
January 20th through February 18th

January 20th Sunday
Moon in Gemini / Cancer

	PST	EST
Moon enters Cancer	12:05 AM	3:05 AM
Sun enters Aquarius	8:43 AM	11:43 AM
Moon opposite Jupiter	12:31 PM	3:31 PM
Moon sextile Saturn	12:45 PM	3:45 PM

Mood Watch: A waxing Cancer Moon brings a focus on defense, and our security and comfort zones are also given a thorough checkup. Moon opposite Jupiter brings an acute awareness of the need to excel and to prosper, and there may be something very tempting calling out to us at this time. It won't be long before Moon sextile Saturn brings a realistic picture of what it will take to summon the discipline and the focus to acquire whatever it is that must be attained. All day our activities are reflected in our emotional state which is also accentuated by strong instinctual urges. The Cancer Moon serves as a good time to brighten up the home and make it feel more comfortable. Reassurance and love are the keys to perfection during a heavily waxing Cancer Moon.

Sun enters Aquarius (Sun in Aquarius Jan. 20 – Feb. 18 PST / 19 EST) Aquarius is ruled by the enigmatic planetary force of Uranus, the often strange villain who forges new clarity and hope through the storms of chaos and disruption. Freedom fighters will remind us always that we must find a solution to every great atrocity that dampens the human spirit. We must always take measures to prevent tomorrow's health crisis and to insure the perpetuity of our species. Aquarius is the "fixed air" sign which represents the sum of human knowledge. It is an old world oppression that we must address in this Aquarian time – through knowledge we will succeed. This is a time for opening up new ideas and possibilities. Aquarians are usually very clever people who love a good challenge.

44

January 21st Monday
Dr. Martin Luther King Junior Day
Moon in Cancer

	PST	EST
Jupiter trine Saturn	1:14 AM	4:14 AM
Moon trine Uranus goes v/c	2:56 AM	5:56 AM
Venus conjunct Pluto begins (see January 23)		

" I believe that unarmed truth and unconditional love will have the final word in reality. That is why right, temporarily defeated, is stronger than evil triumphant. " - Martin Luther King Jr. (1929 – 1968), Accepting Nobel Peace Prize, Dec. 10, 1964

Mood Watch: In the wee small hours, a positive but definitive kind of chaos ensues as Moon trine Uranus prepares us for a pleasant but somewhat disruptive Monday. Emotions rise to restless heights as the nearly full Moon in Cancer remains void-of-course throughout the entire day and night. This will not be an especially easy day to get any kind of production rolling smoothly. In fact, this would be a much more ideal day to accept that emotional confusion and mayhem may tend to be the common denominator in many of our basic interactions. It's a good time to avoid stepping on people's emotional toes on this moody Monday.

Jupiter trine Saturn (occurring Jan. 9 – 31) Jupiter represents joy, attainment, expansion, and the place where economic growth occurs. Saturn is the guard at the edge of time, and represents the work, timing, and responsibility that it takes to generate prosperous growth. These two planets have a natural relationship, as with each bountiful step of attainment there is always the discipline required to maintain it and the duty of labor necessary to keep it expanding in value and quality. Jupiter is now in Capricorn and the retrograde Saturn is in the Mercury-ruled sign, Virgo. The trine aspect of these two planets in the earth signs will bring bountiful and harmonious material wealth, as well as a wealth of material responsibility. Our economy is boosted with breakthroughs in enterprise and financial gifts, especially for the earth signs of the zodiac and for those who are interacting with them. It's no wonder this aspect is occurring in an election year in the USA. North America can probably expect a temporary reign of lower gas prices, and other similar boons, especially as the election gets closer. This is a good time for business, and a good time to take positive steps towards the attainment of health, wealth, and happiness. Enjoy this boost of positive vibrations while you can: this aspect will reoccur August 20 – December 11, reaching its exact aspect two times – first, on September 8, and again on November 21.

January 22nd Tuesday
Moon in Cancer / Leo – FULL MOON in LEO

	PST	EST
Moon enters Leo	2:21 AM	5:21 AM
Moon opposite Sun	5:34 AM	8:34 AM
Mercury conjunct Neptune	5:16 PM	8:16 PM

Mood Watch: Before sunrise, the Moon enters Leo and it's a welcome change, as the long void-of-course Cancer Moon of yesterday may have worn some folks' patience down to a frazzle. Life improves as the **Full Moon in Leo** (Moon opposite

45

Sun) captivates our moods with a wild and instinctual push. There may be an opportunity here to enhance and harmonize friendships and family situations in a fulfilling and enriching manner. Moon in Leo brings out the playful, imaginative, and creative side of our moods. Most of us are easily drawn towards the need to find warmth and affection, or just plain attention.

Mercury conjunct Neptune (occurring Jan. 19 – Feb. 5) This aspect inspires communications on the hypersensitive issues of people's belief systems and the domain of spirituality. Aquarius represents humanity. Neptune in the sign of Aquarius focuses on the essential need for belief in humankind; that is, we must believe in ourselves and our own capabilities in order to survive spiritually. Mercury in Aquarius focuses news, talk, and discussion on human rights issues. Many people, especially Aquarians, are deeply moved to speak about their convictions. This aspect also presents a good time to learn from the news and talk concerning humanitarian issues and, to pray, meditate on, and connect with that higher spirit that dwells within. Due to Mercury's upcoming retrograde period (Jan. 28 – Feb. 18), this aspect will peak again on February 2, and it will also reoccur March 6 - 11, reaching its exact aspect on March 9.

January 23rd Wednesday

Moon in Leo	PST	EST	
Moon opposite Neptune	2:49 PM	5:49 PM	
Moon opposite Mercury	4:13 PM	7:13 PM	
Moon sextile Mars	8:44 PM	11:44 PM	
Venus conjunct Pluto	10:58 PM	1:58 AM	(January 24)
Mercury-trine-Mars-non-exact (see January 31)			

Mood Watch: Our moods are still basking in the playful and inspired energy of a post-Full Leo Moon. Moon opposite Neptune brings especially spiritual moods. Moon opposite Mercury brings particularly talkative moods. Later, Moon sextile Mars brings the potential for some playfully competitive or dominating moods. This is a good time, overall, to utilize creative energies and to focus on personal needs and the needs of family and friends. Many folks will seek entertainment and fun.

Venus conjunct Pluto (occurring Jan. 21 – 26) This conjunction often places affections and love right where they are needed most, the areas of life that are deeply challenging and sometimes traumatic. It also intensifies love related efforts and, at times, our affections may seem overpowering or daunting in some way. Venus represents love and beauty, while Pluto (in Greek myth) represents the god of the underworld, who lured the goddess of love, Persephone, away from heaven with the rich scent of a narcissus flower. Narcissistic love in the modern sense means conceit or excessive love of oneself. Could Persephone have been drawn to the narcissus flower for the pursuit of self-love? As she herself represents love and beauty, was this scent like a mirror to her soul? This single act of peculiar passion lead the youthful goddess into a fateful entanglement that would later force her to descend into the depths of Earth every autumn to join the underworld god until spring season. She represents the life of spring and summer, and when she is absent, planet Earth remains barren or dormant during autumn and winter. Venus (Persephone) conjunct Pluto (Hades) represents the union of beauty and strength. In the end, there is always a rich price to pay for the pursuit of passion, but true love and beauty are everlasting. This is a time when the intensity or hardship of love and attraction create richly striking images and perspectives of which we must eventually let go completely in the hope that love and beauty will transform our lives once again. There is no harm in self-love, as Persephone learned that inner beauty is renewed and can be found in the darkest places, even in the far reaches of the inner soul. Love and beauty are far richer experiences when they are met by the transformation demanded by Plutonian tests; Pluto brings loss through illness, death, and decay. Venus brings love that is renewed through all hardships. This is a time of deep confessions and secrets revealed. One of the powers of love is that we can always find it, even when we are alone, or in a barren or dormant state of being. Venus conjunct Pluto is occurring in Sagittarius at the very brink of the Capricorn cusp. This emphasizes the vast awareness taking place with regard to the transformation process of love and attraction. In just two days, Pluto will enter Capricorn, which is number one on the list of the most important celestial occurrences this year. This is a good time to find love's powers and unite them within. Venus conjunct Pluto will reoccur November 9 – 14, reaching its peak on November 11.

January 24th Thursday
Moon in Leo / Virgo

	PST	EST
Venus enters Capricorn	12:05 AM	3:05 AM
Moon trine Pluto goes v/c	6:43 AM	9:43 AM
Moon enters Virgo	6:49 AM	9:49 AM
Moon trine Venus	7:29 AM	10:29 AM
Moon conjunct Saturn	8:13 PM	11:13 PM
Moon trine Jupiter	10:11 PM	1:11 AM (January 25)

Mood Watch: Moon trine Pluto is not such a bad way to enter a new day and, although the Moon goes void-of-course at the same time, it isn't long before the Leo Moon enters Virgo. As the Virgo Moon trines with Venus, love triumphs over the minor annoyances of the morning, particularly for those who align themselves with a sense of purpose. The Virgo Moon is an excellent time to focus on organization and communication. Moon conjunct Saturn brings serious evening moods that allow for greater concentration. Later, Moon trine Jupiter infuses a sense of joy; this is a really good time to count your blessings.

Venus enters Capricorn (Venus in Capricorn: Jan. 24 – Feb. 17) Now Venus will be grounded in the stoic and serious focuses of Capricorn. Venus in Capricorn brings out an attraction for the staunch and ardent duty of accomplishing goals as well as a love of predictability. This type of expression creates stable ground for the development of relationships, and the general course of affections will be oriented towards making impressions, with a hard and ambitious drive towards providing well for loved ones. This is the time when the general populace is attracted to getting in shape. Venus in Capricorn will certainly bring out a more serious approach to love matters in general, especially while it is conjunct with Pluto (see yesterday). It is important to have respect and maturity in matters of love if we are to be taken seriously by loved ones while Venus is in Capricorn.

January 25th Friday

Moon in Virgo

	PST	EST
Moon opposite Uranus	12:45 PM	3:45 PM
PLUTO ENTERS CAPRICORN	6:38PM	9:38 PM

Mood Watch: Something is brewing. As Moon opposite Uranus will attest, midday and afternoon activities will be laced with radical or unusual feelings. Despite business as usual, the waning Virgo Moon keeps us cautious, suspicious, and carefully poised. This is a good time to focus on the cleansing process of the soul. Today is the big day; Pluto's sign change only occurs once every generation! Today, Pluto enters Capricorn.

Pluto enters Capricorn (Pluto in Capricorn: Jan. 25 – June 13, 2008) For the first time in our lifetime, Pluto now enters Capricorn. Due to Pluto's retrograde pattern, it will initially be in Capricorn for a temporary period, from today until June 13. Pluto will undergo the final stage of traveling back through Sagittarius from June 13 until November 26. Once Pluto has re-entered Capricorn on November 26, it will remain in Capricorn for a good long time – until March 23, 2023. Fifteen years is considered a relatively average cycle for Pluto to travel through one zodiac sign, and this is why it is considered the planet of the generations.

PLUTO REPRESENTS THE GENERATIONS

PLUTO IN LEO GENERATION

Each cycle of Pluto through one particular sign brings a new generation and different schools of thought. Some schools are more advanced in certain ways than others and, certainly, the older generations are more ripened. For instance, the Pluto in Leo generation (1938 to 1958) are the baby boomers who have matured to levels where they have been able to manifest their school of thought quite thoroughly. Leo is ruled by the Sun and this generation is affected by the necessity for its individuals to wholeheartedly identify with life, and to manifest light and creativity from the core of the self, just as the Sun projects light out into our solar system. This has been demonstrated by the attitude of Leo related things such as individuality, natural self expression, independence in business, less formalities, questioning authority, finding more leisure time, expanding the arts and entertainment field, finding joy in work, and applying creativity in the systems of society. Pluto also represents decay, disease, and the annihilation or extinction of things. The Pluto in Leo generation has had to fight heart disease – and interestingly enough, anatomically, Leo is ruled by the heart.

PLUTO IN VIRGO GENERATION

The Virgo generation (1958 to 1972), has also matured enough to make their mark on the world by means of their school of thought. The planet Mercury rules Virgo and it represents communications and the means of processing and storing information. It is no wonder that this generation ushered in the use of fax machines, personal computers, instant messaging, and the age of information. This is the generation that is steeped deeply in the battle against drug and alcohol addictions as well as compulsive disorders. Since Virgo is ruled by the digestive system, it is no wonder that countless colon related diseases are also high on the list of the Virgo generation's trials, as well as the sharp rise in diabetes among average to middle aged adults.

PLUTO IN LIBRA GENERATION

The Libra generation (1972 – 1984) emphasizes society's need for law and order. Libra represents relationships, marriage, psychology, diplomacy, justice and the courts. This is the generation that has fully embraced major changes with regard to the institution of marriage, and the ways in which laws are executed and justice systems operate. No one can deny that these areas of life have taken major turns through the liberal views of this young generation. In a warring world, diplomacy has been the most demanding trial. With any luck, this generation will develop more effective methods of finding peace and harmony among people. In time, they will empower a greater focus on the need for education in a world of increasing illiteracy. As for marriage, not only has the process of wedlock been changed dramatically by the views and practices of this generation, civil rights take the front seat. The big dispute rages on with regard to the lawful union of same-sex partners. It may be a little while yet before the Libra generation addresses the full legal scope of marital partnership. Libra rules the kidneys and, while this generation is surrounded by such grave concerns as a pharmaceutical drug culture, many of the people of this generation will probably battle kidney related diseases and setbacks.

PLUTO IN SCORPIO GENERATION

The Scorpio generation (1984 – 1997) is believed to be the generation of swift change. Pluto, which rules Scorpio, returns home to the major emphasis on such Scorpio related focuses as birth, sex, death, and transformation. It is interesting to note that while Pluto was in Scorpio, the HIV/AIDS virus took root, bringing the symbolic correlation of death by a sexually transmitted disease. Scorpio rules the sex organs, and this generation will have its work cut out for it in the battle against sexually transmitted diseases. As Scorpio also represents birth, it is almost certain that this generation will seed a large growth in population. For them, there will be a strong reckoning with the various aspects of the sex trade, sex changes, sexual psychology and – oh yes – death too. Some believe that a good part of the globe's Pluto in Scorpio generation will be wiped out by war, famine, disease, contaminants, epidemics, and natural disasters. This generation will undoubtedly set a new precedent for the concept of survival and for the mechanism of how true survival works in the 21st century.

PLUTO IN SAGITTARIUS GENERATION

The Sagittarius generation (1996 / 97 – 2008) is completing its birth process. It remains to be seen what this very young generation will do and what they will emphasize in the development and transformation of the world community. This passing time of Pluto in Sagittarius brings a greater increase in global awareness. The Jupiter ruled sign of Sagittarius emphasizes the need for expansion and growth. Sagittarius says: "I see," which also implies a growth in our vision or future outlook. Certainly while global awareness has expanded, by the time this generation comes into full maturity, its members will be much more inclined to world travel, extreme sports, philosophical endeavors, and advanced skills in world trade. Beyond that, it would not be surprising if this generation promotes great effort for space travel. Sagittarius rules the thighs. It is hard to say how thigh related health concerns might permeate the Pluto in Sagittarius generation. Could the increasing battles against obesity cause an unprecedented volume of thigh liposuctions? Maybe there will be some disease which attacks the femur. Perhaps growth disorders, chemical imbalances, or physiological changes will greatly alter the height to which we will grow, and the strength and stamina of our legs may be different somehow. Prosthetic science may introduce new breakthroughs in the course of this generation. From here on, the zodiac signs influence parts of the legs. Legs are what we stand on, and this generation will probably initiate a new understanding of our anatomical evolution.

PLUTO IN CAPRICORN GENERATION

The Pluto in Capricorn generation (2008 – 2023 / 24) will emphasize its school of thought and its focuses on life through such Capricorn related things as corporate growth, architectural feats, monumental achievements, industrial capitalization, environmental control, and many unprecedented forms of success and goal attainment. Capricorn says: "I use," and this produces an emphasis on the necessity for enterprising resourcefulness, employment services, exploitation, consumerism, and capitalization. Capricorn is ruled by the knees, the most complex mechanism of the legs. The Capricorn generation is likely to be strongly affected by major surgical feats and alterations with regard to knee health and knee related technology.

PLUTO IN AN EARTH SIGN

As Pluto always takes many years to traverse completely through any particular sign, we have now reached a place where there will be dynamically strong focuses on the earth and on the physical realm. When Pluto was in Sagittarius, there were times when none of the planets were traveling in any of the earth signs. A distinct lack of earth related influence often means there is less attention on the physical world and more attention on desires, ideas, and emotions. We tend to lose our sense of control over our environment when we become too preoccupied to pay attention to the physical. The generation to come will not have the luxury of ignoring the physical realms. They must – and will – master the physical. Capricorn represents cardinal earth, and is the authority of the earth element. Cardinal earth covers the domains of all types of physical landscapes, especially the world's majestic mountains where the symbol of Capricorn, the mountain goat, resides.

A CHANGE IN LANDSCAPE ♒

The Great Wall of China was the command of Qin Shi Huangdi, the first emperor of China during the Qin (Ch'in) Dynasty (221 BC - 206 BC). Just as it is now, Pluto was on the brink of entering Capricorn when the emperor died. From his vision of this Great Wall, the production of the wall continued to grow; it was built from the 3rd century BC until the beginning of the 17th century. Its enormity made it the one manmade structure on the face of the earth which was predominately visible in the first satellite pictures taken from space. In these days of technologically advanced global images from space, manmade structure will take new forms in the 21st century days of Pluto in Capricorn. Skyscrapers will reach new heights. In fact, this year the highest building ever, the Burj Tower in Dubai, will double the height of any of the tallest buildings now or ever recorded in world history. It will reach a projected height of 800 meters, or 2,625 feet; throw in an antenna and it's a cool enough height to be called "half a mile high." This is some way to kick off the opening of Pluto in Capricorn! This will be an era of architectural feats and advances – some resembling the most imaginative illustrations of science fiction fantasy, the likes of which will spring up around the globe, particularly wherever power and money prevails. These recent years of Pluto in Sagittarius have formed the vision of this pending global development; now this time of Pluto in Capricorn will seal this vision with greater industrialization, capitalization, and astounding growth and development on the physical plane. Pluto represents transformation, and this will be a time when environmentalism will be redefined as the planet Earth – or our earth-bound physical realities – are definitely slated for a strong transformation.

For more on the HISTORY and the FUTURE of Pluto in Capricorn, *see November 26*, when Pluto enters Capricorn on a much more permanent basis.

January 26th Saturday
Moon in Virgo / Libra

	PST	EST
Moon square Mars goes v/c	3:32 AM	6:32 AM
Moon enters Libra	2:36 PM	5:36 PM
Moon square Pluto	2:38 PM	5:38 PM
Moon square Venus	9:25 PM	12:25 AM (January 27)

Mood Watch: Overnight, Moon square Mars, coupled with the Moon going void-of-course, generally brings emotional turmoil and conflict. Fortunately for us in North America, this happens while most are sleeping. However, the entire morning and well into the course of the day, the void-of-course Virgo Moon lingers. It will be best not to hold the very highest of expectations today, as there may be a tendency for people to keep to themselves, or to exhibit a fair range of skepticism or doubt. Although it may seem difficult to keep communications on the up and up, this will be a good time to work on cleaning and organizing. Later, the Libra Moon brings a harmonizing affect to our moods and adds a lot more clarity to our outlook, although Moon square Pluto may bring struggles with regard to permanent changes. Later, Moon square Venus challenges the expression of our affections, and it may hard to experience loving feelings.

51

January 27ᵗʰ Sunday

Moon in Libra

	PST	EST
Moon trine Sun	3:56 AM	6:56 AM
Moon square Jupiter	7:58 AM	10:58 AM
Venus trine Saturn begins (see January 29)		
Mars-trine-Neptune-non-exact begins (see February 1)		

Mood Watch: Moon in Libra brings out an emphasis on the need for balance and harmony, particularly in law and family related matters. This morning's Moon square Jupiter may make it difficult for some folks to get motivated, and many will be inclined to stay home this Sunday. The Libra Moon keeps our senses in a careful pacing pattern. As the search for harmony continues, making balanced decisions regarding loved ones remains the focus of many. Waning Libra Moon often brings the need to release emotional misgivings in order to function peacefully in an imperfect world of complex relationships. There will always be a need for adjustments. Libra also focuses our attention on accessing information and on creating a pleasing and artistic atmosphere. Don't forget the epicurean delights!

January 28ᵗʰ Monday

Moon in Libra

	PST	EST
Moon trine Neptune	8:02 AM	11:02 AM
Mercury goes retrograde	12:31 PM	3:31 PM
Moon trine Mercury	1:20 PM	4:20 PM
Moon trine Mars goes v/c	1:48 PM	4:48 PM

Mood Watch: This waning Moon phase of Libra emphasizes the need to clear up any troubling imbalances that exist between friends. This is a good time to drop grudges and to attempt diplomacy with others. As the Moon goes void-of-course this afternoon, there may be a tendency for indecisiveness. This factor is compounded by the confusion of Mercury going retrograde today (see below). This is a good time to reiterate on absolutely *everything* and to be especially clear with people. You may have to simply warn them that confusion or misinterpretation is likely to screw up even the simplest of plans. They may not believe you at first, but perhaps a good laugh will come out of it in the end.

Mercury goes retrograde (Mercury retrograde: Jan. 28 – Feb. 18) Mercury goes retrograde today in the sign of Aquarius; it will travel back to the beginning of Aquarius before going direct at the eight degree mark of Aquarius on February 18. Mercury retrograde in Aquarius is likely to disrupt communications with misinformation, particularly for topics that cover science, education, human rights issues and philanthropic endeavors. Despite rational and fair minded attempts to spontaneously articulate ingenuous and profound subjects, Mercury retrograde in Aquarius will often leave us dissatisfied and tongue tied. A real test of everyone's patience occurs; this leaves us susceptible to arguments and confusion over scientific developments, and there may be a number of irritating miscommunications over technology related subjects or situations. At first it may be difficult to sit through everyone's excuses and misinformation, but eventually a logical explanation will emerge despite the setbacks. Expect to repeat yourself more than once or twice, and to be persistent as well as patient. For more information on Mercury retrograde, see the section in the introduction about *Mercury retrograde periods.*

January 29ᵗʰ Tuesday
Moon in Libra / Scorpio – LAST QUARTER MOON in SCORPIO

	PST	EST	
Moon enters Scorpio	1:35 AM	4:35 AM	
Moon sextile Pluto	1:47 AM	4:47 AM	
Moon sextile Venus	3:32 PM	6:32 PM	
Moon sextile Saturn	3:50 PM	6:50 PM	
Venus trine Saturn	6:18 PM	9:18 PM	
Moon sextile Jupiter	8:45 PM	11:45 PM	
Moon square Sun	9:03 PM	12:03 AM	(January 30)
Venus conjunct Jupiter begins (see February 1)			

Mood Watch: Besides the Last Quarter Moon aspect, today's lunar events are inspired by the sextile aspect. This implies that the day holds great promise and that opportunities abound. Of course, unless we *act* on this great potential that surrounds us, these opportunities may fall by the wayside. The abundance of sextile aspects occurring today ensures this will be a very busy time for our moods.

The **Last Quarter Moon in Scorpio** (Moon square Sun) occurs later this evening, and it focuses our attention on issues of passion and compassion. It is likely the dark secrets of our life will be touched on somehow. This Moon urges us to release stored up tension, and to find release for our emotions without imposing them on others. Physical workouts are excellent for this, provided safety consciousness is maintained. Safety consciousness of any kind is particularly important during Scorpio Moon. Don't forget to keep an eye out for suspicious activity -- beware of thieves, smooth talkers, and the potential for violent outbreaks.

Venus trine Saturn (occurring Jan. 27 – Feb. 1) This aspect implies that there is a good possibility here for a happy ending. Venus in Capricorn trine Saturn in Virgo brings an earthy, practical, and serious expression of love and commitment to love. Venus in the Saturn ruled sign Capricorn emphasizes the need for a real commitment, a serious one, to the person or thing that holds the greatest attraction. Venus trine Saturn often brings the gift of responsive and enduring love. This aspect may assist in bringing peace to the structure or the closure of a love relationship. This is good time to initiate or enhance a love vow or oath, and to apply the values of devotion and responsive caring. Love is a gift and a responsibility. Genuine love, when given without expectations, will return naturally and bring true love into your life. This aspect will reoccur April 29 – May 4, reaching its exact peak on May 1. It will also reoccur November 27 – December 2, reaching its peak on November 29.

January 30ᵗʰ Wednesday
Moon in Scorpio

	PST	EST
Moon trine Uranus	10:59 AM	1:59 PM
Mars goes direct	2:34 PM	5:34 PM
Moon square Neptune	8:33 PM	11:33 PM

Mood Watch: Today's moods express a deep underlying perception, an intense awareness that laces the events of the day with strong doses of emotion. A waning

Moon in Scorpio calls to us to let go of strong destructive tendencies, and challenges us to cease hurting ourselves and others, and to transform our lower impulses into higher aspirations. Under favorable circumstances, this is a good time to let go of the pain you've been concealing.

Mars goes direct (Mars direct: Jan. 30, 2008 – Dec. 19, 2009) Since November 15, 2007, Mars, "the god of war," has been retrograde. Mars has been traveling back through the signs of Cancer and Gemini, focusing the course of war related activities on such things as the home, territorialism, the media and communications. Mars retrograde through Cancer (November 15 to December 31, 2007) has been quite challenging, especially for the people of the cardinal signs of the zodiac: Cancer, Libra, Capricorn, and Aries. While Mars traveled back through the late degrees of Gemini (December 31, 2007 until now), our toughest challenges have been harnessing energies and conducting activities, This especially affects the mutable signs of Gemini, Virgo, Sagittarius, and Pisces. Here's the good news: Mars now moves *forward* through Gemini (24 degrees), and those who have been heavily challenged during this Mars retrograde period may now more successfully apply their energy levels and activities with much smoother results. The masculine force and vitality of Mars holds the promise of action and represents the principle of will; this shows us that energy can be directed anywhere we choose. While Mars moves forward, the force of the will is less likely to backfire. Mars energy motivates us, summons our need for survival, enables us to act in defense, and awakens the urge to express rage at the apparent offenses of the world. It is best to maintain one's own masculine force with the greatest of dignity and integrity. To live with the vitality of Mars is to serve the life force that lives inside each of us. Mars will now assume a forward moving position around the sun from our geocentric perspective for a nice long time: until December 19, 2009.

January 31st Thursday

Moon in Scorpio / Sagittarius	PST	EST
Moon square Mercury goes v/c	12:33 AM	3:33 AM
Moon enters Sagittarius	2:09 PM	5:09 PM
Mercury-trine-Mars-non-exact		

Mood Watch: The Scorpio Moon continues to wane while bringing strong emotional currents throughout the day. Before the dawn breaks, the Moon goes void-of-course for a number of hours. This morning and afternoon would be a particularly good time to apply some extra caution, especially since the waning void-of-course Moon in Scorpio is often a somewhat risky time to take on dangerous types of jobs. When it comes to important work, stick with skilled practitioners and, by all means, check for credentials. This is especially important while we take this time to adjust to Mercury being newly retrograde (Mercury retrograde: Jan. 28 – Feb. 18). As the Moon enters Sagittarius this afternoon, various philosophical views are revealed to give us a better perspective on matters.

Mercury-trine-Mars-non-exact (occurring Jan. 23 – Feb. 5) Mercury trine Mars comes as close as it can to the trine position today, coming within seconds to a perfect trine aspect. However, due to Mercury retrograde (Jan. 28 – Feb. 18), Mercury doesn't actually reach an exact trine to Mars this time. False starts may occur whenever a demand or a command is launched. The retrograde Mercury is famous for being the cause of misinformation. We must remember that Mercury trine Mars is a beneficial influence and miscommunication may also lead to positive action. This aspect will officially reach an exact peak when it returns to the stage on March 18.

February 1st Friday
National Freedom Day - USA

Moon in Sagittarius	PST	EST	
Venus conjunct Jupiter	3:33 AM	6:33 AM	
Moon square Saturn	4:03 AM	7:03 AM	
Moon sextile Sun	3:10 PM	6:10 PM	
Moon square Uranus	11:36 PM	2:36 AM	(February 2)
Mars-trine-Neptune-non-exact			

" If a nation values anything more than freedom, it will lose its freedom, and the irony of it is that if it is comfort or money that it values more, it will lose that too.
- W. Somerset Maugham (1874 – 1965)

Mood Watch: A new month begins, and the waning Sagittarius Moon opens up our moods to a new perspective on life as we enter the phase of winter that we hail as the Candlemas light, set to begin tomorrow. This is a time of initiation and growth. Waning Sagittarius Moon brings insightfulness and contemplative moods. To gain rich new insights, look for the signs, especially if you're traveling.

Mars-trine-Neptune-non-exact (occurring Jan. 27 – Feb. 9) Mars in Gemini trine Neptune in Aquarius comes as close as it can to reaching an exact trine position today. However, due to the fact that Mars recently went direct, Mars will never actually reach an *exact* trine to Neptune this winter. Despite this, the energy of Mars trine Neptune is still assuredly in full swing. This serves as a good time to initiate creative and imaginative spiritual practices and ceremonies, and to empower your personal outlook with spiritual well being. Mars trine Neptune will fully occur with Mars in Libra; see September 21.

Venus conjunct Jupiter (occurring Jan. 29 – Feb. 4) The influence of beauty, love and attraction (Venus) blends and melds with the powers of production, expansion, and prosperity (Jupiter). In the sign of Capricorn, these two planets are stirring up experiences which are very active and aggressive in nature. Capricorn is associated with industrialization, economic growth, stabilization, and loyalty. This is a time to enhance love relationships and realize the precious value of love in its most limitless sense, since the influence of Jupiter reminds us that the resources of love in the universe are inexhaustible and love's great bounty is designed to be shared. A love for expansion, and the growth of skill (or personal economy), comes out with the conjunction of Venus and Jupiter. Love is infectious. The more love is disseminated the more there is to share and expound on. This aspect will reoccur November 27 – December 4, reaching its exact aspect on December 1.

February 2nd Saturday
Candlemas – Groundhog Day

Moon in Sagittarius	PST	EST
Moon sextile Neptune	8:56 AM	11:56 AM
Moon sextile Mercury	9:29 AM	12:29 PM
Moon opposite Mars goes v/c	2:20 PM	5:20 PM
Mercury conjunct Neptune	4:53 PM	7:53 PM

Mood Watch: Moon in Sagittarius emphasizes the need for adventure and this is a good time for vision quests and visionary work. Let the imagination soar, and enjoy the place of bliss! A philosophical outlook puts us in touch with the abounding forces, and in the early part of the day, opportunity will shine. As the Moon goes void-of-course, moods may appear burned out, and the evening will eventually unfold into a somewhat spacey time. It may be that many folks will seem distracted, lost, or distant. This evening, expect delays when traveling. Don't let imperfection spoil the mood; stick to the bliss!

Today is Candlemas: a celebration of the return of the light. Out of the darkness and into the light -- this represents a time of blossoming knowledge and a time to acknowledge one's own growth. We are now one half of the way through winter season. This holiday is also known as **Imbolc**, the breakthrough of winter's darkness. The days to come bring prismatic sparkling color through crystals suspended from windows. The light awakens and stirs the seeds of hope, and touches us from within. The legendary Irish Saint, Bridget, dons a crown of candles. Light candles and celebrate the return of the light! Today is also Groundhog Day, when the absence or presence of the groundhog's shadow predicts the course of the final half of winter season.

Mercury conjunct Neptune (occurring Jan. 19 – Feb. 5) This aspect usually only occurs once a year, but due to Mercury retrograde from January 28 to February 18, we get to enjoy the influence of Mercury conjunct Neptune for the second time this year. While Mercury is retrograde, it would be wise to be especially careful when relaying spiritual messages. For more details on Mercury conjunct Neptune, see when it first occurred – January 22. This aspect will reoccur March 6 – 11, reaching its exact aspect on March 9.

February 3rd Sunday

Moon in Sagittarius / Capricorn	PST	EST	
Moon enters Capricorn	1:53 AM	4:53 AM	
Moon conjunct Pluto	2:20 AM	5:20 AM	
Moon trine Saturn	2:58 PM	5:58 PM	
Moon conjunct Jupiter	10:25 PM	1:25 AM	(February 4)

Mood Watch: Overnight, the void-of-course Sagittarius Moon enters Capricorn. Our moods are likely to be dominated by a serious phase of expression throughout the day beginning with the intensity of Moon conjunct Pluto. This is an especially good time to tackle and complete a job that has been lurking in the shadows, or to tend to some job that obviously needs to be handled before it gets to be a problem. Moon trine Saturn invites us to accomplish something today, and to feel good about it too! Capricorn Moon keeps our moods focused on important matters and relentlessly reminds us to get a handle on our unfinished business. For some, the important "task" may be the job of resting, but if that's not the case for you, don't use this as an excuse! Enjoy the work!

February 4th Monday
Moon in Capricorn

	PST	EST
Moon conjunct Venus	4:29 AM	7:29 AM
Moon sextile Uranus goes v/c	10:19 AM	1:19 PM

Mood Watch: As the Moon wanes in Capricorn, we are reminded of our unfinished business. There is an air of determination with each matter under consideration. Anything worth doing is best tackled in the early morning. Early today, the Moon goes void-of-course where it remains for the entire day and night. Keeping the foundation of our lives and our work strong and firm is the underlying theme of today's moods. When losing ground, it is difficult to maintain a sense of humor, but humor is an essential part of maintaining one's integrity. Shaky territory requires an overhaul - rebuild and start over again. The commitment to carrying on time honored traditions, and discharging the workload with a sense of accomplishment, brings favorable moods today.

February 5th Tuesday
Moon in Capricorn / Aquarius

	PST	EST
Moon enters Aquarius	11:10 AM	2:10 PM
Sun conjunct Mercury begins (see February 6)		
Venus sextile Uranus begins (see February 6)		

Mood Watch: The morning brings the void-of-course Capricorn Moon and we may be confronted with some of the qualities of yesterday's non-productive and mundanely slow pace. However, by midday, the darkly waning Moon enters Aquarius and our moods begin to open up to a much more receptive and productive quality of expression. Deep contemplative thoughts require brilliant solutions to brighten the mood. Introspective wisdom comes to those who take the time to think things through. A scientific approach to the world around us reminds us that discoveries are made when we choose to experiment. Today will be a good day for research and experimentation. However, experiment wisely; today's darkly waning Moon before tomorrow's solar eclipse may be tiresome for some folks.

February 6th Wednesday
NEW MOON in AQUARIUS – Annular Solar Eclipse

	PST	EST
Sun conjunct Mercury	10:18 AM	1:18 PM
Moon conjunct Mercury	6:17 PM	9:17 PM
Venus sextile Uranus	6:22 PM	9:22 PM
Moon conjunct Sun	7:44 PM	10:44 PM

Mood Watch: **New Moon in Aquarius** (Moon conjunct Sun) is a good time to begin new social and philanthropic endeavors, and to attain new knowledge by learning something new about ourselves or our ever changing world. Moods created by this

New Moon may be bold or daring, with a flair for experimenting with life. This is the time to open up to new feelings and greater comprehension of science and technology and of these changing times, adding to our power.

An **Annular Solar Eclipse in the sign of Aquarius** brings an emphasis on the needs of humanity and the systems by which it operates. This may be a time of technological glitches or accidental breakthroughs. There may also be some form of inspiration or liberating change as a result of longer and harder looks at the way the systems operate. For some, the act of thinking comprehensively may be over-shadowed by the solar eclipse energy, particularly now that Mercury is retrograde. This is a good time to pace ourselves through the motions of this shadowy time.

Sun conjunct Mercury (occurring Feb. 5 – 7) This aspect will occur half a dozen times this year, as it is a common occurrence due to the closeness of Mercury to the Sun. This aspect will create a much more thoughtful, communicative, and expressive year ahead for those Aquarius people celebrating birthdays from February 5 – 7. This is your time (birthday Aquarians) to record ideas, relay important messages, and pay close attention to your imaginative thoughts as they are touched by Mercury, creating the urge to speak and be heard. Birthday Aquarians, your thoughts will reveal a great deal about who you are, now and in the year to come.

Venus sextile Uranus (occurring Feb. 5 – 8) Venus in Capricorn is sextile to Uranus in Pisces. Radically serious kinds of love and aesthetics can be very uplifting at this time, particularly while extreme types of tests are occurring and being stretched beyond the limits in love related matters. Eccentric love may erupt with this aspect. This is the time to work on pent up frustrations with loved ones and to reconcile differences by loving and accepting variation, giving freedom and slack to our loved ones. This aspect will reoccur May 16 – 19, reaching its exact aspect on May 18. Venus will also return to Capricorn on November 12, and with that comes the return of Venus sextile Uranus on November 28.

February 7th Thursday
Moon in Aquarius / Pisces
Chinese New Year: Rat (Year 4706) *Earth Rat*

	PST	EST
Moon conjunct Neptune	2:40 AM	5:40 AM
Moon trine Mars goes v/c	7:49 AM	10:49 AM
Moon enters Pisces	5:47 PM	8:47 PM
Moon sextile Pluto	6:26 PM	9:26 PM
Sun conjunct Neptune begins (see February 10)		

Mood Watch: For a good portion of the day and part of the evening, the Aquarius Moon will be void-of-course. This is classically a time of technological glitches, and some issues may arise with regard to human rights or systems that don't work. This evening, Moon in Pisces brings intuitive and artistic moods a good time to relax.

Happy Chinese New Year! - **Year of the Rat** (occurring: February 7, 2008 – February 6, 2008). Few would suspect that the Rat personality is best known for its charm. Rats are persistent with their efforts to enjoy a full and opulent lifestyle, especially Earth Rats. Rats are hard working and thrifty, but never cheap. As well as being ambitious, Rats also tend to be quite honest, and it may be very difficult to pull one over on them since they are persistently curious and often well apprised of their situation. On the downside, the Rat personality is considered shallow-minded and easily prone to anger, yet they also have pretty good self control, which might lead some folks to think of them as calculating or manipulative. As socialites, Rats tend to be the life of the party, always talking and often gossiping. The earth element greatly tempers the Rat personality with a fair share of practicality and restraint, and they are especially known for their material savvy. The Earth Rat can be extremely seductive and naturally very sensuous. The Year of the Rat is a great time for social engagement, organization and, of course, thrifty persistence towards reaching goals.

February 8th Friday

Moon in Pisces

	PST	EST	
Moon opposite Saturn	5:07 AM	8:07 AM	
Moon sextile Jupiter	2:12 PM	5:12 PM	
Moon conjunct Uranus	11:49 PM	2:49 AM	(February 9)

Mood Watch: Today the Moon in Pisces is beginning the waxing cycle as a newly emerging crescent. This being so, the overall mood begins to awaken our senses to a vague sense of visionary awareness and to initiate the potential for strong psychic intuition. All the while, a glimmer of light barely begins to touch our winter slumber; at last we have made it past Candlemas (Feb. 2), and the light will seem much more prevalent. Something inherently special and often incommunicable touches the heart in the newly waxing inspiration of Pisces Moon. This is the time to recognize an inherent gift that exists within, and to visualize the ways in which that gift can manifest. It is best to get the majority of the workload accomplished today – a portion of tomorrow brings the void-of-course Moon of Pisces. This invariably decreases a sense of progress, but don't be fooled; progress occurs on unseen levels with Moon in Pisces.

February 9th Saturday

Moon in Pisces/ Aries

	PST	EST	
Moon sextile Venus	4:51 AM	7:51 AM	
Moon square Mars goes v/c	1:04 PM	4:04 PM	
Moon enters Aries	10:18 PM	1:18 AM	(February 10)
Moon square Pluto	11:02 PM	2:02 AM	(February 10)

Mood Watch: The Pisces Moon is a good time to use the imagination and focus on artistic and creative endeavors. This afternoon, the Moon goes void-of-course, making this morning the best time to tackle important tasks. Generally speaking, spacey moods are typically what we might expect, and since the Moon will square with Mars when it goes void-of-course, this is a good time to keep an eye out for potential accidents, substance misuse, or temperamental behavior. If at all possible, remember to relax and take it easy, but remain vigilant and cautious. Much later, the Aries Moon motivates us with a strong sense of resolve; at the end of the day, there is eagerness in our moods.

February 10th Sunday

Moon in Aries

	PST	EST
Sun conjunct Neptune	6:02 PM	9:02 PM
Moon square Jupiter	6:55 PM	9:55 PM
Moon sextile Mercury	7:27 PM	10:27 PM
Sun trine Mars begins (see February 14)		

Mood Watch: Waxing Moon represents a time of increasing the awareness of our feelings. Winter restlessness stirs our hearts. The desire to start up new projects is also a symptom of the youthfully waxing Aries Moon. There is another significant occurrence: most of our planets are currently residing in the winter signs of the zodiac, except for two – Mars in Gemini and Saturn in Virgo. As the Moon has now passed through the heavily traversed constellations of winter, the Aries Moon puts a new perspective on our feelings and moods. This Aries Moon now boldly carries our moods beyond the series of planetary conjunctions and emotionally stirring influences of the last week. Aries is a spring sign, and this is the time to initiate a bit of spring, to allow enthusiasm and energetic force to grow.

Sun conjunct Neptune (occurring Feb. 7 – 13) This occurrence of Sun conjunct Neptune particularly affects Aquarius people celebrating birthdays February 7 – 13 with intuitive inclinations and spiritual desires. Your visions (Aquarius birthday folks) will inspire great feats, and the higher, more spiritually refined parts of the soul are going to be speaking to you throughout the upcoming year. Listen! This may be a time to let go of personal attachments and outmoded desires that appear to be going nowhere. Your highly complex Aquarian idealism will work up your spiritual beliefs into a kind of peak performance level, even if you don't believe you have such a thing as spiritual beliefs. Birthday Aquarians, you will continue to encounter a kind of spiritual catharsis and, by the time you've come through this, you'll know what that means. This is all magnified by your ruling planet, Uranus, which has been traveling through the Neptune-ruled sign of Pisces since March 2003. Integrate a listening pattern concerning the Great Spirit in your life; focus on the spiritual part of the self (or higher self) that rules over personal destiny and guides the true desires of the soul. Can you handle that, birthday folks?

February 11th Monday

Moon in Aries

	PST	EST
Moon sextile Neptune	11:31 AM	2:31 PM
Moon sextile Sun	12:49 PM	3:49 PM
Moon square Venus	1:24 PM	4:24 PM
Moon sextile Mars goes v/c	4:59 PM	7:59 PM

Mood Watch: There is a warrior in everyone's heart waiting to tackle the next battle. We're all in the mood to find a leader who will aid us in battle and inspire us to act assertively towards our next move. The leader lives within each of us, and our moods are geared towards confident, swift, and intrepid ability. Positive lunar aspects bring opportunity to the day, except for this afternoon's Moon square Venus; beware of thwarted affections. By evening, the Moon goes void-of-course when Moon sextile Mars occurs. This may be a good time to tap into a nice even pace of energy, but watch out for tendencies towards pessimism, vacillation, delays, impatience, or exhibits of weakness in the self. At each turn, positive reinforcement is the key to success.

February 12ᵗʰ Tuesday

Moon in Aries / Taurus

	PST	EST
Moon enters Taurus	1:34 AM	4:34 AM
Moon trine Pluto	2:23 AM	5:23 AM
Moon trine Saturn	11:52 AM	2:52 PM
Moon square Mercury	7:28 PM	10:28 PM
Moon trine Jupiter	10:38 PM	1:38 AM (February 13)

Mood Watch: Today, the Moon is trine with the big boys (Pluto, Saturn, and Jupiter) and square to Mercury. The Taurus Moon inspires us to face big endeavors with a positive spirit but, by evening, the Moon square Mercury thing leaves us tongue tied. It will be necessary to persevere through our thoughts and to reiterate on all counts; don't forget Mercury is retrograde (Jan. 28 – Feb. 18) and this means that we are deeply challenged by simple communications. The Taurus Moon waxes and our enthusiastic stubbornness to get the job done, despite faulty communications, will make the difference. Overall, our moods are in for a positive day, and the sweet nightcap of Moon trine Jupiter allows us to tap into a sense of joy.

February 13ᵗʰ Wednesday

FIRST QUARTER MOON in TAURUS

	PST	EST
Moon sextile Uranus	6:49 AM	9:49 AM
Moon square Neptune	2:30 PM	5:30 PM
Moon square Sun	7:33 PM	10:33 PM
Moon trine Venus goes v/c	9:04 PM	12:04 AM (February 14)

Mood Watch: **First Quarter Moon in Taurus** (Moon square Sun) brings the pressure to take care of essential needs. Taurus is the *fixed earth* sign, and the nature of Taurus Moon leads many folks to watch their pocketbook and make sure they're getting the most value possible out of all expenditures. There is also a need to let the beauty of our surroundings be accented and appreciated. Somewhere in between the processes of earning and reaping our rewards, a happy medium is struck. The Moon is *exalted* in the place of Taurus, and positive harmony will return satisfaction.

February 14ᵗʰ Thursday

Saint Valentine's Day
Moon in Taurus / Gemini

	PST	EST
Moon enters Gemini	4:20 AM	7:20 AM
Sun trine Mars	8:38 AM	11:38 AM
Moon square Saturn	2:19 PM	5:19 PM
Moon trine Mercury	8:02 PM	11:02 PM

Mood Watch: HAPPY VALENTINE'S DAY! It is appropriate that the Gemini twins are depicted as *the Lovers* in the Tarot. Today's Saint Valentine Moon is in Gemini, and our moods are likely to be reciprocated and playfully romantic. Gemini

Moon can sometimes be very distracting in its playfulness, and fickleness may also be present on some level. Some people may choose to keep their love-play light hearted, and non-committal tendencies may be present in some people's moods. While this afternoon's Moon square Saturn may bring some impatience, or the feeling of limitation, the evening's favorable Moon trine Mercury brings a perfect time to work through our communication blunders and to relay the truth about how we feel. It is important to remember that communication goes both ways; we must listen and speak, but not at the same time.

Sun trine Mars (occurring Feb. 10 – 17) This occurrence of Sun trine Mars particularly affects those Aquarius people celebrating birthdays from February 10 – 17. There will be loads of energy to work with, and a strong need to activate the personality and accomplish goals. Creative work abounds. There are special gifts of triumph for those Aquarius folks who activate their dreams and desires, allowing them to easily utilize existing energy. This is a time to exercise the will and the internal sense of primal might, to stir the personal agenda into a state of action. Heated matters will come to the surface in an advantageous manner. Through the act of making things happen, personal achievement will shine forth like a long needed blessing in the year to come for these birthday folks. Keep it active, Aquarius.

February 15th Friday

Moon in Gemini

	PST	EST	
Moon square Uranus	9:46 AM	12:46 PM	
Moon trine Neptune	5:25 PM	8:25 PM	
Moon conjunct Mars	11:47 PM	2:47 AM	(February 16)

Mood Watch: Trivia Question: What are the two most common things in the universe?*… Sometimes the whirling universe is bursting with more great mystery than one can comprehend. Sometimes the vastness of knowledge cannot be stored with so much detail overloading the system. Sometimes the mind is full and the chattering world won't cease. Gemini moon playfully waxes and loves to play tricks on the mind. Don't overdo the caffeine and take it easy on the nervous system. When in doubt, apply humor. …*Trivia Quiz Answer: Did you guess hydrogen and oxygen? – you were close! Comedy dictates that hydrogen and *stupidity* are the two most common things in the universe! Aquarius Sun and Gemini Moon indicate the need to act with knowledge and to think matters through. There are a lot of things we don't know, but sometimes ignoring the things we do know is a sign of stupidity.

February 16th Saturday

Moon in Gemini / Cancer

	PST	EST
Moon trine Sun goes v/c	2:17 AM	5:17 AM
Moon enters Cancer	7:12 AM	10:12 AM
Moon opposite Pluto	8:13 AM	11:13 AM
Moon sextile Saturn	5:01 PM	8:01 PM

Mood Watch: Moon in Gemini goes void-of-course throughout the dawning hours but, soon enough it slips into Cancer, where our moods are geared towards nurturing and appeasing the emotions. Some do this with an emphasis on food, cooking, and dining. Others may choose to pamper themselves with luxury baths, while others just need to spill the emotional core and let off some steam in the hope that someone will listen sympathetically. The good news: in just a couple of days (Feb. 18) Mercury will go direct and basic communications will be much more easily reconcilable. The bad news: it is often the going into - and coming out of - stage of this Mercury retrograde process that is the most difficult. Hang in there; within a few days after this Mercury retrograde episode ends, communications will be distinctly much clearer. Cancer Moon clearly assists us in feeling our way through situations. There are loads of ways to nurture and give emotional support. Sometimes it's as simple as applying the listening ear.

February 17th Sunday

Moon in Cancer

	PST	EST
Moon opposite Jupiter	5:56 AM	8:56 AM
Venus enters Aquarius	8:22 AM	11:22 AM
Moon trine Uranus goes v/c	1:13 PM	4:13 PM
Sun sextile Pluto begins (see February 19)		

Mood Watch: The waxing Cancer Moon endears home related projects and leisure to us. In the afternoon, the Moon goes void-of-course. This day will seem to bring a stream of distractions, particularly with emotional or mood oriented interruptions. Mood fluctuation is inescapable and this tends to slow down overall progress considerably. All of this moodiness is a natural process, but it can cause forgetfulness, oversensitive or defensive mood swing ellipses... perhaps even senseless attempts at being logical.

Venus enters Aquarius (Venus in Aquarius: Feb. 17 – March 12) Venus in Aquarius creates a fondness for invention, eccentric pleasures, and social life. It puts the focus of attraction and adoration on illuminating kinds of knowledge and on brilliant humanitarian causes and exploits. There is an especially strong attraction to invention – all types of invention – and to new technologies. It is likely to be a beneficial time for the love life of Aquarius people, whose affections and aesthetic pleasures can be enhanced now. By contrast, Scorpio and Taurus people may notice that love related focuses are causing tension in their personal lives – too many complex issues. Leo people, as a general rule, can never get enough love and affection, and they may be particularly aware of their own personal needs for love and beauty while Venus is opposing their natal Sun. Venus in Aquarius is a prime time to perfect and enhance our love of humanity, and to break down the barriers of useless and destructive prejudice and stereotyping.

PISCES
Key Phrase: "I Believe"
Mutable Water Sign
Symbol : The Fishes
February 18th through March 19th

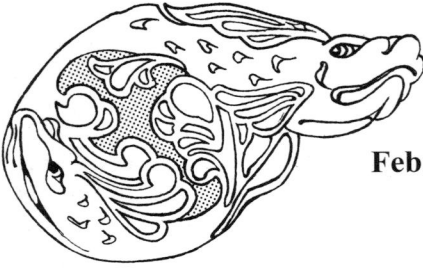

February 18th Monday
Washington's Birthday, USA

Moon in Cancer / Leo	PST	EST	
Moon enters Leo	10:52 AM	1:52 PM	
Moon opposite Venus	1:28 PM	4:28 PM	
Mercury goes direct	6:58 PM	9:58 PM	
Sun enters Pisces	10:49 PM	1:49 AM	(February 19)

Mood Watch: This morning, misdirected moodiness may be a symptom of this Monday void-of-course Moon in Cancer. Eventually the Moon enters Leo and our perspective shifts over to wild and creative kinds of moods. Moon in Leo focuses our moods on personal projects, family matters, and entertainment. Romance is sparked with the drama and spotlights of Leo perfectionism, but we must be careful not to overdo it with Moon opposite Venus. This is a good time to give compliments, stroke the ego until it blushes, to dance, sing, and enjoy letting the wild and beastly side of our natures be free.

Mercury goes direct (Mercury direct: Feb. 18 – May 26) Since January 28, Mercury has been retrograde in the sign of Aquarius, commonly causing communication mix-ups and confusion when relaying information. In Aquarius, the retrograde Mercury often causes communication glitches with regard to social engagements, charity efforts, and technological events. Now we can breathe a greatly needed sigh of relief as Mercury, the planet governing the realms of communication, becomes stationary and will soon begin to move forward. Take note that our faculties and manner of communicating will definitely improve within the next few days. Although perhaps not today – when the stationary Mercury often freezes communication efforts – but very soon our communications will run more smoothly; this will be a good time to begin clearing up various misunderstandings that have occurred over the past few weeks. For more information on this recently completed phase of Mercury retrograde, see February 18. For more on Mercury retrograde patterns throughout this year, see the introduction on *Mercury retrograde periods.*

Sun enters Pisces (Sun in Pisces: Feb. 18 PST /19 EST – March 19 EDT /20 EDT) Pisces is the last sign of the zodiac, representing the completion of a cycle. This mutable water sign is adaptive and Pisceans can absorb all kinds of influence.

64

However, if bogged down by oppressive influences, the Piscean becomes burnt out, oversensitive, and depressed. It is important for the Piscean to find ways to vent heavy feelings of oppression. Pisces people are very psychic as a general rule, and they are also quite artistic and imaginative. The Pisces time of year is a good time to get in touch with divinity.

February 19th Tuesday

Moon in Leo

	PST	EST
Moon opposite Mercury	1:27 AM	4:27 AM
Sun sextile Pluto	2:47 PM	5:47 PM

Mood Watch: Leo Moon brings out the need to relax and keep warm in the midst of winter. The heavily waxing Leo Moon is full of anticipation and excitement, magnifying personal desires as well as family needs. This is a good time to treat oneself to something that will encourage the heart, particularly the childlike aspects of the heart.

Sun sextile Pluto (occurring Feb. 17 – 21) The Sun, barely in Pisces, is sextile Pluto, newly in Capricorn, bringing opportunities that appear both vast and demanding to Pisces/Aquarius cusp born people celebrating birthdays between February 17 – 21. These birthday people are experiencing the sextile aspect of their natal sun to Pluto, giving them opportunities to take charge, to step into positions of power, and to accept and embrace permanent change in their lives. These are powerful transformations which provide opportunities to embody what has been learned from the personal trials of the past. Go thee forth and conquer, master Pisceans and Aquarians! Persist with diligence to resolve the conflicts of your life with self-respect and assurance. Your time to triumph is always available when your will to achieve is balanced by knowledge and hard work. This holds true for all signs of the zodiac. This aspect will re-occur October 19 – 23, reaching its exact aspect on October 21.

February 20th Wednesday

Moon in Leo / Virgo – FULL MOON in VIRGO – Total Lunar Eclipse

	PST	EST
Moon sextile Mars goes v/c	9:53 AM	12:53 PM
Moon enters Virgo	4:07 PM	7:07 PM
Moon trine Pluto	5:22 PM	8:22 PM
Moon opposite Sun	7:30 PM	10:30 PM

Mood Watch: Much of the day, the nearly Full Moon is in Leo, and for awhile, it is void-of-course, causing wild, disorganized, self-oriented moods, and distractions. All of this builds up to the **Full Moon in Virgo** (Moon opposite Sun), which reaches its peak this evening, and reminds us of the need to organize, analyze, and constructively criticize our health and cleanliness practices. Virgo also puts the focus on organization, filing, accounting, preparing taxes, and handling all of life's mundane necessities. Virgo Moon energy purges and purifies our surroundings with sound resourcefulness and simple logic. Virgo rules the intestines of the body and represents the process of elimination. Now is an excellent time to focus on

65

eliminating toxins and purifying the body. This is also a good time to purge the useless, destructive, or outmoded habits of our life. Celebrate your existing health and do something good for your body on this Full Virgo Moon.

Total Lunar Eclipse in Virgo – What we are likely to observe are the darkening psychological affects and the shadowy emotional subtleties of the Virgo Lunar Eclipse. Depression is one commonly noticed symptom of this Virgo Moon phenomenon. Doubt, scrutiny, criticism, and uncertainty may also be the subtle shadows cast upon us. The death of prominent people may be notable. This lunar extravaganza influences priests, divinatory practices, and the worship of gods. The quality of our intuition may seem compromised by doubt, confusion, or by confrontation. The mutable earth sign of Virgo in the ecliptic state also influences earthquakes, hurricanes, floods, storms, drought, thunder and lighting. This is the time to combat emotional doubts and fears, to calm and ease the nerves and the mind with diligent care. Gentle kindness helps.

February 21st Thursday

Moon in Virgo

	PST	EST	
Moon conjunct Saturn	1:56 AM	4:56 AM	
Moon trine Jupiter	6:01 PM	9:01 PM	
Sun opposite Saturn begins (see February 24)			

Mood Watch: It's an all around earthy sort of day – the kind of day that leads us to do such Virgolike things as organizing, secretarial work, statistics and accounting, crafts, collecting and classifying, study and writing. The residual Full Moon energy now subsides, but the crux of the Virgo Moon spirit is just as strong as ever. Virgo is ruled by Mercury, the communications planet. Now that Mercury has been direct for three days, this is a splendid time to work on clearing up communications in a big way, with meticulous, adaptable, and skillful qualities. Tonight, Moon trine Jupiter brings joy!

February 22nd Friday

Moon in Virgo / Libra

	PST	EST	
Moon opposite Uranus	12:44 AM	3:44 AM	
Moon square Mars	6:14 PM	9:14 PM	
Moon enters Libra	11:45 PM	2:45 AM	(February 23)
Mercury conjunct Venus begins (see February 26)			

Mood Watch: It's Moon in Virgo once again. Virgo is the prudent sign of the zodiac, always looking for the loopholes in everything, always questioning, always doubting, scrutinizing, and discerning. Apart from the critic that comes out in all of us, one might notice there is a strong need to pay attention to personal hygiene. Perhaps there is a need to apply some extra effort when brushing the teeth, washing the body and hair, and preparing one's overall appearance and the feeling about this appearance. The trick is to do all this without being overly critical of one's personal state of being. Virgo emphasizes health and daily maintenance, and don't forget the Moon is simply the mood and feeling tone setter of our condition. It is only a temporary state of being and not everyone is focused on their daily moods.

Those that are focused on mood will be the ones to notice the true feeling of what is really going on around them. If we don't wish to appear overly judgmental, we don't always have to react to the things we observe – we can just simply be aware of them.

♓

February 23ʳᵈ Saturday

Moon in Libra

	PST	EST
Moon square Pluto	1:10 AM	4:10 AM
Moon trine Venus	2:32 PM	5:32 PM
Moon trine Mercury	6:09 PM	9:09 PM

Mood Watch: The mood of the day on the celestial chef's menu is about balancing and harmonizing our lives while maintaining a central area of peace in which we seek to dwell. Many of us have our battles to face, while others are truly at work molding and changing the face of justice itself. With so many moral issues at work in the justice system, there is no higher pinnacle from which to create a sense of balance than the very center of our individual being. With this internal equilibrium, there is the potential for us to balance out energies interactively. Libra Moon emphasizes relationships. It is to our advantage that the Moon is trine with both Venus and Mercury. This allows us to harmonize relationships, enjoy pleasurable exploits, and to communicate openly.

February 24ᵗʰ Sunday

Moon in Libra

	PST	EST
Sun opposite Saturn	1:47 AM	4:47 AM
Moon square Jupiter	3:50 AM	6:50 AM
Moon trine Neptune	6:46 PM	9:46 PM

Mood Watch: As the Moon wanes in Libra, we focus on balancing the inconsistencies of relations with partners, loved ones and friends. Libra Moon emphasizes the need for teamwork. There are a number of adjustments being made throughout the entire day and evening. This may also be a crucial time of decision, particularly in making decisions that affect the people who share our life and work. This waning Moon phase of Libra emphasizes the need to clear up any troubling imbalances that exist between friends. This is a good time to drop grudges and attempt diplomacy with others, particularly now that Mercury has finally gone direct (*see Feb 18*).

Sun opposite Saturn (occurring Feb. 21 – 26) This occurrence of Sun opposite Saturn particularly affects those Pisces people celebrating birthdays from February 21 – 26. These birthday folks are undergoing personal challenges with regard to patience, leaving them strongly aware of who and what is in control. These people are mindful of the crucial factors of time, limitations, and timing. Work demands may be overwhelming, and these Pisces folks will have to apply discipline and determination in order to achieve success. Work that requires self motivation may be the most challenging part of applying discipline while Saturn is in Virgo. Pisces birthday folks, this is a most important time in your life to persist! Endure! Keep up the Great Work! Take heart, as this may well be your year, Birthday Pisces, to accomplish something astounding.

67

February 25th Monday

Moon in Libra / Scorpio	PST	EST
Moon trine Mars goes v/c	5:34 AM	8:34 AM
Moon enters Scorpio	10:06 AM	1:06 PM
Moon sextile Pluto	11:40 AM	2:40 PM
Moon sextile Saturn	8:05 PM	11:05 PM
Mars opposite Pluto begins (see March 7)		

Mood Watch: Throughout morning/afternoon, the Moon is void-of-course in Libra causing a lot of issues around making decisions, and there's a tendency for people to disagree on the various matters at hand. Despite confusion, the mood finally breaks as the Moon changes over to the sign of Scorpio. Waning Scorpio Moon emphasizes the need for release of tension and emotional buildups. This is a good time to work on allowing emotional expression to flow, however harsh it may appear on some levels, and trust that the release will bring a greater sense of healing.

February 26th Tuesday

Moon in Scorpio	PST	EST	
Moon trine Sun	12:16 AM	3:16 AM	
Moon square Venus	8:17 AM	11:17 AM	
Moon square Mercury	8:22 AM`	11:22 AM	
Mercury conjunct Venus	9:56 AM	12:56 PM	
Moon sextile Jupiter	4:13 PM	7:13 PM	
Moon trine Uranus	10:13 PM	1:13 AM	(February 27)

Mood Watch: Today will have its ups and downs. Waning Scorpio Moon reminds us to keep a handle on self-criticism, as well as the tendency towards jealousy, suspicion and crimes of hate. Intense moods can be worked out through all kinds of therapy. Dealing with personal truth is important.

Mercury conjunct Venus (occurring Feb. 22 – March 31) Today's conjunction of Mercury and Venus takes place in the ingenious realm of Aquarius. This is often a time when intimate and loving thoughts are shared with inventive and intellectually stimulating flare. With this aspect, loving gestures are usually very sincere and genuine. Hold no expectations in the expression of love, and take no offense if your own attempts to express your love are poorly interpreted. This conjunction will reoccur on March 24 before fading at month's end. It will also occur June 5 – 9, reaching its exact conjunction on June 7. It will reoccur for a final round this year August 14 – September 19, reaching its exact conjunction on August 21, and again on September 14.

February 27th Wednesday

Moon in Scorpio/ Sagittarius	PST	EST	
Moon square Neptune goes v/c	6:53 AM	9:53 AM	
Moon enters Sagittarius	10:23 PM	1:23 AM	(February 28)

Mood Watch: This Scorpio Moon winter day infuses our moods with the need to work through intensity on whatever level it presents itself. All of this is particularly true as the Moon goes void-of-course throughout the day and into the evening. Those who find themselves contending with the forces of inner turmoil or emotional clamor are quite likely to spew forth numerous confessions or complaints in an effort to find relief. Beware of the tendency for some folks to attempt to unload personal troubles on others rather than attempting to deal with them on their own. If your own troubles are full, it can be very frustrating to waste time listening to the troubles of others. Shooting at troubles can never be productive if troubled feelings keep shooting back. The waning Scorpio Moon is a good time to tend to personal troubles that really need addressing.

February 28th Thursday
LAST QUARTER MOON in SAGITTARIUS

	PST	EST
Moon square Saturn	8:06 AM	11:06 AM
Moon square Sun	6:18 PM	9:18 PM

Mood Watch: The morning might start out rather serious, or even somber, with the Moon square Saturn. The **Last Quarter Moon in Sagittarius** (Moon square Sun) is a good time to internalize your new wishes and thoughts about the upcoming season. At the same time, focus on healing disruptive feelings and make a sporting effort to let go of unsatisfactory habits. Sagittarius Moon focuses our attention on such things as fitness, philosophy and travel. This is the time to broaden the mind and allow yourself to go further than anticipated in realizing your vision for the future.

February 29th Friday
Leap Year Day - 2008
Moon in Sagittarius

	PST	EST
Moon sextile Mercury	1:04 AM	4:04 AM
Moon sextile Venus	3:48 AM	6:48 AM
Moon square Uranus	11:00 AM	2:00 PM
Moon sextile Neptune	7:30 PM	10:30 PM

Mood Watch: Moon in Sagittarius puts the emphasis on endeavors such as travel and exercise. This is the time to use the imagination and apply the efforts of visionary work, perhaps even a vision quest, to attain a place of bliss and comfort. Sagittarius Moon is a great time to let the imagination soar, and to apply a philosophical outlook to the abounding forces that have changed and challenged our lives this month.

Leap Year 2008: We close this month with the rare occasion of a Leap Year day. Just like a presidential election, the date of February 29th only rolls around once every four years, and is often celebrated with zeal, particularly among our Pisces friends who celebrate this day as their birth date. In Gilbert and Sullivan's *The Pirates of Penzance (1879)*, the theme of February 29th has a surprising twist, when a main character (Frederic) is bound to carry out his pirate duties until he has reached his 21st birthday. As his supposed 21st birthday approaches, he is shocked to discover that since his birthday of February 29th only occurs once every four years, he is left helplessly at their service for some 84 years in total. Pisceans with this birthday are poignantly reminded that contractual agreements involving their birthday must be painstakingly thought through.

69

March 1st Saturday

Moon in Sagittarius/ Capricorn	PST	EST
Moon opposite Mars goes v/c	8:53 AM	11:53 AM
Moon enters Capricorn	10:34 AM	1:34 PM
Moon conjunct Pluto	12:16 PM	3:16 PM
Moon trine Saturn	7:38 PM	10:38 PM

Mood Watch: These are the mutable days of Pisces. We now commence the exciting month of March when the final weeks of winter give way to a whirlwind of change and to the brighter lengthening of the days. As the waning Sagittarius Moon opposes Mars, it goes void-of-course for awhile, and some folks may find that their hasty ambitions lead them straight into philosophical introspection. Slow down; beware of the potential for accidents. As the Moon enters Capricorn, a serious attitude to ground our energies and maintain our focus develops. This is a time when we tend to put our reactive tendencies aside and carry on in a dutiful, goal oriented canter.

March 2nd Sunday

Moon in Capricorn	PST	EST	
Moon sextile Sun	11:11 AM	2:11 PM	
Moon conjunct Jupiter	5:43 PM	8:43 PM	
Moon sextile Uranus goes v/c	10:15 PM	1:15 AM	(March 3)

Mood Watch: Today's sun in Pisces, coupled with the waning Moon in Capricorn, brings clarity and adaptability to the mood. This is the time to work on completion, to prepare for (or clean up after) late winter storms, and to do today what you might otherwise put off until tomorrow. The majority of planets are in the autumn and winter signs of the zodiac, with the exception of Saturn in Virgo and Mars in Gemini, and this tends to be a time when our focuses are more keenly placed on preservation and general maintenance. In just a few short weeks, winter will come to a close, inviting us to break winter patterns and to take on new exploits. Make the best of this weekend's mood of diligence; tomorrow's exceedingly long void-of-course Moon is likely to hinder progress, and may require extra effort to rectify the slow beginning of March's first work week.

March 3rd Monday

Moon in Capricorn / Aquarius	PST	EST
Moon enters Aquarius	8:25 PM	11:25 PM

Mood Watch: We enter this day with a void-of-course Capricorn Moon, and throughout the entire day and well into the evening, the Moon remains void-of-course in Capricorn. This could put a melancholic spin on the quality of today's overall mood, which may seem to be a lack of any sort of mood at all. Our moods may appear overly serious or heavily laden with work and responsibility. It may be best to hold a stiff upper lip, to carry on as best as possible, and to stay on course – however long the process may take. Later this evening, the Moon enters Aquarius and our moods will shift over to a more innovative perspective as we reflect on the events of the day. Tomorrow holds promise for a better start on the week.

70

March 4th Tuesday

Moon in Aquarius

	PST	EST
Mars enters Cancer	1:57 AM	4:57 AM
Sun sextile Jupiter begins (see March 6)		
Venus conjunct Neptune begins (see March 6)		

Ӿ

Mood Watch: After yesterday's slow start on the week's course of business, the Moon in Aquarius brings a brighter, more optimistic outlook. Moon in Aquarius affects our moods with a sense of humanitarian openness, while a scientific sense of proceeding with caution reminds us to apply our knowledge in all dealings with others. This is a good time to try experimenting with one's way of life, and to apply new methods of living more boldly and freely. With the sun in Pisces, the characteristic dreamy quality of life, coupled with the Moon in Aquarius, makes for a very imaginative and interesting time.

Mars enters Cancer (Mars in Cancer: March 4 – May 9) The fiery drive of force, Mars, now focuses the spirit of action on such Cancerian activities as nurturing and mothering. Mars in Cancer also emphasizes a focus on the home, household improvement or remodeling – possibly even a move to a new home or making the adjustments following a big move. Cancer represents large bodies of water such as the oceans and great lakes, and while Mars is in Cancer, marine activities are emphasized. Military ships will be preparing for battle tests and strategic training. Aquatic sports may become highly popular. Mars in Cancer represents the defenses of the emotions and the tender aspects of our being that we strive so hard to protect. Mars is a natural protector and defender but is also quite capable of offensive attack. Cancer people especially need to be aware of the potential for emotional flare ups, particularly with regard to the home. While Mars is in Cancer, Cancer born people are stirred up with a lot of heat and activity in their lives. Too much worry or fear is likely to lead to some serious anger and defensiveness. Be aware of the potential for heat, fire, and fevers, Cancer folks. Use this energy in your life to keep the flow moving, and to create to your heart's content!

March 5th Wednesday

Moon in Aquarius

	PST	EST
Moon conjunct Mercury	6:06 AM	9:06 AM
Moon conjunct Venus	11:08 AM	2:08 PM
Moon conjunct Neptune goes v/c	1:44 PM	4:44 PM
Sun conjunct Uranus begins (see March 8)		
Jupiter sextile Uranus begins (see March 28)		

Mood Watch: Moon in Aquarius brings intelligent approaches to the forefront of our moods. This morning, as the Moon conjuncts with Mercury, and later with Venus, our day begins with mindfulness and reflective thought, making an interactive outreach towards others likely. The Aquarius Moon always guides us towards making a breakthrough and, as it wanes darkly, it is wise to remember that it is always seemingly darkest before the light. As the day progresses, the Moon conjuncts with Neptune and then goes void-of course for the remainder of the evening. Our evening moods may seem spacey, misdirected, and unfocused — avoid cramming for exams, overexerting the mind, or practicing risky experiments.

March 6th Thursday

Moon in Aquarius / Pisces

	PST	EST
Moon enters Pisces	2:53 AM	5:53 AM
Moon trine Mars	4:03 AM	7:03 AM
Moon sextile Pluto	4:33 AM	7:33 AM
Moon opposite Saturn	10:19 AM	1:19 PM
Sun sextile Jupiter	11:03 AM	2:03 PM
Venus conjunct Neptune	4:02 PM	7:02 PM
Mercury conjunct Neptune begins (see March 9)		

Mood Watch: Early today the Moon enters Pisces as we now pass through the darkest phase of lunar light. The balsamic Moon in Pisces casts a spell of frequent day-dreaming and long moments of internal reflection. Tendencies towards escapism may be strong; nonetheless, busy lunar aspects imply that it will also be a very active and demanding day. As we approach tomorrow's New Moon in Pisces, internal reflection brings rebirth.

Sun sextile Jupiter (occurring March 4 – 8) This aspect brings those Pisces people celebrating birthdays from March 4 – 8 into a favorable natal Sun position to Jupiter. This represents a time of opportunity and expansion for these birthday folks, if they act on their desires and work towards their goals. Skills learned throughout this year will support their overall plans for career advancement and fortune building. This aspect will reoccur November 7 – 12, reaching its exact aspect on November 10, and will have a similar affect on the birthday Scorpios of that time.

Venus conjunct Neptune (occurring March 4 – 9) These two very feminine planets are currently aligned as a higher and lower octave of each other, creating a very fluid and open expression of femininity. Venus represents love, magnetism, and attraction, while Neptune (the higher octave of Venus) represents spiritual love and the melding of spiritual energies. Venus is conjunct with Neptune in the sign of Aquarius. Here the cohesive and melding forces of Venus and Neptune manifest with original, idealistic, and inventive expressions. Beauty and art (Venus) are linked with spirituality and belief (Neptune), much of it focused around humanitarian causes and issues (Aquarius). Science and technology are given more acceptable and aesthetic appearances with this aspect. Venus conjunct Neptune can be utilized to reach a higher vibration of feminine, spiritual love. This aspect allows beauty, femininity, and personal attraction to be connected with the higher spiritual vibrations of the universe. This is an ideal time to connect with one's own guardian angel and spirit guide. Venus conjunct Neptune, if utilized, will bring great wisdom. This conjunction will reoccur December 24–29, reaching exact aspect on December 27.

March 7th Friday

NEW MOON in PISCES

	PST	EST
Mars opposite Pluto	1:10 AM	4:10 AM
Moon sextile Jupiter	7:53 AM	10:53 AM
Moon conjunct Sun	9:13 AM	12:13 PM
Moon conjunct Uranus goes v/c	11:02 AM	2:02 PM

Mood Watch: **New Moon in Pisces** (Moon conjunct Sun) focuses our attention on the need to get in touch with our own beliefs and to inspire those beliefs with devotion and renewed faith. Also, tendencies towards escapism may be strong, particularly for those who are unwilling to let go of the past. This is a time of emotional and spiritual renewal, and the spirit of what is now emerging often represents renewed faith, usually in something divine or omnipotent. The world of magic exists in the melding mutable water of the Piscean expression. Crisp new psychic and intuitive inclinations lead to a spark of inspiration that carries us through the dwindling days of winter towards the renewed light of Spring Equinox (March 20). Let the intuitive and creative process begin! Let the spirit of renewed faith cleanse our beliefs.

Mars opposite Pluto (occurring Feb. 25 – March 15) For the first time this century, Mars in Cancer opposes Pluto in Capricorn, stirring up emotional activities in the home over career related transformations. This aspect last occurred on January 2, when Mars was in Gemini and Pluto was in Sagittarius. Times are changing, especially now; it's fully reflected in this aspect. Oppositions have a strong impact. Combine that fact with two strong planetary influences, Mars and Pluto – the outcome often involves swift, martial transformation. Now that Pluto is in Capricorn, cardinal transformation directly affects leaders and those who have an effect on the economy. This is a time to be vigilant and guarded. Expect swift, permanent changes during this time of Mars opposite Pluto.

March 8th Saturday
Moon in Pisces / Aries

	PST	EST
Moon enters Aries	6:24 AM	9:24 AM
Moon square Pluto	8:01 AM	11:01 AM
Moon square Mars	8:45 AM	11:45 AM
Sun conjunct Uranus	12:19 PM	3:19 PM

Mood Watch: This morning would be an especially good time to apply caution and vigilance as the newly waxing Aries Moon squares off with Pluto and then Mars, bringing the potential for hardship and struggle. Once we're out of the abrupt trials of morning, the rest of the day inspires our moods to push forward. There is perhaps an air of competitiveness or pushiness occurring among friends and foe. There is a restless spirit in the air – a strong desire on the part of many to begin anew, to shake up and break up old business, to start up new projects in preparation for the coming season.

Sun conjunct Uranus (occurring March 5 – 11) This occurrence of Sun conjunct Uranus especially affects people celebrating birthdays March 5 – 11. There may well be a healthy dollop of disruption and chaos in the lives of these folks. Radical breakthroughs that create a sense of freedom will be apparent. Sun conjunct Uranus causes strong rebellious tendencies. There is a stronger than usual Piscean desire to roll with change and take life at a different pace, to fight oppression and injustice, possibly even with an entirely off-the-wall approach to deal with calamity. Where there is knowledge to back this radical new approach, there is a way to achieve a sense of freedom, and there is a good chance to make an impression in the year to come. This will be your year (birthday folks) to express yourselves and your innovative desires and ideas.

March 9th Sunday

DAYLIGHT SAVINGS TIME BEGINS (Turn clocks ahead one hour at 2:00 a.m.)

Moon in Aries

Mercury conjunct Neptune	12:50 AM PST	2:50 AM EDT
	PDT	EDT
Moon square Jupiter	11:51 AM	2:51 PM
Moon sextile Neptune	9:15 PM	12:15 AM (March 10)
Moon sextile Mercury	11:00 PM	2:00 AM (March 10)
Saturn-trine-Pluto-non-exact begins (see April 20)		
Mars sextile Saturn begins (see March 14)		

Daylight Savings Time: Same as last year: instead of the time change occurring on the usual first Sunday in April and last Sunday in October, Daylight Savings Time will begin much earlier and end a bit later this year. Due to the United States' Energy Policy Act of 2005, Daylight Savings Time 2008 begins today and ends on Sunday, November 2.

Mood Watch: It's March; the Moon is waxing in Aries. We're now counting down to the end of winter season and a restless fervor captures our moods. Aries Moon activity breaks the sleepy winter lull with a sudden propensity to cut through the grey areas of life. As a general rule there is very little tolerance for vagueness or uncertainty going around. To be uncertain is to get pushed aside or perceived as being unworthy by the public. Stand up or stand out today, otherwise you might be overlooked. Unless, of course, you wish to lay low, at which point you're bound to be less noticeable.

Mercury conjunct Neptune (occurring March 6 – 11) This aspect usually only occurs once a year, but due to Mercury retrograde, from January 28 to February 18, we get to enjoy the influence of Mercury conjunct Neptune for a third time this year. For more details on Mercury conjunct Neptune, see when it first occurred – January 22.

March 10th Monday

Commonwealth Day, Canada

Moon in Aries / Taurus	PDT	EDT
Moon sextile Venus goes v/c	4:08 AM	7:08 AM
Moon enters Taurus	9:14 AM	12:14 PM
Moon trine Pluto	10:53 AM	1:53 PM
Moon sextile Mars	12:47 PM	3:47 PM
Moon trine Saturn	3:43 PM	6:43 PM

Mood Watch: This morning will have its ups and downs as we find ourselves a bit preoccupied by impatience and distractions during the void-of-course Aries Moon. Our moods soon become more grounded and pragmatic as the Moon enters Taurus. Today's lunar aspects suggest we will have our work cut out for us and activities will be demanding, although fairly positive, in spirit. The Taurus Moon calls out to our need to find comfort and security. With positive and serious effort, we'll get there.

March 11th Tuesday

Moon in Taurus

	PDT	EDT	
Moon trine Jupiter	1:59 PM	4:59 PM	
Moon sextile Uranus	4:19 PM	7:19 PM	
Moon sextile Sun	9:34 PM	12:34 AM	(March 12)
Moon square Neptune	10:58 PM	1:58 AM	(March 12)
Venus sextile Pluto begins (see March 13)			

Mood Watch: Today's Moon in Taurus focuses much of our attention on the perfection of the physical world. As Moon trine Jupiter occurs, we take joy in our riches. This is a time when getting a sense of value or pleasure from our environment and our resources means simplifying the act of beauty. When funds and resources are low, creating the illusion of beauty can have exceptional results if done well. Protecting our environment will also require conservation of our energies and our precious resources; hence, the sooner we simplify our lust for convenience and false luxury, the greater we will benefit from resourceful, simplistic, and practical beauty.

March 12th Wednesday

Moon in Taurus / Gemini

	PDT	EDT
Moon square Mercury	5:27 AM	8:27 AM
Moon square Venus goes v/c	10:26 AM	1:26 PM
Moon enters Gemini	10:55 AM	1:55 PM
Venus enters Pisces	3:51 PM	6:51 PM
Moon square Saturn	5:13 PM	8:13 PM
Venus trine Mars begins (see March 16)		

Mood Watch: The start of the day brings on a couple of troublesome lunar squares as the Taurus Moon then goes void-of-course for a short time and then enters Gemini. It's a busy morning of pleasing (or appeasing) our loved ones. All too swiftly, the Gemini Moon shifts to more complex kinds of moods as we multi-task our way into the afternoon and evening. Gemini Moon brings the need to communicate what has been on our minds. Dual perspectives open up the thinking process.

Venus enters Pisces (Venus in Pisces: March 12 – April 30) Venus, the planet of magnetism and love, will be focusing our attraction on Pisces related subjects. From today through April 30, music, poetry, the arts, psychic phenomena, and spiritual and religious practices will all be endearing and lively pursuits. Over the next few weeks, as Venus crosses over their natal Sun sign, it will touch the personal realms of our Pisces friends with an awareness of the need for love and beauty in their lives. Venus is the feminine planet of love, and Pisces is an extremely feminine, dreamy, and spiritual placement for the love force of Venus. Matters of the heart will emphasize passivity, tenderness, sensitivity and the need for a gentle approach towards love's expression.

March 13th Thursday

Moon in Gemini

	PDT	EDT
Venus sextile Pluto	12:08 PM	3:08 PM
Moon square Uranus	6:45 PM	9:45 PM
Venus opposite Saturn begins (see March 15)		
Mercury sextile Pluto begins (see March 15)		

Mood Watch: Gemini Moon often focuses our attention on those areas of life where we have mixed feelings and there is a tendency to mull things over that have been on our minds. The only lunar aspect of the day, Moon square Uranus, implies that there will be a storm of some kind, be it mental, emotional, physically real or imagined; this storm requires swift and bountiful action to deal with the chaos at hand.

Venus sextile Pluto (occurring March 11 – 15) Venus is in Pisces where the law of attraction is irresistible, easy going, and artistically uplifting. Pluto in Capricorn brings dutiful allegiance to matters of fate. Venus sextile Pluto implies that even in the midst of hardship, opportunities are arising with regard to the things we treasure and are attracted to, and also in matters of love and affection (Venus). These opportunities often are born out of fate or destiny (Pluto), or sometimes are a result of an unpredictable factor. For some, this aspect may be teaching them the lessons of acceptance, of learning to let go of attachments, as well as finding liberation through the transformative process of acceptance, particularly in matters of love. This aspect will reoccur, September 20 – 14, and will reach its peak on September 22 with Venus in Libra and Pluto in Sagittarius.

March 14th Friday

Moon in Gemini / Cancer – FIRST QUARTER MOON in GEMINI

	PDT	EDT
Moon trine Neptune	1:29 AM	4:29 AM
Moon square Sun	3:46 AM	6:46 AM
Moon trine Mercury goes v/c	1:24 PM	4:24 PM
Moon enters Cancer	1:38 PM	4:38 PM
Mars sextile Saturn	2:28 PM	5:28 PM
Moon opposite Pluto	3:27 PM	6:27 PM
Mercury enters Pisces	3:44 PM	6:44 PM
Moon trine Venus	6:04 PM	9:04 PM
Moon sextile Saturn	7:52 PM	10:52 PM
Moon conjunct Mars	8:03 PM	11:03 PM

Mood Watch: Overnight, the **First Quarter Moon in Gemini** (Moon square Sun) brings the necessity for our moods to be changeable and adaptable. Our moods are easily affected by the busy buzz of intellectual focuses and pursuits. The emphasis of covering many details at once becomes the primary objective, but not necessarily the answer to our insatiable curiosity. The act of processing information becomes essential. Do not let gossip and idle chatter be the cause of disruption in your day – thoughtlessness is also a symptom of the Gemini Moon atmosphere. The Gemini Moon puts us in touch with how we feel about our thoughts. If you don't like how you feel about your thoughts, endeavor to alter your way of thinking. Omit thoughts which attempt to defeat your sense of purpose; encourage thoughts that uplift and inspire your spirit. Be careful not to overdo the caffeine. This afternoon, the Moon enters Cancer and a number of lunar aspects brings an emotionally busy time. Take it easy on the emotions and pace yourself today.

Mars sextile Saturn (occurring March 9 – 18) Mars in Cancer is sextile to the retrograde Saturn in Virgo. This is an active time for establishing cleanliness in the home. During this aspect, actions create opportunities, provided there is an application of discipline and timing. Those who are affected by this aspect may feel noticed now. Mars sextile Saturn affects our actions with good timing. Diligently practice your favorite sport, especially those physical activities that demand precision and perfect timing. Offensive and defensive forces tend to work harmoniously with this aspect. Movement and the application of energy (Mars), plus responsibility and awareness of limitation (Saturn), allow the timely qualities of completion and new beginnings to occur. Mars sextile Saturn may be a good time to start a new enterprise, and is an especially opportunistic time to practice control or discipline. This would be the time to end a bad habit or to work to accomplish a goal. This aspect will reoccur October 17 – November 3, reaching its exact aspect on October 30.

Mercury enters Pisces (Mercury in Pisces: March 14 – April 2) Today Mercury enters Pisces and this brings the emphasis of news, media, and communications on our beliefs, spiritual growth, cultural expression, and our tendencies towards escapism and drug use. Today through April 2, Mercury in Pisces brings out the mystic in all of us and adds quite a bit of color and flair to the imagination in relayed messages. This is also a good time to immerse one's self in creative writing and music or to open up the channels to the spirit world, allowing for messages from the other side to penetrate our psyches. Listen and learn from the priests, holy teachers, loved ones, and spirit guides of your choosing. Sometimes the voice of sense and reason needs to give over to the simplicity of just listening in silence.

March 15th Saturday

Moon in Cancer

	PDT	EDT	
Mercury sextile Pluto	10:09 AM	1:09 PM	
Venus opposite Saturn	1:16 PM	4:16 PM	
Moon opposite Jupiter	8:58 PM	11:58 PM	
Moon trine Uranus	10:44 PM	1:44 AM	(March 16)
Mercury opposite Saturn begins (see March 17)			
Mercury trine Mars begins (see March 18)			

Mood Watch: Throughout the day, the waxing Moon in Cancer brings out our maternal instincts, and focuses our moods and feelings on the desire to nurture emotional needs.

Mercury sextile Pluto (occurring March 13 – 16) Communications and discussions are facilitated, with an opportunity to get your message across in negotiations with those in positions of power. Mercury is now in Pisces, ensuring the strong belief behind our topics of communication, while Pluto, one degree into Capricorn, is forcing us to acknowledge our resources and to use them wisely. Vital information regarding treatments for illness or disease may frequent the news, and news in general may well have some critical impact. This is a good time to reach out to those of another generation and make an attempt to communicate something essential. This aspect will reoccur November 2 – 5, reaching its exact aspect on November 3.

Venus opposite Saturn (occurring March 13 – 17) For a brief but notable time, love, beauty, and magnetism are opposed to restrictive discipline. While there is a very strong need to attain a sense of beauty, to stop and smell the roses, there is a constantly compelling and obsessive compulsion to press on with work and vital responsibilities. This may be particularly so because Saturn is currently retrograde (Saturn retrograde: December 19, 2007 – May 2, 2008). Love matters – and the things we are attracted to – are subjected to unavoidable trials and restrictions. There will be folks among us thrust into the challenges of facing jealousy, guilt, offensive outbreaks, anguish, oppression, defeat or despair. There are always lessons where our sheltered passions lie. We must be careful how our passions are stirred or handled. Hold steadfast to all principles of wisdom. Be careful not to bite off more than you can chew, especially with regard to irresistible attractions and restrictive love matters.

March 16th Sunday
Palm Sunday

Moon in Cancer / Leo	PDT	EDT
Venus trine Mars	1:21 AM	4:21 AM
Moon trine Sun goes v/c	11:58 AM	2:58 PM
Moon enters Leo	6:04 PM	9:04 PM

Mood Watch: The morning begins with the Moon in Cancer, a typical time of moodiness, particularly so as the Moon goes void-of-course and remains this way for a fair portion of the day and evening. Warm bubble baths, cosmetic pampering, massage, and delicious nourishing foods are just some of the many delightful ways to soothe one's ills. This evening, the Leo Moon puts a much more cheerful glow on the quality of our moods; sit back, take it easy, and enjoy some good clean fun to help ease the emotional flow.

Venus trine Mars (occurring March 12 – 19) Venus in Pisces is trine Mars in Cancer. Dramatic, passionate, and bold expressions of affection will bring very strong feelings between loved ones. Venus trine Mars brings love in action. When Venus and Mars are well harmonized by this ideal aspect, there is a greater opportunity for peace and healing in relationships, and often gifts are exchanged. These are gifts which help people to understand how masculine and feminine expressions are harmonized. It starts with the effort to make things better, concentrating on the positive, not the negative, and continues with the persistence to bring out the best in your partner – no matter how stubborn at first (s)he may seem. This is the only time Venus trine Mars will occur this year.

March 17th Monday

Saint Patrick's Day

♓

Moon in Leo

	PDT	EDT
Mercury opposite Saturn	2:46 AM	5:46 AM
Sun square Pluto begins (see March 21)		

" A little learning is a dangerous thing, but we must take that risk because a little is as much as our biggest heads can hold. "
– Irish playwright, critic, political activist - George Bernard Shaw (1856 – 1950)

Mood Watch: The waxing Leo Moon brings the spirit of friendship, entertainment, and occasional bouts of excitement, as only a Leo Moon could bring. This is a rewarding time to build on self esteem and confidence. Compliments and flattery will go far today.

Mercury opposite Saturn (occurring March 15 – 19) This aspect brings a very strong awareness of the need to speak out on serious and important subjects. News, talk, discussions and media tend to revolve around matters of closure, deaths, endings, and the establishment of control. There may be an overwhelming tone of command or restriction in some of the more serious subjects being communicated. While Mercury opposes Saturn, be careful where you choose to draw the lines and what you agree to when negotiating. Mercury is in Pisces, where articulate precision is usually complex or abstract in nature. Saturn is in Virgo, where it emphasizes the perimeters and security of our health and other such Virgo-like issues as the need to strive for perfection and to have a clean and practical environment. At this time we may be especially aware of the delicate subject of how rules and laws are affecting our health and our wellbeing.

March 18th Tuesday

Moon in Leo

	PDT	EDT
Mercury trine Mars	4:36 AM	7:36 AM
Moon opposite Neptune goes v/c	11:38 AM	2:38 PM

Mood Watch: Throughout today, playful and bubbly expressions of mood take place. Artistic and imaginative Leo Moon activities can bring memorable pleasures. The watchword for this playful tune of a Moon is "will." If one or more facets of your personal will are purposefully executed and gratefully achieved, you will have experienced a successful Leo Moon time.

Mercury trine Mars (occurring March 15 – 20) Thoughts, words and speech inspire activity, and the messages coming across often give us the incentive to get in on the action. Mercury trine Mars brings news and communications into a most favorable position when it comes to taking action. The trine aspect acts like a gift, and this is a superb time to communicate and to receive positive and uplifting information, which will inspire others to take affirmative action where needed. Back when Mercury was retrograde (Jan. 28 – Feb. 18), this aspect came very close to reaching an exact aspect on January 31.

ARIES

Key Phrase: "I AM"

Cardinal Fire Sign

Symbol: The Ram

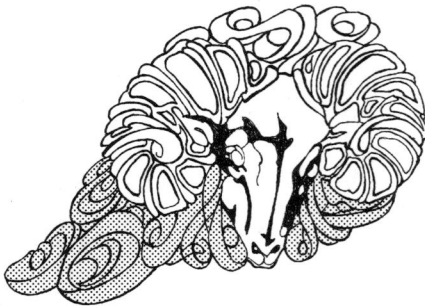

March 19th through April 19th

March 19th Wednesday
Vernal Equinox (PDT)
Moon in Leo / Virgo

	PDT	EDT	
Moon enters Virgo	12:26 AM	3:26 AM	
Moon trine Pluto	2:27 AM	5:27 AM	
Moon conjunct Saturn	6:32 AM	9:32 AM	
Moon sextile Mars	10:38 AM	1:38 PM	
Moon opposite Mercury	1:29 PM	4:29 PM	
Moon opposite Venus	4:31 PM	7:31 PM	
Sun enters Aries	10:48 PM	1:48 AM	(March 20)

Mood Watch: The Virgo Moon is now waxing strongly. Virgo is the prudent sign of the zodiac, always looking for the loopholes in everything, always questioning, always doubting, scrutinizing, and discerning. Have a look around; you shall know them by their expression. A series of strong lunar aspects keeps us busy sorting out the true nature of our feelings. Overall, an active pace is at work. Today marks an auspicious occasion and the perfectionist in us stands out.

Sun enters Aries (Sun in Aries: March 19/20 – April 19) Today, the event classically called **Vernal Equinox**, also known as Spring Equinox, marks the start of a new season and the beginning of the zodiac. This is the time when the daylight hours are equal in length to the hours of the night. Spring arrives when the earth is tilted so the Sun is directly over the equator. In the northern parts of the world, the first day of spring is on or about March 20. In the northern hemisphere we are on the side of the Equinox that returns toward the light, as opposed to Autumnal Equinox when the Sun enters Libra, the opposite of Aries. With Daylight Savings Time already underway since March 9, we now celebrate the continued lengthening of the days.

The Sun in Aries inspires courageous and bold new beginnings, as well as instilling confidence and forcefulness. Many Aries folks have an inherent desire to not only survive, but to exceed, and to make a lasting impression. Aries is the cardinal fire sign that doesn't give up easily. Arians are known for beginning projects with a pioneering zeal. However, they are also infamous for suddenly leaping into a new venture, leaving someone else to complete their original endeavor. Some Aries folks love to start up businesses, but continue into other ventures once the business has been established and requires the dull monotony of upkeep and maintenance. The Aries character typically expresses quality of leadership in the fiery realm of the cardinal signs, and is ruled by the active and vital planet, Mars. Aries boasts of being the first, and works earnestly to defy all who would mock, criticize, or misunderstand their drive to reach a certain self-appointed plateau of excellence. There is a strong sense of devotion to the self and the need to excel in the Arian's chosen field. The Mars ruled Aries person is loaded with fervor and a relentless fortitude that often, at best, motivates and inspires – or, at worst, repels and puts off others around them. Sun in Aries serves as a good time to initiate new projects and apply diligence with inspired ability. The youthful vigor that is characteristic of Arians is reflected in the season, and this springlike sprouting and growth is inspiration for us all.

March 20ᵗʰ Thursday
Vernal Equinox – traditional – (EDT)
Moon in Virgo

		PDT	EDT
Sun enters Aries	(MARCH 19ᵀᴴ - 10:48 PM)		1:48 AM
Moon trine Jupiter		11:20 AM	2:20 PM
Moon opposite Uranus goes v/c		12:29 PM	3:29 PM

Mood Watch: As the Virgo Moon intensifies in its waxing process, tonight is technically the Full Moon Eve, as tomorrow's Full Moon in Libra reaches its peak in the daylight hours. This may be a somewhat sensitive time for our bodies as Virgo emphasizes the digestive system. Smart eating will have its benefits today. Virgo Moon also puts the focus on cleaning, proper hygiene, accounting and filing, preparing taxes, and handling all life's mundane necessities. Unfortunately, the Virgo Moon will go void-of-course for a fair portion of the day and throughout the entire evening, and there may be a tendency for querulous, fussy, pedantic, obsessive, or fault-finding moods. Beware of compulsive or addictive tendencies. Ease the tension with communicative and disciplined persistence.

March 21ˢᵗ Friday
Good Friday / Purim
Moon in Virgo / Libra – FULL MOON in LIBRA

	PDT	EDT	
Sun square Pluto	1:38 AM	4:38 AM	
Moon enters Libra	8:46 AM	11:46 AM	
Moon square Pluto	10:53 AM	1:53 PM	
Moon opposite Sun	11:40 AM	2:40 PM	
Moon square Mars	9:14 PM	12:14 AM	(March 22)

Mood Watch: **Full Moon in Libra** (Moon opposite Sun) brings events that revolve around such things as law, the justice system, friends, and marital partners. Relationships are a balancing act. Friends will share their strengths as well as their weaknesses. Troubled times can strengthen even the weakest links in friendship. Refuse to contribute to the weakness of a friend; nurture friendship with patience, understanding, and encouragement. Use this full Libra Moon energy to empower your relationships. Diplomacy, peace and goodwill can be achieved among loved

81

ones, but a definite effort is required. Today's harsh lunar aspects warn us to be careful and to persevere dutifully.

Sun square Pluto (occurring March 17 – 24) This aspect particularly affects Pisces and early-born Aries people celebrating birthdays this month from March 17 – 24. For them, Pluto squaring their natal Sun brings disruptive changes and many challenges to overcome, such as the pain of loss and the severity of transformation. As well, Virgo and Libra people who are born at the exact opposite of this late Pisces time of year must also change in order to progress through these necessary Pluto-inspired tests of transformation. These tests often involve dealing with illness and loss, irreparable damage, and dramatic life changes. Late-born Sagittarians and early-born Capricorns (Pluto conjunct natal Sun), as well as late-born Geminis and early-born Cancer people (Pluto opposite natal Sun) also know what these tests of Pluto are about, as Pluto continues to trace a slow moving path through the late degrees of Sagittarius and into the earliest degrees of Capricorn. Trying to hold onto the regrets and the pain of the past will only bring greater destruction later. This is the time to persevere through the obstacles of hardship. Yet, the hardships that are taking place now will resurface in time, so do take note of the struggles going on in the life of Pisces/Aries, Virgo/Libra, Gemini/Cancer, and Sagittarius/Capricorn people affected by Pluto's tests. Realize this trend will be repeated, and so necessitates finding methods of release and attitude changes in order to survive the anxiety and stress. Take it one day at a time and do not let fear and worry rule this condition. Know that you are not alone in facing these challenges. Move steadily through the required transformation, as stagnation and fear will only bring extended suffering. This aspect will reoccur September 17 – 27, reaching its exact aspect on September 20, when the Sun will be in Virgo at the cusp of Libra, affecting the Virgo/Libra birthday people of that time.

March 22nd Saturday

Moon in Libra

	PDT	EDT	
Moon square Jupiter	9:34 PM	12:34 AM	(March 23)

Mood Watch: The mood of the day on the celestial chef's menu is about balancing and harmonizing our lives while maintaining a central area of peace in which we seek to dwell. Many of us have our battles to face, as the Sun now in Aries coupled with the post-full Moon in Libra, indicates the need to make strong adjustments and handle important decisions. This is a good time to focus on teamwork and companionship. Tonight, it would be wise to simplify our expectations and to take it easy on excesses, as the Moon square Jupiter tends to challenge our ability to handle a great deal of energy, and some folks may feel short on resources.

March 23rd Sunday

Easter Sunday

Moon in Libra / Scorpio

	PDT	EDT	
Moon trine Neptune goes v/c	5:41 AM	8:41 AM	
Moon enters Scorpio	7:07 PM	10:07 PM	
Moon sextile Pluto	9:20 PM	12:20 AM	(March 24)

Mood Watch: Today brings moods which will tend to revolve around themes of deliberation. Early this morning, the Moon in Libra goes void-of-course causing a great deal of indecisiveness. This may be a time when our patience is tested on some level. Inconveniences may seem challenging but they may also be necessary to create balance. This is a good time to avoid making important decisions; although some folks may feel under pressure socially, it is important not to be hasty with making promises and giving into the whims of others. This evening, Moon in Scorpio is the ticket to some smooth flowing emotional release. Waning Scorpio Moon puts us in touch with our most intense needs and desires; through emotional release, it also mends some of the damaged parts of our emotional core.

March 24th Monday
Easter Monday

Moon in Scorpio	PDT	EDT
Moon sextile Saturn	1:03 AM	4:03 AM
Mercury conjunct Venus	6:28 AM	9:28 AM
Moon trine Mars	10:07 AM	1:07 PM
Sun square Mars begins (see March 30)		

Mood Watch: Scorpio Moon empowers us to face deep emotional concerns, and the waning phase of the Moon is a good time to reflect on the intensity of our emotions with determination to heal, fix, or improve our condition. Today, our moods will be geared towards a focus on regenerative power and healing restoration.

Mercury conjunct Venus (occurring Feb. 22 – March 31) Today's conjunction of Mercury and Venus takes place in the spiritually sensitive realm of Pisces. This is often a time when intimate and loving thoughts are shared with adaptable and finely attuned affection. With this aspect, loving gestures are usually very sincere and genuine. There may be a tendency for love-related communication to seem somewhat instinctual, and possibly abstract, although the need to communicate love is definitely there. This conjunction last occurred in Aquarius on February 26. It will reoccur in Gemini June 5 – 9, reaching its exact peak on June 7. This aspect will reach its peak two more times, on August 21 and again on September 14, before Mercury (the communicator) releases its embrace (the conjunction) with Venus (the lover). By September, Mercury and Venus will both be in Libra, the sign of harmony and balance.

March 25th Tuesday

Moon in Scorpio	PDT	EDT
Moon trine Venus	1:39 AM	4:39 AM
Moon trine Mercury	2:21 AM	5:21 AM
Moon sextile Jupiter	9:45 AM	12:45 PM
Moon trine Uranus	10:13 AM	1:13 PM
Moon square Neptune goes v/c	5:35 PM	8:35 PM
Mercury conjunct Uranus begins (see March 27)		

Mood Watch: The Moon wanes in Scorpio and this continues to be a time of purging and venting strong emotional patterns. The weirdoes appear to be out in droves as the waning Scorpio Moon breeds suspicion and, possibly, paranoia. Strange and unusual patterns are sometimes the course of our moods. On the other hand, Scorpio Moon improves our perception and allows us to make keen distinctions on how we feel about people's manners and behavior. Sun in Aries and Moon in Scorpio brings a regenerative time for us. This evening, as the Moon goes void-of-course, it may be best to lean on the side of caution, as criminal activity is common during the void-of-course Scorpio Moon. Vigilance and awareness will assist you to avoid being a victim.

March 26th Wednesday

Moon in Scorpio / Sagittarius

	PDT	EDT	
Moon enters Sagittarius	7:11 AM	10:11 AM	
Moon square Saturn	12:56 PM	3:56 PM	
Moon trine Sun	9:03 PM	12:03 AM	(March 27)
Mercury sextile Jupiter begins (see March 27)			
Venus conjunct Uranus begins (see March 28)			
Venus sextile Jupiter begins (see March 28)			

Mood Watch: Having both Sun and Moon in fire signs brings a very active and creative time. From Greek mythology, the centaur is the symbol of Sagittarius. Centaurs are a race of creatures that are half human and half horse. They are famous in children's books for being star-gazers, foretellers of the future, and they are also considered to be benevolent and wise, loyal to the very end. Throughout the course of the day, our moods are touched by the need to look ahead and to apply the wisdom and moral self-discipline to overcome the troublesome limitations of a treacherous and uncertain new century. Even when life's continuing difficulties seem insurmountable, the wisdom of the centaur reminds us to hold an optimistic outlook, no matter what.

March 27th Thursday

Moon in Sagittarius

	PDT	EDT	
Mercury sextile Jupiter	11:55 AM	2:55 PM	
Mercury conjunct Uranus	1:06 PM	4:06 PM	
Moon square Venus	9:12 PM	12:12 AM	(March 28)
Moon square Uranus	11:04 PM	2:04 AM	(March 28)

Mood Watch: Sagittarius Moon gives our moods the incentive to explore beyond the usual realms. A very active, fiery, and creative energy is here.

Mercury sextile Jupiter (occurring March 26 – 28) This aspect offers the potential for good news of growth and prosperity, especially for those who are open to broadening their awareness. Mercury brings news and talk, while Jupiter brings wealth and prosperous advancement. The money flows where our attention goes. It may be an advantageous time to ask for a job or a loan. Communicating our dreams (Mercury in Pisces) brings opportunities and the potential for success (the sextile aspect) in the expanding fields of such Capricorn related affluence as career growth, construction, building, banking, architectural feats, estate management, and administrative advancements (Jupiter in Capricorn). Opportunity exists for both the employer and the employee. Mercury sextile Jupiter brings joyful and mind expanding conversations. This aspect will reoccur November 14 – 17, and reaches an exact peak on November 16 with Mercury in Scorpio.

Mercury conjunct Uranus (occurring March 25 – 30) Mercury and Uranus are conjunct in Pisces, giving birth to radical, bright, inspired and intuitive ideas. This may raise some very interesting and unusual questions about what we choose to believe in. Consciousness raising talk is prevalent. Mercury conjunct Uranus magnifies the volume of shocking or question-raising news, and stirs the minds and mouths of rebels and non-conformists who are inspired to speak out. Everyone is crying for some kind of freedom!

March 28th Friday
Moon in Sagittarius / Capricorn

	PDT	EDT	
Moon square Mercury	12:39 AM	3:39 AM	
Moon sextile Neptune goes v/c	6:20 AM	9:20 AM	
Venus sextile Jupiter	3:35 PM	6:35 PM	
Venus conjunct Uranus	3:58 PM	6:58 PM	
Jupiter sextile Uranus	5:17 PM	8:17 PM	
Moon enters Capricorn	7:44 PM	10:44 PM	
Moon conjunct Pluto	9:59 PM	12:59 AM	(March 29)

Mood Watch: Sagittarius Moon keeps us philosophical and, whenever a number of planetary activities are lined up – just like today – you can bet the philosophical approach will allow us to cope with whatever is happening. This evening, the Moon enters Capricorn and the basic mood is somewhat solemn, rather serious, and fully determined.

Venus sextile Jupiter (occurring March 26 – 30) Venus is in Pisces, the place of art and intuitive love play. Jupiter is in Capricorn, bringing a powerful sense of fulfillment and a joyful outreach towards the need to discover love's capabilities. Creative and spiritually uplifting attractions and pleasures (Venus in Pisces) lead us to prosperous opportunities in career related focuses, estate management, engineering, civil service, and corporate business (Jupiter in Capricorn.) This is an excellent time to shower loved ones with gifts and compliments. A lovers' getaway may be just the ticket to recapture some romance. This is the time to allow expansion to occur in love matters, and to take the next step towards enlivening and enhancing life. A greater opportunity for increasing skills or augmenting your livelihood is available, especially if your focus remains on doing what you love most. This aspect will reoccur October 3 – 6, reaching its exact aspect on October 5, when Venus will be in Scorpio.

Venus conjunct Uranus (occurring March 26 – 31) It's no wonder that love matters seem wild or chaotic – this conjunction brings an element of shock value to the expression of love. Venus conjunct Uranus in Pisces creates the potential for lively encounters with spiritual love and affection, wherein there is sometimes an exceedingly wise, though often unusual, counsel of love. A radical or explosive attraction or fascination may occur with this conjunction, opening our senses to a more artistic understanding of chaos. For those who are strongly affected, mischievous, brilliant, outgoing and challenging modes of love and affection now occur. Hang in there. Chaos is often considered a true test of love. Be positive and open to the challenge of love with chaos. This is the only time during the year that Venus will be conjunct with Uranus.

Jupiter sextile Uranus (occurring March 5 – June 12) This is a not so common aspect, actively occurring since March 5 and continuing through June 12. Jupiter affects our sense of prosperity and expansion into new realms of fulfillment and discovery. When Jupiter is in the sextile position to Uranus, it provides us with an opportunity to enhance our revolutionary capabilities and to make large and bountiful breakthroughs towards freedom and abolishing fear. For some folks, this aspect brings the opportunity to introduce a very radical concept or technology into society and have it accepted for use in an expedited fashion. Fads may be liberally incorporated with this aspect. As long as one is working with a process of liberation or is focusing on a freedom quest of some nature, this aspect is giving the active participant the opportunity to expand to great heights and empower the pocketbook despite the inconstant twists in economy. This aspect brings opportunity which must be acted upon, and one must be careful not to take on more than their life's responsibility and commitment levels can afford. Jupiter is in Capricorn and Uranus is in Pisces. This aspect brings a variety of initiations with regard to commerce and our world economy. This is the place to open up one's field of knowledge and attempt to understand without prejudice why certain focuses of life appear out of hand or disruptive. For some, Jupiter sextile Uranus will provide an open porthole to personal freedom. This aspect will reach another exact aspect peak on May 21, before it dissipates completely by June 12. Then it will reoccur later this year, November 1 – 23, reaching its final exact aspect on November 12.

March 29th Saturday
LAST QUARTER MOON in CAPRICORN

	PDT	EDT
Moon trine Saturn	1:07 AM	4:07 AM
Moon square Sun	2:46 PM	5:46 PM
Moon opposite Mars	3:13 PM	6:13 PM

Mood Watch: **Last Quarter Moon in Capricorn** (Moon square Sun) This Moon emphasizes issues of control – whether that means taking control or letting go of it where needed. The waning Capricorn Moon reminds us not to give up, to persist as the mountain goat does, and to find a way to overcome the steep and rocky roads. Capricorn Moon gives moods a serious undertone of needing and wanting to take hold of our goals and create results. Saturn ruled Capricorn emphasizes time and the timeliness of important events. This may be a time to address impending deadlines. Life is so serious with Capricorn Moon in its last quarter state; it reminds us that in order to be in control we must let go of that which we can't control. Attached to success? Persistence wins overall where there is a stubborn drive to excel. How important is success to you?

March 30th Sunday
Moon in Capricorn

	PDT	EDT
Sun square Mars	12:20 AM	3:20 AM
Moon sextile Uranus	11:01 AM	2:01 PM
Moon conjunct Jupiter	11:13 AM	2:13 PM

Moon sextile Venus	3:35 PM	6:35 PM
Moon sextile Mercury goes v/c	9:53 PM	12:53 AM (March 31)

♈

Mood Watch: The feeling of importance is hatching – springtime is here! The Capricorn Moon gives some folks the feeling they could create or crush a whole universe, while the courageous days of Aries lead us fearlessly onward. Capricorn Moon keeps us on the straight and narrow. A determined world of doers sets a busy, but steady, pace. This is the time to take charge, and to get our goals for this week rolling along progressively.

Sun square Mars (occurring March 24 – April 6) This aspect particularly affects those Aries born people celebrating birthdays this year from March 24 – April 6. It creates the illusion that obstacles are constantly getting in the way of the actions (and will) of these people. This may be a time when harnessing energy seems like a chore. It may serve as a good time for these people to lighten up on their expectations of themselves for awhile, and not let such setbacks get in the way of enjoying life. Relax! In time, it will be easier once again to get your personal goals and your willpower into a state of action. This may be an accident prone time in the lives of these birthday folks. The year ahead may bring difficulty when it comes to relating to various events, particularly warlike events, as they occur. Since this year may bring the tendency for accidents and mistakes, this will be a good time for these birthday folks to learn a great deal about how to pace themselves and to work through the obstacles in order to perfect personal visions and goals.

March 31st Monday
Moon in Capricorn / Aquarius

	PDT	EDT
Moon enters Aquarius	6:35 AM	9:35 AM

Mood Watch: As the day begins, the Moon enters Aquarius and our moods enter into a time of scientific foresight. Aquarius Moon gives us the incentive to tackle puzzling problems, and the waning Aquarius Moon often leaves us contemplative over the types of problems that could only be described as "man made." If there's some form of logic that got us into a mess, there is indeed another kind of logic that will get us out of it. The Aquarius Moon gives our moods the extra push to seek out the knowledge that is necessary to succeed.

April 1st Tuesday
April Fool's Day
Moon in Aquarius

	PDT	EDT
Moon sextile Sun	5:27 AM	8:27 AM
Mercury square Pluto begins (see April 3)		

Mood Watch: The Moon wanes in Aquarius. It even howls like a lone human-wolf on this *April Fool's Day*. This Moon gives us the incentive to tackle puzzling problems. Waning Aquarius Moon often leaves us contemplative over the types of problems that could only be described as "man-made." If there's some form of logic that got us into a mess, there is indeed another kind of logic that will get us out of it. Sun in Aries, with the howlin' Aquarius Moon, gives our moods the extra push to seek out the knowledge that is necessary to succeed.

April 2nd Wednesday

Moon in Aquarius / Pisces

	PDT	EDT
Pluto goes retrograde	2:24 AM	5:24 AM
Moon conjunct Neptune goes v/c	2:12 AM	5:12 AM
Mercury enters Aries	10:43 AM	1:43 PM
Moon enters Pisces	1:56 PM	4:56 PM
Moon sextile Pluto	3:36 PM	6:56 PM
Moon opposite Saturn	6:15 PM	9:15 PM

Mood Watch: Minor morning foibles tend to be the way of things as the void-of-course Moon in Aquarius defies all remnants of common sense. Spacey moods bring basic kinds of stupidity. Our patience may be tested when it comes to machines. Later today, as the Moon enters Pisces, our moods shift into a period of fluid adaptability.

Pluto goes retrograde (Pluto retrograde: April 2 – Sept. 8) Processes governed by Pluto take the longest time to go through since, from our perspective, Pluto appears to move the slowest of all the planets because it's the furthest away from us. Pluto goes retrograde today and when it resumes a forward moving course late this summer, it will have traveled only a few degrees in the sky, which is average for a Pluto retrograde period. This means the types of hardships that have been created and brought to our attention in the past five months must be addressed all over again, and that we must acknowledge the evolution of humankind's current condition in order to survive the changes that are occurring on Earth.

Pluto deals with the changes that occur in attitude according to the overall group consciousness of each of the generations. Each generation has its own insight as to what hardship represents. This is a time to make life better by consciously transforming fear into determination and despair into belief in oneself, no matter what condition of fate surrounds you. The destructive habits, prejudices, sufferings and haunts of previous generations must be acknowledged and addressed, and of course altered to enable us to tackle the world of the future. We will all face greater challenges and tests of epic proportions, and outdated concerns must be dealt with so that we may find solutions to the new problems in front of us.

With Pluto's changes we must face tragedies, diseases, losses, shattered dreams, and altered or unexpected doses of reality. Pluto retrograde forces us to look within; this is a good time to confirm our greatest strengths by directing abusive patterns into constructive and useful disciplines which will reshape and bring hope to the emerging outlook on life.

Pluto represents the forces of power and control, which are always in a state of flux due to our mortal tango with fate. Our old concepts and memories of how life once was, or is supposed to be, are dying with the times. Pluto, newly in Capricorn, is making the transition from Sagittarius related changes. Reality and normality are illusions that Pluto sweeps away as its final traversal of Sagittarius opens up global awareness and increases our foresight of worldwide struggles. There are aspects of life that are not meant to be controlled, but how we react to the shifts of this time is something we do control. Pluto retrograde is a time of readdressing universal human problems that take decades to fix.

Pluto, newly in the sign of Capricorn (since Jan. 25), will now move back through to the Sagittarius cusp of Capricorn, and it will reenter Sagittarius on June 13. Pluto will leave Sagittarius for the final time this year on November 26.

Mercury enters Aries (Mercury in Aries: April 2 – 17) Mercury now enters Aries, bringing a focus of communications on selfhood, initiation, new projects, and new ways of seeing and experiencing life. We are all perpetually in the process of being initiated into some aspect of selfhood, particularly given that we are constantly learning, acquiring new skills, growing and aging. Mercury in Aries brings some lively heat to our communications and discussions. Mercury is the messenger, activating information, and Aries is the warrior and the force of nature that takes on life with fearless vigor and aggression. Communications possess a quality of command. Now through April 17, while Mercury is in Aries, talk, news and discussions will be actively focused on the challenging and demanding enterprises and battles that await us.

April 3rd Thursday

Moon in Pisces

	PDT	EDT
Mercury square Pluto	1:53 AM	4:53 AM
Moon trine Mars	10:51 AM	1:51 PM

Mood Watch: The waning Pisces Moon brings reflective, intuitive, and energetic flow to the course of our moods. This is also a time when we may be especially hypersensitive to drugs and alcohol. Other symptoms of the waning Pisces Moon may bring susceptibility to foot problems and stress-related illnesses. This is a good time to seek beneficial health programs and therapeutic practices. Stressful times require a little bit of pampering.

Mercury square Pluto (occurring April 1 – 4) For the first time in our lifetime, Mercury in Aries is square to Pluto in Capricorn. Scrutiny and doubt make it difficult to communicate with those of another generation. This is a particularly difficult time to deal with burdensome issues and discuss them in a manner that relieves tension. Mercury square Pluto often brings harsh and sometimes fatal news. Talk revolves around the corruption of superpowers and the setbacks caused by this corruption. This may be an especially difficult time to discuss matters involving permanent change. Interestingly enough, this aspect usually occurs twice a year like clockwork, but due to Pluto's retrograde pattern through the final degrees of Sagittarius, there will be no exact square of Mercury to Pluto this autumn. This aspect will reoccur August 25 – 29, reaching its peak on August 27, when Mercury is in Virgo and Pluto is in Sagittarius.

April 4ᵗʰ Friday

Moon in Pisces / Aries	PDT	EDT /
Moon conjunct Uranus	12:50 AM	3:50 AM
Moon sextile Jupiter	1:27 AM	4:27 AM
Moon conjunct Venus goes v/c	2:41 AM	5:41 AM
Moon enters Aries	5:28 PM	8:28 PM
Moon square Pluto	7:21 PM	10:21 PM
Venus square Pluto begins (see April 6)		

Mood Watch: If you've got some leisure time, this is the day for you. The darkly waning Pisces Moon goes void-of-course before the day has a chance to begin. The entire mood of the day is likely to be spacey and inattentive. This is good if there's room to be creative, but wherever it is necessary to make progress at week's end, we may find a lack of attentiveness, or cooperation with the universe, to complete tasks and chores on time. By evening, the Aries Moon brings self-assurance and confidence to our moods.

April 5ᵗʰ Saturday

NEW MOON in ARIES	PDT	EDT	
Moon conjunct Mercury	1:24 AM	4:24 AM	
Moon square Mars	2:45 PM	5:45 PM	
Moon conjunct Sun	8:54 PM	11:54 PM	
Venus enters Aries	10:35 PM	1:35 AM	(April 6)

Mood Watch: The **New Moon in Aries** (Moon conjunct Sun) invokes the powers of initiation and newness; it is the essential part of regenerative force to take the initiative and to start anew. This is the time when the new parts of the self begin to emerge, and our moods are encouraged by confidence, motivation, courageousness, and fiery intent. This is the time to generate and promote inspiration and happiness. However, be cautious when Moon square Mars occurs, and beware of confrontational temperaments, as there may be a tendency towards temper tantrums, accidents, or attacks. Overall, the spirit of our moods brings a strong sense of newness and a great deal of activity.

Venus enters Aries (Venus in Aries: April 5 – 30) As Venus enters Aries the expression of beauty, love and attraction assumes a fascination for the warrior spirit. Venus represents magnetic draw and attraction, and now the planet of love and beauty focuses our attention on the force and fire of Aries related interests. This brings sheer love of and appreciation for such activities as competition, rights (or rites) of selfhood, and initiation into new endeavors. Venus in Aries brings out the warrior and conqueror quality in people, and a new sense of life and vitality will be evident. Venus in Aries emphasizes ardent, open and forthright expressions and proposals of love, especially from our Aries friends who may be blinded by the lust for beauty. New hobbies, crafts and talents will spring forth. Remember, Aries rules the head; there are numerous ways you can use your head before plunging head first into love matters. Try not to be too militant in the display of personal defenses and in the expression of true feelings of affection. New love is inspired with Venus in Aries.

April 6ᵗʰ Sunday

Moon in Aries / Taurus

	PDT	EDT	
Moon square Jupiter	3:20 AM	6:20 AM	
Moon sextile Neptune goes v/c	8:00 AM	11:00 AM	
Moon enters Taurus	6:20 PM	9:20 PM	
Moon trine Pluto	8:09 PM	11:09 PM	
Venus square Pluto	8:48 PM	11:48 PM	
Moon trine Saturn	9:57 PM	12:57 AM	(April 7)
Sun square Jupiter begins (see April 10)			

Mood Watch: Aries Moon brings ambitious, energetic, and sometimes competitive moods. This youthful, newly emerging, and newly waxing Moon goes void-of-course this morning and remains void until this evening. For some, false starts may occur as a result of impetuous and hasty behavior. By the time Moon enters Taurus, the ever popular grounding effect brings a comforting temperance to the quality of our moods.

Venus square Pluto (occurring April 4 – 9) Venus in Aries is square Pluto in Capricorn. The energetic, swift and intrepid qualities of our affections are likely to take a pretty good beating. Our concepts of beauty may be challenged as the corruption of superpowers prompts action which threatens or alters the beauty and pleasure in our lives. Venus square Pluto usually involves such difficulties as loss or death of a loved one, the obstacles of rejection, and general oppression for those aspects of life to which we are undeniably attached and which we hold dear. If something of this nature is occurring for you, it is best to recognize that love will triumph in every dimension, despite the pain of separation, or the disease and strife of the beloved. Be both strong and gentle in matters of love. Let the obstacles of love's pain become the building blocks of a better outlook, and a stronger love will supersede these current trials of the heart. This aspect will reoccur August 26 – 31, reaching its exact aspect on August 29, with Venus in Virgo and Pluto in Sagittarius.

April 7ᵗʰ Monday

Moon in Taurus

	PDT	EDT
Moon sextile Mars	4:36 PM	7:36 PM

Mood Watch: The Moon is exalted in the constellation Taurus. The physical world is in a state of reflection with our sensibilities. This is where we turn to environmental awareness, practical sense, business savvy, and the necessities of the body. This is a good time to actively secure those aspects of life that are in need of improvement on the physical level. Taurus governs the neck, throat – including that muscular wonder, the tongue – as well as the taste buds and tonsils, voice box and windpipe, down to the thyroid and parathyroid glands. It's a good time to nurture and care for these parts of the body.

April 8th Tuesday
Holy Day of Thelema (Nuit)
Moon in Taurus / Gemini

	PDT	EDT	
Moon sextile Uranus	2:54 AM	5:54 AM	
Moon trine Jupiter	3:47 AM	6:47 AM	
Moon square Neptune goes v/c	8:12 AM	11:12 AM	
Moon enters Gemini	6:27 PM	9:27 PM	
Moon square Saturn	9:58 PM	12:58 AM	(April 9)

Mercury square Mars begins (see April 10)
Sun trine Saturn begins (see April 21)

"Every man and every woman is a star" -LIBER AL vel LEGIS, 1904

Mood Watch: The early day begins with robust optimism, then, ever so swiftly, the ambitious part of our enthusiasm shifts as we enter into a ten hour phase of the Taurus Moon being void-of-course. It may be easy to see the things we wish to accomplish on the physical level of life, but it is likely to be a little more difficult to summon the energy, or to inspire others to assist in doing the tasks that call out for completion. This evening, the Gemini Moon inspires intellect, communication, and ingenuity.

April 9th Wednesday
Holy Day of Thelema (Hadit)
Moon in Gemini

	PDT	EDT
Moon sextile Venus	12:36 AM	3:36 AM
Moon sextile Mercury	4:48 PM	7:48 PM

"Let the rituals be rightly performed with joy & beauty!"
- LIBER AL vel LEGIS, 1904

Mood Watch: Learn to flip the coin of duality by taking in, hearing and witnessing both sides of the equation. Choose your thoughts integrally and wisely, and on the flip side of the coin, learn to laugh at the comedy of spontaneous confusion in a knowledge driven society full of layered ignorance and unsorted data. Our Gemini Moon moods will play around with new data and allow for new ideas. Get to know your wiser self by choosing your cosmology well. Avoid idle chatter and gossip. New feelings and moods will continually arise because the Gemini Moon has the cauldron of our emotions stirred by our thoughts. Don't put off today what you might not be able to do tomorrow.

April 10th Thursday
Holy Day of Thelema (Ra-Hoor-Khuit)
Moon in Gemini / Cancer

	PDT	EDT	
Moon square Uranus	3:48 AM	6:48 AM	
Moon sextile Sun	4:41 AM	7:41 AM	
Sun square Jupiter	7:10 AM	10:10 AM	
Moon trine Neptune goes v/c	9:11 AM	12:11 PM	
Mercury square Mars	10:12 AM	1:12 PM	
Moon enters Cancer	7:44 PM	10:44 PM	
Moon opposite Pluto	9:37 PM	12:37 AM	(April 11)

Moon sextile Saturn   11:15 PM   2:15 AM (April 11)
Sun sextile Neptune begins (see April 13)
" There is success ! "   - LIBER AL vel LEGIS, 1904

♈

Mood Watch: The long void-of-course Gemini Moon phase of today puts our moods in a perpetual state of mental quandary. We may wish to do and have it all, but without direct focus, we are bound to multitask our way into a thick maze of misunderstandings. Clarity of intent is what counts today. Focus on one thing at a time; modify expectations and temper the impetuous intrusions of the mind. Later, Cancer Moon puts us more directly in touch with our true feelings – time to rest after such a busy day.

Sun square Jupiter (occurring April 6 – 13) This occurrence of Sun square Jupiter will particularly affect those Aries people celebrating birthdays April 6 – 13. This aspect creates difficulties and obstacles to the personal joy and prosperous welfare of these birthday folks. Getting ahead financially or just staying on top of current trends or financial shifts may be personally challenging right now, requiring persistence and determination. Aries folks who are doing well financially may find this aspect is challenging their sense of what makes them happy, or that advancement in the world brings too much complexity and requires a lot of management. Though not all Aries are living as prosperously as they may desire, they do have the ability to come through this and be much better for it. Obstacles create challenges, but do not necessarily dictate an end to efforts to improve our welfare. It is the Aries personality (Sun) that is being challenged (square aspect) in matters of advancement (Jupiter), requiring Arians to make do with less assistance than they had anticipated. This may be a time to redefine and redirect personal goals. Aries birthday folks must reexamine what truly brings prosperity for them in their lives. Libra birthday folks, some of you are next in line to experience this Jupiter square to your natal sun. This aspect will reoccur October 3 – 9, reaching its exact aspect on October 6.

Mercury square Mars (occurring April 8 – 12) Mercury in Aries is square Mars in Cancer. Headstrong thinking creates complications, and indecisiveness or confusion occurs around some activities. Under the influence of this aspect, it is not a good time to lose one's temper. Be especially careful to watch what you say, preferably thinking before you speak; words can be easily taken the wrong way. This aspect stimulates arguments and mental blocks concerning the actions of others. Mercury square Mars makes it difficult for some to justify their actions or explain why they take a certain stand in life. Refrain from making risky comments, and be careful not to misinterpret information as being hostile or personal. Remember, during this complex time of Mercury square Mars, not to shoot the messenger.

April 11ᵗʰ Friday
Moon in Cancer   PDT   EDT
Moon square Venus   6:51 AM   9:51 AM
Moon conjunct Mars   10:51 PM   1:51 AM (April 12)
Mercury square Jupiter begins (see April 13)

Mood Watch: Throughout the day the waxing Moon in Cancer brings out our maternal instincts, and focuses our moods and feelings on the desire to nurture

93

emotional needs. This may be a typical time of moodiness, and the need to complain is just a symptom of wanting to be heard and understood. Moon in Cancer brings a wave of protective and instinctual impulses. For some, motherly cares and concerns come into play. There might well be a steady stream of emotional ups and downs, confirming that we are indeed affected by the tides. Go with the flow and take some good motherly advice.

April 12ᵗʰ Saturday
Moon in Cancer / Leo – FIRST QUARTER MOON in CANCER

	PDT	EDT	
Moon square Mercury	3:37 AM	6:37 AM	
Moon trine Uranus	6:51 AM	9:51 AM	
Moon square Sun goes v/c	11:32 AM	2:32 PM	
Moon enters Leo	11:29 PM	2:29 AM	(April 13)

Mood Watch: The **First Quarter Moon in Cancer** (Moon square Sun) urges us to share our feelings and take care of emotional needs, particularly in the light of our home. Home focused activities bring warm expressions of contentment. With First Quarter Cancer Moon the emotional current tends to be magnified. Nurturing foods and trustworthy company are important components of today's activities. Treating ourselves and others in a nurturing way becomes the key to enhancing or cleansing our emotional perspective. Be careful not to push the buttons of sensitive people and use words wisely while considering the feelings of yourself and others.

April 13ᵗʰ Sunday
Moon in Leo

	PDT	EDT
Sun sextile Neptune	12:30 AM	3:30 AM
Mercury square Jupiter	10:48 AM	1:48 PM
Moon trine Venus	4:36 PM	7:36 PM
Mercury sextile Neptune begins (See April 14)		
Sun conjunct Mercury begins (see April 16)		

Mood Watch: Leo Moon moods are energetic and openly focused on identity. The sun and moon are both in fire signs and archetypes abound with tales of the self, bursting with character and ego. A waxing Moon in Leo uplifts our moods with entertainment, magnetism and stimulation. It's good time to do something special for yourself and to reinforce your own integral outlook on the importance of living life according to will power. Get in touch with a sense of personal vitality and call it your own.

Sun sextile Neptune (occurring April 10 – 15) This occurrence of Sun sextile Neptune creates an opportunistic time for those Aries people celebrating birthdays from April 10 – April 15. These Aries folks are experiencing an opportunity to awaken in the realm of spirituality and creativity. There is an awareness of the self that goes deep here, and these birthday people are likely to appear distracted and difficult to reach while this phenomenon of great depth is occurring. This will be your year, birthday folks, to explore personal opportunities of spiritual growth. It may be a time to get away from it all, and find a sanctuary in which to meditate and open up to some valuable answers to old questions. These folks are in a place that gives them an opportunity to better understand the work of their path, but this is probably only true if they act on their own intuitive sensibilities, without the influences of others. That shouldn't be too hard for the enterprising and self-motivated Aries natures among us. This will be your year (Aries birthday people) to enhance and strengthen your intuition and primal instincts by tapping into them while they are easily available. This aspect will reoccur December 11 - 15, reaching its exact aspect on December 13, when the Sun will be in Sagittarius.

Mercury square Jupiter (occurring April 11 – 14) During this aspect it may be best to hold off on a job request, asking for a raise, or signing any binding contracts concerning long term investment and payment schedules. It may be an especially difficult time to communicate during travels, and it may be best to double check travel schedules. This aspect has a tendency to create expensive misunderstandings when it comes to large scale investments. This may also be a difficult time to raise money for charities. Dig harder and investigate more thoroughly the details associated with long term investments. This aspect will reoccur on three more occasions this year; first, September 5 - 10, reaching its exact aspect on September 7. Next, it occurs October 4 – 9, reaching its exact position on October 6. Finally, it occurs October 23 – 28, with its last exact aspect on October 26.

April 14th Monday

Moon in Leo

	PDT	EDT	
Mercury sextile Neptune	3:09 PM	6:09 PM	
Moon opposite Neptune	6:34 PM	9:34 PM	
Moon trine Mercury	7:13 PM	10:13 PM	
Moon trine Sun goes v/c	9:57 PM	12:57 AM	(April 15)

Mood Watch: This is a good time to work on developing one's personal image and to work on improving personal strengths. Leo Moon also focuses our attention on family and friends – those people in our lives who tend to play a big role in the course of self-development. We hope to get encouragement from those who are a part of us, and those who are considered to be our extended family, but we know from experience it doesn't always work that way. Leo Moon reminds us that it is ultimately up to each individual to empower personal integrity for the self – what follows naturally is the encouragement of others.

Mercury sextile Neptune (occurring April 13 – 15) Mercury in Aries sextile Neptune in Aquarius brings bold, independent messages that inform us of opportunities for spiritual growth in humanity. This is an opportunistic time to cautiously attempt communication with regard to beliefs and spiritual matters. Mercury is in Aries adding a fiery urgency to the question of how to face such Neptune related subjects as spiritual strength, guidance, and inspiration. Address addiction problems with helpful instruction. Prayers, channeling, and spells are all very effective with Mercury sextile Neptune. This is the time to get the word out to Great Spirit, and to reinforce a sense of faith or an acceptance of the way life is going. Mercury sextile Neptune allows us to verbalize and share beliefs in a way that encourages people. This aspect will reoccur December 5–8, reaching its exact aspect on December 6.

April 15ᵗʰ Tuesday

Moon in Leo / Virgo

	PDT	EDT
Moon enters Virgo	6:07 AM	9:07 AM
Moon trine Pluto	8:10 AM	11:10 AM
Moon conjunct Saturn	9:45 AM	12:45 PM
Mars trine Uranus begins (see April 22)		

Mood Watch: As we shake aside the beastly concerns of a long void Leo Moon night, the morning brings a Moon in Virgo mood. Virgo is the prudent sign of the zodiac, always looking for the loopholes in everything, always questioning, doubting, scrutinizing, and discerning one thing or another. Apart from the critic that comes out in all of us, one might notice that there is a strong need to pay attention to personal hygiene. It's a good time to apply some extra effort when brushing the teeth, washing the body and hair, and collaborating on one's overall appearance and the feelings about this appearance.

April 16ᵗʰ Wednesday

Moon in Virgo

	PDT	EDT	
Sun conjunct Mercury	12:23 AM	3:23 AM	
Moon sextile Mars	4:32 PM	7:32 PM	
Moon opposite Uranus	9:25 PM	12:25 AM	(April 17)
Moon trine Jupiter goes v/c	10:59 PM	1:59 AM	(April 17)
Mercury trine Pluto begins (see April 18)			

Mood Watch: Virgo Moon contentment can occur when we tend to personal needs without being overly critical of the self. Virgo emphasizes health and daily maintenance, and – don't forget – the Moon is simply the emotional barometer of our condition. It is only a temporary state of being and not everyone is focused on their daily moods. In order not to seem overly judgmental, we don't always have to react to the things we observe – we can simply be aware of them.

Sun conjunct Mercury (occurring April 13 – 18) This aspect will create a much more thoughtful, communicative and expressive year ahead for those Aries folks celebrating birthdays April 13 - 18. This is your time (birthday Aries) to record ideas, relay important messages, and pay close attention to your imaginative thoughts as they are touched by Mercury, creating the urge to speak and be heard. Birthday Aries, your thoughts will reveal a great deal about who you are, now and in the year to come.

April 17ᵗʰ Thursday

Moon in Virgo / Libra

	PDT	EDT
Mercury enters Taurus	2:06 PM	5:06 PM
Moon enters Libra	3:11 PM	6:11 PM
Moon square Pluto	5:16 PM	8:16 PM
Mars opposite Jupiter begins (see April 24)		

Mood Watch: Waxing Moon in Virgo brings industrious and communicative moods leading us to push past all the clutter and put the immediate universe at hand into some form of order. Later today as the Moon enters Libra, the need for teamwork is emphasized.

Mercury enters Taurus (Mercury in Taurus: April 17 – May 2) Mercury moves into the sign of Taurus, and communications will focus on manifesting sales and generating economic growth. It is a good time to clarify matters involving valuables, and to focus on documents, contracts, speeches, and business procedures. Mercury in Taurus brings on a new wave of discussion about the natural beauties and luxuries that surround us, and there is also an equal concern for practicality. Mercury is the messenger, the speaker and the director of the subject matter at hand. Mercury is also classically known as "The Merchant," "The Trickster," and "The Thief." In the fixed earth sign of Taurus, Mercury inspires the inclination to buy, sell, trade, and barter. Issues of ownership and, undoubtedly, a "steal of a deal" will appear in the arena of barter. Resourceful thinking and information processing can lead to the extra buck. This is a time to accurately record practical matters and events, and to communicate about finances.

April 18th Friday

Moon in Libra

	PDT	EDT	
Mercury trine Pluto	2:21 AM	5:21 AM	
Mercury trine Saturn	11:10 AM	2:10 PM	
Moon opposite Venus	10:25 PM	1:25 AM	(April 19)

Mood Watch: Libra Moon focuses our attention on research and court related matters, as well as specialty foods and culinary delights. Libra Moon emphasizes the pleasures of the learning and teaching processes. This is a good day to focus on business as usual, to take the time to show some appreciation for good friends, and to enjoy the contents of your latest favorite book.

Mercury trine Pluto (occurring April 16 – 19) Mercury in Taurus is trine to Pluto in Capricorn. Resourceful thoughts and communications will bring powerful results. This aspect brings hope like a gift, and the myth of Pandora's Box shows us that hope regenerates our senses and fills us with the potential for triumph over difficulties. Mercury in Taurus gives a very practical and logical quality to our methods of communicating. This would be a good time to share tales of triumph, spreading those miraculous stories that remind us of the great potential of winning against all odds. This positive aspect aids communication about struggles with fate, trouble, loss, and fatal illnesses. This is a good time to express encouraging words and reinforce the troubled people of our world with a sense of hope. This aspect will reoccur August 7 – 11, reaching its exact aspect on August 9 with Mercury in Leo.

Mercury trine Saturn (occurring April 17 – 19) Mercury is in Taurus where the emphasis of information is placed on the need for practicality in business. Mercury in Taurus trine Saturn in Virgo brings favorable communication which tells us how, and where, to draw the lines for ourselves. This is a good time to make an impression, to teach, and to communicate to others those important matters that must be clarified. This is a great time to study or practice memorization skills. Timely information and news represents a gift or blessing. News concerning the end of a long and arduous task brings relief. Mercury trine Saturn occurs again this December with Mercury in Capricorn and Saturn in Virgo. This aspect will reoccur December 24 – 28, reaching its exact aspect on December 26.

TAURUS

Key Phrase: "I HAVE"
Fixed Earth Sign
Symbol: The Bull
April 19ᵗʰ through May 20ᵗʰ

April 19ᵗʰ Saturday

Moon in Libra

	PDT	EDT
Moon square Mars	5:12 AM	8:12 AM
Moon square Jupiter	9:41 AM	12:41 PM
Sun enters Taurus	9:51 AM	12:51 PM
Moon trine Neptune goes v/c	1:54 PM	4:54 PM
Venus square Mars begins (see April 23)		

Mood Watch: Libra Moon brings moods focused on balancing matters that arise between friends and loved ones. Later today, the Moon is void-of-course, and this may cause some delays, particularly when it comes to making decisions. There may be a tendency for people to disagree on various matters at hand. It's a Full Moon eve and emotional tension builds. This is no time to make hasty or irrational decisions about something as important as relationships and friendships. Give Peace a Chance.

Sun enters Taurus (Sun in Taurus: April 19 – May 20) Taurus is a Venus ruled sign whose attraction to beauty is second nature. As a general rule, Taurus energy promotes a strong desire to keep physically fit, and to keep possessions and personal effects shining and looking good. Taurus has a very matter-of-fact way of looking at life, and likes to keep the surroundings neat and functional as well as aesthetically pleasing and socially acceptable. This is not to say that Taurus folks are orderly according to the rest of the world! They have a very sensitive and often sentimental side, and find it difficult to change and adapt swiftly when their lives seem to be in perfect order. Taurus loves stability and security. Taurus folks have a knack for smelling money and for finding the value in all things. Taurus says "I have," and Taurus folks are interested in preserving and enhancing what they have attained and acquired in the course of their lives.

April 20ᵗʰ Sunday

Passover begins (ends April 27)
Moon in Libra / Scorpio – FULL MOON in SCORPIO

♉

	PDT	EDT
Moon enters Scorpio	2:01 AM	5:01 AM
Moon opposite Sun	3:25 AM	6:25 AM
Moon sextile Pluto	4:07 AM	7:07 AM
Moon sextile Saturn	5:37 AM	8:37 AM
Sun trine Pluto	11:56 AM	2:56 PM
Moon opposite Mercury	2:48 PM	5:48 PM
Saturn-trine-Pluto-non-exact	- - - no exact aspect - - -	

Mood Watch: **Full Moon in Scorpio** (Moon opposite Sun) reaches its peak overnight, and throughout this morning our moods are – for lack of a better word – intensified. The brink of this lunar fullness has already commenced and yesterday's dramas are diminishing, although in many cases they are still being played out. The Full Scorpio Moon is a good time for garden lovers to transplant flowers and shrubs as well as planting seeds. Sex appeal is strongly highlighted. Intense desires are often our deepest secrets. Silly entertaining fun, and off-the-cuff kinds of play and humor are good medicine. Safe physical exercises and activities are excellent avenues of release.

Sun trine Pluto (occurring April 17 – 23) Positive, life altering changes are occurring, particularly in the lives of those Aries/Taurus cusp born people celebrating birthdays this year from April 17 – 23. These folks are currently undergoing the favorable trine aspect of Pluto to their natal Sun, bringing out experiences that involve transformation, and encounters with greater powers and with fate. It is always difficult to speculate just how the Pluto experience will manifest. For some of these birthday folks, the concept of receiving gifts and empowerment in the midst of fateful events may seem rocky and not particularly advantageous. Have no fear; this is a time to get in touch with your power, birthday Aries/Taurus! It is wise to remember Pluto moves slowly in our cosmos, and powerful encounters that seem deadly or harsh are actually a necessary process. Though unavoidable, matters involving fate can be positive, and the trine aspect does represent a gift being bestowed. Aries/Taurus birthday people, be grateful this is the trine aspect that brings power issues into your life in a more positive fashion with Pluto, and the work of destiny will bestow untold gifts this year. This is a time of positive transformation. Sun trine Pluto will reoccur August 17 – 24, reaching its exact aspect on August 20.

Saturn-trine-Pluto-non-exact (occurring March 9 – June 11) Today, and over the next couple of days, this is as close as we come to the Saturn trine Pluto aspect. Although the books do not count this aspect as technically occurring this year, we are in fact under its influence for three months. This long winded aspect represents a blessing. We have come a long way since Saturn was in the opposition to Pluto in 2001, an aspect that was popularly attributed to the breath-taking 911 incidents. Now, Saturn in Virgo is in the favorable trine position to Pluto, which is newly in the sign of Capricorn. Down-to-earth accomplishment is the key to this aspect, and there will be many astonishing shifts in focus, as down-to-earth needs become much more apparent. During this time, carefully considered plans and disciplines will be carried out with a power-packed force to back them. All of this occurs as we acknowledge the influence of world powers, contemplate the wave of the future, and focus on our health and well being. When it comes to accomplishing goals, matters of fate will now turn to a considerably more practical level of application. New disciplines and responsibilities, which will probably appear very physical in nature, will become a necessary part of our future and our sense of security.

April 21st Monday
Moon in Scorpio

	PDT	EDT	
Sun trine Saturn	6:04 AM	9:04 AM	
Moon trine Mars	7:32 PM	10:32 PM	
Moon trine Uranus	8:00 PM	11:00 PM	
Moon sextile Jupiter	9:47 PM	12:47 AM	(April 22)

Venus square Jupiter begins (see April 23)

Mood Watch: The intensity of tiredness, or strife, or of being confronted by mundane yet annoying disturbances is sometimes the curse of a post full Scorpio Moon. Fortunately, today's lunar aspects, although intensely energetic, are upbeat and very positive in nature.

Sun trine Saturn (occurring April 8 – 24) This aspect particularly affects Aries and Taurus people celebrating birthdays April 8 – 24. This is a positive time for these Aries and Taurus folks to get a handle on their lives, and it may be easier for them to take on the responsibilities of life with fewer complications and less difficulty in the year to come. These birthday folks may notice more acceptable forms of control, responsibility and work occurring in their lives. Now is your time (birthday people) to successfully work on putting some structure into your life; the kind of structure you've needed and wanted awaits you in the coming year. It is possible that time (Saturn) is on your side to make that move you've wanted to make.

April 22nd Tuesday
Earth Day
Moon in Scorpio / Sagittarius

	PDT	EDT
Moon square Neptune goes v/c	1:53 AM	4:53 AM
Mars trine Uranus	7:47 AM	10:47 AM
Moon enters Sagittarius	2:08 PM	5:08 PM
Moon square Saturn	5:41 PM	8:41 PM

"The goal of life is living in agreement with nature."
 - Zeno (335 BC – 264 BC), from Diogenes Laertius, Lives of Eminent Philosophers

Mood Watch: A post-full void-of-course Scorpio Moon emphasizes the need for safety, security, and protection. Keep an eye on suspicious characters. Later, as the Moon enters Sagittarius, our moods are geared towards finding a cohesive and acceptable perspective on matters. Sagittarius Moon invites us to apply "vision" and creative awareness in order to make sense of it all.

Mars trine Uranus (occurring April 15 – 28) Mars in Cancer trine Uranus in Pisces brings heated activities concerning very sensitive emotional matters and the radical tendencies that are seen in art and spiritual practices. It is through this aspect that emotional breakthroughs may occur. This is a battle that arrives on an apparently emotional level, with the two planets in water signs. Then it turns into explosive and radical events, creating a long run of favorable gifts and triumphs due to the congenial nature of the trine aspect. Since when is destructive macho energy favorable? These particularly masculine planets are tempered in the feminine watery signs. Watch, meditate and observe; the answers are out there. This is a good time to tackle the breakdown of unwanted barriers that stifle the human spirit from evolving in chosen ways. Mars trine Uranus is bound to create fire somewhere, and the heat often can be worked to our advantage. In the triumph mode, Mars trine Uranus creates fireworks of celebration. There is a certain sense of truly being alive with regard to home life, the demand for spiritual freedom and rights, and the need to bring an artistic form of relief to those who have experienced the challenge of emotional and spiritual battles. This aspect will reoccur October 27 – November 4, reaching its exact aspect on October 31 with Mars in Scorpio.

April 23rd Wednesday
Moon in Sagittarius

	PDT	EDT
Venus square Mars	11:07 AM	2:07 PM
Venus square Jupiter	6:35 PM	9:35 PM
Venus sextile Neptune begins (see April 25)		

Mood Watch: Despite love related trouble with Venus (see below), this may be a good time to think about travel options in the coming season. Waning Sagittarius Moon is also a time to focus on introspective visionary awareness.

Venus square Mars (occurring April 19 – 27) Venus square Mars creates tension and obstacles between the forces of love and the forces of defense. The archetypal images of Venus and Mars are largely that of feminine and masculine counterparts, and this aspect may bring stress between people in love relationships. The pain of separation or the sorrow of unrequited love may be a symptom of this time, as the rocky boat of romance is due to have some notable ups and downs. On the other hand, the difficulties of these tests may strengthen the power of love and, although it is sometimes very difficult to endure love related conflicts, it is also a necessary process to ensure the authenticity of our love experience.

Venus square Jupiter (occurring April 21 – 26) Venus in Aries is square to Jupiter in Capricorn. A love for independence and competition, as well as the pursuits of comforting beauty and affection are challenged by the need to handle escalating economic obligations or social debts. Our experiences of beauty and affection may be tested by the difficulty of attracting or acquiring prosperity. Some might say that the act of appreciating beauty is a form of prosperity in itself. Unfortunately, this aspect may create an obstacle to acknowledging the expenses incurred by our attractions and love-needs. This aspect reminds us that something more than love's blindness is required in order for us to fully realize our riches and the value of what we care about most. Venus square Jupiter will reoccur September 7 – 11, reaching its exact aspect on September 9, when Venus will be in Libra.

101

April 24th Thursday

Moon in Sagittarius

	PDT	EDT
Mars opposite Jupiter	6:22 AM	9:22 AM
Moon square Uranus	8:51 AM	11:51 AM
Moon trine Venus	12:27 PM	3:27 PM
Moon sextile Neptune goes v/c	2:37 PM	5:37 PM

Mood Watch: Physical activity or indulging in a favorite sport is an excellent outlet on a Sagittarius Moon day. However, the morning may be the time to proceed with caution, as certain types of chaotic energies will seem like a chore to overcome. A sense of pleasure increases in the afternoon, and then the Moon goes void-of-course for the rest of the evening. Delays when traveling may be evident; you'll know who's affected by their dazed look.

Mars opposite Jupiter (occurring April 17 – 30) Heated activities and those areas of life where we wage battles (Mars) are at odds with our economic welfare and outlook (Jupiter). Mars in Cancer opposes Jupiter in Capricorn. This aspect may bring domestic squabbles over money and career related topics. Initiatives, when activated, will quickly come up against high levels of curiosity coupled with over-whelming market demands. This aspect brings an abrupt awareness of economic oppression or shortcomings. Fortunes may be mishandled due to unanticipated or accidental circumstances. While Mars is opposed to Jupiter, active forces are diametrically opposed to expansive fortitude, and sometimes our anger is spurred due to a lack of flow or growth in our economic resources. This is a very busy and often overwhelming time to attempt to excel in business endeavors, especially in actively trading markets. While Mars is opposing Jupiter it is wise to remember that when you're roused to anger, you must take heed not to "bite the hand that feeds you."

April 25th Friday

Moon in Sagittarius / Capricorn

	PDT	EDT
Moon enters Capricorn	2:47 AM	5:47 AM
Moon conjunct Pluto	4:48 AM	7:48 AM
Moon trine Saturn	6:15 AM	9:15 AM
Venus sextile Neptune	9:33 AM	12:33 PM
Moon trine Sun	2:57 PM	5:57 PM

Mood Watch: Keeping the foundation of our life strong and firm is the underlying theme of today's moods. When losing ground it is difficult to maintain a sense of humor, but it's an essential part of maintaining one's integrity. Commitment to tradition, work, and completion brings favorable moods today.

Venus sextile Neptune (occurring April 23 – 27) Venus in Aries brings love, attraction, beauty, and the nature of feminine expression into prominence. Neptune in Aquarius is a time to awaken human spirituality and to excel in creative expression through music, art, writing, etc. Spread this healing power around for all to share! This time also holds the potential for one to realize the profound beauty and the depths of which true love is capable. This aspect last occurred January 14 – 18, reaching its exact aspect on January 16. It will also reoccur on November 3 – 6, reaching its exact aspect on November 5.

April 26th Saturday

♉

Moon in Capricorn

	PDT	EDT	
Moon trine Mercury	4:58 PM	7:58 PM	
Moon sextile Uranus	9:14 PM	12:14 AM	(April 27)
Moon conjunct Jupiter	10:59 PM	1:59 AM	(April 27)
Mercury sextile Uranus begins (see April 27)			
Mercury trine Jupiter begins (see April 28)			

Mood Watch: Capricorn Moon focuses our moods on the importance of diligence, persistence, and discipline. There is a need to get things done, to finish business, and handle whatever comes along with serious intent. There is great potential to accomplish much today as long as everyone remains focused on their tasks and watches their time. Drop fears concerning financial security. Risk becomes greater when nothing is done to change one's condition. Get to work! Hope comes with diligent effort.

April 27th Sunday

Moon in Capricorn / Aquarius

	PDT	EDT
Moon opposite Mars	1:35 AM	4:35 AM
Moon square Venus goes v/c	7:17 AM	10:17 AM
Moon enters Aquarius	2:28 PM	5:28 PM
Mercury sextile Uranus	7:36 PM	10:36 PM
Mercury square Neptune begins (see April 29)		

Mood Watch: A waning Capricorn Moon goes void-of-course this morning, and our moods may seem motionless; we're frozen in time. Eventually, the Moon enters Aquarius and our moods begin to focus more directly on the necessity for knowledge and expertise.

Mercury sextile Uranus (occurring April 26 – 28) Sensationalism may be played up in the news during this aspect. Mercury is in Taurus focusing talk, information and news on such practical matters as the value and cost of things, while Uranus is in Pisces, blowing all practicality right out of the water and stirring up chaos in the arts and religion. Mercury sextile Uranus gives us the opportunity to freely speak our minds and to address the turmoil that exists in our lives. This aspect will reoccur December 23 – 25, reaching its exact aspect on December 24, with Mercury in Capricorn.

April 28th Monday

LAST QUARTER MOON in AQUARIUS

	PDT	EDT
Mercury trine Jupiter	6:40 AM	9:40 AM
Moon square Sun	7:12 AM	10:12 AM
Mercury sextile Mars begins (see April 29)		
Venus trine Pluto begins (see May 1)		

Mood Watch: This morning we come to the **Last Quarter Moon in Aquarius** (Moon square Sun), and this Aquarius Moon encourages our conscience to have compassion for our kin. Common courtesy calls to us. The drive to sort out what this means – to assist and guide others – is often a questionable sport, given that most folks don't always know what's good for them. A kind word or a sympathetic ear has great healing power and often this promotes greater peace.

Mercury trine Jupiter (occurring April 26 – 29) This most favorable aspect brings good news of expansion and prosperity to those who are open to broadening their awareness. Ask and you shall have! Mercury in Taurus trine Jupiter in Capricorn inspires practical communication which can lead to career breakthroughs, adventure, great achievements, happiness and wellbeing. This is an excellent time to learn new skills which will improve one's livelihood and better one's outlook. This is also a great time for salespeople to make sales. Mercury brings news, while Jupiter brings wealth and prosperous change. Mercury trine Jupiter is often considered to be an advantageous time to advertise and put information out there, and to ask for a job or a loan. Look openly for opportunity when sharing information, and promote yourself and your capabilities. This aspect will reoccur August 15 – 19, reaching its exact aspect on August 17 with Mercury in Virgo.

April 29ᵗʰ Tuesday

Moon in Aquarius / Pisces

	PDT	EDT	
Mercury square Neptune	6:10 AM	9:10 AM	
Moon conjunct Neptune	12:13 PM	3:13 PM	
Moon square Mercury	1:15 PM	4:15 PM	
Mercury sextile Mars	3:20 PM	6:20 PM	
Moon sextile Venus goes v/c	10:23 PM	1:23 AM	(April 30)
Moon enters Pisces	11:11 PM	2:11 AM	(April 30)
Venus trine Saturn begins (see May 1)			

Mood Watch: This is the time when many will be making social connections. The signs of the times are all around us, applying some very interesting twists and turns in the ventures and knowledge of humankind. On some level, the desire for freedom or personal breakthrough calls out to some folks. The restlessness of spring season stirs our hearts. Sun in Taurus and Moon in Aquarius is an important time to banish fear and test the realms with one's own sensibilities. There's enough love and beauty to go around for everyone.

Mercury square Neptune (occurring April 27 – 30) This aspect often brings difficulty in communications with the spirit world, and with understanding human spirituality and beliefs. As a result, talk and discussion concerning what we believe in and strive for may be greatly misunderstood. Neptune is in Aquarius, stirring up the issue of human divinity and the structure of humanity's beliefs in the confusing shifts of this dawning age. While Mercury in Taurus is squaring Neptune, pragmatic thought and divinity will be tested, and relaying information on these subjects may seem very difficult. Anticipate religious or belief related arguments and disputes. Deep subjects must not be treated lightly while Mercury squares Neptune. This aspect will reoccur November 15 – 19, reaching its peak on November 17 with Mercury in Scorpio.

Mercury sextile Mars (occurring April 28 – May 1) Clear communications regarding the manner in which actions are taken may make this a superb time to seek employment. Mercury in Taurus demands the practical delivery of communications and is an excellent time to carry out promises or proclamations. Mars in Cancer demands heartfelt action. Mercury sextile Mars brings out opportunities which can be received, recognized, communicated and acted upon. News or information may lead to immediate action, and commands made with conviction are quickly acted upon. It's an advantageous time to apply one's word with a full backing of action for a very favorable outcome. This aspect will repeat on June 8, when Mercury will be retrograde in Gemini and Mars will be in Leo. Finally, Mercury sextile Mars occurs for the third time this year on July 15 with Mercury in Cancer and Mars in Virgo.

♉

April 30th Wednesday
Moon in Pisces

	PDT	EDT
Moon sextile Pluto	12:53 AM	3:53 AM
Moon opposite Saturn	2:13 AM	5:13 AM
Venus enters Taurus	6:34 AM	9:34 AM
Moon sextile Sun	7:07 PM	10:07 PM

Mood Watch: It's the eve of May Day and the Moon in Pisces opens our moods to all possibilities and imaginative hope. For many, this is a time of indulgence and fantasy, and a time to preoccupy the senses with something special and memorable for our spirits.

Venus enters Taurus (Venus in Taurus: April 30 – May 24) Venus in Taurus is the time of an extraordinary attraction to beauty. Here in Taurus, Venus is at home nurturing us with sensual pleasure and enhancing our appreciation of nature and earthly bounty, as well our as appreciation for quality and specialty craftsmanship. Venus in Taurus brings out aesthetic awareness, and places a greater emphasis on the love of having valuable items, wealth, and abundance. Venus attracts and draws, and Taurus represents material acquisition and attainment. Taurus people will be touched by the need for love and affection in their lives as Venus crosses over their natal Sun. Now is the time to acquire, polish, clean, and beautify things that give a sense of truly having something. To create beauty around oneself is to enhance one's sense of wellbeing. Beauty, of course, varies according to the eye of the beholder. Simple pleasures are the best – an effort to enjoy the beauties of life is not necessarily expensive.

May 1st Thursday
Beltane / May Day
Moon in Pisces

	PDT	EDT
Venus trine Pluto	12:48 AM	3:48 AM
Moon conjunct Uranus	1:12 PM	4:12 PM
Moon sextile Jupiter	2:39 PM	5:39 PM
Venus trine Saturn	3:20 PM	6:20 PM
Moon trine Mars	8:56 PM	11:56 PM
Mercury square Saturn begins (see May 3)		

Mood Watch: The waning Pisces Moon is a time to be aware of many people's need for escapism and overindulgence. Dreamy, somewhat spacey and artistic moods ebb and flow like the sea. This is a time when our moods tend to reflect on our beliefs.

Happy **May Day**! This is a traditional old world solar holiday, also known as **Beltane**. We have now reached the half-way mark – and the height – of the spring season. This holiday celebrates the dance of the Maypole, fertility, beauty, rapturous love, and the various types of youthful frolic appropriate to spring. May Day represents the awakening of the passion and the youthfulness in all of life. This time calls to us to take joy in the fertilization of those parts of ourselves and our lives that need to be brought to fruition.

Venus trine Pluto (occurring April 28 – May 3) Venus in Taurus is trine to Pluto in Capricorn, and both of these planets are on the cusp at zero degrees. Beauty can be found in all aspects of existence. Venus trine Pluto represents a love or fascination for the workings of fate and power. This aspect often allows a breakthrough to occur for those who are under stress from hardship. There is hope yet that we will acquire an appreciation for the not-so-glamorous aspects of existence. This is also an aspect that allows for adoration and loving energy to flow more easily between generations, despite all the differences that have separated us in these fast changing times. This aspect will reoccur August 2–7, reaching its exact aspect on August 4.

Venus trine Saturn (occurring April 29 – May 4) Venus in Taurus brings a strong attraction to the comforting luxuries and natural beauties of the physical world. Saturn in Virgo gives us the inclination to organize and structuralize, as well as communicate. The favorable trine position of these two planets helps to inspire the desire – and the discipline – necessary to cultivate and keep those luxuries. This aspect brings the timely gift of love. Paradoxically, it also allows for some peace in the closure of a love relationship. Remember, when extending love, it is best not to have expectations about the need to receive it in return. Genuine love, when given without expectation, will return naturally, and bring love into your life. This aspect reoccurs November 27 – December 2, reaching its exact aspect on November 29.

May 2ⁿᵈ Friday

Moon in Pisces / Aries

	PDT	EDT
Moon sextile Mercury goes v/c	2:32 AM	5:32 AM
Moon enters Aries	3:52 AM	6:52 AM
Moon square Pluto	5:23 AM	8:23 AM
Mercury enters Gemini	1:00 PM	4:00 PM
Saturn goes direct	8:08 PM	11:08 PM

Mood Watch: It's an Aries Moon day and there is eagerness in our moods. We have a strong need to stand out and be on top and in control of situations. This may be a difficult time to ignore pushy aggressors; being aware of this behavior and attempting to avoid it by watching for the signs, before the oppressor gets out of hand, may well be in your favor today.

Mercury enters Gemini (Mercury in Gemini: May 2 – July 10) Mercury is the ruling planet of two astrological signs, Gemini and Virgo. When in Gemini, Mercury is known to increase our attention to detail and to cover a wide range of interesting topics. Mercury in Gemini directs and orchestrates information – like food for the brain – in an interesting and captivating way. Mercury in Gemini, the mutable air sign, is the best time to inspire a storyteller who is often looking for ways to make the story more interesting. Talk, discussion, stories, gossip, and the news media all generate flashes designed to captivate one's interest even if only for one moment. Mercury in Gemini brings out the two sides of every story. The well developed story has merit as a description of the course of our own existence. Pay heed to the message if the storyteller happens to be telling *your* story while Mercury is in Gemini. Mercury will go retrograde on May 26, causing it to remain in Gemini for an extended period of time, until July 10.

♉

Saturn goes direct (Saturn direct: May 2 – December 31) Saturn, which represents time, restriction, responsibility, and disciplinary acts, has been retrograde since December 19, 2007 and will go direct today until December 31 this year. Saturn retrograde often requires us to backtrack on many previous, as yet unfulfilled, obligations and disciplines. Since December last year, Saturn retrograde has been a time of implementing, testing and correcting various types of security measures in our lives, and many sacrifices were made in order for us to feel a sense of completion and accomplishment. Today Saturn goes direct at the one degree mark of Virgo and will remain in Virgo until October 29, 2009. This is a good time to regenerate the discipline of our senses, to end destructive habits, particularly bad health practices, as well as to make new lifestyle choices and changes. As Saturn begins to move forward, this may be the time for Virgo folks to move forward towards positive endings and new beginnings as Virgo related focuses become society's priority. Saturn in Virgo focuses on the power of research, statistics, accounting, communication and the dexterity of the mind. It also focuses on such Virgo-like matters as the quality and purity of one's environment, crafts, academic studies, agricultural disciplines, and systems analysis. Saturn in Virgo brings a greater emphasis on practical focuses and health related disciplines. Virgo says: "I analyze." While Saturn travels through Virgo, structure and discipline when applied to analysis and forethought, brings magnanimous results. Here, there is no room for Virgo's ability to question or to cast doubt. Here, it is skill, persistence, and indefatigable management that will support grand feats of accomplishment for Virgo.

May 3ʳᵈ Saturday
Moon in Aries

	PDT	EDT
Mercury square Saturn	12:51 PM	3:51 PM
Moon square Jupiter	4:38 PM	7:38 PM
Moon sextile Neptune	7:32 PM	10:32 PM

Mood Watch: Waning Aries Moon is an excellent time to reiterate personal affirmations and to prepare for the reinventing process of the self. This means weeding out and dropping the old tendencies and habits that are holding back the emergence of the new self. Most importantly, this is a time of abolishing self doubt.

Mercury square Saturn (occurring May 1 – 5) Mercury in Gemini square Saturn in Virgo creates tension in communications. Under the influence of this aspect, the battle to maintain accurate or precise information may be strongly evident. There may also be a tendency for "foot-in-mouth disease" as people may say the wrong things at the wrong time. It is wise to use caution when attempting communications during Mercury square Saturn, especially concerning matters of time and timing. It is also wise to be careful not to misinterpret health related information.

While Mercury is square to Saturn, beware of the tendency for people to make uninformed assumptions about the conclusion or outcome of important matters. This aspect will reoccur December 4 – 8, reaching its exact aspect on December 6, when Mercury will be in Sagittarius.

May 4ᵗʰ Sunday

Moon in Aries / Taurus

	PDT	EDT
Moon square Mars goes v/c	12:14 AM	3:14 AM
Moon enters Taurus	4:59 AM	7:59 AM
Moon trine Pluto	6:22 AM	9:22 AM
Moon trine Saturn	7:38 AM	10:38 AM
Moon conjunct Venus	1:20 PM	4:20 PM

Mood Watch: Early a.m. (4:59) on the west coast and later in the morning (7:59) on the east coast, the Moon enters Taurus and the stubborn stampeding attitude of the bull sets matters straight with less-than-subtle tactics. Now that the Moon wanes darkly before it settles into newness (tomorrow morning), stubbornness and determination abound. The wise old soul puts us in touch with a sense of value. Taurus Moon puts us in touch with getting our finances in order. This is a good day for bargain hunters.

May 5ᵗʰ Monday

Cinco de Mayo
NEW MOON in TAURUS

	PDT	EDT
Moon conjunct Sun	5:18 AM	8:18 AM
Moon sextile Uranus	3:05 PM	6:05 PM
Moon trine Jupiter	4:16 PM	7:16 PM
Moon square Neptune	7:04 PM	10:04 PM

Mood Watch: **New Moon in Taurus** (Moon conjunct Sun) emphasizes the acquisition of new possessions, or it could mean there is a need to restore, replenish, and maintain the old ones. Personal contentment counts with new possessions. Search for the value of what you need and want. This serves as a good time to clean the bad energy off misguided objects of power. New Moon in Taurus is exalted and calls to us to enjoy the beauty that surrounds us, shut down the noise and go celebrate nature!

May 6ᵗʰ Tuesday

Moon in Taurus / Gemini

	PDT	EDT
Moon sextile Mars goes v/c	1:21 AM	4:21 AM
Moon enters Gemini	4:18 AM	7:18 AM
Moon square Saturn	6:56 AM	9:56 AM
Moon conjunct Mercury	2:31 PM	5:31 PM

Mood Watch: The youthfully waxing Gemini Moon fills our moods with an intrusion of mutable thoughts and busy ideas. Springtime frenzy is changing the rate at which we are able to plan and keep track of matters. Getting an earful of everyone else's affairs can seem tedious, but it's just a way for folks to vent that extra nervous energy. Gemini Moon reminds us to filter through all the trivia and take it in stride.

108

Prioritize the important stuff. As if it were a game, learn to enjoy setting straight all the minor details.

♉

May 7ᵗʰ Wednesday
Moon in Gemini

	PDT	EDT
Moon square Uranus	2:37 PM	5:37 PM
Moon trine Neptune goes v/c	6:36 PM	9:36 PM

Mood Watch: How playful we are today. Despite some struggles with late afternoon chaos, this time invites us to apply the good medicine of laughter and joy. Gemini Moon waxes and puts many people into curious, talkative, and interactive moods. Spontaneous and random tidbits of information will draw our attention and highlight the need for correspondence and communication. This is a good time to bounce ideas off others. This is also an important time to pace ourselves on the mental level and not to overtax our nervous systems with too much sugar or caffeine, especially in those instances when we're under mentally challenging pressure. This evening's void-of-course Moon will be a good time to try to rest the mind.

May 8ᵗʰ Thursday
Moon in Gemini / Cancer

	PDT	EDT	
Moon enters Cancer	4:02 AM	7:02 AM	
Moon opposite Pluto	5:22 AM	8:22 AM	
Moon sextile Saturn	6:48 AM	9:48 AM	
Moon sextile Venus	9:25 PM	12:25 AM	(May 9)
Sun trine Jupiter begins (see May 12)			

Mood Watch: Deep feelings run through our moods with Moon in Cancer, and there may be a tendency for some people to be very distracting with their moodiness. For the most part this is simply a time when many of us need a little more reassurance and love. Strong feelings will be necessary today, bringing determination and a powerful willingness to get to the source of what we are feeling and how it is affecting us.

May 9ᵗʰ Friday
Moon in Cancer

	PDT	EDT
Jupiter goes retrograde	5:12 AM	8:12 AM
Moon sextile Sun	12:19 PM	3:19 PM
Mars enters Leo	1:19 PM	4:19 PM
Moon trine Uranus	4:04 PM	7:04 PM
Moon opposite Jupiter goes v/c	5:06 PM	8:06 PM
Sun sextile Uranus begins (see May 11)		

Mood Watch: A waxing Cancer Moon brings a focus on our defenses, and our security and comfort zones are also given a thorough check. The entire day's activities gear up our senses with deep emotional expressions and focus our attention on nurturing and instinctual urges. This serves as a good time to brighten up the home and make it feel more comfortable. Lazy evening moods come with the void-of-course phase of the Moon; beware of a tendency towards bingeing.

Jupiter goes retrograde (Jupiter retrograde: May 9 – Sept. 7) The planet of expansion and prosperity now begins to recede back through the degrees of the zodiac today through September 7. The planet Jupiter itself does not go backwards; it is only the apparent shift in our orbital position to Jupiter that makes it appear this way. Most planets orbiting around the Sun eventually go into a retrograde pattern from our geocentric view of planetary movement. Jupiter in Capricorn brings prosperity and expansion to such areas of life as construction, building, banking, corporate growth, architectural feats, estate management, and administrative expertise. This is a time when marketing strategies often employ the themes of corporate development, real estate growth, and engineering. Jupiter retrograde is not the best time for the growth of large scale funds and investments, but it is a good time to meditate, and to observe carefully, what truly makes us happy in the realms of fortune seeking. A clearer sense of growth will occur through internal processing and through personal skill development. It is an important time to apply wisdom and caution in this area of our lives, and in our livelihood, so that we may see future growth. While Jupiter is retrograde through Capricorn this spring and summer, the economy may appear to be receding or to be progressing slowly at times, while unpredictable or volatile market trends may occur.

Mars enters Leo (Mars in Leo: May 9 – July 1) Leo is a fearless place for the planet Mars; sheer action is stimulated and animated here. Now through July 1, Leo people will have a lot of extra energy and some of them will be forced to reckon with their temper. Leo folks, be creative with this extra energy while you have it. In the meantime, while traveling through Leo, Mars will go into the square position to the signs Taurus and Scorpio. Taurus and Scorpio people may have an accident prone time, or they may need to steer clear of heated disputes, particularly with Leos. Aquarius people may be overwhelmed by brazen activity in their lives while Mars opposes their natal Sun. Mars in Leo generally brings positive and fortifying energy to the scope of all action.

May 10th Saturday
Moon in Cancer / Leo

	PDT	EDT
Moon enters Leo	6:11 AM	9:11 AM
Moon conjunct Mars	6:50 AM	9:50 AM

Mood Watch: Waxing Leo Moon brings playfulness, and many people seem to be self absorbed or independent. Others may display their sense of importance by being entertaining and attention grabbing. Many will be focused on building up their talents and willpower. This is a great time to seek entertainment and personal pleasures.

May 11ᵗʰ Sunday

Mother's Day

♉

FIRST QUARTER MOON in LEO

	PDT	EDT	
Moon sextile Mercury	4:07 AM	7:07 AM	
Moon square Venus	5:51 AM	8:51 AM	
Moon square Sun	8:47 PM	11:47 PM	
Sun sextile Uranus	9:32 PM	12:32 AM	(May 12)
Sun square Neptune begins (see May 14)			

Mood Watch: The expression of a **First Quarter Moon in Leo** (Moon square Sun) places our moods in states of playfulness, self indulgence, and the need for expression and adoration. Today's attractions tend to be towards those areas of life that we identify with the most. With the Sun in Taurus, the Moon in Leo is most likely expressed by the act of flashing around our best toys. Moods reflect on the contest of who has the best, the biggest, the shiniest, and the most expensive toys, cars, clothes, house and garden. Entertainment value and quality of presentation are just as important. Bonus points go out to those who not only have the finest trimmings, but know how to use what they have in an imaginative, original, and creative manner. Cool is always "in," and requires the assurance of the proper attitude.

Sun sextile Uranus (occurring May 9 – 14) This occurrence of Sun sextile Uranus particularly affects those Taurus folks celebrating birthdays May 9 – 14. These birthday people are being given an opportunity to blow off some chaotic steam and to reach for qualities of freedom that may have been absent in their recent past. This will be your time to make radical breakthroughs, birthday Taurus; your natal Sun is currently sextile Uranus for a good reason – to find a liberating balance in the midst of the chaos. Once you've done this, you'll be ready to take the next step. Right now, there is no holding back, so go for it; discover your freedom. The victory of creative change will bring a more optimistic outlook on life. This aspect last occurred on January 6, covering the period of January 4 – 8, when the Sun was in Capricorn.

May 12ᵗʰ Monday

Moon in Leo / Virgo

	PDT	EDT
Moon opposite Neptune goes v/c	1:09 AM	4:09 AM
Sun trine Jupiter	10:28 AM	1:28 PM
Moon enters Virgo	11:49 AM	2:49 PM
Moon trine Pluto	1:11 PM	4:11 PM
Moon conjunct Saturn	3:05 PM	6:05 PM

Mood Watch: The morning brings a void-of-course Leo Moon. For some, there may be a struggle with personal identity. As the waxing Moon enters Virgo, there is a need for practicality. Sun in Taurus and Moon in Virgo brings out definite spring cleaning urges for those who are ever inclined in this fashion. There is a need to account for what we have. This is an especially good time to ground out and apply important physical health practices.

Sun trine Jupiter (occurring May 8 – 15) This aspect brings those Taurus people celebrating a birthday from May 8 – 15 to a favorable natal solar position with relation to Jupiter. This will be a time of gifts and expansion for these birthday folks, and there are good times ahead for them in the coming year. This aspect will

111

bring a better sense of what it means to expand and attain one's personal desire. Be sure to take the time right now (Taurus birthday people) to enjoy and appreciate life, which will definitely improve for those who are being given the gifts of joy this aspect often brings. Sun trine Jupiter will reoccur with the Sun in Virgo, September 1 – 7, reaching its peak on September 4.

May 13th Tuesday

Moon in Virgo	PDT	EDT
Moon square Mercury	4:20 PM	7:20 PM
Moon trine Venus	7:02 PM	10:02 PM

Mood Watch: The Moon waxes in Virgo, and a sense of the necessity to be more resourceful and prudent overcomes many. Moon in Virgo places an emphasis on accounting for what's around us and cleaning up the physical disruption in our midst. This really is a good time to tidy up the home and apply health practices such as dental hygiene, etc. This Moon emphasizes a great deal of commotion around issues of communication and resources. This evening's Moon trine Venus brings pleasurable moods.

May 14th Wednesday

Moon in Virgo / Libra	PDT	EDT	
Moon opposite Uranus	5:08 AM	8:08 AM	
Moon trine Jupiter	5:56 AM	8:56 AM	
Sun square Neptune	8:50 AM	11:50 AM	
Moon trine Sun goes v/c	9:38 AM	12:38 PM	
Moon enters Libra	8:57 PM	11:57 PM	
Moon square Pluto	10:08 PM	1:08 AM	(May 15)

Mood Watch: This morning's Virgo Moon brings hard working, practical moods. However, as the Moon goes void-of-course, our moods are less work oriented and more scrupulous, doubtful, and skeptical at times throughout the day. Tonight, the Libra Moon sheds some balance on our defensive moods, and people will be a little more congenial.

Sun square Neptune (occurring May 11 – 17) This occurrence of Sun square Neptune especially affects those Taurus people celebrating birthdays from May 11 – 17. Neptune, in the square position to these folk's natal Sun, brings a perception that obstacles are getting in the way of Spirit, the spiritual path, or the acknowledgment of one's beliefs. The challenge for these Taurus birthday folks is to overcome the doubts and confrontations that interfere with their beliefs. Over the next year, there will undoubtedly be some spiritual adjustments, and perhaps a change of belief is required for those encountering birthdays at this time. Taurus change? Never! Well, unless it suits them, of course. This aspect will reoccur November 10 – 16, reaching its exact aspect on November 13, when the Sun will be in Scorpio, affecting the lives and beliefs of some Scorpio people.

May 15th Thursday

ŏ

Moon in Libra

	PDT	EDT
Moon sextile Mars	2:36 AM	5:36 AM
Venus trine Jupiter begins (see May 18)		

Mood Watch: Waxing Libra Moon brings the potential for positive progress to be made among friends and with marital partners. This is a good time to review decisions that have to be made and to work towards making adjustments and compromises with others. Libra Moon activities emphasize the need for sound logic and clear objectives. There may be a strong need to research or to investigate the feasibility of our plans. There is also a need for us to understand the current laws and rules of the situations we face. Libra Moon requires balanced thinking and acting, as well as benevolent and civilized approaches to creating harmony and camaraderie in the midst of carrying out our objectives.

May 16th Friday

Moon in Libra

	PDT	EDT
Moon trine Mercury	7:12 AM	10:12 AM
Moon square Jupiter	4:36 PM	7:36 PM
Moon trine Neptune goes v/c	8:28 PM	11:28 PM
Venus sextile Uranus begins (see May 18)		

Mood Watch: Leadership is emphasized on this Libra Moon day, and true leaders must be patient as well as convincing. Certainly no one can do absolutely everything alone, for without the corroboration of others, even the decisions of the most assertive leaders have no staying power. This is especially important later today, as the Moon squares with Jupiter, bringing a tendency for people to struggle with the need to prosper. A good leader overlooks the less ambitious moods and forges forward with ardent optimism.

May 17th Saturday

Moon in Libra / Scorpio

	PDT	EDT
Moon enters Scorpio	8:00 AM	11:00 AM
Moon sextile Pluto	9:17 AM	12:17 PM
Moon sextile Saturn	11:43 AM	2:43 PM
Moon square Mars	4:48 PM	7:48 PM

Mood Watch: While the Moon is void-of-course in Libra, the early part of the morning may be strained by tendencies towards indecisiveness. Soon enough, the Moon enters Scorpio and our moods shift over to a much clearer perspective on where they are headed. Scorpio Moon puts us in touch with our powers of perception. Clairvoyance and sensibility work together to provide a better understanding of what we are feeling.

May 18th Sunday

Moon in Scorpio

	PDT	EDT
Venus sextile Uranus	4:22 AM	7:22 AM
Venus trine Jupiter	8:17 AM	11:17 AM
Mercury-square-Uranus-non-exact begins (see below)		

Mood Watch: Physically and emotionally charged energy is extremely high on this Full Scorpio Moon Eve. There is a risk of elevated levels of crime and violence, particularly in high crime areas, but also in the unexpected places. Despite the fact that there are no significant lunar aspects occurring today, a full list of celestial events, coupled with the nearly Full Moon, keeps our Scorpio Moon emotions going strong.

Mercury-square-Uranus-non-exact (occurring May 18 – June 2) Throughout this time, Mercury square Uranus comes as close as it can to the square position, but due to the pending Mercury retrograde (May 26 – June 19), Mercury doesn't actually reach an exact square to Uranus this time. False starts may occur whenever a demand or a command is launched. Mercury retrograde is famous for being the cause of misinformation, and while it is *almost* in the unfavorable square position to Uranus, misunderstandings may lead to wasted energy, or chaotic activity. During this time, it would be wise to refrain from spouting out radical or offensive comments which may well create explosive reactions from people. This aspect will officially reach an exact peak when it returns to the stage on July 5, when Mercury in Gemini will no longer be retrograde.

Venus sextile Uranus (occurring May 16 – 19) Venus in Taurus is sextile to Uranus in Pisces. Natural beauty takes on a radical or unusual kind of expression. Eccentric love may erupt with this aspect. Venus sextile Uranus can encourage us to break useless tendencies and habits, and also may bring an opportunity for love related matters to transcend the restriction of unmet personal needs. Venus sextile Uranus last occurred February 5 – 8, reaching its exact aspect peak on February 6, when Venus was in Capricorn. Venus will also return to Capricorn on November 12, and with that comes the return of Venus sextile Uranus on November 28.

Venus trine Jupiter (occurring May 15 – 20) Valuable and inspiring gifts of love and affection come with this aspect. Love (Venus) is harmoniously placed with prosperity and opportunity (Jupiter). Venus in Taurus trine Jupiter in Capricorn brings practical love and affection, inspirational natural beauty, stable growth, and prosperity. This is a great time to give gifts of love, and for many, it offers an expansive outlook of love's power. Getting ahead in life, in this case, has everything to do with appreciating and loving those areas of life in which we want to expand and prosper. A positive outlook can indeed help make this happen. This year we will be graced with the presence of this delicious tango of Venus and Jupiter again from August 14 – 18, reaching its exact aspect peak on August 16.

May 19th Monday
Victoria Day, Canada
Moon in Scorpio / Sagittarius – FULL MOON in SCORPIO

♉

	PDT	EDT	
Moon trine Uranus	4:17 AM	7:17 AM	
Moon sextile Jupiter	4:35 AM	7:35 AM	
Moon opposite Venus	6:59 AM	9:59 AM	
Moon square Neptune	8:41 AM	11:41 AM	
Moon opposite Sun goes v/c	7:11 PM	10:11 PM	
Moon enters Sagittarius	8:19 PM	11:19 PM	
Venus square Neptune	11:27 PM	2:27 AM	(May 20)
Sun square Saturn begins (see May 22)			

Mood Watch: **Full Moon in Scorpio** (Moon opposite Sun) reaches its peak this evening, and throughout the day our moods are, for lack of a better word, intensified. As this lunar fullness builds to a crescendo of emotional dramas, our emotional patterns are being played out in interesting ways. Intense desires – and what provokes them – reveal a lot about who we are and what we need to appease the satisfaction-hungry inner child. Silly entertaining fun, and off-the-cuff kinds of play and humor are good medicine. The Full Scorpio Moon is a good time for garden lovers to transplant flowers and shrubs as well as plant seeds. Safe physical exercises and activities are excellent avenues of release. Later, as the Moon enters Sagittarius, a much more philosophical mood comes to light.

Venus square Neptune (occurring May 17 – 22) Venus in Taurus is square to Neptune in Aquarius. Earthy pleasures, love, and expressions of beauty and femininity run up against the obstacles represented by the higher, more refined goddess image that humanity expects. A conflict of beliefs about womanhood is common with this aspect, and sometimes women, artists, and very attractive people are placed on high pedestals. Despite this, the human element usually leads them to certain error and they suffer great delusions. It is here that beauty suffers a spiritual conflict. The expectation and conditioning of others has created a false image of beauty, and the person on whom it is imposed is likely to be suffocated by the beliefs of others. With Venus square to Neptune, what we want is challenged by what we know is best for us. Consequently, it may be difficult for some people to make a personal connection with spiritual attractions. Beliefs concerning love matters may be tested. Despite the conflicts, this is a time to rise to the challenge of believing in love and loving your own choice of spiritual path. As for the art of love, the influences of this aspect are not as harsh for those who understand that true beauty is found in the core of feminine wisdom, and that magnetic attraction goes beyond temporal beauty. This aspect will repeat reoccur October 9 – 13, reaching its exact aspect peak on October 11 with Venus in Scorpio.

GEMINI

Key Phrase: "I THINK"

Mutable Air Sign

Symbol: The Twins

May 20th through June 20th

May 20th Tuesday

Moon in Sagittarius

	PDT	EDT
Moon square Saturn	12:13 AM	3:13 AM
Moon trine Mars	8:08 AM	11:08 AM
Sun enters Gemini	9:00 AM	12:00 PM

Mood Watch: Although the intensity of the Full Moon reached its peak last night, the lunar energy now in the sign of Sagittarius is basking in strength and the urge to break out of the usual routine. The philosophical clarity of Sagittarius allows us to look at the bigger picture of where energy goes and how to make the most of our situation. Though all of this energy is still strong, it is now beginning to dissipate, and this is a good time to reflect and push past all the intensity with a clearer and calmer vision.

Sun enters Gemini (Sun in Gemini: May 20 – June 20) Gemini people love to think. They're often thinking of ways to change the picture and to make it brighter and more detailed. The mutable and adaptable mind must be free to roam with different concepts and ideas that haven't been fully integrated into the big picture. Gemini weaves tapestries of thought; great storytellers, Geminis are often articulate and eloquent speakers, captivating audiences with details and keen observations. Duality is the key factor that shapes the Gemini perspective, and there is always a need to explore the two sides of life.

May 21st Wednesday

Moon in Sagittarius

	PDT	EDT	
Jupiter sextile Uranus	11:03 AM	2:03 PM	
Moon opposite Mercury	2:01 PM	5:01 PM	
Moon square Uranus	5:03 PM	8:03 PM	
Moon sextile Neptune goes v/c	9:19 PM	12:19 AM	(May 21)

Mood Watch: The Moon wanes in Sagittarius and the general course of our moods will now focus on the wider picture of life and on global occurrences, while the need to shake off some restless energy persists to affect our senses. This may be a good time to think about what type of travel will take place in the coming season. Waning Sagittarius Moon is also a time for introspective visionary awareness.

116

Jupiter sextile Uranus (occurring March 5 – June 12) This aspect reached an exact peak on March 28, and occurs again today for the second time during its prolonged period of existence. Jupiter sextile Uranus will reoccur for a shorter time, November 1 – 23, reaching its final exact aspect peak on November 12. For more information on today's repeat aspect of Jupiter sextile Uranus, see March 28, when it last occurred.

May 22nd Thursday

Moon in Sagittarius / Capricorn

	PDT	EDT
Moon enters Capricorn	8:56 AM	11:56 AM
Moon conjunct Pluto	10:00 AM	1:00 PM
Sun square Saturn	11:25 AM	2:25 PM
Moon trine Saturn	12:59 PM	3:59 PM

Mood Watch: The morning may seem a little spacey, or it may seem difficult to find our way through various situations as the waning Moon in Sagittarius is void-of-course. Soon enough though, the Moon enters Capricorn and our Moon moods tend to be very serious. There is a strong sense of responsibility and involvement in whatever matter is at hand.

Sun square Saturn (occurring May 19 – 25) This occurrence of Sun square Saturn especially affects those Taurus/Gemini cusp born people who are celebrating birthdays May 19 – 25. These folks may be experiencing some personal challenges such as impatience, loss of control, a poor sense of timing, or difficulty identifying with current obligations. The challenge is therefore to overcome those obstacles that intrude on one's control of discipline and accuracy. Since Saturn has moved into Virgo (Sept. 2, 2007) the square aspect of Saturn affects the lives of Gemini and Sagittarius people, and this will continue until Oct. 29, 2009, when Saturn enters Libra. These challenges will pass, and for those folks who have uplifting and positive aspects occurring in their lives, these (Saturn) challenges may seem insignificant. Overall, these folks will have a good look at what really matters in life, and hopefully, they will honor and appreciate it. Saturn represents those things in life that we are willing to work for and maintain. Don't give up, Taurus/Gemini birthday folks – conserve your energies and take losses and difficulties in stride! Through the tests, a stronger human being emerges to take on future tests with greater confidence and ability. Avoidance of responsibilities or hardships now will only make life more difficult later. This aspect will re-occur December 9 – 15, reaching its exact aspect peak on December 12, affecting the birthday Sagittarians of that time.

May 23rd Friday

Moon in Capricorn

Mercury-trine-Neptune-non-exact (occurring May 23 – 29)

Mood Watch: There are no exact celestial aspects occurring today, which means that we can expect a fairly smooth day of work-oriented focuses while the Moon wanes in Capricorn. This is an excellent time to focus on completion, and to reap the rewards of a genuine feeling of accomplishment as we finish up this week's workload – in spades.

117

Mercury-trine-Neptune-non-exact (occurring May 23 – 29) Due to Mercury retrograde (May 26 – June 19), this aspect will never actually reach an exact peak during this time. However, although non-exact, the affects of Mercury in Gemini trine Neptune in Aquarius are definitely enlivening our spiritual views and communications. While Mercury is retrograde, internal dialog with regard to spiritual enhancement is likely to be rewarding, while external attempts at communicating about the spirit world may be positive in nature, but confusing nonetheless for its recipient. For more information on Mercury trine Neptune, see July 6, when this aspect reaches its first true peak this year while Mercury is in Gemini. This busy aspect will also occur on September 19, September 28, and October 29, when Mercury will be in Libra.

May 24th Saturday

Moon in Capricorn / Aquarius

	PDT	EDT
Moon conjunct Jupiter	5:02 AM	8:02 AM
Moon sextile Uranus	5:25 AM	8:25 AM
Venus enters Gemini	3:51 PM	6:51 PM
Moon trine Venus goes v/c	3:53 PM	6:53 PM
Moon enters Aquarius	8:52 PM	11:52 PM
Moon trine Venus	9:24 PM	12:24 AM (May 25)

Mood Watch: The waning Moon in Capricorn brings clear, focused, work-oriented moods that allow us to filter out all the cloudy, uncertain perspectives impeding our sense of progress. By late afternoon/early evening, the Capricorn Moon goes void-of-course for a five hour period; at this point there is little tolerance for moodiness and people may become somewhat lazy or unaccommodating. By the time the Moon enters Aquarius, a much more humanitarian kind of mood fills the air.

Venus enters Gemini (Venus in Gemini: May 24 – June 18) Venus, the influence of love, magnetism and attraction now enters Gemini, the personification of duality. Love desires may be split and suffer from ambivalence and schisms. Gemini people will focus more intently on personal attractions and love related matters, while Sagittarius folks may be overwhelmed by love concerns as Venus opposes their natal Sun. Virgo and Pisces people are also likely to feel affection related challenges or difficulties in their life as Venus squares their natal Sun positions. Librans and Aquarians will find things a little easier. With Venus in Gemini, there is an attraction to writing, speaking about, and recording extraordinary experiences and stories, especially about beauty and love. Gossip and talk about love matters will be especially prevalent. Venus in Gemini shows us the two sides of love – the giving and the taking. As attractions appear more diverse, concerns may arise among those with a jealous nature. Love related changes are rampant – to some it's a challenge, while for others, it's a breath of fresh air.

May 25th Sunday

Moon in Aquarius

	PDT	EDT
Moon trine Sun	6:04 AM	9:04 AM
Moon opposite Mars	2:01 PM	5:01 PM

Mood Watch: On some level the desire for freedom or personal breakthrough calls

118

out to some folks. The restlessness of spring season stirs our hearts. People we haven't seen in some time are starting to come out in droves. Untested theories and certain types of knowledge can sometimes be illusions; this is an important time to banish fear and test the realms with one's own sensibilities. With the Moon and Sun both now in air signs, there will be a lot on our minds and much to talk about.

May 26th Monday
Memorial Day, USA
Moon in Aquarius

	PDT	EDT
Mercury goes retrograde	8:48 AM	11:48 AM
Neptune goes retrograde	9:15 AM	12:15 PM
Venus square Saturn	10:10 AM	1:10 PM
Moon trine Mercury	2:37 PM	5:37 PM
Moon conjunct Neptune goes v/c	7:48 PM	10:48 PM

Mood Watch: The Aquarius Moon reminds us of the necessity to apply knowledge wisely, and to not take miscommunications to heart. It is the first few days coming into – and going out of – the Mercury retrograde period that cause so much misunderstanding. This is a time to be diligently cautious when communicating.

Mercury goes retrograde (Mercury retrograde: May 26 – June 19) For the next few weeks (until June 19), Mercury will be retrograde in one of the primary places it rules, Gemini. Mercury retrograde in Gemini is likely to bring disruption to gossipy communication and there are likely to be numerous misunderstandings. Be on the lookout for frequent bouts of dyslexia, and other communication mistakes in such Gemini related activities as writing, speaking, journalism, and overall communications. During this time it will be best to attempt communications more than once or twice, and to be persistent as well as patient. At first it may be difficult to sit through everyone's excuses and misinformation, but eventually there will be a logical explanation to Mercury related setbacks. For more information on Mercury retrograde, see the section in the introduction about *Mercury retrograde periods.*

Neptune goes retrograde (Neptune retrograde: May 26 – Nov. 1) Like clockwork, every year, the planet Neptune goes retrograde for about five months. Today Neptune goes retrograde in Aquarius. Neptune governs the spiritual dimensions and, when in Aquarius, it inspires a special interest in the spiritual development of humanity. While Neptune is retrograde, many of the spiritual issues that have come up in the last five to six months will reoccur. Neptune harmonizes spiritual vibrations and represents intuition and higher feminine wisdom. For the next five months, be aware of the frequency of escapist tendencies, and of the inclination to internalize deep-rooted spiritual matters. Being firm with your own spiritual center will allow for progressive spiritual growth. Be careful not to blindly disrupt the core of another's belief system, nor to become ensnared by someone else's blindness with regard to your own beliefs during Neptune's retrograde months.

Venus square Saturn (occurring May 23 – 28) Venus in Gemini is square to Saturn in Virgo. This will probably be a difficult time to express love and affection in a serious or timely fashion, especially while Mercury (also in Gemini) is retrograde (see above). No matter how much one prioritizes their focus of love, it is still likely to be misinterpreted on some level during Venus square Saturn. The basic expression of love will flow more easily without the limitations of expectations or demands. Love related dramas may be taken too seriously. This aspect last occurred January 3 – 8, and it reached its peak on January 6. This aspect will reoccur once more, October 31 – November 5, reaching its exact aspect peak on November 3.

May 27th Tuesday
Moon in Aquarius / Pisces – LAST QUARTER MOON in PISCES

	PDT	EDT
Moon enters Pisces	6:39 AM	9:39 AM
Moon sextile Pluto	7:26 AM	10:26 AM
Moon opposite Saturn	10:44 AM	1:44 PM
Moon square Venus	1:14 PM	4:14 PM
Moon square Sun	7:56 PM	10:56 PM

Mood Watch: **Last Quarter Moon in Pisces** (Moon square Sun) brings entranced wonder. There is a dreamy, mysterious, enchanting and – some might perceive – fearful depth to the word "entranced." This is the place where the imagination roams with steady accuracy and our beliefs are profoundly touched. People can be entranced by an endless number of things. Those areas of our life that bring depth and meaning are often brought out on a Pisces Moon. At times like this, many may choose to be intoxicated on substances that block pain and fear in an effort to escape. Emotional, spiritual, and artistic moods set the tone of the day as the season of spring progresses. The Moon is always at work on some level of the subconscious. This serves as a good time to cleanse the spiritual cobwebs of our own lives and to reinforce personal fortitude with the strength to overcome addictions using sheer willpower and belief in oneself.

May 28th Wednesday
Moon in Pisces

	PDT	EDT	
Moon square Mercury	9:32 PM	12:32 AM	(May 29)
Moon sextile Jupiter	10:21 PM	1:21 AM	(May 29)
Moon conjunct Uranus goes v/c	11:21 PM	2:21 AM	(May 29)
Sun conjunct Venus begins (see June 8)			

Mood Watch: The world is full of subliminal messages, working to capture our mood. This is why the waning Pisces Moon sometimes causes the desire to block it all out and let the imagination wander elsewhere. This is all fine and well when one has the luxury of doing so. While some of us are striving to keep it together, others are allowing themselves to be carefree and to let loose, and others still might only find comfort in a hidden sanctuary. For the most part the waning Pisces Moon leads our moods into complexity and challenging feelings. Pisces Moon teaches us how to adapt to a wide range of emotions.

May 29th Thursday
Moon in Pisces / Aries

	PDT	EDT
Moon enters Aries	12:53 AM	3:53 PM
Moon square Pluto	1:30 PM	4:30 PM

Ⅱ

Mood Watch: Sun in Gemini and Moon in Aries brings incisive and keen moods that require a strong dose of self-respect and a high morale. Our interactions are likely to be inclined towards, or dominated by, rapid thinking and swift decision making. If you're inclined in this fashion, it's a good time to get things done. However, Moon square Pluto in the afternoon may bring unexpected challenges in overcoming some of life's biggest obstacles. The waning Aries Moon helps us to adapt swiftly to urgent situations and attend to personal development.

May 30th Friday
Moon in Aries

	PDT	EDT
Moon sextile Venus	12:12 AM	3:12 AM
Moon sextile Sun	5:07 AM	8:07 AM
Moon trine Mars	8:29 AM	11:29 AM

Mood Watch: Waning Aries Moon encourages our hearts to let go of grudges and all of those minor and irritating defense modes holding us back from applying our more positive and constructive capabilities. This is the time to reincorporate personal confidence through self assurance. Positive lunar aspects bring positive moods.

May 31st Saturday
Moon in Aries / Taurus

	PDT	EDT
Moon sextile Mercury	12:06 AM	3:06 AM
Moon square Jupiter	1:33 AM	4:33 AM
Moon sextile Neptune goes v/c	5:53 AM	8:53 AM
Moon enters Taurus	3:19 PM	6:19 PM
Moon trine Pluto	3:49 PM	6:49 PM
Moon trine Saturn	7:12 PM	10:12 PM

Mood Watch: The waning Aries Moon goes void-of-course this morning and our moods may be inclined towards false starts, impulsiveness, and disagreement. A busy and hurried energy fills the day, but there may not be a lot of progress for all the hot air. Once we've pushed our way past these aggressive moods, the Taurus Moon brings a grounded spirit. Relaxation and physical comforts bring balance, healing, and timely care.

June 1st Sunday
Moon in Taurus

	PDT	EDT
Moon square Mars	11:38 AM	2:38 PM

Mood Watch: This is a time of preparation and refinement. Taurus Moon fixates our moods on the important focuses of the physical world. Starting a new month with the Moon in Taurus works hand 'n' hand with the process of – and common practice of – assessing our finances. The need to continue spring cleaning prac-

121

tices calls to us. There is also an emphasis on selling, buying, shifting and moving physical possessions. This means having to face a lot of "emotional baggage" attached to letting go of physical possessions that have piled up in our lives. Taurus Moon often brings a sentiment which is attached to the things on which we fix our energy. Don't forget: less is more.

June 2nd Monday

Moon in Taurus / Gemini	PDT	EDT
Moon trine Jupiter	1:41 AM	4:41 AM
Moon sextile Uranus	3:09 AM	6:09 AM
Moon square Neptune goes v/c	6:02 AM	9:02 AM
Moon enters Gemini	3:06 PM	6:06 PM
Moon square Saturn	7:02 PM	10:02 PM
Venus sextile Mars begins (see June 6)		

Mood Watch: Our moods appear stable and grounded at first, but gradually, the Taurus Moon day turns lazier and lazier. Progress may seem slow at times, or it may seem physically demanding as the day turns to evening. Later, as the Moon enters Gemini, deep, almost philosophically rooted thoughts and moods transcend time. The balsamic Gemini Moon wanes darkly, bringing pensive moods. The busy days of Gemini have taken wing.

June 3rd Tuesday

NEW MOON in GEMINI	PDT	EDT
Moon conjunct Venus	9:53 AM	12:53 PM
Moon conjunct Sun	12:22 PM	3:22 PM
Moon sextile Mars	12:43 PM	3:43 PM
Moon conjunct Mercury	9:05 PM	12:05 AM (June 4)

Mood Watch: The **New Moon in Gemini** (Moon conjunct Sun) allows for new thoughts and ideas to flow, and new feelings about the way we are thinking will begin to emerge. New Moons are like clean slates. It's time to begin a process of strengthening and celebrating your energy and to plan new vistas for growth, particularly in the area of emotional well-being. It's a time to pay attention to those newer thoughts, ideas and caprices in the wind. This would be a good time to initiate a new round of creative writing or to apply a new mental discipline in a manner which will eventually become more personally beneficial. Making a new attempt at reaching out to an old friend or opening up communications with a new circle will bring great new insights to one's field of knowledge at this time.

June 4th Wednesday

Moon in Gemini / Cancer	PDT	EDT
Moon sextile Mars	1:34 AM	4:34 AM
Moon square Uranus	2:20 AM	5:20 AM
Moon trine Neptune goes v/c	5:08 AM	8:08 AM
Moon enters Cancer	2:16 PM	5:16 PM
Moon opposite Pluto	2:38 PM	5:38 PM
Moon sextile Saturn	6:25 PM	9:25 PM

Mood Watch: Early this morning, the Gemini Moon goes void-of-course, starting off the day with scattered thoughts and indecisive moods. There may be a tendency for delays, distractions, and mix-ups to occur. Later today, as the Moon enters Cancer, our moods are fortified by nurturing foods and comforting care.

June 5th Thursday

Moon in Cancer

	PDT	EDT
Moon opposite Jupiter	12:25 AM	3:25 AM
Sun conjunct Mercury begins (see June 7)		
Mercury conjunct Venus begins (see June 7)		

Mood Watch: This young crescent Moon in Cancer has a subtle but assuring way of apprising us of the underlying truth behind what we are feeling. Although we often mask our true feelings, our moods are affected by the shifts of the Moon and are shared collectively by those we encounter. Cancer Moon reminds us that our inner feelings do eventually change and new feelings need to emerge. Today many folks will be inclined to give hints and clues about these new feelings through the basic mood around us. This is the time to give newer feelings a chance to be felt.

June 6th Friday

Moon in Cancer / Leo

	PDT	EDT
Venus sextile Mars	1:15 AM	4:15 AM
Moon trine Uranus goes v/c	2:33 AM	5:33 AM
Moon enters Leo	3:01 PM	6:01 PM
Mercury sextile Mars begins (see June 8)		

Mood Watch: Disoriented feelings are a common symptom of a long void-of-course Cancer Moon day. This is a busy time, and for some the pressure comes out today in an emotional form of release. Later, the evening commences with the Moon in Leo. Animal instincts are strong. Waxing Leo Moon brings playfulness and the need on the part of many people to be self-absorbed or independent. Others may display their sense of importance by being entertaining and attention grabbing. Many will be focusing on building up their talents and willpower.

Venus sextile Mars (occurring June 2 – 9) Mischievous, talkative, and outgoing kinds of affection are evident while Venus is sextile to Mars. Venus in Gemini sextile Mars in Leo brings curious attractions and ambitious displays of playfulness. It is here that feminine (Venus) and masculine (Mars) forces have an opportunity (the sextile aspect) to support each other. The Mars influence emphasizes the awareness and application of action, movement, involvement, and also harnesses strength and energy. Venus reminds us to draw towards ourselves the pleasures we desire. Here we have the incentive to apply action with love. Make good use of this positive aspect; this is the only time it will occur this year.

June 7th Saturday

Moon in Leo	PDT	EDT	
Sun conjunct Mercury	8:26 AM	11:26 AM	
Mercury conjunct Venus	2:03 PM	5:03 PM	
Moon conjunct Mars	6:38 PM	9:38 PM	
Moon sextile Mercury	7:58 PM	10:58 PM	
Moon sextile Venus	8:48 PM	11:48 PM	
Moon sextile Sun	9:20 PM	12:20 AM	(June 8)

Mood Watch: This Moon in Leo and Sun in Gemini spring day enlivens our spirits as our childlike qualities come out and play. Waxing Leo Moon brings on self-awareness and the desire to feel important and look good.

Sun conjunct Mercury (occurring June 5 – 9) This aspect will create a much more thoughtful, communicative, and expressive year ahead for those Gemini folks celebrating birthdays June 5 – 9. This is your time (birthday Geminis) to record ideas, relay important messages, and pay close attention to your imaginative thoughts as they are touched by your ruling sign, Mercury, creating the urge to speak and be heard. Your thoughts will reveal a great deal about who you are, now and in the year to come.

Mercury conjunct Venus (occurring June 5 – 9) When these two planets are conjunct, the energy suggests the need to communicate love. Today's conjunction of Mercury and Venus takes place in the curious and intellectually playful sign, Gemini. For some folks, there may be a tendency for love related communication to seem somewhat reserved, or overly internalized, although the need to communicate love is definitely there. While Mercury is retrograde (May 26 – June 19), there may be a tendency for love related matters to be easily misinterpreted. It would be best to communicate love without getting too hung up on commitment or performance. Hold no expectations in the expression of love, and take no offense if your own attempts to express your love are poorly interpreted. This may be an especially important time to make sure people are clear on what is important and valuable. This busy aspect occurred on February 26 and March 24, and will reoccur August 14 – September 19, reaching its exact aspect peak marks on August 21, and again on September 14.

June 8th Sunday

Moon in Leo / Virgo	PDT	EDT	
Moon opposite Neptune goes v/c	8:41 AM	11:41 AM	
Mercury sextile Mars	11:28 AM	2:28 PM	
Moon enters Virgo	7:02 PM	10:02 PM	
Moon trine Pluto	7:15 PM	10:15 PM	
Sun conjunct Venus	9:19 PM	12:19 AM	(June 9)

Mood Watch: A long void-of-course Leo Moon day brings a tendency towards laziness and rest. Our moods may be beastly at times, but it's probably due to a lack of attention or a lack of output. Later, as the Moon enters Virgo, we become more diligent, inquisitive and resourceful. Virgo Moon tickles our curiosity.

Mercury sextile Mars (occurring June 6 – 10) Mercury sextile Mars brings opportunities that can be recognized, received, communicated and acted upon. News or information may lead to the taking of immediate action. Bear in mind that Mercury is currently *retrograde* (May 26 – June 19) and communications have the potential of being misunderstood. As for now, Mercury in Gemini moves in a pattern that creates thoughtful and intellectually stirring introspection, while Mars in Leo puts high demands on family related activities. Careful deliberation leads to effective action. Applying active communication has the potential for a very favorable outcome. This aspect last occurred when Mercury was *direct* on April 29, and it will repeat for a final time this year on July 15, when Mercury will be *direct* again.

Sun conjunct Venus (occurring May 28 – June 20) The Sun and Venus are conjunct in Gemini. This aspect particularly affects the love lives of those Gemini people celebrating birthdays from May 28 – June 20. These birthday folks are being filled with the need to have or express love as best as they can and this is the year for them to address the love matters in their lives. There is an attraction which draws us to beauty, romance, and love when Venus connects with the natal solar degrees. The issue of love is unavoidable, and these birthday folks' love needs become evident whether they wish to acknowledge them or not. It is through the attraction magnet of Venus that the personality (Sun sign) is assured of that with which they choose to identify, be affected by, and attracted to. Sometimes sheer magnetism is unavoidable and an event or relationship cannot be chosen – it just happens. This can encompass not only love matters, but also other areas such as the arts, aesthetics or appreciation of beauty. This will be a year of love, birthday Gemini people.

June 9ᵗʰ Monday

Moon in Virgo

	PDT	EDT
Moon conjunct Saturn	12:12 AM	3:12 AM
Venus square Uranus begins (see June 12)		
Sun square Uranus begins (see June 12)		

Mood Watch: The young waxing Moon of Virgo encourages us to put important matters into order. Curious and investigative moods abound. Record keeping and reference guides are all around us. Analytical tendencies are brought out on Virgo Moon. Today will be a good day to organize and get the work week started off right.

June 10ᵗʰ Tuesday

FIRST QUARTER MOON in VIRGO

	PDT	EDT
Moon square Mercury	12:00 AM	3:00 AM
Moon square Sun	8:04 AM	11:04 AM
Moon square Venus	8:53 AM	11:53 AM
Moon trine Jupiter	9:24 AM	12:24 PM
Moon opposite Uranus goes v/c	12:42 PM	3:42 PM
Venus trine Neptune begins (see June 13)		

Mood Watch: There is a strong investigative curiosity at work with the Sun in Gemini and the Moon in Virgo. This is the **First Quarter Moon in Virgo** (Moon square Sun). Both of these Mercury ruled signs (Gemini and Virgo) emphasize the need to keep things flowing both on a logical and practical level of application,

125

particularly when passing on information. This is often a busy time of spring when the "quickening" of summer is upon us, and the preparation for the long days of the sun turns the energy once more towards the fruition and maintenance of the warmer days ahead.

June 11th Wednesday

Moon in Virgo / Libra

	PDT	EDT
Moon enters Libra	2:56 AM	5:56 AM
Moon square Pluto	3:04 AM	6:04 AM
Sun trine Neptune begins (see June 14)		

Mood Watch: The Moon in Libra brings forth moods focused on harmony and the decision making process which will no doubt tug at us all day. The Sun and the Moon are in air signs, emphasizing the need to apply logic and mental clarity to the things we do. Sun in Gemini keeps us keen on the two sides to everything we observe, allowing us to be more open and adaptable in our decision making process.

June 12th Thursday

Moon in Libra

	PDT	EDT	
Venus square Uranus	12:38 AM	3:38 AM	
Moon trine Mercury	7:26 AM	10:26 AM	
Moon sextile Mars	4:03 PM	7:03 PM	
Moon square Jupiter	7:06 PM	10:06 PM	
Sun square Uranus	10:24 PM	1:24 AM	(June 13)
Moon trine Sun	11:09 PM	2:09 AM	(June 13)

Mood Watch: Moon in Libra focuses our moods around social and moral issues. Group harmony and the need for balance in relationships is emphasized.

Venus square Uranus (occurring June 9 – 14) Venus, the planet that governs love and magnetism, is square Uranus, the planet of chaos and disruption. It may be difficult for love (Venus) to flourish in a spontaneous and carefree fashion. Venus in Gemini is square to Uranus in Pisces. Some folks are likely to become too easily affronted by radical or explosive kinds of magnetism. This influence may be testing the power of love to withstand the chaos of extremes and sudden change. While Mercury is retrograde in Gemini (May 26 – June 19), it may be wisest to refrain from communicating radical messages with regard to loved ones. This aspect last occurred January 9 – 14, reaching its exact peak on January 12. Venus square Uranus will reoccur once more this year, October 31 – November 5, reaching its exact position on November 3.

Sun square Uranus (occurring June 9 – 16) This occurrence of Sun square Uranus particularly affects those Gemini people celebrating birthdays June 9 – 16. The square of Uranus to these Gemini folks' natal Sun brings a strong dose of unrestrained chaos and challenging events. This may be the year for you, Gemini birthday folks, to surrender to those aspects of life that are truly out of your control, and to concentrate more rationally on those facets of life over which you do have control. Sometimes the aftermath of Uranus influence is an improvement, but with the square aspect at work, it is likely that these people will feel personally challenged. It is important to understand that some types of personal challenges are best left alone, while others must be confronted directly without causing destructive damage, particularly to one's self. On the other hand, birthday Gemini folks, if your life has no foundation, there is no point in holding on to the illusion of stability at this juncture of your sojourn. Albeit slowly, this aspect will pass in due time. Try to be detached from chaotic events as they occur, and the outcome will seem less costly. It is vital not to give rapid change too much resistance, lest you be subject to the reversals of trying to fight chaos with logic at a time when resistance is futile. Project the picture of peace and it will be there for you at the other end. This aspect will reoccur December 7 – 13, reaching its peak on December 10 with the Sun in Sagittarius.

June 13ᵗʰ Friday
Moon in Libra / Scorpio

	PDT	EDT	
Moon trine Venus	1:37 AM	4:37 AM	
Moon trine Neptune goes v/c	2:15 AM	5:15 AM	
Venus trine Neptune	7:53 AM	10:53 AM	
Moon enters Scorpio	1:53 PM	4:53 PM	
Moon sextile Pluto	1:54 PM	4:54 PM	
Moon sextile Saturn	8:14 PM	11:14 PM	
Pluto enters Sagittarius	10:12 PM	1:12 AM	(June 14)

Mood Watch: Our moods will seem busy but positive on this fortunate *Friday the thirteenth*. Lunar aspects are generally positive today. Ever so early, the void-of-course Libra Moon brings indecisiveness. Soon enough however, the Moon enters Scorpio. The waxing Scorpio Moon enlivens our passion for life.

Venus trine Neptune (occurring June 10 – 15) Venus in Gemini is trine Neptune in Aquarius. This brings detail oriented feminine love right in harmony with ingenious kinds of spiritual expression. Artistic endeavors will shine with spiritual brilliance. This aspect brings calmness and tranquility that are vitally needed, particularly in love related matters, and especially while Venus is square Uranus *(see yesterday)*. When coming from a place of love, it is easier to draw down a spiritual enhancement of that love with Venus trine Neptune. Enjoying beauty is a way to acquire gifts of the spirit world. This is a good time to actively engage in peaceful, pleasurable, and spiritual love. This aspect will reoccur September 14 – 19, reaching its peak on September 17 when Venus will be in Libra.

Pluto enters Sagittarius (Pluto in Sagittarius: June 13 – Nov. 26) Today, the retrograde Pluto enters Sagittarius for the very last time in our lives. Here's our chance to recognize and acknowledge the concurrent qualities of the Pluto in Sagittarius cycle. It is not until eleven more generations pass (the year 2242) that Pluto returns full circle to the constellation Sagittarius. This is a time of completion, and a time when the last of the children of this generation will be born. In a couple of decades, when these Pluto in Sagittarius children have grown up, they will establish a more strongly connected global awareness in the world. They will also establish a bold sort of philosophical awareness, and a clearer picture of the future of the 21ˢᵗ century, and consequently, what we will need to do to meet the challenges of this future.

127

June 14th Saturday
Flag Day, USA

Moon in Scorpio	PDT	EDT
Sun trine Neptune	2:01 PM	5:01 PM

Mood Watch: The waxing Scorpio Moon emphasizes the need to apply life's passion. Today is a superb day for garden work. This is a time of intensity, a time when the fruition of our desires are emphasized and when limitations are confronted and embraced through emotional release.

Sun trine Neptune (occurring June 11 – 17) This occurrence of Sun trine Neptune particularly affects those Gemini people celebrating birthdays from June 11 – 17. These Geminis are experiencing the favorable trine aspect of Neptune to their natal Sun, bringing gifts of spiritual encounters and awareness, as well as a calming effect on life. This serves as a good time (particularly for these birthday folks) to seek visions, apply prayer and meditation, and to explore spiritual avenues and beliefs that are being presented. This aspect will reoccur October 11 – 17, reaching its peak on October 14 with the Sun in Libra.

June 15th Sunday
Father's Day

Moon in Scorpio	PDT	EDT
Moon sextile Jupiter	6:45 AM	9:45 AM
Moon square Mars	7:13 AM	10:13 AM
Moon trine Uranus	11:22 AM	2:22 PM
Moon square Neptune goes v/c	2:29 PM	5:29 PM

Mood Watch: Psychic buildups are addressed and personal enemies tend to surface during the intensity of waxing Scorpio Moon. Some folks are awakened abruptly on the emotional plane, and they are reminded of the fine line of survival and the need to come in contact with one's own limitations, as well as the daunting urge to overcome limitations. Later today, the Scorpio Moon goes void-of-course and brings a good time to be cautious and alert.

June 16th Monday

Moon in Scorpio / Sagittarius	PDT	EDT
Moon enters Sagittarius	2:20 AM	5:20 AM
Moon square Saturn	9:06 AM	12:06 PM
Mars opposite Neptune begins (see June 21)		

Mood Watch: Electrical magnitude and energetic forces begin to build towards the Full Sagittarius Moon, set to occur this week. Sagittarius Moon moods, when raised to full peaks, can gift us with powerful visions and rich insights. These insights show us the way to the future and give us an opportunity to look outside ourselves and see what's coming. Life is not always that cut and dry, but it is times like this that open the porthole to new adventure. The point of the Sagittarius experience is to experiment with exploration, to go beyond the tangible and defy the odds of logic.

June 17th Tuesday

Moon in Sagittarius

	PDT	EDT	
Moon opposite Mercury	4:54 AM	7:54 AM	
Moon trine Mars	10:56 PM	1:56 AM	(June 18)
Venus opposite Pluto	11:45 PM	2:45 AM	(June 18)
Sun opposite Pluto begins (see June 20)			

Mood Watch: Moon in Sagittarius will reinforce our desires to expand and progress in a forward moving, battery charged fashion. Charge! The Full Moon Eve is upon us!

Venus opposite Pluto (occurring June 15 – 20) Venus in Gemini now opposes the retrograde Pluto in Sagittarius. Matters concerning love, beauty, and affection may be overwhelmed by powerful forces or unforeseeable twists of fate. These fateful forces may be intruding somehow on the objects or people we love and admire. This could include just about any kind of scenario – from being shattered over the loss of a loved one, to a terminal disease, to the process of learning how to fully accept and support some kind of total transformation of a loved one. Some people find it difficult to support loved ones through severe kinds of hardship, yet now is the time to offer support to them, despite the opposing forces that appear too harsh or overwhelming. This aspect may well bring on an acute awareness of the desire that some have for power, and the need to have power over loved ones. No one, no matter how powerful, can justifiably tell us what we love, who we love, or how we are to love. Deep in our hearts dwells the truth. When the going gets tough, look to your heart! This is the only time this year Venus will oppose Pluto.

June 18th Wednesday

Moon in Sagittarius / Capricorn – FULL MOON in SAGITTARIUS

	PDT	EDT	
Moon square Uranus	12:01 AM	3:01 AM	
Venus enters Cancer	1:48 AM	4:48 AM	
Moon sextile Neptune	3:01 AM	6:01 AM	
Moon opposite Sun	10:30 AM	1:30 PM	
Moon conjunct Jupiter goes v/c	2:36 PM	5:36 PM	
Moon enters Capricorn	2:52 PM	5:52 PM	
Moon opposite Venus	2:41 PM	5:41 PM	
Moon trine Saturn	9:57 PM	12:57 AM	(June 19)

Mood Watch: The **Full Moon in Sagittarius** (Moon opposite Sun) brings new insights about life, and emotional energy runs very high throughout the day. For many, there is a tendency to go way out beyond the usual bounds and discover new territory as a matter of circumstance. How we chose to perceive and develop our understanding of this new territory has a lot to do with what stage in our life we have come to, and what kind of philosophy best suits our own individual needs. By afternoon (PST) / evening (EST), the Moon goes void-of-course then swiftly enters Capricorn. The Capricorn Moon allows us to get a more grounded picture of how we might choose to profit from our insightful outlook.

Venus enters Cancer (Venus in Cancer: June 18 – Aug. 5) Venus now enters the nurturing sign of Cancer, an appropriate place for the expression of love and affection. It invites those with rocky love relationships to patch things up, and to do so with more heart and less uncertainty. Venus will be in Cancer today through August 5, encouraging our affections and affinities to be carefully placed and nurtured. When attractions occur, they will have a lasting impression and will seem very strong and emotionally sound. Venus in Cancer brings out a love for such things as the ocean, leisurely aquatic sports, motherly care and expression, and all varieties of nurturing. While Venus travels over their natal Sun, those folks born in the sign of Cancer will be especially aware of their love life and their needs for pleasure.

June 19th Thursday

Moon in Capricorn

	PDT	EDT
Mercury goes direct	7:32 AM	10:32 AM
Venus sextile Saturn begins (see June 21)		

Mood Watch: The Moon wanes and the workload before us may appear demanding. Despite this, Capricorn Moon urges us to work hard and in a disciplined fashion, applying some diligent and concentrated effort. A troubling and somewhat overwhelming sense of pressure to do the impossible strikes our moods; nonetheless, the intensely earthy Capricorn Moon also inspires us to do the impossible.

Mercury goes direct (Mercury direct: June 19 – Sept. 24) Since May 26, Mercury has been retrograde in the sign of Gemini, commonly causing communication mix-ups and confusion when relaying information. In Gemini, the retrograde Mercury often causes communication mix-ups with regard to talk in general, discussions, stories, gossip, and news media information. This has undoubtedly been an especially difficult time for Gemini people or those with Mercury in Gemini. Now we can breathe a greatly needed sigh of relief as Mercury, the planet governing the realms of communication, becomes stationary and will soon begin to move forward. Take note that our faculties and manner of communicating will definitely improve within the next few days. Although perhaps not today – when the stationary Mercury often freezes communication efforts – but very soon, our communications will run more smoothly; this will be a good time to begin clearing up various misunderstandings occurring over the past few weeks. For more information on this recently completed phase of Mercury retrograde, see May 26. For more on Mercury retrograde patterns throughout this year, see the introduction on *Mercury retrograde periods*.

CANCER

Key Phrase: "I FEEL"
Cardinal Water Sign
Symbol: The Crab
June 20th through July 22nd

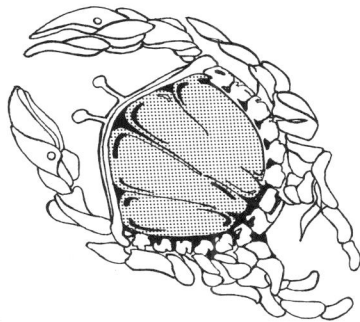

June 20th Friday
Summer Solstice
Moon in Capricorn

	PDT	EDT
Moon conjunct Jupiter	6:22 AM	9:22 AM
Moon sextile Uranus goes v/c	12:01 PM	3:01 PM
Sun opposite Pluto	12:42 PM	3:42 PM
Sun enters Cancer	4:59 PM	7:59 PM

Mood Watch: The Moon, although waning, is still rather full. Capricorn Moon says to keep a steady head, and to handle the emotional process professionally.

Sun opposite Pluto (occurring June 17 – 23) The Sun is at the midsummer cusp of Gemini/Cancer, and while it spends its last hours in Gemini, it is in opposition to Pluto, in the late degrees of Sagittarius. Geminis and early born Cancer folks having birthdays from June 17 – 23 are undergoing the effects of Pluto being in a lengthy opposition to their natal Sun sign. Birthday folks, with Pluto in opposition to your identity, this is the time to accept transition, however overwhelming the circumstances. Persist in recognizing the empowering differences each generation embodies. Gemini folks – here's the good news: it won't be that much longer for Pluto to be in opposition to the sign of Gemini. Pluto has been teaching Gemini people about the necessity of regeneration, and the shifting of the powers that be. Gemini is aware of irreversible change and the power of new generations of thinkers who will defy much of the logic of the previous generation. These transformative visions will alter our perceptions, and expand our awareness of travel, disease, permanent loss, nuclear realities, and the cruelty in the world. These challenges appear threatening and are often perceived as a painful process of loss and destruction. Late Gemini and early born Cancer birthday folks, do not get hung up on high expectations of life or you are likely to burn out. These lessons are meant to be, so open up to the need for endurance and perseverance during this time – use wisdom as your guide. Survival counts! Use your senses and your sensibilities well, but do not resist the forces of great change. Surviving all this means the best of life is yet to come, as you will grow to appreciate life in a delightfully transformed way. This is also true for your opposites, the Sagittarians and early born Capricorns, who are feeling the conjunction of Pluto to their natal Sun. This will be the last time this century that the Sun in Gemini will oppose Pluto in Sagittarius.

131

Sun enters Cancer (Sun in Cancer: June 20 – July 22) This is the time when Summer Solstice enthusiasts are out celebrating old traditions and creating new ones while thanking the Sun for life and light. The dominion of the sign of Cancer is expressed by cardinal water, affecting people in deep and unconscious ways. Cancer people are extremely intuitive and often very psychic or perceptive. Cancers value and prize their deep emotional attachments and treasured memories and feelings. Cancer is a home oriented sign, and making the home a well-loved place calls out to us. Barbeques, home improvements, and other home based events are the focuses of many folks during the days of Sun in Cancer.

June 21ˢᵗ Saturday

Moon in Capricorn / Aquarius

	PDT	EDT
Venus sextile Saturn	2:14 AM	5:14 AM
Moon enters Aquarius	2:34 AM	5:34 AM
Mars opposite Neptune	8:31 AM	11:31 AM

Mood Watch: Moon in Aquarius turns our moods towards a thoughtful mode of expression and emphasizes the role of science, technology, and integrated systems. Moods are directed towards finding the most knowledgeable source available to save oneself a lot of time and trouble getting important projects off the ground.

Venus sextile Saturn (occurring June 19 – 22) Venus in Cancer sextile Saturn in Virgo brings the security of nurturing and reassuring expressions of love which are being amicably shared between lovers and friends. Venus emphasizes the vibrations of love, magnetism, and beauty, and while in Cancer, it brings an emphasis on the need for a peaceful retreat or a stable home environment. Saturn's influence emphasizes the awareness of time, responsibility, and dedication; while this planet is in Virgo, it inspires the need for a wholesome diet and good health practices, outdoor recreation, and relaxing hobbies. Saturn reminds us that beauty is temporary but with proper maintenance, it can also be preserved. This is a good time to capture a glimpse of beauty that will leave a lasting mark. This aspect will re-occur October 5 – 8, reaching its exact aspect peak on October 6, when Venus will be in Scorpio.

Mars opposite Neptune (occurring June 16 – 26) Individual integrity (Mars in Leo) is challenged by, or opposed to (opposite), humanity's belief in science (Neptune in Aquarius). Mars activates and stirs up action, while Neptune calms and dissolves all concern. When in opposition these two planets create an acute awareness of our spiritual beliefs and the manner in which those beliefs are acted upon and absorbed. For some this aspect can create a spiritual breakthrough, while for others it may be that events are forging a strong spiritual awareness challenging personal beliefs. Sometimes we lash out at the world for draining so much of our energy. Perhaps this is a healthy sign that we need to re-structure our priorities, to take action towards finding a peaceful sanctuary where we can recharge our batteries. With Mars in Leo and Neptune in Aquarius, actions which relate to the self and the family are sometimes at odds with outside beliefs, or beliefs imposed by society. Establishing a more healthy attitude towards defending the self, and one's own beliefs, is the best remedy for the opposing outbursts that affect our spiritual well being.

June 22nd Sunday

Moon in Aquarius

	PDT	EDT
Moon trine Mercury	4:31 AM	7:31 AM
Sun sextile Saturn begins (see June 24)		

Mood Watch: The Moon now wanes in Aquarius and the general course of moods emphasizes the need to break out of routines. A bit of the eccentric or risk taker comes out in our moods, and there is a need for some to go off track for a little while in order to gather a sense of what it is to be on track again. Knowledge is empowered and confirmed initially from within. Unusual capabilities are there for those who choose to be aware and apply their talent.

June 23rd Monday

Moon in Aquarius / Pisces

	PDT	EDT
Moon conjunct Neptune	1:13 AM	4:13 AM
Moon opposite Mars	3:15 AM	6:15 AM
Moon sextile Pluto goes v/c	12:03 PM	3:03 PM
Moon enters Pisces	12:33 PM	3:33 PM
Moon trine Sun	6:00 PM	9:00 PM
Moon opposite Saturn	7:56 PM	10:56 PM

Mood Watch: The morning sparks our moods in Aquarian ways with the waning Aquarius Moon. There is a general fascination for innovative thinking and technology. By afternoon, the Moon goes void-of-course for a short time and then enters Pisces. Waning Moon in Pisces puts the emphasis of our moods on spiritual matters, in some cases moral and religious focuses, and for those that care not about such things, the wild abandon of parties and escapism also takes the stage. Waning Pisces Moon may also cause some folks to become introverted and meditative. This is a good time to look within and clean up any issues which create personal turmoil or possibly depression.

June 24th Tuesday

Moon in Pisces

	PDT	EDT
Moon trine Venus	2:27 AM	5:27 AM
Moon square Mercury	2:50 PM	5:50 PM
Sun sextile Saturn	10:00 PM	1:00 AM (June 25)

Mood Watch: Throughout today, the waning Pisces Moon puts us in touch with our intuitive feelings. This may also be a time to release emotional baggage that has built up, or to be aware of the tendency towards escapism.

Sun sextile Saturn (occurring June 22 – 27) This occurrence of Sun sextile Saturn particularly affects those Cancer people celebrating birthdays between June 22 – 27, helping them focus their energy and disciplines with greater clarity throughout the year. As Saturn enters the sextile aspect to the natal Sun of these Cancer people, they will have a greater sense of making progress through discipline, and they may very well begin to see the rewards of their diligent labor in the coming year. This is

133

only true, however, as long as they apply themselves to their work and maintain a vigilant and persistent effort to master personal discipline and training. Birthday Cancer folks of this time must remember: greater control comes with genuine effort. This aspect will reoccur November 9 – 13, reaching its exact aspect peak on November 11, when the Sun will be in Scorpio.

June 25th Wednesday

Moon in Pisces / Aries

	PDT	EDT
Moon sextile Jupiter	12:19 AM	3:19 AM
Moon conjunct Uranus	6:34 AM	9:34 AM
Moon square Pluto goes v/c	7:16 AM	10:16 AM
Moon enters Aries	7:50 PM	10:50 PM
Mars trine Pluto begins (see June 30)		

Mood Watch: This morning, the waning Pisces Moon goes void-of-course and then swiftly enters Aries. The void-of-course Pisces Moon can be disorienting, but by the time the Moon enters Aries, our moods will be more ambitious and determined to push past all vagueness and uncertainty. Waning Aries Moon is a good time to work on self-confidence and to make an effort to drop or change undesirable personality traits.

June 26th Thursday

LAST QUARTER MOON in ARIES

	PDT	EDT	
Moon square Sun	5:09 AM	8:09 AM	
Moon square Venus	2:19 PM	5:19 PM	
Uranus goes retrograde	5:01 PM	8:01 PM	
Moon sextile Mercury	10:38 PM	1:38 AM	(June 27)

Mood Watch: We now come to the **Last Quarter Moon in Aries** (Moon square Sun). Obstacles occur between one's emotions and one's sense of personal identity due to the square aspect. This Moon in Aries expression of mood has very little trouble manifesting new energies. Last Quarter Moon requires disengaging from intensified emotional energy. Dropping problems with the ego becomes the key to this moon. One cannot change the stubbornness and selfishness of others, but one can make a difference by setting the right example individually. Be true to yourself.

Uranus goes retrograde (Uranus retrograde: June 26 – Nov. 27) Uranus, the outer planet representing revolution, chaos, explosive energy, and big changes, now appears to turn back through the zodiac in the sign of Pisces. Since March 10, 2003, Uranus in Pisces has been stirring up a revolution in religion, music, the arts, poetry, psychic research, occultism, movie making and plays. Outer planets move slowly, and this one will take five months to backtrack only four degrees before it moves forward once again. Uranus influences chaos and volatile or abrupt energies, and inspires the need for change and breakthroughs in the pursuit of freedom. When retrograde, the influence of Uranus teaches us to handle uncertainty, particularly internal chaos. Many aspects of chaos tend to be sporadically repeated until the boundaries of restriction loosen enough so we can move more freely. Uranus retrograde is a time when humanity as a whole must backtrack over their revolutionary practices in order to make breakthroughs in the long run. Uranus liberates, although for some people the retrograde process may seem to be excessively inhibiting, particularly if one's surroundings do not allow for much freedom. For rebels, contemplation and internalization bring greater inner strength. While Uranus is retrograde, be sure to set a standard for a certain degree of freedom in your life, so that you can stop and smell the flowers this summer and into the days of autumn. Don't let this valuable time of the year slide by without allowing your inner rebel to kick up his or her heels once in awhile. Freedom is a worthy thing to claim.

June 27th Friday

Moon in Aries / Taurus

	PDT	EDT	
Moon square Jupiter	5:04 AM	8:04 AM	
Moon sextile Neptune	1:38 PM	4:38 PM	
Moon trine Mars	8:17 PM	11:17 PM	
Moon trine Pluto goes v/c	11:12 PM	2:12 AM	(June 28)
Moon enters Taurus	11:51 PM	2:51 PM	(June 28)

Mood Watch: Today's waning Moon in Aries sets the tone for many people to push their way through traffic and shopping lines, and to focus on themselves and their own interests. While some are assured they know exactly what they want, others seem baffled at the tenacity and the fortitude behind the push and drive of selfish desires. Selfhood is okay to sport around and we are a self-oriented culture, feeling our way through to find our identities and maintain our egos with some sort of pride. We're doing okay as long as we are not completely oblivious to the needs of others. This is indeed a time when selfhood is touched upon, and our general moods are based on our own personal needs as well as those pushy or powerful enough to come first! Avoid butting heads if that's not what you're looking for, since it's very easy to do on an Aries Moon.

June 28th Saturday

Moon in Taurus

	PDT	EDT	
Moon trine Saturn	7:02 AM	10:02 AM	
Moon sextile Sun	12:14 PM	3:14 PM	
Moon sextile Venus	10:57 PM	1:57 AM	(June 29)

Mood Watch: Positive lunar aspects bring a good day. A waning Taurus Moon focuses our moods on practical needs, esthetic surroundings, and the process of having, attaining, financing and paying for those material desires that persist to keep us working. Overall, the day progresses into the sheer pleasures of nature loving tendencies and earthy moods.

June 29th Sunday

Moon in Taurus

	PDT	EDT	
Moon trine Jupiter	6:47 AM	9:47 AM	
Moon sextile Uranus	1:10 PM	4:10 PM	
Moon square Neptune	3:17 PM	6:17 PM	
Moon square Mars goes v/c	11:42 PM	2:42 AM	(June 30)

Mood Watch: Summer smells are rich and vibrant. Taurus is the place of exaltation for the Moon, and this is a good time for us to enjoy our favorite pleasures. The waning Moon in Taurus puts us in touch with the reassurance of satisfying practical needs, as well as the desire to enjoy and appreciate luxurious beauty. Here, our moods are affected by down-to-earth matters. Enjoying the simple things in life is part of what makes it feel rich.

June 30th Monday

Moon in Taurus / Gemini

	PDT	EDT
Moon enters Gemini	1:04 AM	4:04 AM
Moon square Saturn	8:14 AM	11:14 AM
Mars trine Pluto	3:56 PM	6:56 PM
Venus opposite Jupiter begins (see July 2)		

Mood Watch: Gemini Moon puts the focus of our moods on communicating and receiving information. Activities revolve around writing, speeches, conversations, and secretarial duties. On the surface a lot of the information sifts past our ears, through seemingly meaningless detail, and eventually more significant, more useful and practical information is attained, especially now that Mercury is direct since June 19.

Mars trine Pluto (occurring June 25 – July 5) Mars in Leo is trine to Pluto in Sagittarius. Confident, independent action leads to positive and powerful transformations. Actions taken now are more likely to have favorable results or to be influential with higher powers. This is a good time to resolve personal aggression directed towards the views and differences of another generation or established powers. This is also a good time for vital discoveries in the fight against diseases. Mars trine Pluto brings opportunity for favorable direct action that may well make a powerful and impressionable impact. Youthful or strong new influences will reach places of power, and a new generation will take many seats of power in political offices of the world. Mars, the god of war, and Pluto, the underworld god (or hell raiser), may actually be reaching some favorable kind of truce.

July 1st Tuesday

Canada Day

Moon in Gemini

	PDT	EDT
Moon conjunct Mercury	6:37 AM	9:37 AM
Mars enters Virgo	9:21 AM	12:21 PM
Moon square Uranus	1:11 PM	4:11 PM
Moon trine Neptune	3:12 PM	6:12 PM

Mood Watch: The Gemini Moon picks up our moods with a lot more chatter and talk. Gemini Moon brings curious moods and a more lively level of interest in the world of unending trivia.

Mars enters Virgo (Mars in Virgo: July 1 – Aug. 19) Today through August 19, Mars will be in Virgo creating heat, energy, and activity in the lives of Virgos. There will also be quite a bit of action taking place in the lives of Pisces people, as Mars opposes their natal sun during this time. Gemini and Sagittarius people may notice a lot of conflict in the area of keeping up energy levels and possibly dealing with bouts of temper, while Mars is in the square position to their natal sun signs. Mars in Virgo, in general, causes the heat of our activities to be focused on such Virgo-like tasks as communications, accounting, analyzing, and nitpicking perfection. Resourcefulness and cleverness are emphasized.

July 2nd Wednesday
Moon in Gemini / Cancer – NEW MOON in CANCER

	PDT	EDT	
Moon opposite Pluto goes v/c	12:08 AM	3:08 AM	
Moon enters Cancer	12:53 AM	3:53 AM	
Moon sextile Mars	1:31 AM	4:31 AM	
Moon sextile Saturn	8:18 AM	11:18 AM	
Moon conjunct Sun	7:18 PM	10:18 PM	
Venus opposite Jupiter	10:17 PM	1:17 AM	(July 3)
Mercury square Uranus begins (see July 5)			

Mood Watch: The **New Moon in Cancer** (Moon conjunct Sun) beckons to our moods to tune into new feelings about ourselves. The New Cancer Moon invites new experience and brings new desires to nurture the child within and build up a fresh outlook on our home life. Cancer focuses on the nurturing strength of the mother. This is a good time to bring new things to the home and brighten up one's outlook with nurturing and uplifting moods and feelings.

Venus opposite Jupiter (occurring June 30 – July 5) Venus in Cancer brings a love for emotional security, domestic comforts, and nurturing love, while the retrograde Jupiter in Capricorn focuses on the need for financial security, career advancement, and those areas of our lives where work is required. Venus opposite Jupiter brings on a significant awareness of the dynamics of attraction and wealth. Custody battles are hard fought under these circumstances. The process of overcoming personal loss requires a great deal of effort to attain the healing power of love. Money related tests and troubles in relationships are often a factor under this aspect. Venus opposite Jupiter increases awareness of the need for joy in relationships.

July 3rd Thursday
Moon in Cancer

	PDT	EDT
Moon opposite Jupiter	6:03 AM	9:03 AM
Moon conjunct Venus	6:49 AM	9:49 AM
Moon trine Uranus goes v/c	1:14 PM	4:14 PM

Mood Watch: The youthfully waxing Cancer Moon envelops our moods with intuitive hunches and revealing perspectives about how we are feeling. Our instincts are hard at work as we take the time to nurture the heart, pamper the soul, and

137

enjoy the best there is in a comforting home environment. In the privacy of the home, we can work out a number of kinks in our lives, and we are at liberty to display a wider variety of moods and feelings. This is the time to process those feelings and let them tell us what we need to know about those emotional planes of existence. Once the Cancer Moon goes void-of-course this afternoon, it may be especially important to look out for defensiveness and moodiness throughout the remainder of the day.

July 4th Friday

Independence Day, USA

Moon in Cancer / Leo	PDT	EDT
Moon enters Leo	1:16 AM	4:16 AM
Venus trine Uranus begins (see July 6)		
Mars conjunct Saturn begins (see July 10)		

Mood Watch: The newly waxing Moon in Leo puts us in touch with our pride and our joy. There is pride in the self, pride in the family, and pride in the way we put our own signature on things. Strength, self assurance and vitality are worthy focuses on a newly waxing Leo Moon. Sharing affection and playful interactions can be infectious.

July 5th Saturday

Moon in Leo	PDT	EDT
Mercury square Uranus	4:05 AM	7:05 AM
Moon sextile Mercury	4:20 PM	7:20 PM
Moon opposite Neptune	5:22 PM	8:22 PM

Mood Watch: Playfulness of moods allow for jovial encounters with the youthfully waxing Leo Moon. If the lion does not sleep or play, his hunger leads him into the most serious venture of stalking. Keep your bellies full and your spirits light and there won't be much trouble keeping peace on the plains.

Mercury square Uranus (occurring July 2 – 7) This aspect last occurred May 18 – June 2, but due to the retrograde pattern of Mercury at that time, it never actually reached its exact peak. However, Mercury square Uranus was certainly at work influencing us then, and probably more harshly in some ways, due to the fact that Mercury retrograde often requires that we reiterate and correct communication mistakes. As a general rule, this aspect creates excessive disruptions in communications. Mercury in Gemini is square to Uranus in Pisces. Communications, talks, discussions and news are troubled and challenged by unusual or explosive circumstances. It is also possible that important news of a radical nature will be obscured by sensationalism or overlooked as insignificant. Mercury in the sign of Gemini emphasizes the need to communicate about absolutely everything, while Uranus in the sign of Pisces emphasizes the need to deal with the revolutionary processes of beliefs, religion, and spiritual matters. The two focuses are creating a tension between people as they discuss their beliefs. Religious debates bring out the two sides of an issue repeatedly. Be careful what you say and how you say it; stirring up chaos can sometimes cause disruptive damage that is not really necessary and, in this case, may be a contributing factor that costs some folks their jobs or something else important to them. This aspect will reoccur on one more occasion this year, December 2 – 6, reaching its exact position on December 4 with Mercury in Sagittarius.

July 6th Sunday

Moon in Leo / Virgo

	PDT	EDT
Moon trine Pluto goes v/c	3:05 AM	6:05 AM
Mercury trine Neptune	3:44 AM	6:44 AM
Moon enters Virgo	4:04 AM	7:04 AM
Moon conjunct Mars	9:19 AM	12:19 PM
Venus trine Uranus	11:31 AM	2:31 PM
Moon conjunct Saturn	12:59 PM	3:59 PM
Sun opposite Jupiter begins (see July 9)		

Mood Watch: Virgo Moon moods focus our attention on the need to hold back, reassess, and devise a much more grounded strategy for living up to the high expectations we have set for ourselves. This is a good time to do some planning.

Mercury trine Neptune (occurring July 3 – 8) This aspect first occurred May 23 – 29, but it never reached its exact aspect due to Mercury's retrograde movement at that time *(see May 23).* Today, the forward moving Mercury in Gemini is trine to Neptune in Aquarius. Thoughtful discussions bring intuitive knowledge. Communicate about spiritual needs with helpful counsel and receive gifts of renewed faith in your own beliefs. Accept that some messages are there to spiritually uplift you. Mercury trine Neptune will reoccur three more times this year: first, September 14 – October 2, reaching its peak on September 19 and again on September 28, and October 27 – 31, reaching its peak on October 29 with Mercury in Libra.

Venus trine Uranus (occurring July 4 – 8) Venus in Cancer is trine Uranus in Pisces. Tender hearted and motherly kinds of love and attraction will make positive breakthroughs in matters of belief and believing. Venus trine Uranus brings a favorable attraction to revolutionary concepts. This is a time of freedom fighters and rebel love, and youth is easily attracted to the spirit of rebellion. Dangerous love and taking chances become common occurrences. This aspect creates an attraction to the unusual, yet it allows a harmony to exist in love related matters while chaotic occurrences are taking place. Love at first sight is explosive at this time, but not necessarily long lasting. This aspect will reoccur October 7 – 12, reaching its exact aspect peak on October 9 with Venus in Scorpio.

July 7th Monday

Moon in Virgo

	PDT	EDT
Moon sextile Sun	8:23 AM	11:23 AM
Moon trine Jupiter	11:41 AM	2:41 PM
Moon opposite Uranus	8:44 PM	11:44 PM

Mood Watch: Once priorities are straight and strategies are in place, anything is possible – that is, anything that will not defy the laws of physics or the doubtful and scrutinizing perfectionism of the Virgo demeanor. The Moon keeps warning us: be cautious, be prudent, be accurate, and be precise. It's summer and it's hard to heed such warnings. As long as we learn to read the signs, listen to our instincts, and apply the laws of the elements properly, the best experience can be possible.

July 8th Tuesday
Moon in Virgo / Libra

	PDT	EDT
Moon sextile Venus	12:15 AM	3:15 AM
Moon square Mercury	3:58 AM	6:58 AM
Moon square Pluto goes v/c	9:21 AM	12:21 PM
Moon enters Libra	10:32 AM	1:32 PM
Mercury opposite Pluto begins (see July 10)		

Mood Watch: The Virgo Moon morning keeps us curious and cautious. For an hour, the Moon will be void-of-course, creating some degree of doubt and confusion. By the time the Moon enters Libra, our moods will become more balanced and much more amicably interactive. Today would be a good day to empower friendship.

July 9th Wednesday
FIRST QUARTER MOON in LIBRA

	PDT	EDT	
Sun opposite Jupiter	12:39 AM	3:39 AM	
Moon square Jupiter	7:45 PM	10:45 PM	
Moon square Sun	9:35 PM	12:35 PM	(July 10)

Mood Watch: The Sun is in Cancer emphasizing activities of the home, the world of our feelings, and the need to preserve our emotional attachments; the **First Quarter Moon in Libra** (Moon square Sun) encourages us to harmonize with our partners and friends. This is the Moon that brings out a wide range of focuses on the need to create balance in various kinds of relationships, particularly those relationships of a close nature. It's all about making adjustments.

Sun opposite Jupiter (occurring July 6 – 11) Cancer birthday people, celebrating birthdays from July 6 – 11, are experiencing the opposition of Jupiter to their natal Sun. This brings an acute awareness of the shifts in personal economic conditions and issues, for better or worse. There is a strong personal awareness, or perhaps an obsession, at work to obtain a sense of wealth, joy, and well being. The need for peace in the shifting economy of these times is strong for these Cancer birthday folks. Use your best techniques, birthday Cancer, to abstain from impulse buying or credit card use. Governing your expenditures with wisdom instead of impetuosity will assuredly bring you around to the place you know you need to be. While it all comes at you at an overwhelming pace, remember this, Cancer – you can have (just about) anything you want – you just can't have *everything*. This aspect only occurs once this year.

July 10ᵗʰ Thursday

Moon in Libra / Scorpio

	PDT	EDT	
Mercury opposite Pluto	2:48 AM	5:48 AM	
Moon trine Neptune	8:14 AM	11:14 AM	
Mars conjunct Saturn	11:11 AM	2:11 PM	
Mercury enters Cancer	1:16 PM	4:16 PM	
Moon square Venus	3:10 PM	6:10 PM	
Moon sextile Pluto goes v/c	7:13 PM	10:13 PM	
Moon enters Scorpio	8:35 PM	11:35 PM	
Moon trine Mercury	9:40 PM	12:40 AM	(July 11)

Mood Watch: This Libra Moon day loads us up with busy and somewhat difficult aspects, and this may be the time to review decisions that have to be made and to work towards making adjustments and compromises with others. Later, the Scorpio Moon emphasizes the need for regenerative focuses such as rest or therapy. Pace yourself today.

Mercury opposite Pluto (occurring July 8 – 11) Mercury in Gemini opposes Pluto in Sagittarius. Dual perspectives of the intense and grotesque aspects of the news may be emphasized, causing horror, fascination, realization, and for some people, a kind of triumph as well. The news highlights power issues and the ensuing struggles for a breakthrough. This aspect will only be evident for a short time, but the long term affects for some folks may be unforgettable. Mind boggling awareness abounds now as the need to comprehend awakening powerful issues comes through in our thoughts and discussions.

Mars conjunct Saturn (occurring July 4 – 16) This aspect unites the forces of action itself (Mars), with the diligence to take this action to the limit (Saturn). This is the perfect time to apply discipline. In the striking of forces in battle, this aspect often brings swift and abrupt endings. It is always important to pay attention to those aspects of one's life that are active and hold the potential for accidents. Keep the fire extinguisher on hand. The popular old adage of *"look before you leap"* may not be a bad meditation to apply during this crucial time of Mars conjunct Saturn. Overall, when applying caution and discipline as a basis for constructive activity, Mars conjunct Saturn is an excellent time to put the all-important theory to practice. In fact, with Mars and Saturn in Virgo, this is an ideal time to practice, practice, and practice until you get it precisely right, especially with regard to action which requires perfect timing. Mars is the fire of our actions being precisely contained and preserved by the crucible: Saturn. Saturn is there to teach us about our limitations, and our sense of control is exercised through applying discipline. With practice, we can call up great strength through our disciplines. This may be just the right starting point to get the lazy rear in gear, so to speak.

Mercury enters Cancer (Mercury in Cancer: July 10 – Aug. 10) The shift in communications turns our attention from an emphasis on details and logic (Mercury in Gemini) to a focus on feelings and senses (Mercury in Cancer). This is a time when many people will appear to intuit their way through conversations. Thoughts may blend with mood as the emphasis on emotional expression takes the stage. As Mercury goes through the sign of Cancer, take special note of a tendency for people to talk more specifically about their feelings, defenses, and the need to be

141

nurtured. Mercury in Cancer makes some people more intuitive to the thoughts of others, and this may be an easier time to interpret people's thoughts by observing their emotional body language. Through Cancer, thoughts and communications are shaped by the course of our complex world of emotions.

July 11th Friday

Moon in Scorpio

	PDT	EDT
Moon sextile Saturn	7:33 AM	10:33 AM
Moon sextile Mars	8:27 AM	11:27 AM
Sun trine Uranus begins (see July 14)		

Mood Watch: The Sun is in Cancer and the Moon is in Scorpio – these are water signs and the general theme of today focuses on the emotional flow of our senses. This is a great weekend for garden work. Waxing Scorpio Moon puts our senses and defenses on the line, and our capacity for greater awareness and intuitive perception is often increased. Sexual prowess and the passion of Eros and Psyche are ascending on the horizon. Summer excitement and drama are in full swing.

July 12th Saturday

Moon in Scorpio

	PDT	EDT
Moon sextile Jupiter	6:41 AM	9:41 AM
Venus enters Leo	11:38 AM	2:38 PM
Moon trine Sun	2:24 PM	5:24 PM
Moon trine Uranus	5:46 PM	8:46 PM
Moon square Neptune goes v/c	8:05 PM	11:05 PM
Mercury sextile Saturn begins (see July 14)		

Mood Watch: Scorpio Moon awakens our moods to strong depths of emotion with the Sun in Cancer. Emotional currents tend to run deep and there is a strong need to express and unleash personal tension. This is a creative time of emotional healing for the soul.

Venus enters Leo (Venus in Leo: July 12 – Aug. 5) Venus in Leo brings out the more playful side of love. Venus represents the expression of love and affection; it is the influence of magnetism, beauty, and of feminine refinement. In the sign of Leo, Venus brings out desires and needs for personal attention. Magnetism is one of Leo's most endearing traits, and it is this magnetism that brings what Leos want most: loving attention. The entertainment industry will be highlighted as music, poetry, art, singing and acting are all enhanced with heartfelt expression. Leos will be more aware of their need for love. The love of looking good, having the best, and being the best is alluring to the ego. Wild lust will abound and the love of fantasies will be enhanced. Love affairs may be torrid and dramatic, while affections, when first initiated, can seem very ardent and sincere. One might be hesitant to believe that a too-good-to-be-true relationship is actually occurring. On the other hand, if it doesn't feel harmonious, it may be because the love affair is more focused on the demands and needs of just one person. Leo demands a lot of affection and, when Venus comes into play, the need for attention sometimes outweighs the need to reciprocate that attention. It is always wise not to have expectations in love matters and to be sure that the joys of exchanging love are balanced.

142

July 13th Sunday

Moon in Scorpio / Sagittarius

	PDT	EDT
Moon enters Sagittarius	8:50 AM	11:50 AM
Moon trine Venus	11:16 AM	2:16 PM
Moon square Saturn	8:31 PM	11:31 PM
Mercury sextile Mars begins (see July 15)		

Mood Watch: This morning's void-of-course Moon in Scorpio may seem a little intense. Soon enough however, the Moon enters Sagittarius and our moods become much more philosophical, adventurous, and outgoing. The Sagittarius Moon inspires us to reaffirm our sense of vision with insightful fortitude. This is a time to build on our talents and skills, and we are drawn towards the need to explore and find opportunity wherever possible.

July 14th Monday

Moon in Sagittarius

	PDT	EDT
Moon square Mars	12:09 AM	3:09 AM
Mercury sextile Saturn	1:34 AM	4:34 AM
Sun trine Uranus	8:03 AM	11:03 AM

Mood Watch: There is a great deal revealed to us through our moods. Sagittarius says: "I see," and today's overall activities call for vision and creative effort to enjoy this valuable summer time.

Mercury sextile Saturn (occurring July 12 – 15) Mercury in Cancer is sextile Saturn in Virgo. Mercury in Cancer requires accurate but sensitive communications over vital subjects. Meanwhile, Saturn demands prudent and carefully analyzed measures with regard to setting up perimeters and implementing rules. This tends to be a time when struggles and difficulties are discussed, and people draw collective conclusions on how best to handle their problems or responsibilities. This is an opportunistic aspect for communicating work skills, particularly with regard to home related tasks and chores. Make use of it while the opportunity is here. Mercury sextile Saturn will reoccur November 15 – 17, reaching its exact aspect peak on November 16, when Mercury will be in Scorpio.

Sun trine Uranus (occurring July 11 – 17) This occurrence of Sun trine Uranus favorably affects our Cancer friends celebrating birthdays July 11 – 17. It puts the radical forces of Uranus in the favorable trine position to the natal Sun of these Cancer folks. This is the time for these birthday people to make the breakthrough. Don't hold back, Cancer folks; chaos is here to stay for awhile, and the apparent madness occurring in your lives is there for a reason. Let the experience be positive as long as this aspect brings gifts. Expect restless desires for freedom and a heart-felt need to break out of your personal prison. These challenges are a necessary part of Cancer folks' growth patterns, and the resultant changes are positive in nature, though on the surface they may seem harsh and overbearing. Freedom knocks loudly and the course of change for these people is inevitable in the next year. The trine aspect bestows gifts of triumph, and this could be a good time to let chaos be the force that brings freedom. This aspect will reoccur November 7 – 13, reaching its exact aspect peak on November 10, and affecting Scorpio birthday people.

July 15th Tuesday

Moon in Sagittarius / Capricorn	PDT	EDT	
Moon square Uranus	6:18 AM	9:18 AM	
Moon sextile Neptune	8:33 AM	11:33 AM	
Mercury sextile Mars	2:09 PM	5:09 PM	
Moon conjunct Pluto goes v/c	7:43 PM	10:43 PM	
Moon enters Capricorn	9:20 PM	12:20 AM	(July 16)

Mood Watch: The waxing Sagittarius Moon invites us to see things openly, optimistically, and there's no holding back the creative and energetic spirit of our moods. Later tonight, the Moon enters Capricorn and our moods take on a cooler, calculating perspective on the week ahead.

Mercury sextile Mars (occurring July 13 – 17) Mercury in Cancer sextile Mars in Virgo brings heartfelt messages of physical triumphs and actions. Mercury sextile Mars presents opportunities which can be received, recognized, communicated and acted upon. News or information may lead to immediate action, especially now that Mercury is *direct* (since June 19). It's an advantageous time to apply one's word with a full backing of action for a very favorable outcome. Mercury sextile Mars last occurred on June 8, when Mercury was retrograde. This aspect also occurred on April 29, when Mercury was in Taurus and Mars was in Cancer.

July 16th Wednesday

Moon in Capricorn	PDT	EDT
Moon trine Saturn	9:24 AM	12:24 PM
Moon trine Mars	3:39 PM	6:39 PM
Moon opposite Mercury	6:47 PM	9:47 PM

Mood Watch: The waxing Capricorn Moon prepares us for its fullness, set to reach its peak at the close of the week. This intensely earthy Moon is a good time to apply some diligent and concentrated effort. Today will be a day of progress.

July 17th Thursday

Moon in Capricorn	PDT	EDT
Moon conjunct Jupiter	6:00 AM	9:00 AM
Moon sextile Uranus	5:57 PM	8:57 PM

Mood Watch: Diligence and serious intent affect the mood pattern which is building at this time. Tonight marks the eve of the Full Moon and there is no doubt that the wolves are howling - somewhere. Today serves as a good day to get some work done. Tonight is a good time to celebrate the beautiful Moon.

144

July 18th Friday
Moon in Capricorn / Aquarius – FULL MOON in CAPRICORN

	PDT	EDT
Moon opposite Sun goes v/c	12:58 AM	3:58 AM
Moon enters Aquarius	8:41 AM	11:41 AM
Mercury opposite Jupiter begins (see July 19)		

Mood Watch: The **Full Moon in Capricorn** (Moon opposite Sun) always suggests a time of celebration, and the earthy Capricorn expression focuses on the accomplishment of goals through the application of persistence and diligence. The gold is in your integrity and work, but this morning, the Full Moon will be void-of-course and a slow start on the day causes us to pause and be more observant than active. Early in the day, the Moon enters Aquarius and our moods shift over to an intense desire to investigate the unknown factors of life that brought through this busy Full Moon phase of July.

July 19th Saturday
Moon in Aquarius

	PDT	EDT
Moon opposite Venus	12:12 AM	3:12 AM
Mercury opposite Jupiter	12:53 PM	3:53 PM

Mood Watch: The Moon, though still quite full, now wanes in Aquarius. Innovative thoughts and ideas spark our moods as we contemplate experimental ways to handle the unusual aspects of our life.

Mercury opposite Jupiter (occurring July 18 – 20) Mercury in Cancer is opposite Jupiter in Capricorn bringing impressionable observations about overwhelming visions, career goals, and aspirations. We may find ourselves bartering for things that cannot be sold. An economic shift may bring financial or political awareness, and the incessant chatter which fills the airwaves has a further effect on the sharp movements occurring in the stock market. This aspect also focuses news on the opulent lifestyles of the rich and famous, as people find themselves unable to stop talking about their financial situation or their need for advancement, a raise, or an income. Wealth is highlighted, and there is considerable debate as to what wealth really represents. Most of the time wealth is an illusion, and people really don't know what they're talking about when they make assumptions about the apparent well being of others. As class separation continues, it is a time of acute concern in this realm. This short-lived aspect only occurs once this year.

July 20th Sunday
Moon in Aquarius / Pisces

	PDT	EDT
Moon conjunct Neptune	5:54 AM	8:54 AM
Moon sextile Pluto goes v/c	2:24 PM	5:24 PM
Moon enters Pisces	6:08 PM	9:08 PM

Mood Watch: The first part of the day brings social, imaginative, intellectually stimulating moods. Once the Moon goes void-of-course, puzzling moods make it difficult to think clearly at times. Tonight's Pisces Moon puts the emphasis of our moods on spiritual matters, in some cases moral and religious focuses, and for those that care not about such things, the wild abandon of parties and escapism also takes the stage.

July 21st Monday

Moon in Pisces

	PDT	EDT	
Moon opposite Saturn	6:24 AM	9:24 AM	
Moon opposite Mars	4:59 PM	7:59 PM	
Moon sextile Jupiter	11:34 PM	2:24 AM	(July 22)
Mercury trine Uranus begins (see July 22)			

Mood Watch: Pisces Moon gives no boundaries to the scope of the feelings. The imagination is strong and feelings are absorbed from all around while they are also busy addressing all of the post-full-moon changes in the air. Throughout the day the Moon in Pisces brings imaginative, poetic and deeply feminine images to the forefront of our emotional awareness. Pisces Moon brings out our need to quench thirsts, connect with aquatic life forms, and release feelings through art and music. Addictive or impulsive behavior is strong at this time.

LEO

Key Phrase: "I WILL"

Fixed Fire Sign

Symbol: The Majestic Lion

July 22nd through August 22nd

July 22nd Tuesday

Moon in Pisces

	PDT	EDT	
Sun enters Leo	3:54 AM	6:54 AM	
Moon trine Mercury	11:05 AM	2:05 PM	
Moon conjunct Uranus	11:34 AM	2:34 PM	
Mercury trine Uranus	2:09 PM	5:09 PM	
Moon square Pluto goes v/c	11:37 PM	2:37 AM	(July 23)
Mars trine Jupiter begins (see July 26)			

Mood Watch: A dreamy, rather psychic expression of awareness takes place with Moon in Pisces. Throughout the day moods remain somewhat spacey, very clairvoyant, and quite artistic and full of belief, prayer, and meditation.

146

Sun enters Leo (Sun in Leo: July 22 – Aug. 22) Leo, the sign ruled by the Sun, fills the season with strong, instinctive fervor and deep, fiery desire. Leo focuses on will, identity, truth, selfhood, integrity, pride, and strength. Yours is a lustful time of year, Leo, and your totem, the lion, is one of the most self-assured of the zodiac's symbols. Sun in Leo focuses our attention on Sun related frolic and play, outdoor activities for children and families, and the entire entertainment industry. This is the time for self-development and fulfillment. Leo says, "I Will," and it is important for a Leo to be expressive in the act of will. The Leo part within us must remember with a true affirmation of will we can have *anything* we want – we just can't have *everything*. Choose what is true to the self!

Mercury trine Uranus (occurring July 21 – 23) Mercury, emphasizing the transmission of news and information, is now in the favorable trine position to Uranus, representing disruption and chaos. This aspect brings news of disorder and calamity which (through the trine aspect) represents a gift, probably one of freedom or a break in the mundane routine. There are many premature or radical breakthroughs waiting in the wings, and Mercury trine Uranus often brings news of these discoveries. Mercury is in Cancer trine to Uranus in Pisces. Talk will be generated about changes in our belief structures and in the arts. Catch phrases, or radical concept statements and ideas, are often born under this aspect, and are more easily absorbed. Mercury trine Uranus also allows for brilliant concepts to shine through and be worded in a way that radically makes sense. This is a good time to record thoughts and appreciate brilliant thinking. This aspect will reoccur November 14 – 17, reaching its peak on November 15 with Mercury in Scorpio.

July 23rd Wednesday
Moon in Pisces / Aries

	PDT	EDT
Moon enters Aries	1:23 AM	4:23 AM
Moon trine Sun	3:00 AM	6:00 AM

Mood Watch: The Moon wanes in Aries bringing out a sense of urgency to proceed through the day. This is a time when new projects are developing. Waning Aries Moon brings out the warrior in all of us. Sometimes we must stand up to the things that get us in a knot and make our will be known. Self-importance is both the key and the burden of our sojourn. On one hand we must fight for our rights and be true to our own being, hence, self-importance is aright! On the other hand, too much self-importance can be very foreboding to others, and those who do claim supremacy and leadership must have something that captivates and appeals to their subjects. Fear can captivate, while charm can appeal. It doesn't much matter how the commander storms into town, either way he/she shall seem very important!

July 24th Thursday
Moon in Aries

	PDT	EDT
Moon trine Venus	2:51 AM	5:51 AM
Moon square Jupiter	5:05 AM	8:05 AM
Moon sextile Neptune	6:49 PM	9:49 PM

Mood Watch: Aries Moon brings out self-awareness and self-assertiveness, and focuses our attention on pushing forward with force and vigor, with strength and intent. Aries Moon often inspires us to focus on something new or delve into our work with a new spirit of determination. It calls to us to get motivated, however small the cause.

July 25th Friday
Moon in Aries / Taurus – LAST QUARTER MOON in TAURUS

	PDT	EDT
Moon square Mercury	2:09 AM	5:09 AM
Moon trine Pluto goes v/c	4:29 AM	7:29 AM
Moon enters Taurus	6:15 AM	9:15 AM
Moon square Sun	11:40 AM	2:40 PM
Moon trine Saturn	6:20 PM	9:20 PM

Mood Watch: The **Last Quarter Moon in Taurus** (Moon square Sun) focuses the general course of our moods on creating some sense of order in our financial situations, and encourages the need for creature comforts and esthetically pleasing or luxurious surroundings. There is often a focus on cleaning up and/or selling various useful artifacts that have collected in our lives. The Last Quarter Taurus Moon often advocates the activities of yard sales, auctions and flea markets. This is a good time to transform one's atmosphere into a more useful and practical working order. Letting go of attachment to material things that have bogged one down with too much maintenance or disruptive costs may very well be the best move, and if ever there is a time to do this, it is during the Last Quarter Moon of Taurus. Certain kinds of sacrifice produce some very remedial freedom.

July 26th Saturday
Moon in Taurus

	PDT	EDT	
Moon trine Mars	7:59 AM	10:59 AM	
Moon trine Jupiter	8:20 AM	11:20 AM	
Moon square Venus	11:31 AM	2:31 PM	
Mars trine Jupiter	3:04 PM	6:04 PM	
Moon sextile Uranus	8:05 PM	11:05 PM	
Moon square Neptune goes v/c	9:51 PM	12:51 AM	(July 27)
Sun conjunct Mercury begins (see July 29)			

Mood Watch: The waning Taurus Moon brings continued efforts to perfect our surroundings and to enjoy luxurious pleasures. Not only do many have to assess their material possessions, sometimes the physical body and the vitality of one's health are in question; it is vitally important to make healthy choices and apply the labor or rest necessary to keep the body, the beloved temple of our life, in good working order.

Mars trine Jupiter (occurring July 22 – 30) Mars is in Virgo activating a strong focus on health, communications, business, and placing an all-around emphasis on the power of success. Jupiter is in Capricorn, expanding our economic growth through career awareness, diligent effort, and special skills. Act on opportunities as they arise and set visions and dreams into a feasible plan that holds the potential for favorable actions to occur. The drive to create some expansion of our livelihood involves resourceful awareness. Mars activates and stirs action, while Jupiter represents not only economy and advancement, but our sense of philosophic and visionary awareness as well. While Jupiter is retrograde, introspective reflections will help us to realize new talents and new means of livelihood, and perhaps even some prosperity, joy and well being. For some people this aspect brings gifts of inheritance; for all of us it brings opportunities for growth. Mars trine Jupiter allows us to activate a stronger grasp of our domain, and gives many folks the extra energy and spark to boost their sense of achievement and advancement. This most auspicious aspect only occurs once this year, so it will be best to take advantage while the action is, potentially, the most lucrative.

July 27th Sunday
Moon in Taurus / Gemini

	PDT	EDT
Moon enters Gemini	8:56 AM	11:56 AM
Moon sextile Mercury	1:43 PM	4:43 PM
Moon sextile Sun	5:44 PM	8:44 PM
Moon square Saturn	8:59 PM	11:59 PM

Mood Watch: The void-of-course Taurus Moon brings a lazy Sunday morning. Soon enough, the Moon enters Gemini and our moods become considerably upbeat, curious, communicative, and intellectually stimulated. This is a great day to make connections.

July 28th Monday
Moon in Gemini

	PDT	EDT	
Moon square Mars	12:01 PM	3:01 PM	
Moon sextile Venus	5:49 PM	8:49 PM	
Moon square Uranus	9:32 PM	12:32 PM	
Moon trine Neptune	11:15 PM	2:15 AM	(July 29)

Venus opposite Neptune begins (see July 31)

Mood Watch: Gemini Moon can bring nervous energy, and the restlessness of this factor may cause many folks to be preoccupied with getting to the point and cutting through the chatter in order to obtain some sense of peace and well being. Joking and small talk are all a part of getting through this nervous clamor – so if your heart is restless, chatter on!

July 29th Tuesday
Moon in Gemini / Cancer

	PDT	EDT	
Moon opposite Pluto goes v/c	8:25 AM	11:25 AM	
Moon enters Cancer	10:12 AM	1:12 PM	
Sun conjunct Mercury	1:04 PM	4:04 PM	
Moon sextile Saturn	10:29 PM	1:29 AM	(July 30)

Mood Watch: The void-of-course Gemini Moon morning may be disorienting at times. Soon enough, the Moon enters Cancer and our moods will become notably more emotional. This is a good time to stick to nourishing foods and to find a comforting place, like home, to ease emotional burdens. Everyone needs a space they can call their own.

Sun conjunct Mercury (occurring July 26 – Aug. 1) This aspect will create a much more thoughtful, communicative, and expressive year ahead for those Leo folks celebrating birthdays July 26 – August 1. This is your time (birthday Leos) to record ideas, relay important messages, and pay close attention to your imaginative thoughts as they are touched by Mercury, creating the urge to speak and be heard. Your thoughts will reveal a great deal about who you are, now and in the year to come.

July 30th Wednesday

Moon in Cancer

	PDT	EDT	
Moon opposite Jupiter	10:28 AM	1:28 PM	
Moon sextile Mars	3:13 PM	6:13 PM	
Moon trine Uranus goes v/c	10:31 PM	1:31 AM	(July 31)

Mood Watch: The waning Cancer Moon commonly brings introspective exploration over emotional matters. Cancer Moon puts us in touch with the need to care and nurture ourselves – but, of course, it's always darkest before the dawn, and this may seem like a time when it becomes necessary to weed out bad habits and poor judgment that trigger negative emotional responses. This is prominently one of those times when we are reminded of the need overcome temptation and do the right thing.

July 31st Thursday

Moon in Cancer / Leo

	PDT	EDT
Venus opposite Neptune	9:29 AM	12:29 PM
Moon enters Leo	11:22 AM	2:22 PM

Mood Watch: The New Moon (Sun conjunct Moon) mark approaches early tomorrow morning, at which point the process of mulling over useless or negative emotional tendencies becomes more of a rebirthing kind of experience for our emotional process. The void-of-course waning Cancer Moon is a time to dump useless emotional baggage. As the day progresses, the Moon enters Leo, and now the fun begins. It is the New Leo Moon that starts up a new month tomorrow. Playful Leo energy is bountiful. Must play!

Venus opposite Neptune (occurring July 28 – Aug. 2) Venus in Leo is opposing Neptune in Aquarius. What we are attracted to may be opposed to what we (or others) believe in. Selfishness conflicts with philanthropy. Wild and instinctual expressions of love and beauty are at odds with universal beliefs. This aspect brings an awareness of the dichotomy between fashion's feminine archetypes versus a natural or spiritual expression of femininity. The feminine spirit needs to be free and connect with a more divine image of womanhood; however, the goddess that lives within may seem distant or hard to reach. Nonetheless, the feminine parts of the spirit (Venus) are being made acutely aware of the divine parts of the spirit (Neptune) in one way or another. The opposition of Venus to Neptune may seem like an overwhelming time to try to make a spiritual connection with large groups of people, especially through the mediums of art, music, and theater. There may be a desire to create a spiritual refuge or retreat – an attractive, sensual, and aesthetically pleasing sanctuary. This opposition only occurs once this year.

150

August 1ˢᵗ Friday
Lammas / Lughnassad
NEW MOON in LEO – Total Solar Eclipse

𝒮𝓁

	PDT	EDT
Moon conjunct Sun	3:13 AM	6:13 AM
Moon conjunct Mercury	8:52 AM	11:52 AM
Mars opposite Uranus begins (see August 6)		

Mood Watch: The **New Moon in Leo** (Moon conjunct Sun) encourages our moods to acquire a new outlook on our personal image. Some may be strongly touched by the need to get a new lease on life. The desire for new attire and a focus on hair is commonplace for this sort of mood setting. If low self-esteem sets you back on this solar ecliptic New Moon, remember that you aren't inherently a failure – that's just an old pattern of behavior. A new pattern of positive self-image and dignity can be created and the old beastly pattern will have to be tempered and corrected. Image comes from within and is generated by the sheer magnitude of one's will. Everyone has room to grow if they take the time to apply self worth, self respect, and discipline.

A **Total Solar Eclipse in the sign of Leo** brings an emphasis on controversies rooted in our individuality and our personal needs. For some, feelings of self confidence may seem overshadowed, but it must be remembered that this is only a brief shadow. Eclipses are believed to threaten the lives and liberty of leaders and special figures in society. Every time there is a Solar Eclipse, there is always a Lunar Eclipse within two weeks — *see **Partial Lunar** Eclipse, August 16*. This Eclipse duo will have another Eclipse pair at the opposite time of year – *see Annular Solar Eclipse in Aquarius, February 6, and the Total Lunar Eclipse in Virgo, February 20*. Although this may not feel like a particularly easy time for starting anew, the Solar Eclipse touches our lives with a fluid and accepting kind of assertiveness to move through the greatest obstacles. Beware of the tendency for some people to lean towards substance abuse, depression, and emotional instability.

August 2ⁿᵈ Saturday
Moon in Leo / Virgo

	PDT	EDT
Moon opposite Neptune	2:19 AM	5:19 PM
Moon conjunct Venus	6:18 AM	9:18 AM
Moon trine Pluto goes v/c	11:59 AM	2:59 PM
Moon enters Virgo	2:00 PM	5:00 PM
Venus trine Pluto begins (see August 4)		

Mood Watch: The morning Leo Moon opens our hearts with optimism and playfulness as the newly waxing Moon completes its cycle in Leo. This afternoon, the Moon goes void-of-course for a couple of hours and beastly moods, laziness, or a lack of punctuality may cause some minor setbacks. As the Moon enters Virgo, a more cautious and discerning quality of mood begins to take over. Virgo Moon keeps us focused on accounting for our resources and making ends meet. This evening brings a good time to plan and organize.

151

August 3rd Sunday

Moon in Virgo

	PDT	EDT
Moon conjunct Saturn	3:58 AM	6:58 AM
Moon trine Jupiter	3:17 PM	6:17 PM

Mood Watch: New feelings concerning organization and making important connections persistently emerge with the freshly waxing Virgo Moon. This is the time to enjoy the fruits of summer and take in healthy foods as well as implementing more thorough health practices. Look for good deals, make connections with others, and plan out the rest of the summer.

August 4th Monday

Civic Holiday / Provincial Day, Canada

Moon in Virgo / Libra

	PDT	EDT	
Moon conjunct Mars	2:14 AM	5:14 AM	
Moon opposite Uranus	5:02 AM	8:02 AM	
Moon square Pluto goes v/c	5:16 PM	8:16 PM	
Moon enters Libra	7:28 PM	10:28 PM	
Venus trine Pluto	9:53 PM	12:53 AM	(August 5)
Mercury opposite Neptune begins (see August 6)			

Mood Watch: Today the waxing Virgo Moon brings the need for pragmatism. A wholesome diet, outdoor recreation, and relaxing hobbies are great ways to enhance the mood. This evening, cautious and skeptical moods may slow down the pace as the Moon goes void-of-course for a couple of hours. Later, the Libra Moon brings the opportunity to balance our skepticism with the reassurance of loved ones.

Venus trine Pluto (occurring Aug. 2 – 7) For the last time in our lifetime, Venus in Leo is trine to Pluto in Sagittarius. Family ties are made stronger in the art of love as they wade through their hardships. Venus trine Pluto is certainly exciting – with fate, power, love, and intensity at work! This aspect represents a love or fascination occurring with regard to the work of fate as well as power. Venus trine Pluto allows a breakthrough to occur for those who have trouble accepting the work of fate. Loving energy flows more easily between generations. Love triumphs over all, especially with Venus trine Pluto. This is a great time to let love cure the pain. This aspect last occurred April 28 – May 3, reaching its exact peak on May 1.

August 5th Tuesday

Moon in Libra

	PDT	EDT	
Venus enters Virgo	9:19 PM	12:19 AM	(August 6)
Moon sextile Sun	9:50 PM	12:50 AM	(August 6)
Moon square Pluto	10:00 PM	1:00 AM	(August 6)

Mood Watch: Waxing Libra Moon focuses our moods on the need to create harmony and beauty in our lives, and to get on with the necessity to create some order with our sense of progress. Friends and partners often become the highlights of our moods and focuses during the waxing Libra Moon.

Venus enters Virgo (Venus in Virgo: Aug. 5 – 30) Venus now enters the sign of Virgo, where love and attraction are highlighted with such Virgo-like traits as shyness, prudence, purity, and virginal beauty. While Venus is in Virgo, the expression of love and beauty will be analyzed and reflected upon, and love related activities are more often reserved or calculated than they are acted upon. Venus in Virgo is referred to as "the fall," a less ideal position for Venus and a time when disappointment in love matters may be felt by some folks. Keep faith in your affections, despite the cooling of passions.

August 6th Wednesday

Moon in Libra

	PDT	EDT
Mars opposite Uranus	11:37 AM	2:37 PM
Mercury opposite Neptune	11:40 AM	2:40 PM
Moon trine Neptune	3:00 PM	6:00 PM
Moon sextile Mercury	3:38 PM	6:38 PM

Mood Watch: Waxing Libra Moon is an excellent time to kick back with a friend or partner and enjoy the lazy Leo sun energy of summertime. Friendship is highlighted and this is a good time to enjoy artful cuisine as well as cultural and social endeavors.

Mars opposite Uranus (occurring Aug. 1 – 11) This aspect puts the fiery Mars in Virgo, into the acutely aware position to the radical and explosive power of Uranus in Pisces. If there was ever an aspect that most aptly described the term "fighting fire with fire," this is the one. The potential for harsh action is very strong with this aspect, and we may encounter such travesties as explosions, the fires of war backfiring, rampant building and forest fires, and atrocious hate crimes against minorities and underdogs. Fiery violence is just a matter of course with this aspect; however, because these two planets of a fiery and active nature are tempered in earth and water signs, the level of action we may see take place is likely to be emphasized over the qualities of the Virgo/Pisces polarity. There is intensity in the air concerning our delicate national budget and resources, as well as the freedom and rights necessary to exercise and express our individual beliefs. Take caution regarding risky undertakings that may rock the boat of fiery activity. Those who are affected by this aspect are likely to be stir-crazy and in strong need of a revolution or revolt. Anger and frustration can be stifling at times, causing the need for freedom and a definite breakthrough when it comes to matters of where to place one's faith. Fortunately, this opposition only occurs once this year.

Mercury opposite Neptune (occurring Aug. 4 – 7) Mercury opposite Neptune makes us acutely aware of discussions concerning religious beliefs. Beliefs go beyond the physical to the metaphysical realms, where information is accessed and spiritual fortification occurs. It is wisest to be clear on one's own beliefs, and not to put oneself in a position of having to defend or expose those beliefs before a pack of merciless critics. Spiritual growth and enlightenment are not easy things to relay in conversation, and during this aspect it may seem particularly overwhelming for some folks to try to communicate effectively, or to comprehend what others are trying to communicate about spiritual matters. This opposition only occurs once this year..

153

August 7th Thursday

Moon in Libra / Scorpio

	PDT	EDT	
Moon sextile Pluto goes v/c	2:02 AM	5:02 AM	
Moon enters Scorpio	4:27 AM	7:27 AM	
Moon sextile Venus	7:54 AM	10:54 AM	
Moon sextile Saturn	9:19 PM	12:19 AM	(August 8)
Mercury trine Pluto begins (see August 9)			

Mood Watch: Waxing Scorpio Moon calls to our passionate center. Sun is in Leo, Moon is in Scorpio, drama of some sort is bound to happen. Energy rises to the occasion. Scorpio Moon focuses our energies on the need for a positive and uplifting outlook. Physical exertion will help to defuse intense emotions. Spirit releases a death cry, peace is restored. Sales and thefts soar high in the market place.

August 8th Friday

FIRST QUARTER MOON in SCORPIO

	PDT	EDT
Moon sextile Jupiter	8:01 AM	11:01 AM
Moon square Sun	1:20 PM	4:20 PM
Moon trine Uranus	1:59 PM	4:59 PM

Mood Watch: The **First Quarter Moon in Scorpio** (Moon square Sun) arouses our moods in deep and impassioned ways. Intensity of exchange between people comes through with an impressionable attitude. Throughout today, this waxing quarter Moon of Scorpio persists to bring our moods to a strange and intense level of existence. Today is the eighth day of the eighth month of the eighth year of the century. The Qabalistic significance of this number points to the eighth sphere on the Tree of Life, which represents Mercury. Symbolically this suggests a good time to make change occur in conformity with willpower. Put the message out there and it will be answered. Get in touch with your creative and imaginative side, and celebrate your passion.

August 9th Saturday

Moon in Scorpio / Sagittarius

	PDT	EDT
Moon square Neptune	2:06 AM	5:06 AM
Moon sextile Mars	3:28 AM	6:28 AM
Mercury trine Pluto	11:18 AM	2:18 PM
Moon square Mercury goes v/c	2:02 PM	5:02 PM
Moon enters Sagittarius	4:11 PM	7:11 PM

Mood Watch: The waxing Moon in Scorpio puts us in touch with deep rooted subjects and feelings. Throughout today, it emphasizes a mystical sort of drama as the interplay of moods are intensified with vigilant and undaunted emotionality; our feelings may confuse or mystify us at times while the Moon is void-of-course. Later, the Moon in Sagittarius brings clarity of vision, optimism, and resilience.

Mercury trine Pluto (occurring Aug. 7 – 11) Mercury in Leo trine Pluto in Sagittarius brings the message of hope. Mercury in Leo gives a very colorful and theatrical flare to our methods of communication. Mercury trine Pluto brings greater definition to the meaning of fate, and allows us to more easily communicate about the power struggles occurring collectively around the world. Mercury is the communications tower that transmits information. Pluto's disruptive energy is focusing our attention on such issues as contagious diseases, senseless crime, misunderstandings between cultures, facing up to addiction, and many other painful realities. This is a good time to express encouraging words and reinforce the troubled people of our world with a sense of hope. This aspect last occurred April 16 – 19, reaching its exact peak on April 18.

August 10ᵗʰ Sunday

Moon in Sagittarius

	PDT	EDT
Moon square Venus	2:39 AM	5:39 AM
Mercury enters Virgo	3:53 AM	6:53 AM
Moon square Saturn	10:07 AM	1:07 PM
Venus conjunct Saturn begins (see August 13)		

Mood Watch: The Sun and Moon are both in fire signs, igniting creative and energetic expression, and giving us a very lively perspective on the events of the day. Despite the square of lunar aspects occurring today, the waxing Sagittarius Moon brings zealous, hopeful, and outgoing moods. This is a good time to contemplate future plans. Sagittarius Moon helps to provide visionary awareness.

August 11ᵗʰ Monday

Moon in Sagittarius

	PDT	EDT
Moon trine Sun	7:06 AM	10:06 AM
Moon square Uranus	12:21 PM	3:21 PM
Moon sextile Neptune	2:30 PM	5:30 PM
Moon square Mars	7:23 PM	10:23 PM
Sun opposite Neptune begins (see August 15)		

Mood Watch: The waxing Sagittarius Moon encourages us to focus our moods on a visionary process. The need to see ahead is strong, and we are often empowered when we also take an insightful look at the way our recent past – and sometimes distant past – has manifested in our lives. Sagittarius Moon encourages us to reach out to new realms of possibility and advancement. Still, we must pace ourselves with the ups and downs of today's energy charged lunar aspects.

August 12ᵗʰ Tuesday

Moon in Sagittarius / Capricorn

	PDT	EDT	
Moon conjunct Pluto goes v/c	2:03 AM	5:03 AM	
Moon enters Capricorn	4:43 AM	7:43 AM	
Moon trine Mercury	1:20 PM	4:20 PM	
Moon trine Venus	9:56 PM	12:56 AM	(August 13)
Moon trine Saturn	11:03 PM	2:03 AM	(August 13)
Mars square Pluto begins (see August 16)			

Mood Watch: An industrious mood captivates us as the waxing Moon enters Capricorn. Throughout the day, a sense of keen focus and a serious determination to get things done makes this an excellent time to complete tasks and make some

155

progress on important projects and work loads. Positive lunar aspects bring favorable communications, pleasures, and achievements.

August 13ᵗʰ Wednesday

Moon in Capricorn

	PDT	EDT	
Moon conjunct Jupiter	7:42 AM	10:42 AM	
Venus conjunct Saturn	10:03 AM	1:03 PM	
Moon sextile Uranus	11:56 PM	2:56 AM	(August 14)

Mercury conjunct Saturn begins (see August 15)

Mood Watch: Today is the day to focus on getting the work done, as tomorrow's long void-of-course Moon day may prove to be nonproductive. Moon in Capricorn demands a firm guard on the emotional side of our moods. Sound, resourceful and earnest labor will be the emphasis of the day.

Venus conjunct Saturn (occurring Aug. 10 – 16) Venus and Saturn are conjunct in Virgo and this creates subtly affectionate, communicative, and serious bonding between loved ones. This aspect brings a favorable time to apply discipline in the arts and in love related matters. Venus conjunct Saturn represents our commitment and responsibility to the people we love and care about. It may also indicate there is a strong timely quality about love matters taking place, or that love matters are undergoing a restriction, or possibly even closure of some kind. This aspect can go either way on the positive-negative scale, since the loving attraction of Venus can be either encouraged or thwarted by the responsible, serious, and limiting discipline of Saturn's energy. This is the only time Venus will be conjunct with Saturn this year.

August 14ᵗʰ Thursday

Moon in Capricorn / Aquarius

	PDT	EDT
Moon trine Mars goes v/c	10:08 AM	1:08 PM
Moon enters Aquarius	3:57 PM	6:57 PM

Venus trine Jupiter begins (see August 16)
Mercury conjunct Venus begins (see August 21 and September 14)

Mood Watch: Just when the positive urge to take action occurs, contingencies and setbacks tend to get in the way of the work. The Moon goes void-of-course in Capricorn and this tends to slow down progress, causing many of us to take every little matter that comes up more seriously than is probably necessary. Relax! Take it in stride. The Moon is waxing towards fullness (this Saturday) and the resulting tension bursts with determination, obscured uneasiness, and shrewd persistence. Expect some unnecessary commotion at times in the early part of the day. Later today, as the Moon enters Aquarius, innovative thoughts and ideas spark our moods.

August 15ᵗʰ Friday

Moon in Aquarius

	PDT	EDT
Sun opposite Neptune	12:42 AM	3:42 AM
Mercury conjunct Saturn	1:00 PM	4:00 PM
Mercury trine Jupiter begins (see August 17)		

Mood Watch: Moon in Aquarius is waxing towards fullness, and the energy at this time is busy and strong. Aquarius Moon puts the focus on the need to apply knowledge. A hunger for knowledge and investigation brings a surge of social gatherings.

Sun opposite Neptune (occurring Aug. 11 – 18) This occurrence of Sun opposite Neptune especially affects those Leo people celebrating birthdays from August 11 – 18. Neptune in opposition to these folks' natal Sun brings a strong awareness of Spirit, the spiritual path, and the acknowledgment of one's beliefs. The challenge facing these Leo birthday folks is to confront and overcome all disruptive personal doubts that cause them to question the practice of believing. These people will be eminently aware this year of the vast shifts in spiritual beliefs, and they may feel quite overwhelmed by the confusion and fluctuations of their own spiritual awareness. This is no surprise – it is occurring for numerous people at this time – Leos will just experience it more directly. This is the time to go to a personal sanctuary of choice and tune into Spirit.

Mercury conjunct Saturn (occurring Aug. 13 – 17) Mercury conjunct Saturn will bring talk about putting an end to the useless or unwanted components of our lives. When occurring in Virgo, this conjunction implies that strong rules or guidelines will be established with regard to business communications, and also health related restrictions and disciplines will be communicated. There is a discerning quality at work with Mercury conjunct Saturn, making this aspect a very good one for speakers and writers to inspire, initiate and capture vital thoughts. News concerning the end of a cycle is likely to occur. Examples include retirement announcements, job loss, and possibly even the news of a notable death. Overall, Mercury conjunct Saturn tends to bring out a strong tone of seriousness in communications. There is a restriction, a discipline, a carefully considered emphasis of thoughts placed on our communications, and there is a serious intent to get the word across in no uncertain terms. Governments and corporations may make new and restrictive proclamations for order. There is the strong implication at work that we must be seriously responsible for what we say, particularly around authority and in official public statements. "Anything you say can and will be used against you..."

August 16th Saturday
FULL MOON in AQUARIUS – Partial Lunar Eclipse

	PDT	EDT	
Moon conjunct Neptune	11:22 AM	2:22 PM	
Moon opposite Sun	2:15 PM	5:15 PM	
Venus trine Jupiter	5:15 PM	8:15 PM	
Moon sextile Pluto goes v/c	10:13 PM	1:13 AM	(August 17)
Mars square Pluto	11:15 PM	2:15 AM	(August 17)

Mood Watch: The **Full Moon in Aquarius** (Moon opposite Sun) enlivens our senses with the need to apply clarity and definition. The mood of the day is likely to be blanketed in bizarre and unusual occurrences, and it's often focused on modern technological breakthroughs and invention. People may seem idealistic and generous in some respects of this lunar expression, or out of hand and downright unrealistic in others. This is a good time to celebrate knowledge.

Today, a **Partial Lunar Eclipse in Aquarius** brings an emphasis on the needs of humanity and the systems by which mankind operates. This may be a time of technological glitches or vicarious breakthroughs. There may also be some form of inspiration or liberating change as a result of intense scrutiny at the way systems operate. For some, the act of thinking comprehensively may be overshadowed by the lunar eclipse energy. This is a good time to pace ourselves.

Venus trine Jupiter (occurring Aug. 14 – 18) Love (Venus) is harmoniously placed with prosperity and opportunity (Jupiter). Venus in Virgo trine Jupiter in Capricorn brings pure and wholesome affection that inspires serious, undemonstrative – but abiding – prosperity. Under this influence, love may grow and expand in practical and secure ways. This is a great time to give gifts of love and, for many people, it offers an expansive outlook. Without love in your life and a love for what you are doing, an expanding empire will eventually lose its luster. Venus trine Jupiter reminds us fortune can be realized with simple aesthetics and quality moments. This aspect last occurred May 15 – 20, reaching its exact peak on May 18, when Venus was in Taurus.

Mars square Pluto (occurring Aug. 12 – 21) Mars in Virgo square Pluto in Sagittarius brings carefully premeditated battles over the seemingly unchangeable realities of global power structures. Mars emphasizes all forms of action while Pluto represents the transformational powers of destiny. These two planets in the square position spell out the potential for trouble with regard to our actions. Strong disputes and war related action between generations, and among those of different cultures, are likely to occur. This aspect does imply a more likely time for an attack from groups seeking to take power, but with such attacks there will be struggles. These actions against or conflicts with higher powers are likely to backfire – it is best not to bluff those of a higher or unanticipated authority at this time, as taking action in an attempt to create a transformation may be very dangerous. This may be a particularly difficult time to fight addiction, disease, and war related stress – it is also the most crucial time not to give up the fight. Thankfully, this is the only time this year we will have to endure the Mars square Pluto experience.

158

August 17th Sunday

Moon in Aquarius / Pisces

	PDT	EDT
Moon enters Pisces	12:47 AM	3:47 AM
Mercury trine Jupiter	6:23 PM	9:23 PM
Moon opposite Saturn	6:46 PM	9:46 PM
Sun trine Pluto begins (see August 20)		

Mood Watch: A dreamy, rather psychic expression of awareness takes place with Moon in Pisces. Throughout the day moods remain somewhat spacey, very clairvoyant, and quite artistic and full of belief, prayer, and meditation. The Pisces Moon, although now waning, remains in essence very full. For some, this may be a highly emotional time requiring the release of emotional expression. Be aware of the tendency towards escapism and of people seeking to indulge their fantasy world or addictions.

Mercury trine Jupiter (occurring Aug. 15 – 19) Mercury gets the message out there, the trine aspect brings gifts and positive breakthroughs, and Jupiter brings prosperity. This most favorable aspect brings good news of expansion and prosperity to those who are open to broadening their awareness. Ask and you shall have! Mercury in Virgo trine Jupiter in Capricorn brings carefully perfected words which can lead to a gold mine of happiness and wellbeing. This is an excellent time to learn new skills that will improve one's livelihood and better one's outlook. This is also a great time for salespeople to make sales, and for everyone to advertise and put information out there. For some folks, Mercury trine Jupiter is an advantageous time to ask for a job or a loan, or to provide a service that may have a bearing on a potential promotion. Look openly for opportunity when sharing information, and promote yourself and your capabilities. This aspect last occurred April 26 – 29, reaching its exact peak on April 28, when Mercury was in Taurus.

August 18th Monday

Moon in Pisces

	PDT	EDT
Moon sextile Jupiter	1:00 AM	4:00 AM
Moon opposite Mercury	1:58 AM	4:58 AM
Moon opposite Venus	4:25 AM	7:25 AM
Moon conjunct Uranus	4:12 PM	7:12 PM

Mood Watch: The Pisces Moon puts us in touch with our beliefs. As the stardust of the Full Ecliptic Aquarius Moon now settles, today's Moon in Pisces has some intense features. The Moon wanes as it sides with Uranus. Yesterday the Moon was opposite to Saturn, meanwhile, today the Moon opposes Mercury and Venus, and tomorrow the Moon will oppose Mars. All this lunar opposition energy aids us as it brings the reaction, response, attraction, and action that is reflective of our keenly heightened moods. As the Moon in Pisces opposes so many planets in Virgo, our mood patterns are synchronized by the immense change that Uranus activity demands. Here we learn the tender art of siding with chaos and accepting its challenges while we attempt to make sense of it.

August 19th Tuesday

Moon in Pisces / Aries

	PDT	EDT
Mars enters Libra	3:03 AM	6:03 AM
Moon square Pluto goes v/c	4:20 AM	7:20 AM
Moon enters Aries	7:10 AM	10:10 AM
Moon opposite Mars	7:21 AM	10:21 AM

Mood Watch: A somewhat spacey early morning fog captures the mood as the Pisces Moon goes void-of-course for a few hours. It isn't long before the Aries Moon kicks our moods into action. This will be an action-packed Tuesday, full of vibrant, willful, energy.

Mars enters Libra (Mars in Libra: Aug. 19 – Oct. 3) Mars in Libra now focuses more heat on the necessity for harmony in relationships. Heated energy will be directed to law related matters – particularly domestic disputes. Mars in Libra is often considered a detrimental position for the planet, especially given that Mars, the planet of war, is in the sign opposite to Aries, the place it rules. Libra folks will have an abundance of hot energy during this time, and will be quick to settle matters to the full extent of the law – matters that may disrupt the Libra's personal sense of harmony. Beware Libra people; with Mars in your sign, you may also be susceptible to fevers, accidents, or temper tantrums. Remember Mars represents activity; don't waste this energy with indecision. Now is the time to work towards making peace. When discord seems evident among loved ones, it is best to try to defuse and creatively redirect anger before irrational actions become a source of regret. Look for the signs of relationship trouble, anticipate trouble before it happens, and actively divert potential trouble – these are some of the best ways to manage the Mars-in-Libra days. It may be best, though difficult, to be a careful observer, but to withhold judgments about relationships right now.

August 20th Wednesday

Moon in Aries

	PDT	EDT	
Moon square Jupiter	6:14 AM	9:14 AM	
Moon sextile Neptune	10:58 PM	1:58 AM	(August 21)
Sun trine Pluto	11:50 PM	2:50 AM	(August 21)

Venus opposite Uranus begins (see August 23)
Jupiter trine Saturn begins (see September 8 and November 21)

Mood Watch: Sun in Leo and Moon in Aries emphasize the power of selfhood. This is indeed a time when selfhood is touched upon, and our general moods are based on our own personal needs, as well as the needs of those who are pushy or powerful enough to come first! Avoid butting heads if that's not what you're looking for, since it's very easy to do on a waning Aries Moon.

Sun trine Pluto (occurring Aug. 17 – 24) Positive, life-altering changes are occurring in the lives of Leo and Virgo cusp born people celebrating birthdays this year from August 17 – 24. They are currently undergoing the favorable trine aspect of Pluto to their natal Sun, bringing out experiences that involve transformation and encounters with greater powers and fate. It is always difficult to speculate just how the Pluto experience will manifest itself. Have no fear; this is a time to get in touch with your power, birthday Leos and Virgos! Pluto moves slowly in our cosmos, and powerful encounters that seem deadly or harsh are actually a necessary part of the process. Matters involving fate can be positive, and the trine aspect does represent a gift being bestowed – however unlikely it may seem. Be grateful this trine brings power issues into your life in a more positive fashion, leading to positive transformation. Finding out how to benefit from this power is a big part of discovering Pluto's gifts. This aspect last occurred April 17 – 23, reaching its exact peak on April 20, affecting the Aries/Taurus cusp born folks of that time.

August 21st Thursday

Moon in Aries / Taurus

	PDT	EDT
Mercury conjunct Venus	8:45 AM	11:45 AM
Moon trine Pluto	9:10 AM	12:10 PM
Moon trine Sun goes v/c	9:52 AM	12:52 PM
Moon enters Taurus	11:38 AM	2:38 PM
Mercury opposite Uranus begins (see August 22)		

Mood Watch: Early in the day, the Aries Moon goes void-of-course for a short while, and this may be a time of impatient behavior due to long lines, heavy traffic, and similar obstacles. As the Moon enters Taurus, our moods may appear more cautious, thorough and logical, rather than quick. A truthful, resolute mentality brings resilience to our moods as we steadily take care of business throughout the day and move on swiftly towards evening comforts.

Mercury conjunct Venus (occurring Aug. 14 – Sept. 19) Today's conjunction of Mercury and Venus takes place in the practical and reserved realm of Virgo. This is often a time when intimate and loving thoughts are shared with subtle or shy affection. With this aspect, loving gestures are usually very sincere and genuine. There may be a tendency for love related communication to seem somewhat reserved, or overly internalized, although the need to communicate love is definitely there. This aspect last occurred June 5 – 9, reaching its exact peak on June 7. It also occurred earlier this year, February 22 – March 31, reaching two exact peaks on February 26 and March 24. This aspect will reach its final peak one more time, on September 14, before Mercury (the communicator) releases its embrace (the conjunction), with Venus (the lover). By September, Mercury and Venus will no longer be in Virgo, they will be in Libra, the sign of harmony and balance.

VIRGO

Key Phrase: " I ANALYZE "

Mutable Earth Sign

Symbol: The Virgin

August 22nd through

September 22nd

August 22nd Friday

Moon in Taurus

	PDT	EDT	
Moon trine Saturn	5:22 AM	8:22 AM	
Moon trine Jupiter	9:51 AM	12:51 PM	
Sun enters Virgo	11:02 AM	2:02 PM	
Mercury opposite Uranus	11:13 PM	2:13 AM	(August 23)
Moon trine Venus	11:32 PM	2:32 AM	(August 23)

Mood Watch: The waning Taurus Moon inspires us to appreciate the beauty and the comforts all around us. The summer Sun crosses the line from the Sun-ruled sign, Leo, to the Mercury-ruled sign, Virgo. A series of lunar trines brings a couple of joyous days.

Sun enters Virgo (Sun in Virgo: Aug. 22 – Sept. 22) Virgo's key phrase is "I analyze," and the pragmatic spirit of Virgo examines all avenues of life. It is just like Virgo to pick everything apart, detail by detail, and yet Virgo strives to get as much of an overview of the whole picture as possible. Virgo questions, Virgo doubts, and Virgo demands proof. The Mercury ruled mutable sign of earth is keen, sharp-witted, and not so quick to believe any sort of random information, unless it's painstakingly researched by some reputable sources. Virgo will question the source every time. Virgos are famous for their ability to count, calculate, and measure everything that must be accounted for, which is why Virgo is chosen to watch over the vital and bountiful harvest season.

Mercury opposite Uranus (occurring Aug. 21 – 24) Mercury in Virgo opposes Uranus in Pisces. Explosive events under discussion are testing our ability to trust or be convinced. Many will approve openly but will still maintain a healthy dose of skepticism. Ideas may seem bigger than life, and talk seems to focus on concepts which have not been fully grasped, but appear to be presented with assured confidence. Shocking or liberating statements tend to come out with this aspect. There is an acute awareness of the need to speak out for freedom, and the dialogue may appear sharp; radical and sometimes vulgar language may erupt. Outrageous claims and verbal presumptions made at this time may bring fiery or irrational flare-ups in discussion groups and chat rooms. This is a really good time to watch your mouth. Fortunately, this only occurs once this year.

August 23rd Saturday
Moon in Taurus / Gemini – LAST QUARTER MOON in GEMINI ♍

	PDT	EDT
Moon sextile Uranus	12:21 AM	3:21 AM
Moon trine Mercury	12:30 AM	3:30 AM
Moon square Neptune goes v/c	2:19 AM	5:19 AM
Venus opposite Uranus	8:48 AM	11:48 AM
Moon enters Gemini	2:49 PM	5:49 PM
Moon square Sun	4:49 PM	7:49 PM
Moon trine Mars	7:52 PM	10:52 PM

Mood Watch: The **Last Quarter Moon in Gemini** (Moon square Sun) brings talkative moods and informative interaction. People will have a lot on their minds today and intellectual pursuits are emphasized. This is the time to enjoy games, puzzles, and social conversations. Waning Gemini Moon is a good time to release frustrating and confusing mixed emotions. Ease the mind by not using it so much to stir those emotions!

Venus opposite Uranus (occurring Aug. 20 – 25) Venus in Virgo opposes Uranus in Pisces. Prudent love is tested by radical beliefs. Conflict may surface as love relationships are tested by fundamental differences of belief or by drug related problems. On the up side, exciting and unusual kinds of pleasure bring radical new awareness. On the down side, this type of love is explosive in nature, creating radical obsessions – some healthy and some not. Although they are often short lived, this aspect allows for unusual, exciting, and torrid love affairs. This is a good time for artists to make breakthroughs and for eccentric expressions of affection. Issues of freedom are likely to be raised in love related disputes. Strong psychic connections will occur more rapidly, invoking hypersensitivity that could easily get out of hand. No matter how you look at it, issues of love are surely being activated with a broadening sense of awareness.

August 24th Sunday
Moon in Gemini

	PDT	EDT
Moon square Saturn	8:42 AM	11:42 AM

Mood Watch: Sun in Virgo and Moon in Gemini puts the focus on business details and strategies. Varied viewpoints and perspectives will arise today. Both Virgo and Gemini are ruled by Mercury, the famous messenger of the gods. It's all in the message and how that message is received and reciprocated. This is a good time to feed the brain, and to get as much rest as possible – tomorrow's long day of the Moon in Gemini may seem much more nerve-racking than we might expect.

August 25th Monday

Moon in Gemini / Cancer

	PDT	EDT	
Moon square Uranus	2:51 AM	5:51 AM	
Moon trine Neptune	4:50 AM	7:50 AM	
Moon square Venus	6:56 AM	9:56 AM	
Moon square Mercury	9:02 AM	12:02 PM	
Moon opposite Pluto goes v/c	2:52 PM	5:52 PM	
Moon enters Cancer	5:19 PM	8:19 PM	
Moon sextile Sun	10:58 PM	1:58 AM	(August 26)
Mercury square Pluto begins (see August 27)			

Mood Watch: Due to a number of square aspects, the Gemini Moon brings challenging morning moods. We may be challenged by how we think and how we communicate. For a time, the waning Gemini Moon goes void-of-course, and talk may seem somewhat senseless. This evening, as the Moon enters Cancer, we are reminded of the need to give motherly affection where it is needed. Avoid the compulsive overeating of junk foods, thoughts fuelled by fears, and stop trying to make sense where senselessness reigns supreme. Domestic comforts and nourishing foods will help to alleviate the pressure.

August 26th Tuesday

Moon in Cancer

	PDT	EDT
Moon square Mars	12:42 AM	3:42 AM
Moon sextile Saturn	11:34 AM	2:34 PM
Moon opposite Jupiter	2:46 PM	5:46 PM
Venus square Pluto begins (see August 29)		

Mood Watch: Cancer Moon reminds us to address emotional currents. Nurturing love is essential at this time, as motherly love and attention are strongly emphasized. This can be done so effectively with a hug, either a symbolic hug to yourself, or literal hugs to all those important folks around you who need some extra reassurance. This will be a good day to handle numerous domestic affairs and to cover a lot of ground.

August 27th Wednesday

Moon in Cancer / Leo

	PDT	EDT
Moon trine Uranus	5:11 AM	8:11 AM
Moon sextile Venus	2:10 PM	5:10 PM
Moon sextile Mercury goes v/c	5:13 PM	8:13 PM
Mercury square Pluto	6:37 PM	9:37 PM
Moon enters Leo	7:51 PM	10:51 PM

Mood Watch: The waning Cancer Moon encourages our moods to work out the unsettled parts of our emotional stability. This is a time to recognize the importance of letting people's moodiness run a natural course without taking personal offense. Tonight, the Moon goes void-of-course for less than a couple of hours. Despite the moodiness, take this time to nurture yourself and those you care for with homey gestures of love. As the Moon enters Leo, self-assurance and affection wins the heart of the mood.

Mercury square Pluto (occurring Aug. 25 – 29) Mercury in Virgo is square to Pluto in Sagittarius. Scrutiny and doubt make it difficult to communicate with those of another generation. This is a particularly difficult time to deal with burdensome issues and discuss them in a manner that relieves tension. Mercury square Pluto often brings harsh and sometimes fatal news. Talk revolves around the corruption of superpowers and the setbacks caused by this corruption. This may be a particularly difficult time to discuss matters involving permanent change. This aspect last occurred on April 1 – 4, reaching its peak on April 3, when Mercury was in Aries and Pluto was in Capricorn.

August 28th Thursday
Moon in Leo

	PDT	EDT
Moon sextile Mars	5:44 AM	8:44 AM
Mercury enters Libra	7:52 PM	10:52 PM

Mood Watch: This Leo Moon day brings the expression of playfulness and the need to keep life interesting and entertaining. Late August Leo Moon instills the need to get the very best out of summer, and to indulge the senses in something delicious, appeasing, and completely satisfying. Do something good for yourself today.

Mercury enters Libra (Mercury in Libra: Aug. 28 – Nov. 4) Mercury in Libra aligns us with diplomacy, tact, and the need to connect with friends and loved ones. Libra is the autumn sign that emphasizes balance and adjustment. Today through November 4, Mercury in Libra will bring a focus on harmonizing with the changing season. This is a good time for people to communicate by gathering important information, as our decision making process kicks into high gear. Due to the retrograde pattern of Mercury this autumn (Sept. 23 – Oct. 15), Mercury will remain in Libra for an extended period of time.

August 29th Friday
Moon in Leo

	PDT	EDT	
Venus square Pluto	2:51 AM	5:51 AM	
Moon opposite Neptune	10:14 AM	1:14 PM	
Moon trine Pluto goes v/c	8:44 PM	11:44 PM	
Moon enters Virgo	11:19 PM	2:19 AM	(August 30)

Mood Watch: Sun in Virgo and Moon in Leo calls us to find a practical outlet for creative skills, public recognition, encouragement and appreciation. As the Moon wanes in Leo and eventually goes void-of-course, we must beware of a tendency to tackle too much for our own wellbeing. By this evening, introspection becomes more grounding as we reach the balsamic phase (darkest stage) of the Moon, set to be a New Moon in Virgo tomorrow. Tonight, we can expect to see our moods become more cautious, yet we are instinctually willing to communicate our doubts.

Venus square Pluto (occurring Aug. 26 – 31) Venus is in Virgo squaring to Pluto in Sagittarius. Love is sometimes confronted with sheer madness. Often, with this aspect, something valuable and pure is being corrupted or trampled on by another generation's way of thinking and behaving. Venus square Pluto can involve such difficulties as loss or death of a loved one, and it challenges our attachments to

165

many things in life we hold dear. If something of this nature is occurring to you, it is best to recognize love will triumph in every dimension despite the pain that life inevitably brings. Denying these processes of life (rejection, death, disease and loss) is to prolong pain and delay the necessary transformations we must make. As with any hardship, acceptance comes with time. Let the obstacles of love's pain become building blocks towards a better outlook; stronger love will supersede the current trials of the heart. This aspect last occurred April 4 – 9, reaching its exact peak on April 6, when Venus was in Aries.

August 30th Saturday
Moon in Leo / Virgo – NEW MOON in VIRGO

	PDT	EDT	
Venus enters Libra	7:41 AM	10:41 AM	
Moon conjunct Sun	12:58 PM	3:58 PM	
Moon conjunct Saturn	7:21 PM	10:21 PM	
Moon trine Jupiter	9:31 PM	12:31 AM	(August 31)

Mood Watch: The **New Moon in Virgo** (Moon conjunct Sun) invites us to start all over again with the growing process of our feelings. New Moon in Virgo calls to our feelings to apply a new form of skepticism, a new way of analyzing, and to apply caution. How about a new way of accounting? Or a new set of health practices? School season will soon come, and children experience this practice of preparing for the new by acquiring and contemplating new school supplies and learning tools. New Virgo Moon prepares us for the changes that occur around us in the physical world.

Venus enters Libra (Venus in Libra: Aug. 30 – Oct. 18) Venus enters Libra and now the course of magnetism, affection and feminine perception begins to focus on harmonizing and balancing relationships, marriages, and friendships. Venus will be in Libra today through October 18, stimulating our Libra friends with a strong sense of affection, and focusing our love relationships towards the goal of creating a more harmonized and balanced state of being. Venus is at home in Libra, and brings out a love of libraries, of scholarly works, and there is a greater attraction to large bodies of information. Venus in Libra emphasizes the love of books, education, law and order, friends and loved ones, and particularly, a love and desire for balance wherever possible. As late summer continues, our nesting instincts grow deeper, and relationships that aren't stable enough to undergo the responsibilities and tests of autumn are likely to break off, as Venus in Libra strives to apply diplomacy as tactfully as possible. As for the delicacy of love matters, in order to settle on the best choices and decisions possible, Libra strives hard to apply a great wealth of knowledge, common law, history, and helpful information with regard to relation-ships. Attraction is a mystery; Libra seeks to decode the mystery.

August 31st Sunday

Moon in Virgo

	PDT	EDT
Moon opposite Uranus	12:44 PM	3:44 PM

Sun conjunct Saturn begins (see September 3)

Mood Watch: New feelings about organization and making important connections persistently emerge with the freshly waxing Virgo Moon. This is the time to enjoy the fruits of summer and take in healthy foods as well as implementing more thorough health practices. Astute thoughts and feelings blend together to create a mood of resourcefulness and caution. Today's thriftiness and persistence bring great end-of-the-month deals.

September 1st Monday

Labor Day, USA / Labour Day, Canada

Moon in Virgo / Libra

	PDT	EDT
Moon square Pluto goes v/c	2:02 AM	5:02 AM
Moon enters Libra	4:45 AM	7:45 AM
Moon conjunct Venus	9:23 AM	12:23 PM
Moon conjunct Mercury	1:56 PM	4:56 PM
Moon conjunct Mars	8:58 PM	11:58 PM

Sun trine Jupiter begins (see September 4)

Mood Watch: September opens with the waxing Moon in Libra; it's all about making adjustments and finding that quintessential balance between friends, loved ones and partners. The Libra Moon is conjunct with Venus, Mercury, and Mars today and our moods are touched by the need for partnership, a sense of connection or communication with others, and our moods are also touched by the need to take action.

September 2nd Tuesday

Ramadan begins (ends October 1)

Moon in Libra

	PDT	EDT	
Moon trine Neptune	10:23 PM	1:23 AM	(September 3)

Mars square Jupiter begins (see September 7)
Mercury conjunct Mars begins (see September 8 and 23)

Mood Watch: The youthfully waxing Libra Moon gears up our moods toward wrapping up the affairs of last month and preparing for the autumn season ahead in these busy final weeks of summer. This is a good time to review decisions that have to be made and to work towards making adjustments and compromises with others. Harmony and peace abound.

September 3rd Wednesday

Moon in Libra / Scorpio

	PDT	EDT
Moon sextile Pluto goes v/c	10:09 AM	1:09 PM
Moon enters Scorpio	1:02 PM	4:02 PM
Sun conjunct Saturn	6:59 PM	9:59 PM

Mood Watch: This morning brings the harmonizing effects of the final hours of the

167

Libra Moon. For a couple of hours the Moon goes void-of-course, creating a time of indecision and occasional confusion. This afternoon the Moon enters Scorpio, and our moods are intensified with the compelling draw of undaunted passion.

Sun conjunct Saturn (occurring Aug. 31 – Sept. 7) This occurrence of Sun conjunct Saturn in Virgo especially affects those Virgo people celebrating birthdays August 31– September 7. These birthday people are experiencing a perfect time to focus on change. Saturn is also reminding you birthday folks to take charge of your life more responsibly, and to recognize the importance of your limitations. Maybe it's time for an overhaul, Virgo – at least until certain areas of your life become more comfortable again. Saturn is urging you to connect with a sound dose of responsibility that fits your lifestyle and energy level. This may be the time to tune into the body and give it what it needs, and to deal succinctly with health matters. This year, it may be best for these birthday Virgos to incorporate a healthy exercise and diet routine that is fun and effective. Don't be so hard on yourself either, Virgo; try to remember to reward yourself throughout this year with each measure of your progress – it's good for the soul. Make up for lost time, and apply some self-love and nurturing to your renewed self-discipline. Hang in there and keep up the work, birthday folks, and don't be so glum; the tedious work in which you are now immersed will bring you genuine rewards later on. You'll see. Note: Just a year and a day ago, Saturn entered Virgo. Now, Saturn is a considerable distance (nearly 12 degrees) through the constellation of Virgo; Saturn will enter Libra on October 29, 2009.

September 4th Thursday

Moon in Scorpio

	PDT	EDT
Sun trine Jupiter	10:41 AM	1:41 PM
Moon sextile Saturn	12:25 PM	3:25 PM
Moon sextile Jupiter	1:29 PM	4:29 PM
Moon sextile Sun	1:44 PM	4:44 PM

Mood Watch: The waxing Scorpio Moon sets the tone of mood with a sense of urgency and drama. The many sextile aspects of the Moon make this a positive and promising day. Scorpio Moon opens up such rich emotional issues as birth, sex, death, and transformation.

Sun trine Jupiter (occurring September 1 – 7) Virgo people celebrating a birthday from September 1 – 7 are undergoing a favorable natal solar position with relation to Jupiter. This will be a time of gifts and expansion for these birthday folks, and there are good times ahead for them in the coming year. This aspect will bring a better sense of what it means to expand and attain one's personal desire. This is especially good news for those Virgos who are experiencing the challenging struggle to maintain life with the conjunction of Saturn to their natal sun *(see: September 3, Sun conjunct Saturn)*. Be sure to take the time right now, Virgo birthday people, to enjoy and appreciate life. Despite control issues or struggles, life will definitely improve for those who are being given the gifts of joy this aspect often brings. This aspect last occurred May 9 – 15, reaching peak on May 12, when the Sun was in Taurus.

September 5th Friday

♍

Moon in Scorpio

	PDT	EDT
Moon trine Uranus	6:08 AM	9:08 AM
Moon square Neptune goes v/c	8:45 AM	11:45 AM
Mercury square Jupiter begins (see September 7)		

Mood Watch: Early this morning, the final hours of the Scorpio Moon bring swiftness to our moods. Then all too soon, the Moon goes void-of-course and many aspects of our moods appear to come to a grinding halt. Insecurity, jealousy, and sneaky underhandedness may be some of the less desirable symptoms of this endless void-of-course Moon day. Stay alert today, and avoid falling victim to petty crimes.

September 6th Saturday

Moon in Scorpio / Sagittarius

	PDT	EDT	
Moon enters Sagittarius	12:11 AM	3:11 AM	
Moon sextile Venus	6:34 PM	9:34 PM	
Moon sextile Mercury	11:19 PM	2:19 AM	(September 7)
Venus conjunct Mars begins (see September 11)			

Mood Watch: While the last weeks of summer wind down to a close, the general moods of this day and night are winding up with a fiery fervor. Our moods now shift towards a restless inquisitiveness and visionary awareness as the Sagittarius Moon waxes. Sports and outdoor activities are emphasized and there is a need to push beyond the usual bounds and explore.

September 7th Sunday

FIRST QUARTER MOON in SAGITTARIUS

	PDT	EDT	
Moon sextile Mars	12:42 AM	3:42 AM	
Moon square Saturn	1:01 AM	4:01 AM	
Moon square Sun	7:04 AM	10:04 AM	
Mars square Jupiter	2:05 PM	5:05 PM	
Moon square Uranus	6:18 PM	9:18 PM	
Moon sextile Neptune	9:02 PM	12:02 AM	(September 8)
Jupiter goes direct	9:17 PM	12:17 AM	(September 8)
Mercury square Jupiter	10:10 PM	1:10 AM	(September 8)
Venus square Jupiter begins (see September 9)			

Mood Watch: Moon in Sagittarius puts the emphasis on such endeavors as travel and vision quests. With this visionary process comes the desire to expand. While the Virgo sun reminds us to budget our resources for the coming of the changing season, Sagittarius Moon reminds us to reach out there while the brilliant beauty of summer is still happening. Pace yourself today; the many square aspects of the Moon imply there will be complex struggles throughout the afternoon and evening.

Mars square Jupiter (occurring Sept. 2 – 12) When Mars squares Jupiter, various activities are met with the obstacles of economic oppression and shortfall. This is a very difficult time to excel in business endeavors, especially in actively trading

169

markets. This aspect warns us that there will be trouble when approaching the job market aggressively. Trying to make progress using headstrong attitudes and unwarranted self-confidence might impede progress. This aspect brings no-nonsense demands or increases in our workload. Mars in Libra suggests the need for aggressive law enforcement, which is likely to become expensive while Mars is square to Jupiter. Difficulties may arise from bold competitive moves that may end up looking like corporate takeovers. Jupiter is in Capricorn, focusing on the expansion of wealth through corporate industry, agriculture, and career development. The square aspect of these two planets creates a challenging dynamic in the struggle to grow economically. Expect to work a lot harder and perhaps a lot longer in order to smooth the rough edges of the financial empire while Mars in Libra squares Jupiter in Capricorn. Fortunately for us, this aspect only occurs once this year.

Jupiter goes direct (Jupiter direct: Sept. 7, 2008 – June 14, 2009) Since May 9, Jupiter has been retrograde in the sign of Capricorn Let us celebrate as the planet Jupiter moves forward! Jupiter represents skill, fortune, luck, wealth, expansion, well being, and joviality; it's also associated with advancement, prosperity, opportunity, fulfillment, and inheritance. The process of Jupiter retrograde is sometimes difficult for systems, and for the predictability of economic growth, such as business and market control. Jupiter has been in Capricorn since December 18, 2007, emphasizing advancements in such Capricorn related things as big business, agriculture, and career enhancement. Jupiter engages one with a sense of happiness and fulfillment. Now that Jupiter goes direct, advancement goes from an internalized process to an externalized process, which is how Jupiter operates best. Blessed are the Capricorn people, as the prosperity planet, Jupiter, has been and will continue to be sweeping through Capricorns' personal realm, giving them the opportunities and tools for growth needed to advance, and also bestowing a sense of joy. Next year will be Aquarius' year to identify with prosperity and happiness, as Jupiter enters the sign of Aquarius on January 7, 2009.

Mercury square Jupiter (occurring Sept. 5 – 10) This aspect may bring discussions or complaints which revolve around the difficulties of getting funds or capital to grow. Mercury is in Libra squaring to Jupiter in Capricorn, and this may be a difficult time to make breakthroughs with even the most balanced types of investments, to get extensions for business contracts. This aspect sometimes creates a difficult relationship between the communications industry and the sponsors of expansive production. The block in this energy flow occurs between the powers of Mercury represented as the salesman, informant, or negotiator, and the powers of Jupiter represented as the sources that allow wealth to flow (i.e., the manufacturer, banker, fund raiser, etc.) This is the place where value is realized and assessed, and the potential for growth is emphasized, but a whole lot of effort will be required to work through the obstacles. This aspect last occurred April 11 – 14, and it reached its peak on April 13. Due to the retrograde patterns of Mercury, this aspect will reoccur on two more occasions; October 4 – 9, reaching its exact aspect peak on October 6, and, October 23 – 28, reaching its exact aspect on October 26. Mercury will also be in Libra during those times.

September 8th Monday

♍

Moon in Sagittarius / Capricorn

	PDT	EDT
Moon conjunct Pluto goes v/c	5:42 AM	8:42 AM
Mercury conjunct Mars	10:47 AM	1:47 PM
Moon enters Capricorn	12:45 PM	3:45 PM
Jupiter trine Saturn	4:18 PM	7:18 PM
Pluto goes direct	8:14 PM	11:14 PM

Mood Watch: Early today the Sagittarius Moon goes void-of-course, and it may be easy to go off track and get lost at some point. Later today, as the Moon enters Capricorn, our moods are tempered by the necessity to get things done. A productive time has come.

Mercury conjunct Mars (occurring Sept. 2 – 26) This aspect brings the forces of communication (Mercury) together with the forces of action (Mars). This is not a very good time to bluff! This aspect brings words and deeds together, and in this case, the greatest action occurs with communication and is empowered in the expression of the message. This is an excellent aspect to get others motivated through speech. This may also be a time of angry words being spoken. Heated discussions are most likely to occur with this aspect, especially now as these two planets are conjunct in the politically conscientious – and intellectually crafty – sign of Libra. Some might say, the best way to win an argument is to begin by being right; taking this approach during this aspect is likely to win you favors but not friendship. Take caution with your words; if they are intended to incite a battle, this would be a marvelous time to put that message out there! Note: due to Mercury retrograde this month (Sept. 24 – Oct. 15), this aspect will reoccur on September 23. It will also occur for a third time, November 25 – December 2, reaching its exact aspect peak on November 28.

Jupiter trine Saturn (occurring Aug. 20 – Dec. 11) Jupiter in Capricorn is trine Saturn in Virgo. Prudent and safe investments are ideal tools to use at this time. The upcoming season will be the time to take advantage of all kinds of gifts – gifts of skill, opportunity, and perfect timing in business. The fruits of our labor will be rewarded with the enthusiasm and determination created by this most advantageous aspect. Jupiter and Saturn are the two social planets of our solar system. This will serve as an excellent time to enjoy the fruits of our economic growth and to implement sound investments towards future growth. Notoriously, in order to stimulate voter morale, the US presidential election will bring a boom of economic growth in America. This aspect last occurred January 9 – 31, and it reached its peak on January 21. This favorable aspect reaches an exact peak today, and it will also reach another peak again on November 21, before it dissipates completely by December 11.

Pluto goes direct (Pluto direct: Sept. 8, 2008 – April 4, 2009) After the long – but common – retrograde period of Pluto (April 2 – September 8), the planet of transformation now moves into a smooth, direct pattern for the rest of the year. Since April, Pluto has been going back through the late degrees of Sagittarius. Now that it is direct, we can better acknowledge the evolution of humankind's condition in order to survive the challenges that are occurring on planet Earth. This transformation is about consciousness, without which we would not be. This is not a time

171

to take life for granted; rather, it is a time to participate in making life better by consciously transforming fear into determination and despair into belief in oneself. Pluto in Sagittarius (since 1996) is changing both our global community and our awareness of it, transforming our point of view. From January 25 to June 13, Pluto was in Capricorn and inspired a new journey for the generations of mankind. Then on June 13, Pluto entered Sagittarius for the last time in our lifetime, where it currently resides near the cusp of Capricorn. Now that Pluto moves direct, the last days of Pluto in Sagittarius are upon us. To read more about the Pluto transit from Sagittarius to Capricorn, see January 25 and November 26.

September 9th Tuesday

Moon in Capricorn

	PDT	EDT
Venus square Jupiter	1:12 PM	4:12 PM
Moon conjunct Jupiter	1:53 PM	4:53 PM
Moon square Venus	1:58 PM	4:58 PM
Moon trine Saturn	2:06 PM	5:06 PM
Moon square Mars	4:37 PM	7:37 PM
Moon square Mercury	5:40 PM	8:40 PM

Sun opposite Uranus begins (see September 12)

Mood Watch: Today's waxing Capricorn Moon brings the extra determination to tackle this especially busy time – the third day of long-winded aspects. Some things will take longer to do, and we must be persistent to work out the rough edges of the day's moods. That said, today will be much more productive than tomorrow.

Venus square Jupiter (occurring Sept. 7 – 11) Venus in Libra is square to Jupiter in Capricorn. A love for harmony and friendship may be interrupted or challenged by the need to handle such costly economic pursuits as career advancement, business and commerce. Love relationships complicated by difficult money issues may be prevalent. Don't let money matters spoil the beauty of loving affection, but expect the strong possibility that this might well be the case with others. This aspect reminds us that something more than love's blindness is required in order for us to fully realize our riches and the value of what we care about most. Venus square Jupiter last occurred April 21 – 26, reaching its exact peak on April 23, when Venus was in Aries.

September 10th Wednesday

Moon in Capricorn

	PDT	EDT
Moon trine Sun	12:41 AM	3:41 AM
Moon sextile Uranus goes v/c	6:14 AM	9:14 AM

Mood Watch: What a difficult thing a void-of-course Capricorn Moon can be when it is extended for an entire day and night. This Moon is creating a strong need for things to get done, while at the same time, there is little cooperation in the universe to focus on the goals and tasks that require completion. This is a time to remember it is futile to let such setbacks be taken so seriously.

September 11ᵗʰ Thursday

ℳ

Moon in Capricorn / Aquarius

	PDT	EDT
Moon enters Aquarius	12:20 AM	3:20 AM
Venus conjunct Mars	7:05 PM	10:05 PM

Mood Watch: Moon in Aquarius waxes strongly as it brings a focus on knowledge and learning new skills. This is a time of fairs, social endeavors, conventions, as well as philanthropic and fund raising events.

Venus conjunct Mars (occurring Sept. 6 – 17) This aspect brings together the feminine and the masculine in the sign of Libra. Venus conjunct Mars in Libra brings out a tendency towards the ever popular "balancing act," where masculine and feminine counterparts will be attempting to produce harmony on many levels. This conjunction also puts us in touch with the power of love in action and active attraction. This will undoubtedly serve as a good time to express love ardently and sincerely, and to receive love just as well. This is also a good time for an individual to get in touch with both the masculine and feminine aspects of the self, and to create peace between those active and passive parts of the personality. While Venus and Mars are conjunct in Libra, lovers will benefit strongly from the act of sharing and expressing their diplomacy. Having a relationship with masculine and feminine imbalances often requires experimenting with and adopting new activities, or taking action to enliven the dormant aspects of the male and female relationship. In some cases, this conjunction of Venus and Mars in Libra creates an even-tempered energy which leads to a greater appreciation in companionship. This is a time of integration between the feminine and masculine forces – it is best done in stride and with care. Fortunately, the Libra spirit is inclined this way. Masculine expression has less of a chance here, while Mars is in the detrimental position of Libra; however, Venus in Libra is right at home, soothing the feminine approach to diplomacy with a great deal more grace and tact. This is a good time to empower love relationships with the greatest respect. This is the only conjunction of Venus and Mars this year.

September 12ᵗʰ Friday

Moon in Aquarius

	PDT	EDT
Moon trine Mars	6:13 AM	9:13 AM
Moon trine Venus	6:46 AM	9:46 AM
Moon trine Mercury	8:45 AM	11:45 AM
Moon conjunct Neptune	6:27 PM	9:27 PM
Sun opposite Uranus	7:21 PM	10:21 PM

Mood Watch: The general mood on this Aquarius Moon day is positive, outgoing, and eccentric. Thoughts and ideas will be unusual and inspired. This is a good time to enjoy social outings and appreciate the late summer with our most inspired friends and comrades as the Moon waxes towards its fullness in the next few days.

Sun opposite Uranus (occurring Sept. 9 – 15) This occurrence of Sun opposite Uranus particularly affects Virgos celebrating birthdays September 9 – 15. The opposition of Uranus creates an acute awareness of the revolutionary forces in one's life. There will undoubtedly be a lot of chaos, and the challenge (in part) may be to accept the rebel within you, and to persevere through the drastic and edgy discord. This is the time to go with the flow of unusual and unpredictable occurrences. It's also a good time to learn the Tao of chaos, and to understand that this awakening force is enlivening a sense of freedom. The only alternatives are to break through, or to break down if one resists. Survival counts; use your senses and your sensibilities well but do not resist the forces of great change. In the year to come, Uranus in opposition to Virgo will both challenge and strengthen our Virgo (birthday) friends to live a life of freedom. This may be particularly challenging given the fact that Virgos must now face the traverses of Saturn through their natal sun sign. It may seem overwhelming; however, as long these birthday Virgos avoid staying attached to the way things once were, all will be well. All of this might be likened to a Virgo trying to describe, in the most technical terms, just how a dramatic tornado works while simultaneously experiencing it. Uranus opposite the Virgo Sun teaches Virgo the value in allowing for a greater range of possibilities. This will be an exciting and, at times, exhausting year ahead for these Virgo folks.

September 13th Saturday

Moon in Aquarius / Pisces

	PDT	EDT
Moon sextile Pluto goes v/c	6:18 AM	9:18 AM
Moon enters Pisces	9:05 AM	12:05 PM

Mood Watch: This morning our moods and technical equipment may appear to have an unpredictable edge with the Moon void-of-course in Aquarius. Soon enough, the Moon enters Pisces and our moods will become artistic, intuitive, and mystical in nature. Pisces Moon draws many people to the heart of their beliefs and needs. Addictive tendencies may lead to overindulgence. The creative process of performing and enjoying music and fine art is a superb way to celebrate the nearly full Pisces Moon.

September 14th Sunday

Moon in Pisces

	PDT	EDT	
Moon sextile Jupiter	7:55 AM	10:55 AM	
Moon opposite Saturn	9:05 AM	12:05 PM	
Mercury conjunct Venus	6:35 PM	9:35 PM	
Moon conjunct Uranus	10:08 PM	1:08 AM	(September 15)
Venus trine Neptune begins (see September 17)			
Mercury trine Neptune begins (see September 19 and 28)			

Mood Watch: Full Moon Eve in Pisces is a mystical time that brings strong psychic inclinations and a wide range of emotional expression. Dreamy moods will be prevalent throughout the day and evening.

Mercury conjunct Venus (occurring Aug. 14 – Sept. 19) For the fifth and final time this year, Mercury is conjunct with Venus. Today's conjunction of Mercury and Venus takes place in the harmonious and fair-minded realm of Libra. A strong urge to communicate about the things and people we love brings a lyrical time of joyous expressions and open kindness. This is a great time to communicate love or take a love vow. This conjunction previously occurred on August 21, June 7, March 24, and February 26.

September 15ᵗʰ Monday
Moon in Pisces / Aries – FULL MOON in PISCES

	PDT	EDT
Moon opposite Sun	2:12 AM	5:12 AM
Moon square Pluto goes v/c	12:02 PM	3:02 PM
Moon enters Aries	2:40 PM	5:40 PM

Mood Watch: The **Full Moon in Pisces** (Moon opposite Sun) brings out the psychic in everyone. People can be very sensitive, and as a result, some people express themselves in very artistic or perhaps nonsensical manners. Enchantment sets the stage for Full Pisces Moon activity early in the day. This afternoon the Moon goes void-of-course for some time, causing extremely spacey moods. Later as the Moon enters Aries, our moods may become slightly impatient, and many folks may appear somewhat self-absorbed.

September 16ᵗʰ Tuesday
Moon in Aries

	PDT	EDT	
Moon square Jupiter	12:28 PM	3:28 PM	
Moon opposite Mars	10:45 PM	1:45 AM	(September 17)

Mood Watch: The post-full Moon wanes in Aries, bringing out a sense of urgency and evoking the warrior in all of us. This is a time when new projects are developing. This kind of lunar expression brings out a reflection of the self and urges one to look toward their own sense of importance, guidance, and leadership. Self-respect is an acceptable practice for the peaceful warrior.

September 17ᵗʰ Wednesday
Moon in Aries / Taurus

	PDT	EDT
Moon opposite Mercury	1:54 AM	4:54 AM
Moon opposite Venus	4:10 AM	7:10 AM
Moon sextile Neptune	4:25 AM	7:25 AM
Venus trine Neptune	6:58 AM	9:58 AM
Moon trine Pluto goes v/c	3:25 PM	6:25 PM
Moon enters Taurus	5:57 PM	8:57 PM
Sun square Pluto begins (see September 20)		
Mars trine Neptune begins (see September 21)		

Mood Watch: The Aries Moon is a time when selfhood is touched upon and our general moods are based on our own personal needs. Strong lunar aspects keep us busy individually. Later this evening, as the Moon enters Taurus, our moods become preoccupied with the necessity for creature comforts, aesthetics, and basic securities.

Venus trine Neptune (occurring Sept. 14 – 19) Venus in Libra trine Neptune in Aquarius enhances spiritual love. This aspect brings well balanced and generous kinds of love into harmony with a very ingenious kind of spiritual expression. It delivers a calmness and tranquility that are vitally needed, and there is a greater potential to create a spiritually enhanced atmosphere. Wherever there is spiritual turmoil, Venus trine Neptune helps to ease our woes with a support network of feminine kindness. Visiting or meditating upon sacred places and favorite sanctuaries brings visions and inner wisdom. Peaceful, pleasurable, and spiritual love is possible with this aspect, which last occurred June 10 – 15, reaching its exact peak on June 13, when Venus was in Gemini.

September 18ᵗʰ Thursday

Moon in Taurus	PDT	EDT
Moon trine Jupiter	3:19 PM	6:19 PM
Moon trine Saturn	5:07 PM	8:07 PM

Mood Watch: Waning Taurus Moon brings on a cool pace of rummaging through piles of material goods. What we put off doing all summer now needs to be addressed. This is the time to focus on buying important necessities and to clean up the homestead. Earthy focuses are the key today, as the physical realities of this time of year urge us to collect what we need and get to work on making our surroundings comfortable and secure.

September 19ᵗʰ Friday

Moon in Taurus / Gemini	PDT	EDT
Moon sextile Uranus	4:13 AM	7:13 AM
Moon square Neptune	6:49 AM	9:49 AM
Moon trine Sun goes v/c	3:51 PM	6:51 PM
Moon enters Gemini	8:17 PM	11:17 PM
Mercury trine Neptune	8:24 PM	11:24 PM

Mood Watch: While the Sun is in Virgo urging us to be prudent, the Moon is in Taurus reminding us constantly of our imminently pressing needs. This is a time of focus on the material world. Later, when the Taurus Moon goes void-of-course, lazy or tired moods may be evident and traffic will be slow. Tonight's Gemini Moon brings pensive curiosities, and will be a good time to enjoy social gatherings and communications.

Mercury trine Neptune (occurring Sept. 14 – Oct. 2) This is a superb aspect for discussing personal philosophies and metaphysical subjects, and a good time to communicate with the spirit world. Mercury trine Neptune brings gifts of encouraging news from Spirit. Out of the upheaval will come a much needed boon. Those who are open to communication and prayer will have a spiritual channel attuned to their hearts and minds where peace and tranquility can be found. Mercury in Libra is trine to Neptune in Aquarius. Diplomacy in speech brings intuitive and uplifting knowledge. Communicate about spiritual needs with helpful counsel and receive gifts of renewed faith in your own beliefs. Recognize that some messages are there to spiritually uplift you. This aspect occurred on two earlier occasions this year; first, May 23 – 29, but it never actually reached an exact trine peak due to Mercury retrograde. It also occurred July 3 – 8, reaching its exact peak on July 6. As Mercury will go retrograde (Sept. 24 – Oct. 15), Mercury trine Neptune will reach a second peak during this cycle on September 28. This aspect will occur one more time, October 27 – 31, reaching its final peak on October 29.

♍

September 20ᵗʰ Saturday
Moon in Gemini

	PDT	EDT
Moon square Saturn	7:52 PM	10:52 PM
Sun square Pluto	8:45 PM	11:45 PM
Venus sextile Pluto begins (see September 22)		

Mood Watch: The Sun is in Virgo and the Moon is in Gemini, and this brings a strong emphasis on communications, organization, and resources. This is the time to make connections with others.

Sun square Pluto (occurring Sept. 17 – 23) This occurrence of Sun square Pluto particularly affects those Virgo and early born Libra cusp people celebrating birthdays from September 17 – 23. For them, Pluto squaring their natal Sun brings disruptive changes and many challenges to overcome, such as the pain of loss and the severity of transformation. These tests often involve illness, irreparable damage, and dramatic life changes. Trying to hold onto the regrets and the pain of the past will only bring greater destruction later. This is the time to persevere through the obstacles of hardship. The hardships that are taking place now will resurface again in time, and that necessitates finding methods of release and of attitude adjustment in order to survive the anxiety and stress. Take it one day at a time, and do not let fear and worry rule you. Know you are not alone in facing these challenges. Move steadily through the required transformation, as stagnation and fear will only bring extended suffering. This aspect last occurred March 17 – 24, reaching its exact peak on March 21, affecting the Pisces/Aries birthday people of that time.

September 21ˢᵗ Sunday
Moon in Gemini / Cancer – LAST QUARTER MOON in GEMINI

	PDT	EDT	
Moon square Uranus	6:27 AM	9:27 AM	
Moon trine Mars	8:35 AM	11:35 AM	
Moon trine Neptune	9:08 AM	12:08 PM	
Moon trine Mercury	10:05 AM	1:05 PM	
Moon trine Venus	6:32 PM	9:32 PM	
Mars trine Neptune	7:56 PM	10:56 PM	
Moon opposite Pluto	8:20 PM	11:20 PM	
Moon square Sun goes v/c	10:04 PM	1:04 AM	(September 22)
Moon enters Cancer	10:49 PM	1:49 AM	(September 22)

Mood Watch: The majority of this morning's lunar aspects are very positive in nature. The **Last Quarter Moon in Gemini** (Moon square Sun) brings talkative moods and informative interaction. People will have a lot on their minds today and intellectual pursuits are emphasized. This is the time to enjoy games, puzzles, and social conversations.

Mars trine Neptune (occurring Sept. 17 – 26) This aspect creates an active trend to empower our beliefs. Mars in Libra is trine to Neptune in Aquarius. Actions taken to create balance will be well received, especially with regards to the necessity of upholding our faith in humanity. This will be an active time of obtaining spiritual gifts and helpful guidelines from the spirit world. Mars guarantees activities will occur, and with Neptune in the trine position, these activities will be favorably stirred up with spiritual and psychic awareness, bringing gifts from Neptune. This serves as a good time to initiate creative and imaginative spiritual practices and ceremonies; to empower the personal outlook and spiritual well being. Mars trine Neptune almost reached a peak earlier this year (Jan. 27 – Feb. 9); see February 1, Mars-trine-Neptune-non-exact.

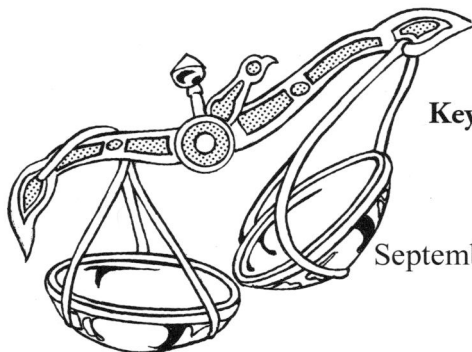

LIBRA

Key Phrase: "I BALANCE"
Cardinal Air Sign
Symbol: The Scales
September 22nd through October 22nd

September 22nd Monday

Autumnal Equinox
Moon in Cancer

	PDT	EDT	
Sun enters Libra	8:45 AM	11:45 AM	
Venus sextile Pluto	3:24 PM	6:24 PM	
Moon opposite Jupiter	8:46 PM	11:46 PM	
Moon sextile Saturn	11:12 PM	2:12 AM	(September 23)

Mood Watch: The Moon is in Cancer and the entire day gears up our senses with deep emotional expressions and focuses our attention on nurturing and instinctual urges. This serves as a good time to brighten up the home and make it feel more comfortable.

Sun enters Libra (Sun in Libra: Sept. 22 – Oct. 22) It's the magical time of Autumnal Equinox. This time of year calls to us to reach out to each other and create a support system and a network of helpful friends to prepare for the busy season ahead and the darker and colder days yet to come. The Sun now enters Libra and this is a Venus ruled sign that focuses our attention on the power of teamwork and partnership. The key phrase for Libra is, "I balance," and the key to Libra's happiness comes with a sense of balance. Another factor to take into account for our Libran friends is the perpetual state of adjustment required to meet that balance. Libra could therefore easily say, "I adjust." The cornucopia of life is

178

full of expressions of harmony and beauty. Libra focuses on libraries and accesses data and knowledge, particularly concerning law. May this new autumn season be pleasurable and fruitful for you and all your loved ones!

♎

Venus sextile Pluto (occurring Sept. 20 – 24) Venus is in Libra focusing on the need for harmony, and for the empowerment of friendship and balance in love matters. Pluto is in Sagittarius allowing us to expand and grow through hardship, to empower our visions, and the visions of the generations to come. It is altering our perception of travel and extreme sports, and expanding our awareness of the diseases and cruelties of the world. There was a time when Pluto, the god of the underworld, seized Persephone, who was a symbol of youth, fertility and Venusian beauty. Many have viewed this myth as a power play on the part of the underworld king. Others view it as the well understood destiny of Beauty and the Beast. Venus sextile Pluto may bring exceptional breakthroughs in relationships. Sometimes the death of a power figure occurs, and the love of that figure is empowered by the impact of their fate. This may be the place where we discover the true power of love. Sometimes this aspect helps us to recognize the devotion of our loved ones, to see the acceptance of the difficulty and hardship that comes with their devotion. This is a good time to recognize and acknowledge the efforts of loved ones. Through this, greater devotion will shine. This aspect may allow someone to find true love by virtue of some unexpected twist of fate. It is here that the beauty and the beast surprise us when, through some form of trial or sacrifice, harmony and strength in love can be found. This aspect occurred earlier this year, March 11 – 15, reaching its peak on March 13, when Venus was in Pisces and Pluto was in Capricorn.

September 23rd Tuesday
Moon in Cancer

	PDT	EDT
Mercury conjunct Mars	3:44 AM	6:44 AM
Moon trine Uranus	9:24 AM	12:24 PM
Moon square Mercury	1:49 PM	4:49 PM
Moon square Mars	2:17 PM	5:17 PM
Moon square Venus goes v/c	8:00 PM	11:00 PM

Mood Watch: Deep feelings run through our moods with a waning Moon in Cancer, and there may be a tendency for some people to be distracted and moody. For the most part, this is simply a time when many of us need a little more reassurance and love, especially during the afternoon and evening when the lunar aspects become more challenging.

Mercury conjunct Mars (occurring Sept. 2 – 26) This Mercury/Mars conjunction first reached its peak on September 8. Now that Mercury is about to go *retrograde (see tomorrow)*, this aspect is repeating for a second time this year. While Mercury is retrograde, communications are likely to be misunderstood, and information that is going around at this time may not only be inaccurate, but is likely to spur some folks to lash out with annoyance or rage. Mercury conjunct Mars in Libra may bring a great deal of legal action, or may create a lot of tension between diplomats and peace negotiators. Take all information with a grain of salt at this time, and attempt to avoid volatile subjects, talk, and discussions. This aspect will reoccur for a third

179

time, November 25 – December 2, reaching its peak on November 28; however, by that time, Mercury and Mars will be in the mutable fire sign, Sagittarius.

September 24th Wednesday

Moon in Cancer / Leo	PDT	EDT
Mercury goes retrograde	12:17 AM	3:17 AM
Moon enters Leo	2:14 AM	5:14 AM
Moon square Venus	2:50 AM	5:50 AM
Moon sextile Sun	5:23 AM	8:23 AM

Mood Watch: The Leo Moon wanes and puts us in touch with the beastly side of our nature. Although we have just entered the autumn season, we still might need to let out the last whooping cries of wild abandon and summertime blues fury. The summer spirit dies hard. Nonetheless, we must begin to rehearse our next moves. The actor in each of us begins to portray new characters in an effort to address the new stage before us. This is a time of change, and today we do what we can to strengthen our self image and honor our choices for the days ahead.

Mercury goes retrograde (Mercury retrograde: Sept. 24 – Oct. 15) Hold on to your thinking caps – today Mercury goes retrograde in Libra until October 15. Mercury retrograde in Libra will likely cause numerous miscommunications between friends and among partners. Negotiations among friends and marital partners may be confusing and frustrating, and it may be difficult to make decisions. Try to give speakers a decent chance before jumping all over their words. Interruptions and tensions are likely to occur during discussions. Peace talks among diplomats may seem useless. Cancellations and postponements of court cases and judicial processes may be prevalent. A key to getting through the Mercury retrograde period is to be attentive to important details, to inquire often, and to listen carefully. For more on Mercury retrograde, see the section in the introduction about *Mercury retrograde periods.*

September 25th Thursday

Moon in Leo	PDT	EDT	
Moon opposite Neptune	4:24 PM	7:24 PM	
Moon sextile Mercury	5:52 PM	8:52 PM	
Moon sextile Mars	9:19 PM	12:19 AM	(September 26)

Mood Watch: The Leo Moon continues to keep us in a state of autumn denial and summer playfulness. This is a good time to focus on family and friends and to work on improving your self-esteem. Leo Moon captivates our moods with childlike play and fun. Don't forget – Mercury is retrograde (see yesterday); it will probably take a few days to adjust to the frequent miscommunications and misunderstandings of this time.

September 26th Friday

Moon in Leo / Virgo

	PDT	EDT
Moon trine Pluto goes v/c	4:20 AM	7:20 AM
Moon enters Virgo	6:53 AM	9:53 AM
Moon sextile Venus	12:44 PM	3:44 PM

Mood Watch: For a short time this morning the waning Leo Moon goes void-of-course, causing our moods to be preoccupied and somewhat beastly. Soon enough, the Moon enters Virgo and shifts our moods into a curious state. The Virgo Moon is ruled by Mercury, the planet of communications. Needless to say, the main issue of the day revolves around the tendency for communications to be inaccurate due to Mercury retrograde. The Virgo Moon will keep us fastidious about correcting our mistakes.

September 27th Saturday

Moon in Virgo

	PDT	EDT
Moon trine Jupiter	6:22 AM	9:22 AM
Moon conjunct Saturn	9:29 AM	12:29 PM
Moon opposite Uranus	6:57 PM	9:57 PM

Mood Watch: Throughout the day, the darkly waning Virgo Moon keeps our moods somewhat skeptical, curious, questioning and communicative. Virgo Moon is a good time to take in healthy foods as well as to implement more thorough health practices. Keeping track of matters and accounting for what's going on is an important part of ringing in the new season. Sun in Libra and Moon in Virgo strongly emphasize making decisions and preparing schedules.

September 28th Sunday

Moon in Virgo / Libra

	PDT	EDT
Mercury trine Neptune	5:19 AM	8:19 AM
Moon square Pluto goes v/c	10:31 AM	1:31 PM
Moon enters Libra	1:06 PM	4:06 PM
Mars sextile Pluto begins (see October 1)		

Mood Watch: This morning our moods may seem testy, affecting our ability to organize. The Moon is void-of-course in Virgo, but not for long. By afternoon the Moon enters Libra, and this brings us to the New Moon eve. The darkly waning Libra Moon brings intense desires to master partnership and friendship. While Mercury is retrograde, we must take extra measures to say the right things and correct our indiscretions.

Mercury trine Neptune (occurring Sept. 14 – Oct. 2) This aspect first occurred May 23 – 29, but it never reached its exact aspect due to Mercury's retrograde movement at that time. Mercury trine Neptune reoccurred two more times this year; first, July 3 – 8, reaching its peak on July 6, and also September 14 – October 2, reaching its second peak on September 19. Today the retrograde Mercury brings this trine with Neptune back to another peak once again. This trine will also occur October 27 – 31, reaching its final peak on October 29. For more information on Mercury in Libra trine Neptune in Aquarius, see September 19.

September 29ᵗʰ Monday

NEW MOON in LIBRA

	PDT	EDT
Moon conjunct Sun	1:13 AM	4:13 AM
Moon square Jupiter	1:44 PM	4:44 PM

Mood Watch: The **New Moon in Libra** (Moon conjunct Sun) is a time of reaffirming and harmonizing our relationships with friends and partners, as well as a time of new friendship as the shift to autumn activities creates a new working environment for many people. New rules also set the standard for how to create a more harmonious environment in the autumn days to come. October is almost here, and the commitment to the unfolding trends of autumn is starting to sink into our mood-set.

September 30ᵗʰ Tuesday

Rosh Hashana

Moon in Libra / Scorpio

	PDT	EDT	
Moon trine Neptune	5:42 AM	8:42 AM	
Moon conjunct Mars	5:20 PM	8:20 PM	
Moon sextile Pluto goes v/c	6:47 PM	9:47 PM	
Moon enters Scorpio	9:27 PM	12:27 AM	(October 1)

Mood Watch: Today's Libra Moon emphasizes the need to make adjustments and work things out with friends and loved ones. The newly waxing Libra Moon brings an excellent time to make decisions and plans, however, be sure to check the facts while Mercury is retrograde. Later tonight, the Scorpio Moon brings extraordinary will-power fuelled by passion.

October 1ˢᵗ Wednesday

Moon in Scorpio

	PDT	EDT	
Moon conjunct Venus	3:54 PM	6:54 PM	
Mars sextile Pluto	9:01 PM	12:01 AM	(October 2)
Moon sextile Jupiter	11:30 PM	2:30 AM	(October 2)

Mood Watch: Scorpio Moon classically brings a strong underlying emotional current to the tone of our moods. This is a time for renewal, or a sharpening of the senses. For many people, a new perspective emerges and there is a better understanding of the transformational processes in their lives.

Mars sextile Pluto (occurring Sept. 28 – Oct. 4) Mars, the planet of action is in a favorable position to Pluto, the planet of the generations. Mars is in the late degrees of Libra sextile to Pluto in the late degrees of Sagittarius. This is a superb time to take up activities with people of a different culture, or with someone who is of a different level of maturity or experience. This is also potentially a good time to reconcile differences. Those who are not in accordance with others at this time are likely to stand out – quite obviously. This may be a beneficial aspect for successfully recuperating from an illness. Mars represents the masculine push of our personal lives, the area where we activate our will, strength, and vitality; this brings opportunity, optimism, and the added boost to face otherwise tense situations and predicaments. The activities of Mars sextile Pluto will teach us about hardships and what we can learn from other generations. Some will make breakthroughs during this time. Some may choose to be more forgiving of the destructive behaviors of previous generations. All around, tender care is advised in your efforts to create peace.

♎

October 2ⁿᵈ Thursday

Moon in Scorpio

	PDT	EDT
Moon sextile Saturn	3:22 AM	6:22 AM
Moon trine Uranus	12:12 PM	3:12 PM
Moon square Neptune goes v/c	3:46 PM	6:46 PM

Mood Watch: The Moon waxes in Scorpio, and our moods become intent on deeper emotional feelings and concerns. A sense of secrecy and cautious suspicion fills the air, and many restless souls are on the prowl to satiate personal desires. Later today the Moon goes void-of-course, and this evening will be a good time to be cautious, patient, and to avoid touching on sensitive subjects that may cause some folks to overreact.

October 3ʳᵈ Friday

Moon in Scorpio / Sagittarius

	PDT	EDT	
Moon enters Sagittarius	8:15 AM	11:15 AM	
Mars enters Scorpio	9:33 PM	12:33 AM	(October 4)
Venus sextile Jupiter begins (see October 5)			
Sun square Jupiter begins (see October 6)			

Mood Watch: Enthusiastic moods brighten our outlook on this new month as the waxing Sagittarius Moon invites us to explore all avenues of possibility.

Mars enters Scorpio (Mars in Scorpio: Oct. 3 – Nov. 16) Mars in Scorpio brings a very passionate and daring edge to our activities. In Scorpio, the execution of activity (Mars) is done with precision and intense clarity. Mars in Scorpio often brings out aggressive acts in people, but not necessarily ones that are cruel or destructive. When tension builds, it is often best to channel aggressive impulses into sports or outdoor activities. Scorpio people will have a lot of extra energy and strength, perhaps even anger or fever, as Mars connects with their natal Sun. Scorpios, use this extra energy constructively.

October 4ᵗʰ Saturday

Moon in Sagittarius

	PDT	EDT
Moon sextile Sun	7:50 AM	10:50 AM
Moon square Saturn	3:52 PM	6:52 PM
Moon sextile Mercury	4:44 PM	7:44 PM
Mercury square Jupiter begins (see October 6)		

Mood Watch: If we are astute and willing to watch for the signs, a vision of the month ahead illuminates our senses. A picture or a vision can be magnified with a positive affirmation. Perfect and empower the vision. Sagittarius Moon is a great time to explore.

183

October 5th Sunday

Moon in Sagittarius / Capricorn

	PDT	EDT	
Moon square Uranus	12:09 AM	3:09 AM	
Venus sextile Jupiter	1:22 AM	4:22 AM	
Moon sextile Neptune	3:55 AM	6:55 AM	
Moon conjunct Pluto goes v/c	6:08 PM	9:08 PM	
Moon enters Capricorn	8:49 PM	11:49 PM	
Moon sextile Mars	11:40 PM	2:40 AM	(October 6)
Sun conjunct Mercury begins (see October 6)			
Venus sextile Saturn begins (see October 6)			

Mood Watch: The waxing Sagittarius Moon keeps us busy exploring and adventuring. Later tonight the Moon enters Capricorn, and a serious or more pensive tone of mood brings the evening to a close. We must be practical; October's storms will come and we must be ready.

Venus sextile Jupiter (occurring Oct. 3 – 6) Venus is in Scorpio where beauty and attraction are emphasized with deep and passionate levels of care and concern. Jupiter is in Capricorn, bringing a powerfully clear and focused sense of adventure and a joyful outreach to discover love's capabilities. A devotion to passion (Venus in Scorpio) leads us to prosperous and rewarding opportunities in careers (Jupiter in Capricorn). This is an excellent time to shower loved ones with gifts and compliments, to allow expansion to occur in love matters, and to take the next step towards enlivening and enhancing life. A greater opportunity for increasing skills or augmenting your livelihood is available, especially if your focus remains on doing what you love most. This aspect last occurred March 26 – 30, reaching its exact peak on March 28, when Venus was in Pisces.

October 6th Monday

Moon in Capricorn

	PDT	EDT	
Sun square Jupiter	9:52 AM	12:52 PM	
Sun conjunct Mercury	1:53 PM	4:53 PM	
Mercury square Jupiter	4:46 PM	7:46 PM	
Venus sextile Saturn	10:42 PM	1:42 AM	(October 7)

Mood Watch: This very busy Monday brings loads of work with the waxing Moon in Capricorn. Numerous aspects bring an especially daunting time for some folks. The Capricorn Moon gives us the edge to carry on without our moods being too affected.

Sun square Jupiter (occurring Oct. 3 – 9) This aspect particularly affects those Libra people celebrating birthdays October 3 – 9. Sun square Jupiter creates difficulties with and obstacles to the personal joy and prosperous welfare of these birthday folks. For these people, getting ahead financially or just staying on top of current trends or financial shifts may be personally challenging right now. Jupiter is in Capricorn, demanding extra effort in our work. To stay on top of financial matters, persistence and determination are essential. Although some Librans are not living as prosperously as they may desire at this time, they do have the ability to come through this and be much better for it. Hang in there, Librans, your hard

184

work will pay off eventually. Obstacles create challenges, but do not necessarily dictate an end to efforts to improve our welfare. It is the Libra personality (Sun) that is being challenged (square aspect) in matters of advancement (Jupiter), requiring Libras to make do with less than they were anticipating. This may be a time to redefine and redirect personal goals, and Libra birthday folks must reexamine what truly brings prosperity for them in their lives. This aspect occurred earlier this year, April 6 – 13, reaching its peak on April 10, affecting the birthday Aries folks of that time. Ω

Sun conjunct Mercury (occurring Oct. 5 – 7) This is the fifth time, out of a half a dozen times, that the Sun will be conjunct with Mercury this year. Today's conjunction will create a much more thoughtful, communicative, and expressive year ahead for those Libra folks celebrating birthdays October 5 – 7. This is your time (birthday Libras) to record ideas, relay important messages, and pay close attention to your imaginative thoughts as they are touched by Mercury, creating the urge to speak and be heard. Your thoughts will reveal a great deal about who you are, now and in the year to come.

Mercury square Jupiter (occurring Oct. 4 – 9) During this aspect it may be best to hold off on a job request, asking for a raise, or signing any binding contracts concerning long term investment and payment schedules. Due to Mercury retrograde (September 24 – October 15), this aspect has occurred over extended periods. It occurred last month, September 5 – 10, reaching its peak on September 7. Mercury square Jupiter will occur again October 23 – 28, reaching its peak on October 26. For more details on Mercury square Jupiter, *see September 7.*

Venus sextile Saturn (occurring Oct. 5 – 8) Venus is in Scorpio sextile to Saturn in Virgo. Venus in Scorpio invites an attraction to sharing secrets, daring love play, and passionate encounters. Venus sextile Saturn brings the opportunity for us to gain some control of our love relationships, and to better understand our boundaries and limitations. Saturn in Virgo is bringing a prudent and meticulously planned approach to applying disciplines and setting limits. It is through this aspect that love relationships are given an opportunity for stronger levels of commitment and responsibility. This is the time to protect loved ones with guidance, and to teach them about discipline. Perfect timing brings pleasure. Venus sextile Saturn teaches us how to hold on to and maintain the things we love – those places, people, and things that matter to us. True love has a binding and lasting affect, and this aspect often shows us the ways in which love stands the test of time. This aspect last occurred June 19 – 22, reaching its peak on June 21, when Venus was in Cancer sextile to Saturn in Virgo.

October 7th Tuesday
FIRST QUARTER MOON in CAPRICORN

	PDT	EDT
Moon square Mercury	12:03 AM	3:03 AM
Moon conjunct Jupiter	12:49 AM	3:49 AM
Moon square Sun	2:03 AM	5:03 AM
Moon trine Saturn	5:10 AM	8:10 AM
Moon sextile Venus	5:50 AM	8:50 AM
Moon sextile Uranus goes v/c	12:36 PM	3:36 PM
Venus trine Uranus begins (see October 9)		

Mood Watch: The **First Quarter Moon in Capricorn** (Moon square Sun) strongly emphasizes the need for serious labor. Some staunch determination is required. There is a steadily mounting concern to achieve a notable level of accomplishment or completion in projects. The late harvest ripens and the physical labor force of the world is hard at work. October festivals and banquets require a tremendous amount of preparation. People's moods are greatly moved by the acknowledgement of merits. The need to hunt for a steady job, a marketing edge, or a secure investment, keeps us vigilant and focused. Punctuality in business is stressed. Some may feel isolated by constant work and no play. No one likes feeling rushed, particularly when high standards must be met.

October 8th Wednesday
Moon in Capricorn / Aquarius

	PDT	EDT
Moon enters Aquarius	9:03 AM	12:03 PM
Moon square Mars	3:21 PM	6:21 PM

Mood Watch: Brilliant moods come with the Moon in Aquarius. Although Mercury is retrograde (Sept. 24 – Oct. 15), which brings a challenge to our communications, Aquarius Moon brings clever ideas, inspirational thoughts, and humanitarian kindness. However, later in the day there will probably be some testy moods while the Moon squares with Mars. Sun and Moon in air signs will help us to think matters through, but this may not be the time to set matters straight with communications.

October 9th Thursday
Yom Kippur
Moon in Aquarius

	PDT	EDT	
Moon trine Mercury	6:31 AM	9:31 AM	
Moon trine Sun	6:16 PM	9:16 PM	
Venus trine Uranus	10:47 PM	1:47 AM	(October 10)
Moon square Venus	11:06 PM	2:06 AM	(October 10)
Venus square Neptune begins (see October 11)			

Mood Watch: A busy shuffle rustles through the halls of large institutions. Waxing Aquarius Moon puts the spotlight on science, charities and humanitarian based causes and issues. Eccentric people are spurred to expose their creative genius.

186

Venus trine Uranus (occurring Oct. 7 – 12) Venus in Scorpio is trine Uranus in Pisces. Passionate love and attraction will allow people to make breakthroughs in relationships and in artistic disciplines. Venus trine Uranus brings a favorable attraction to revolutionary concepts. Harmony can exist in love related matters even while chaos is occurring. This is a time of freedom fighters, rebel love, and attraction to the unusual. Youth is attracted to and more highly susceptible to rebellion during this aspect. Dangerous love and taking chances become common occurrences. Love at first sight is explosive at this time, but not necessarily long lasting. This aspect last occurred July 4 – 8, reaching its peak on July 6, when Venus was in Cancer.

♎

October 10th Friday
Moon in Aquarius / Pisces

	PDT	EDT
Moon conjunct Neptune	2:48 AM	5:48 AM
Moon sextile Pluto goes v/c	4:12 PM	7:12 PM
Moon enters Pisces	6:32 PM	9:32 PM

Mood Watch: The general mood is outgoing and eccentric. Moon in Aquarius opens us to learn and explore new perspectives on the people around us. Later, the Aquarius Moon goes void-of-course for a couple of hours, and this may be a difficult time to get through technical problems and minor setbacks. As the Moon enters Pisces, intuitive moods lead to a wide variety of ever changing feelings.

October 11th Saturday
Moon in Pisces

	PDT	EDT
Moon trine Mars	3:33 AM	6:33 AM
Venus square Neptune	1:20 PM	4:20 PM
Moon sextile Jupiter	8:34 PM	11:34 PM

Sun trine Neptune begins (see October 14)

Mood Watch: Today's Moon in Pisces will draw many people to the heart of their beliefs and needs. The waxing Pisces Moon reminds us to keep a close check on addictive tendencies which, for some people, will require careful monitoring.

Venus square Neptune (occurring Oct. 9 – 13) This may be a difficult time to be drawn to or to meditate on spiritual matters or activities. Art with a spiritual approach may appear more phony than ethereal. Feminine expression may be set back by antiquated beliefs. Love matters could be rocky due to a conflict of beliefs. Venus is in Scorpio, which intensifies the art of attraction, while Neptune is in Aquarius, formulating a new spiritual outlook for humankind. Venus influences beauty, attraction, and magnetism. Neptune is the higher spiritual vibration of the feminine spirit, the higher octave of Venus herself – the imperfect yet alluring mortal versus the perfect and irresistible goddess. When these two planets are in conflict, it is a time when women are being sent mixed messages about how to live up to a higher standard of the self. The influences of this aspect are not as harsh for those who understand that true attraction and beauty are found in the core of feminine wisdom, and that magnetic attraction goes beyond temporal beauty. This aspect last occurred May 17 – 22, reaching its peak on May 19, when Venus was in Taurus.

October 12ᵗʰ Sunday

Moon in Pisces

	PDT	EDT	
Moon opposite Saturn	12:34 AM	3:34 AM	
Moon conjunct Uranus	5:53 AM	8:53 AM	
Moon trine Venus	11:25 AM	2:25 PM	
Moon square Pluto goes v/c	10:01 PM	1:01 AM	(October 13)
Saturn opposite Uranus begins (see November 4)			

Mood Watch: Pisces Moon brings on a mystical time of strong psychic inclinations and a wide range of emotional expressions. Bubbly, artistic, enchanting, and dreamy moments allow us to access some hidden sanctuary where the soulful or prayerful part of ourselves is unleashed. Today many folks will be drawn to seek out a favorite space or refuge from the mundane, to find a place that recharges the batteries and allows the faith to be renewed.

October 13ᵗʰ Monday

Columbus Day, USA / Thanksgiving Day, Canada

Moon in Pisces / Aries

	PDT	EDT
Moon enters Aries	12:08 AM	3:08 AM
Moon opposite Mercury	1:40 PM	4:40 PM

Mood Watch: It's Full Moon Eve. Aries Moon initiates – and very rarely finishes the task – as the spirit of cardinal fire burns through to the next stage of life, leaving in its path unfinished business and a creative or impulsive course of action, which often brings new light to a situation. This almost Full Moon in Aries is a restless and impatient time for some. There is a competitive air increasing in many folks. This is a good time to take initiative with autumn projects that need to be started. While the spirit of Aries Moon may seem relentless to some, the necessity to forge the will with precision and expertise brings a better sense of well being. Taking action towards personal goals is the most natural way to channel this hard driving energy of Aries.

October 14ᵗʰ Tuesday

Sukkot begins (ends October 20)

FULL MOON in ARIES

	PDT	EDT
Moon square Jupiter	12:50 AM	3:50 AM
Sun trine Neptune	6:18 AM	9:18 AM
Moon sextile Neptune	12:33 PM	3:33 PM
Moon opposite Sun	1:01 PM	4:01 PM

Mood Watch: The **Full Moon in Aries** (Moon opposite Sun) reaches its peak this afternoon and charges our spirits with an extra dose of energy. All the high pomp and hype of this time comes to a crescendo, marked with the burning and willful force of Aries Moon activity. A warrior spirit touches us all, particularly with regard to the personal challenges in our lives.

Sun trine Neptune (occurring Oct. 11 – 17) This occurrence of Sun trine Neptune particularly affects those Libra people celebrating birthdays October 11 – 17. These

Librans are experiencing the favorable trine aspect of Neptune to their natal Sun. This brings gifts of spiritual encounters and awareness, as well as a calming effect on one's life. It also serves as a good time (particularly for these birthday folks) to seek visions, apply prayer and meditation, and to explore spiritual avenues and beliefs that are being presented. This aspect last occurred June 11 – 17, reaching its peak on June 14, when the Sun was in Gemini.

♎

October 15th Wednesday

Moon in Aries / Taurus

	PDT	EDT
Moon trine Pluto goes v/c	12:35 AM	3:35 AM
Moon enters Taurus	2:32 AM	5:32 AM
Mercury goes direct	1:06 PM	4:06 PM
Moon opposite Mars	3:37 PM	6:37 PM

Mood Watch: The Moon in Taurus urges us to address our finances, shop wisely, and to seek out practical measures in meeting personal demands.

Mercury goes direct (Mercury direct: Oct. 15, 2008 – Jan. 11, 2009) Since September 24, Mercury has been retrograde in the sign of Libra, commonly causing communication glitches and confusion when relaying information. In Libra, the retrograde Mercury often causes communication mix-ups with regard to making decisions, arranging social affairs, harmonizing relationships, and when attempting to make compromises. Now we can breathe a greatly needed sigh of relief as Mercury, the planet governing the realms of communication, becomes stationary and will soon begin to move forward. Take note that our faculties and manner of communicating will definitely improve within the next few days. Although perhaps not today, when the stationary Mercury often freezes communication efforts, but very soon our communications will run more smoothly; this will be a good time to begin clearing up various misunderstandings occurring over the past few weeks. For more information on this recently completed phase of Mercury retrograde, see September 24. For more on Mercury retrograde patterns throughout this year, see the introduction on *Mercury retrograde periods.*

October 16th Thursday

Moon in Taurus

	PDT	EDT
Moon trine Jupiter	2:40 AM	5:40 AM
Moon trine Saturn	6:21 AM	9:21 AM
Moon sextile Uranus	10:14 AM	1:14 PM
Moon square Neptune	1:40 PM	4:40 PM

Mood Watch: Stable and practical security calls to us on this waning Taurus Moon day. In order to feel balance in our life and to make adjustments in this Libra time of year, we must address money related matters and take care of practical concerns. Taurus Moon puts us in touch with our sensibilities and lets us know what we will need to outfit ourselves for the season.

October 17th Friday

Moon in Taurus / Gemini

	PDT	EDT
Moon opposite Venus goes v/c	12:33 AM	3:33 AM
Moon enters Gemini	3:26 AM	6:26 AM
Moon trine Mercury	4:25 PM	7:25 PM

Mood Watch: The spirit of the Gemini Moon shifts our moods towards a curious and communicative outlook. Many folks will be confronted with mixed feelings concerning the issues that are being raised at this time. Gemini Moon gets us looking at both sides of matters and raises important questions. The Gemini Moon guides us to readdress communications now that Mercury has gone direct (see yesterday). However, it often takes a couple of days to overcome the shift from Mercury retrograde to Mercury direct.

October 18th Saturday

Moon in Gemini

	PDT	EDT	
Moon square Saturn	7:37 AM	10:37 AM	
Moon square Uranus	11:05 AM	2:05 PM	
Venus enters Sagittarius	11:30 AM	2:30 PM	
Moon trine Neptune	2:38 PM	5:38 PM	
Moon trine Sun	10:21 PM	1:21 AM	(October 19)

Mood Watch: The Sun is in Libra and the Moon is in Gemini; this is a time of research, teaching, and speeches. The attention of the world focuses on law, and at times like this, we commonly seek to have a say in every jurisdiction that directly affects our lives.

Venus enters Sagittarius (Venus in Sagittarius: Oct. 18 – Nov. 12) Now the planet of love and of the expression of affection is enhanced by the inspired character of Sagittarius. Venus in Sagittarius brings out a love of the arts, travel, philosophy, cultural exploration and sports achievements. With this comes a positive and optimistic spirit of camaraderie among people in general, and the effort to take affections beyond the usual bounds is certainly present. Philosophical theories justify love matters. Venus in Sagittarius will help to boost the love life and affections of our Sagittarius friends. This is your time, Sagittarius people, to reaffirm your visions of how to enhance the beauty and the love you are enjoying in your lives.

October 19th Sunday

Moon in Gemini / Cancer

	PDT	EDT	
Moon opposite Pluto goes v/c	2:52 AM	5:52 AM	
Moon enters Cancer	4:41 AM	7:41 AM	
Moon square Mercury	8:00 PM	11:00 PM	
Moon trine Mars	11:03 PM	2:03 AM	(October 20)
Sun sextile Pluto begins (see October 21)			

Mood Watch: The waning Cancer Moon is a good time to apply cleansing practices, particularly emotional cleansing, and to make the home sparkle with beautiful accents and inviting specialty foods. Be careful not to indulge unduly – overeating is a common way to combat feelings of not being loved and to drown out personal troubles or family conflicts. Feed the hunger, nurture the soul.

October 20ᵗʰ Monday

Moon in Cancer

♎

	PDT	EDT
Moon opposite Jupiter	6:19 AM	9:19 AM
Moon sextile Saturn	10:06 AM	1:06 PM
Moon trine Uranus	1:13 PM	4:13 PM

Mood Watch: Moody Monday has arrived. Moodiness is the essence of the lunar expression, and Cancer is the Moon's attributed domain. This is the time to apply the motherly touch. Bundle up and stay warm today. Nurture all ills and wounds, and focus on emotional health and well being. A comforting home atmosphere is a fine way to overcome today's basic moodiness.

October 21ˢᵗ Tuesday

Moon in Cancer / Leo – LAST QUARTER MOON in CANCER

	PDT	EDT
Moon square Sun goes v/c	4:55 AM	7:55 AM
Moon enters Leo	7:36 AM	10:36 AM
Moon trine Venus	2:08 PM	5:08 PM
Sun sextile Pluto	5:23 PM	8:23 PM

Mood Watch: Early this morning we come to the **Last Quarter Moon in Cancer** (Moon square Sun). The emotional concerns surfacing at this time require that extra bit of nurturing and understanding. Feelings must surface at times during the morning, particularly as the Moon goes void-of-course for a couple of hours. As the Moon enters Leo, bold self-expression and alertness entice our moods to be playful and friendly.

Sun sextile Pluto (occurring Oct. 19 – 23) The Sun, at the tail end of Libra, is sextile Pluto, which is finishing its final trek through Sagittarius. This brings opportunities that appear both vast and demanding to Libra and Scorpio cusp born people who are celebrating birthdays October 19 – 23. These birthday people are experiencing the sextile aspect of their natal sun to Pluto, giving them opportunities to take charge, to step into positions of power, and to accept and embrace permanent change in their lives. These are powerful transformations which provide opportunities to embody what has been learned from the personal trials of the past. Go thee forth and conquer, master Librans and Scorpions! Persist with diligence to resolve the conflicts of your life with self-respect and assurance. Your time to triumph is always available when your will to achieve is balanced by knowledge and hard work. This holds true for all signs of the zodiac. This aspect occurred earlier this year, February 17 – 21, reaching its peak on February 19.

SCORPIO

Key Phrase: " I CREATE " or
"I DESIRE"
Fixed Water Sign
Symbol(s): The Scorpion,
The Eagle, and The Phoenix
October 22nd through
November 21st

October 22nd Wednesday

Moon in Leo

	PDT	EDT	
Moon sextile Mercury	3:05 AM	6:05 AM	
Moon square Mars	5:30 AM	8:30 AM	
Sun enters Scorpio	6:08 PM	9:08 PM	
Moon opposite Neptune	9:24 PM	12:24 AM	(October 23)

Mood Watch: Waning Leo Moon creates a hunger for attention, and quite often there is a need for acknowledgment of individual efforts. This is a good time to encourage people around us by acknowledging them with compliments and praise for their recent efforts. A small compliment can go a long way and reassure someone that their efforts are not in vain. Credit where credit is due, but by all means, give credit!

Sun enters Scorpio (Sun in Scorpio: Oct. 22 – Nov. 21) This time of year, like the Scorpio personality, creates an air of mystery and mysticism. This is a time when people are more likely to focus on their hidden agendas and their need to get in touch with their own passion. Scorpio focuses our attention on the most important events of life: birth, sex, death and regeneration or transformation, as this sign is ruled by the underworld god known as Pluto. Scorpio represents the powers of hidden meaning, the need for secrecy, and the deeper psychologically ensnaring struggles with the self-destructive nature of humans and beasts. The totem of the sign of Scorpio is classically the desert arachnid known as the scorpion. The scorpion sting can kill; this is the violent or criminal side of the Scorpio personality. There are other totems – the Eagle and the Phoenix. These higher aspects of the Scorpio personality relate to the eagle's ability to observe from very far away and see a larger and more objective picture of life while noting all the details essential to life itself. The Phoenix totem represents the ability to rise above the burning rays of the sun as a transformed and enlightened being. Pushing through and surviving the perilous difficulties and dangers of life is practically a personality trait of the sign of Scorpio. The Scorpio archetype demands some respect. Scorpios are often stereotyped for having a desire to live richly and often dangerously. There is always the vast and more esoteric version, too – the way of spirit, the mystical and spiritual path, or the acknowledgment of one's own truth.

♏

October 23rd Thursday
United Nations Day

Moon in Leo / Virgo	PDT	EDT
Moon trine Pluto goes v/c	10:53 AM	1:53 PM
Moon enters Virgo	12:41 PM	3:41 PM
Moon sextile Sun	2:10 PM	5:10 PM
Mercury square Jupiter begins (see October 26)		
Mars sextile Jupiter begins (see October 27)		

Mood Watch: The Sun in Scorpio and the Moon in Leo brings creative and entertaining intensity. For a couple of hours this morning, the void-of-course Leo Moon leaves many of us preoccupied with personal desires, and such things as service and work performance will tend to be lessened in quality. This is a good time to reassure others with compliments, but not so much as to distract them from doing their work. As the Moon enters Virgo, our moods shift over towards the need for more pragmatic and realistic strategies for our approach to life.

October 24th Friday

Moon in Virgo	PDT	EDT	
Moon square Venus	12:52 AM	3:52 AM	
Moon sextile Mars	2:29 PM	5:29 PM	
Moon trine Jupiter	5:33 PM	8:33 PM	
Moon conjunct Saturn	9:26 PM	12:26 AM	(October 25)
Moon opposite Uranus	11:43 PM	2:43 AM	(October 25)

Mood Watch: Virgo Moon focuses our moods on the need to communicate and tend to practical concerns, personal hygiene, and the focus of collecting and distributing necessary resources. Prudent resourcefulness allows us to squeeze pennies from unknown sources and eventually account for the hidden gold. Don't spend it now – simply account for it. See what you've got, and apply your rational sensibility as you picture all the ways your money could be spent. This doesn't mean business can't be done; it just means it may be wiser at this time to put off spending until you've got all the facts in order.

October 25th Saturday

Moon in Virgo / Libra	PDT	EDT
Moon square Pluto goes v/c	6:02 PM	9:02 PM
Moon enters Libra	7:48 PM	10:48 PM

Mood Watch: Virgo Moon keeps our moods busy working on matters requiring keen focused attention. Our health consciousness calls to us during a waning Virgo Moon to flush toxins, decrease bad health habits, and clean up our surroundings. Later, the Moon goes void-of-course and creates a somewhat skeptical period for our moods. As the Moon enters Libra, amicable moods allow us to interact more freely, and with less doubt.

October 26th Sunday

Moon in Libra

	PDT	EDT
Mercury square Jupiter	5:13 AM	8:13 AM
Moon sextile Venus	2:15 PM	5:15 PM

Mood Watch: Waning Libra Moon focuses our moods on the need for peace and forgiveness. Relationships that need mending at this time require structure and some ground rules in order to generate trust. This is the time to banish those moods and emotions that prevent us from harmonizing and generating good feelings with others.

Mercury square Jupiter (occurring Oct. 23 – 28) Mercury in Libra is square Jupiter in Capricorn. During this aspect it may be best to hold off on a job request, asking for a raise, or signing any binding contracts concerning long term investment and payment schedules. Due to Mercury retrograde (September 24 – October 15), this aspect has occurred for extended periods. Mercury square Jupiter occurred last month, September 5 – 10, reaching its peak on September 7. Due to Mercury retrograde (Sept. 23 – Oct. 14), this aspect also occurred earlier this month, October 4 – 7, reaching its peak on October 6. For more details on Mercury square Jupiter, *see September 7.*

October 27th Monday

Moon in Libra

	PDT	EDT
Moon square Jupiter	2:17 AM	5:17 AM
Moon conjunct Mercury	4:37 AM	7:37 AM
Moon trine Neptune	12:24 PM	3:24 PM
Mars sextile Jupiter	1:29 PM	4:29 PM
Mars sextile Saturn begins (see October 30)		
Mars trine Uranus begins (see October 31)		

Mood Watch: Libra Moon now wanes towards the darkest phase. All imbalances that exist between friends seem to surface at this time, requiring an effort to create some harmony.

Mars sextile Jupiter (occurring Oct. 23 – 31) Mars in Scorpio is sextile Jupiter in Capricorn. Passionate and instinctual actions, when taken, have the opportunity to go profoundly far and be very successful in the long run. Those who act on specific urges and impulses to achieve their heart's desire are more likely to make a breakthrough during this aspect. This is a time to make true efforts to promote career skills or to enhance a career move. Remember – action is required; mere good intentions will get you nothing while this aspect is in full force. This is a good time to go adventuring and exploring while Mars sextile Jupiter promotes opportunities.

October 28th Tuesday

Moon in Libra / Scorpio – NEW MOON in SCORPIO – *Hecate's Moon*

	PDT	EDT
Moon sextile Pluto goes v/c	3:06 AM	6:06 AM
Moon enters Scorpio	4:48 AM	7:48 AM
Moon conjunct Sun	4:14 PM	7:14 PM

194

Mood Watch: Some may say that *"Hecate's Moon"* is the **New Moon in Scorpio** (Moon conjunct Sun), others may say it's the New Moon closest to *All Hallows (Halloween / October 31st)*, others still may say its the New Moon of October that represents Hecate's Moon. As for this *New Moon of Hecate*, all of that is true. The moon known as Hecate's Moon always happens around the new moon of the witches' New Year holiday, Halloween. Hecate is the Wiccan goddess of the underworld who leads us through death towards a cycle of rebirth. She guides the lost souls to their final destiny, and can be called on at this time to guide those who have passed on, especially those who have met their end in a demeaning and challenged way, such as violent death or suicide. Hecate cures the ills that surround death. To honor her, take eggs, black bread, and beer to a Y-shaped path or road where an old tree stands. Give this offering to her and ask her to oversee the souls who have died that we want to see safely through to the other side. Honor her with respect – she is a serious and powerful spirit to call up, and no immature or insincere request will be granted by this goddess of the dark moon. If the wind kicks up or you receive a chill on the back of your neck, fear not; that's the spirit of Hecate confirming her presence. She will not hurt you as long as you respect her. New Moon in Scorpio puts us in touch with a new understanding of the passionate depths of life that we experience through birth, sex, death and transformation.

October 29th Wednesday

Moon in Scorpio

	PDT	EDT	
Moon sextile Jupiter	12:59 PM	3:59 PM	
Moon conjunct Mars	3:17 PM	6:17 PM	
Moon sextile Saturn	4:45 PM	7:45 PM	
Moon trine Uranus	6:01 PM	9:01 PM	
Moon square Neptune goes v/c	10:45 PM	1:45 AM	(October 30)
Mercury trine Neptune	11:10 PM	2:10 AM	(October 30)

Mood Watch: The Moon is still dark, still new, although now waxing in Scorpio. This is a time for renewal and for many, a place to come to new terms with regard to transformation. There is an initiation process of the soul taking place for those who are open to rebirth. Mystery and intrigue ring strongly throughout the day. New Moon in Scorpio is a splendid time to drop late autumn seeds expected to rise next spring. There are also seeds of dreams and seeds of the heart. This could be the day to accomplish something new – something that feels right.

Mercury trine Neptune (occurring Oct. 27 – 31) Mercury in Libra is trine to Neptune in Aquarius. This aspect occurred on four earlier occasions this year; first, May 23 – 29, when Mercury was in Gemini, but it never actually reached an exact peak due to Mercury retrograde. Second, it occurred July 3 – 8, reaching its exact peak on July 6. Third, Mercury trine Neptune occurred September 14 – October 2, and it reached the third peak on September 19 and a fourth peak on September 28. As it reaches its final peak today, this aspect is now occurring for the fifth time. For a recap on the story of this advantageous aspect, see September 19, when it first occurred with Mercury in Libra.

October 30ᵗʰ Thursday

Moon in Scorpio / Sagittarius   PDT   EDT
Moon enters Sagittarius   3:42 PM   6:42 PM
Mars sextile Saturn   8:51 PM   11:51 PM
Mars square Neptune begins (see November 3)

Mood Watch: A good portion of this day brings the void-of-course Moon in Scorpio. This is a good time to apply caution and keep an eye out for danger and theft. Emotional ups and downs may be the trend of the early part of the day. As the Moon enters Sagittarius, positive and upbeat moods inspire us to be more open minded.

Mars sextile Saturn (occurring Oct. 27 – Nov. 3) Mars in Scorpio is sextile Saturn in Virgo. This is an active time for establishing emotional stability and cleanliness. While Mars is in Scorpio, there may be quite a bit of internal turmoil occurring with regard to emotional security. During this aspect, actions create opportunities, provided there is an application of discipline and timing. For the second time this year, Mars sextile Saturn brings opportunities for perfect timing to occur. This is a good time to remain optimistic and not to let fear or worry rule the conditions of our lives. This aspect occurred earlier this year, March 9 – 18, reaching its peak on March 14.

October 31ˢᵗ Friday

All Hallows (Halloween) / Samhain / Witches' New Year
Moon in Sagittarius   PDT   EDT
Mars trine Uranus   1:32 PM   4:32 PM
Venus square Saturn begins (see November 3)
Venus square Uranus begins (see November 3)

Mood Watch: Halloween marks the half-way point of the autumn season. Sagittarius Moon keeps our sights open to all the visionary possibilities as the autumn unfolds. A philosophical outlook arises due to the need to get a handle on the rapid changes emerging. Moon in Sagittarius allows for exploratory moods and adventurous feelings. Studious efforts will go far today. As the wind kicks up, anticipation of the Halloween fun begins, and the long line of estranged images allures our imagination.

Mars trine Uranus (occurring Oct. 27 – Nov. 4) Mars in Scorpio trine Uranus in Pisces brings heated activities concerning very sensitive emotional matters and the radical tendencies that are seen in art and spiritual practices. It is through this aspect that emotional breakthroughs may occur. Be careful what you stand for or you'll fall for anything in this atmosphere of active yet favorable destruction. This is a good time to tackle the breakdown of unwanted barriers that stifle the human spirit from evolving in chosen ways. Mars trine Uranus is bound to create fire somewhere and the heat can be worked to our advantage. In the triumph mode, Mars trine Uranus creates fireworks of celebration, and there is a certain sense

of truly being alive with regard to the demand for spiritual freedom and rights, ♏
and the need to bring an artistic form of relief to those who have experienced
the challenge of emotional and spiritual battles. This aspect occurred earlier this
year, April 15 – 28, reaching its peak on April 22, when Mars was in Cancer.

November 1ˢᵗ Saturday
All Saints Day / Day of the Dead

Moon in Sagittarius	PDT	EDT	
Moon conjunct Venus	12:36 AM	3:36 AM	
Moon square Saturn	5:14 AM	8:14 AM	
Moon square Uranus	5:55 AM	8:55 AM	
Moon sextile Neptune	10:53 AM	1:53 PM	
Moon sextile Mercury	7:56 PM	10:56 PM	
Neptune goes direct	11:39 PM	2:39 AM	(November 2)
Jupiter sextile Uranus begins (see November 12)			

Mood Watch: The earliest morning lunar aspects may be a bit trying and complex,
but by the time the day progresses, our outlook will become more positive and
optimistic. The waxing Sagittarius Moon prepares us for the darker half of the
autumn season, and allows us to see more clearly through the deeper and more
complex parts of our lives. There is in excess of a couple of billion people alive
on our planet now, and it is reported there will be many more than that before
we know it. Nevertheless, there are still more dead folks than living ones. The
Day of the Dead is a superb time to call upon the spirits of our ancestors, and
the wisdom of those folks who have passed before us. Honor and celebrate their
wisdom today, and it will assist you to make wise decisions.

Neptune goes direct (Neptune direct: Nov. 1, 2008 – June 1, 2009) Neptune
resumes a direct-moving course after five months (since May 26) of being
retrograde. This will regenerate our spiritual and intuitive work and facilitate
our development. Neptune is in Aquarius, influencing the flow of the Aquarian
age and the evolutionary processes of belief systems. Neptune is the master of
illusion, while Aquarius demands scientific proof. As Neptune proceeds further
into Aquarius, we will learn to achieve a higher and freer sense of spiritual
awareness – a sense that something divine is occurring, even though it cannot be
explained in mortal terms. What many of us are finally coming to acknowledge
is the notion that we are spiritual beings having a human experience, not human
beings having a spiritual experience. A good meditation, when sincerely applied,
helps to discharge our emotional baggage. Neptune's calming and forgiving
nature will help us to let go of malicious and non-productive thoughts, and will
melt away cold-heartedness. Frequently invoke the spiritually uplifting medita-
tions that work for you. This practice will lead you to a positive and regenerative
place in your own spiritual evolution. Neptune moving direct allows us to move
freely forward, using divine wisdom and our spiritual aspirations as guides.

November 2nd Sunday

DAYLIGHT SAVING TIME ENDS (**Turn clocks back one hour at 2:00 a.m.**)

Moon in Sagittarius / Capricorn	PST	EST
Moon conjunct Pluto goes v/c	2:41 AM	5:41 AM
Moon enters Capricorn	3:14 AM	6:14 AM
Mercury sextile Pluto begins (see November 3)		

Mood Watch: We will have already entered Daylight Saving Time by the time the Moon goes void-of-course in Sagittarius. Before dawn, the Moon enters Capricorn, bringing a sense of duty to the important business of this time. Tomorrow's long list of aspects shows that we are sensing the immensity of work and swift change that stands before us. This is a good time to focus on setting the week's pace, and to plan on a busy time of mixed ups and downs.

November 3rd Monday

Moon in Capricorn	PST	EST	
Venus square Saturn	12:41 AM	3:41 AM	
Moon sextile Sun	2:21 AM	5:21 AM	
Venus square Uranus	3:18 AM	6:18 AM	
Moon conjunct Jupiter	2:22 PM	5:22 PM	
Moon trine Saturn	5:40 PM	8:40 PM	
Moon sextile Uranus	5:46 PM	8:46 PM	
Mercury sextile Pluto	9:31 PM	12:31 AM	(November 4)
Moon sextile Mars goes v/c	10:46 PM	1:46 AM	(November 4)
Mars square Neptune	11:44 PM	2:44 AM	(November 4)
Venus sextile Neptune begins (see November 5)			

Mood Watch: Intense kinds of ups and downs swing into play as the highly antici-pated US election week begins to unfold. The Capricorn Moon keeps determined to move through our experiences without much reaction time in between.

Venus square Saturn (occurring Oct. 31 – Nov. 5) This aspect creates obstacles and restrictions concerning the timely expression of love. Venus in Sagittarius is square to the Saturn in Virgo. It may be difficult to engage in romance, particularly when traveling, as it might seem that something is always getting in the way of basic pleasures. Venus square Saturn sometimes creates blocks in the flow of care and love due to external responsibilities and restrictions that create separation. Sometimes people are distracted from properly providing care and concern where it is most needed due to the high demands of the world at large. While this aspect is occurring, it is wisest to work a little harder for the things that attract us, and at love related matters. This aspect first occurred January 3 – 8, and it reached its peak on January 6. Then it happened for a second round, May 23 – 28, and last reached its peak on May 26.

Venus square Uranus (occurring Oct. 31 – Nov. 5) Venus is in Sagittarius squaring to the retrograde Uranus in Pisces. A love for travel may be stifled by chaotic changes. This aspect tends to put obstacles between love and freedom. Be careful not to become too personally affronted by explosive or radical love matters. This influence may be testing the power of love to withstand chaos. Be assured in self-

love and empower affection with personal integrity and a strong loving vision. ♏
People are changing at a rapid rate and it is essential to let love take its course
concerning issues of personal freedom. This aspect last occurred on June 12, when
Venus was in Gemini. Before that, Venus in Sagittarius squared to Uranus in Pisces
on January 12.

Mercury sextile Pluto (occurring Nov. 2 – 5) This aspect brings an opportunity for
us to get the message across to people in strong positions of power and authority.
Mercury is currently in Libra, focusing discussions on matters of law and diplomacy. Will the scales of justice be tipped once again? Pluto in Sagittarius is forcing
us to see beyond the norm by creating a long term transformation of our views on
the quality and understanding of life. Mass media may well be entranced by news
concerning world superpowers and/or challenging power issues, particularly with
regard to changes in the law. This is an opportunistic time to reach out to those of
another generation and make an attempt to communicate something vital. This
aspect last occurred March 13 – 16, and it reached its peak on March 15.

Mars square Neptune (occurring Oct. 30 – Nov. 8) Heated activities run into
obstacles concerning the work of Great Spirit and the fulfillment of spiritual
harmony. Mars is in Scorpio and there may be emotional disruption that intrudes
on or impedes our spiritual level of experience. Martial forces are bursting through
temples, belief systems, and holy moments. Active aggression occurs around spiritual groups and religious institutions, often targeting the belief systems of others.
Mariners at sea may run into challenging storms. This aspect also brings the potential for accidents and temper tantrums, especially with regard to opinions about
substance abuse and sacred matters. It is important not to get so wrapped up in the
spiritual side of things that physical world realities, such as fire, are overlooked.
Angry outbursts are likely to affect sacred land or the personal territory of spiritual
sentiment. While Mars is square to Neptune, it is best to anticipate confrontations
concerning moral or spiritual issues. As this aspect passes, it will be easier to put
spiritual beliefs and practices back on course without much conflict or interference.
Meanwhile, stay aware and ready to deal with whatever comes along.

November 4ᵗʰ Tuesday

Election Day, USA
Moon in Capricorn / Aquarius

	PST	EST
Saturn opposite Uranus	5:35 AM	8:35 AM
Mercury enters Scorpio	7:59 AM	10:59 AM
Moon enters Aquarius	4:02 PM	7:02 PM
Moon square Mercury	5:16 PM	8:16 PM

Mood Watch: Today's moods will wear a poker face at first, as the Capricorn Moon
has been void-of-course since last night. It might look like an endless haul to get
through the immense workload and the obstacles that appear to stand in the way
throughout the core of the day. Numerous delays will dull our bewildered senses
as we observe the big changes that affect today's US election. Voter turnout may
seem staggeringly slow at first, but as the day progresses, the big election altering
votes will start to soar by the time the Moon enters Aquarius. Excitement will

199

really build as surprising and remarkable changes occur while the waxing Aquarius Moon boosts the patriotic morale of the American people. Mayhem will ensue with conflicting news reports in the early evening. Unsettled chatter will keep us curious throughout the night.

Saturn opposite Uranus (occurring Oct. 12, 2008 – March 23, 2009) The slow moving Saturn in Virgo has finally reached an orbital opposition to the even slower moving Uranus in Pisces. This process will last quite a number of months, since Saturn will go retrograde on December 31, 2008 through mid-May 2009. This aspect will affect us a number of times in the next few years to come, but then it will dissipate completely until the middle of the 21st Century (the year 2056) when it returns. The stark reality of this aspect suggests Saturn, which represents order and structure, is indeed the very opposite kind of energy in the very opposite position to its opponent, Uranus, which represents chaos and disorder. What might be the result of all this polarization? Which of the two masters' energy will outweigh the other? Saturn being control, and Uranus being disruption, one might surmise the very best to hope for would be an elaborate exercise in learning to control the uncontrollable. From storms, earthquakes, shifts of ocean currents, and volcanic activity, come all kinds of earth shifts. Saturn is in an earth sign, the *mutable earth* sign, Virgo. This represents the mutability and the adaptability of the physical world, and the shifting of the physical realm will be unpredictable and chaotic while Uranus's opposing influence brings immense and irreparable change.

Mercury enters Scorpio (Mercury in Scorpio: Nov. 4 – 22) Mercury in Scorpio is often a time when communications are veiled in secrecy, and talk revolves around matters of intensity and sensitivity. Passionate issues are communicated with creativity and intuition. This is also a time to be aware that a sharp tongue may easily cause a violent or challenging reaction. It is through this medium of Mercury in the sign of Scorpio that the expression of communications is seemingly fearless, obstinate, reckless, and passionate. From indecent babble to the subtle perfection of clear articulation, discussions frequently deliver a powerful punch. Not only our words but also our appearance, mannerisms and attitudes all send out the message of who we are. The mask we choose for the grand masquerade of autumn's darkening days teaches us much about ourselves.

November 5th Wednesday
FIRST QUARTER MOON in AQUARIUS

	PST	EST
Venus sextile Neptune	4:56 AM	7:56 AM
Moon square Sun	8:02 PM	11:02 PM

Mood Watch: We have now reached the **First Quarter Moon in Aquarius** (Moon square Sun). Waxing Aquarius Moon puts the spotlight on eccentric and unusual breakthroughs of humankind. The eccentric quality of this Moon is perfect for addressing the startling results of yesterday's US presidential election. Controversial subjects are strongly at work as we cross this threshold of American history. This time is intensely affected by the very busy pile-up of celestial traffic. We are all aware of great shifts of energy and the Aquarius Moon will assist our moods to meet and formally address humanity's newest challenges.

200

Venus sextile Neptune (occurring Nov. 3 – 6) Venus in Sagittarius brings adventure to the law of attraction. Neptune in Aquarius brings a powerfully intelligent higher feminine vibration to our driving search for perfect love. This aspect can have a strong healing effect on the soul, and reaches into the feminine parts of our being with a calm fortitude. Faith and belief in love matters may be rewarded at this time, and will be enhanced where similar beliefs are shared. This is a great time to take your love to a special place, or sanctuary of divine countenance, where the depth of tranquility can be accessed. This aspect first occurred January 14 – 18, reaching its exact aspect on January 16. It also occurred on April 23 – 27, reaching its exact peak on April 25.

♏

November 6th Thursday

Moon in Aquarius	PST	EST
Moon conjunct Neptune	10:22 AM	1:22 PM
Moon sextile Venus	1:31 PM	4:31 PM
Moon square Mars	1:53 PM	4:53 PM

Mood Watch: There is an ancient saying of magicians and the like: *"As Above, So Below."* Complexity has been building in the heavens; meanwhile, here on planet Earth we ride the wave. Moon in Aquarius steadily waxes, increasing our awareness and putting us in touch with the awakening pace of events now rising to the occasion of the high celestial traffic. We are all aware of great shifts of energy at this time.

November 7th Friday

Moon in Aquarius / Pisces	PST	EST
Moon sextile Pluto goes v/c	1:31 AM	4:31 AM
Moon enters Pisces	2:44 AM	5:44 AM
Moon trine Mercury	12:25 PM	3:25 PM
Sun sextile Jupiter begins (see November 10)		
Sun trine Uranus begins (see November 10)		

Mood Watch: Moon in Pisces allows us to get more easily in touch with our intuition, our dreams, and our beliefs. Sun in Scorpio and Moon in Pisces often brings deeply penetrating wet weather; a watery, rainy, cloudy, snowy, and all around damp cast to the North American landscape brings misty moods. Hot delicious drinks will bring comfort to the soul.

November 8th Saturday

Moon in Pisces	PST	EST
Moon trine Sun	9:41 AM	12:41 PM
Moon sextile Jupiter	12:11 PM	3:11 PM
Moon conjunct Uranus	1:39 PM	4:39 PM
Moon opposite Saturn	2:29 PM	5:29 PM

Mood Watch: This will most likely be a day to work on emotional issues, particularly with regard to addictive tendencies, and the need to escape or alter reality. This is also a good time to tap into creativity and art, and to use personal skills and talents to ease the senses. A wide host of subconscious concerns that have finally begun to surface are appearing before us as strong symbols and signs. Go with the flow and look for the signs.

November 9th Sunday

Moon in Pisces / Aries

	PST	EST
Moon trine Mars	12:38 AM	3:38 AM
Moon square Venus	2:39 AM	5:39 AM
Moon square Pluto goes v/c	8:27 AM	11:27 AM
Moon enters Aries	9:27 AM	12:27 PM
Sun sextile Saturn begins (see November 11)		
Venus conjunct Pluto begins (see November 11)		

Mood Watch: For a brief time this morning, the Pisces Moon goes void-of-course, and our early Sunday morning moods may appear especially spacey and difficult to interpret. Soon enough, the Moon enters Aries and our moods will become more confident. A brisk new mood is in the air as the waxing Moon in Aries invites us to take charge and get in tune with leadership and self-reliance.

November 10th Monday

Moon in Aries

	PST	EST	
Sun sextile Jupiter	12:54 AM	3:54 AM	
Sun trine Uranus	1:21 PM	4:21 PM	
Moon square Jupiter	4:59 PM	7:59 PM	
Moon sextile Neptune	10:02 PM	1:02 AM	(November 11)
Sun square Neptune begins (see November 13)			

Mood Watch: Many of the more impatient people among us are no longer putting up with inadequacy, and are now taking matters into their own hands. A competitive, confident, and enterprising level of productivity picks up our moods.

Sun sextile Jupiter (occurring Nov. 7 – 12) This aspect brings those Scorpio people celebrating birthdays from November 7 - 12 into a favorable natal Sun position to Jupiter. It's a time of opportunity and expansion for these birthday folks if they act on their desires and work towards their goals. Skills learned throughout this year will support their overall plans for career advancement and fortune building. This aspect last occurred March 4 – 8, reaching its peak on March 6, bringing a similar affect to the birthday Pisces of that time.

Sun trine Uranus (occurring Nov. 7 – 13) This occurrence of Sun trine Uranus favorably affects our Scorpio friends celebrating birthdays November 7 – 13. It puts the radical forces of Uranus in the favorable trine position to their natal Sun. It is time for these people to make a breakthrough. Don't hold back, birthday Scorpios; chaos is here to stay for awhile. Let the experience be positive as long as this aspect brings gifts. Expect restless desires for freedom and the need to break out of your personal prison. Freedom knocks loudly, and the course of change is inevitable in the coming year. Change is necessary for growth. These influential changes are positive in nature, though on the surface they may seem harsh. Birthday people, the apparent madness occurring in your life is there for a reason. You will find a clearer picture in the long run by keeping up the good fight to preserve your inspiration, intelligence, and Scorpio passion. The trine aspect gives gifts of triumph, and this may be a good time to let chaos be the force that brings freedom. This aspect last occurred July 11 – 17, reaching its peak on July 14, affecting the birthday Cancer folks of that time.

♏

November 11ᵗʰ Tuesday
Veteran's Day, USA / Remembrance Day, Canada

Moon in Aries / Taurus	PST	EST	
Sun sextile Saturn	6:24 AM	9:24 AM	
Moon trine Venus	10:21 AM	1:21 PM	
Moon trine Pluto goes v/c	11:16 AM	2:16 PM	
Moon enters Taurus	12:06 PM	3:06 PM	
Venus conjunct Pluto	9:54 PM	12:54 AM	(November 12)

Mood Watch: Throughout the morning the Aries Moon brings a courageous warrior-like spirit. For less than an hour, the Aries Moon goes void-of-course and there may be a tendency for people to be self-absorbed, pushy, and possibly bossy. As the Moon enters Taurus, practical needs call out to us, a sense of duty is instilled, and we are drawn to the necessity to take care of business.

Sun sextile Saturn (occurring Nov. 9 – 13) This occurrence of Sun sextile Saturn particularly affects those Scorpio people celebrating birthdays November 9 – 13, helping them focus their energy and discipline with greater clarity throughout this year. As Saturn traverses the sextile aspect to the natal Sun of these Scorpio people, there is a sense of making progress through discipline, and they may very well begin to see the rewards of their diligent labor in the coming year. This is only true as long as they apply themselves to their work, and maintain a vigilant and persistent effort to master personal discipline and training. For the birthday Scorpio folks of this time, greater control comes with genuine effort. This aspect last occurred June 22 – 27, reaching its peak on June 24, presenting better opportunities and allowing more control in the lives of some Cancer folks.

Venus conjunct Pluto (occurring Nov. 9 – 14) This conjunction unites the power of love (Venus) with the unrelenting, transformational sting of fate (Pluto). For the second time this year, Venus in the late degrees of Sagittarius unites with Pluto. This conjunction last occurred January 21 – 26; for a recap on the story of how this conjunction affects us, *see January 23*, when Venus conjunct Pluto last occurred.

November 12ᵗʰ Wednesday

FULL MOON in TAURUS	PST	EST	
Venus enters Capricorn	7:24 AM	10:24 AM	
Moon opposite Mercury	9:13 AM	12:13 PM	
Moon trine Jupiter	6:24 PM	9:24 PM	
Moon sextile Uranus	6:26 PM	9:26 PM	
Moon trine Saturn	7:49 PM	10:49 PM	
Jupiter sextile Uranus	9:39 PM	12:39 AM	(November 13)
Moon opposite Sun	10:16 PM	1:16 AM	(November 13)
Moon square Neptune	10:41 PM	1:41 AM	(November 13)

Mood Watch: The **Full Moon in Taurus** (Moon opposite Sun) invites us to celebrate the beauty and the perfection of the valuable elements of the earth, and brings appreciation for the beauty in nature. The Taurus totem is the bull, and in its splendor, the bull is a marvelous and classically stubborn creature of habit. This Full Moon reminds us to take the time to enjoy and create beauty around us, and to indulge a little bit in some luxurious pleasures or leisure time. For those who realize the importance of celebrating planet Earth, now is the time to reflect on what you do have and how it is that these physical gifts of Earth can be enjoyed. Ask Mother Moon to bring you what you need and she will teach you how to sow for the harvest of your desire.

Venus enters Capricorn (Venus in Capricorn: Nov. 12 – Dec. 7) For the second time this year, Venus (the planet of love) enters the high and lofty domains of Capricorn. For more information on Venus in Capricorn, *see January 24.*

Jupiter sextile Uranus (occurring Nov. 1 – 23) This aspect occurred earlier this year, March 5 – June 12, reaching two exact peaks during that time, once on March 28, and again on May 21. For more information on today's repeat aspect of Jupiter sextile Uranus, *see March 28*, when it first occurred.

November 13th Thursday

Moon in Taurus / Gemini

	PST	EST
Sun square Neptune	4:31 AM	7:31 AM
Moon opposite Mars goes v/c	9:12 AM	12:12 PM
Moon enters Gemini	12:12 PM	3:12 PM

Mood Watch: Taurus is the place of exaltation for the Moon, and as yesterday's Full Taurus Moon now begins to wane, the fullness of its blessings can still be felt this morning. As the Taurus Moon goes void-of-course for a few hours early in the day, there may be a lot of back-tracking over material and money related matters. As the Moon enters Gemini, the need for a good conversation calls out to our moods.

Sun square Neptune (occurring Nov. 10 – 16) This occurrence of Sun square Neptune especially affects Scorpio people who are celebrating birthdays November 10 – 16. Neptune in the square position to these birthday folks' natal Sun brings a sense of obstacles getting in the way of Spirit or the acknowledgement of spiritual beliefs. The challenge for these Scorpio birthday folks is to overcome the interfering doubts and confrontations. This especially applies to overcoming those extremely dangerous and destructive addictive tendencies. Remember, Scorpio, spiritual lessons do not have to be life threatening! Over the next year, there will undoubtedly be some spiritual adjustments, and perhaps a change of belief is required. This aspect last occurred May 11 – 17, reaching its peak on May 14, affecting the Taurus birthday people.

November 14th Friday

Moon in Gemini

	PST	EST	
Moon square Uranus	5:59 PM	8:59 PM	
Moon square Saturn	7:39 PM	10:39 PM	
Moon trine Neptune	10:18 PM	1:18 AM	(November 15)
Mercury trine Uranus begins (see November 15)			
Mercury sextile Jupiter begins (see November 16)			

Mood Watch: Throughout the day, the waning Gemini Moon keeps us busy making connections and weighing out the pros and cons of our decisions. This is a good

204

time for writing, networking, secretarial organization, and communications. The nature of the Gemini Moon keeps us curious and inquisitive as well as oriented towards collecting details and sharing ideas. ♏

November 15th Saturday

Moon in Gemini / Cancer

	PST	EST	
Moon opposite Pluto goes v/c	11:17 AM	2:17 PM	
Moon enters Cancer	11:53 AM	2:53 PM	
Moon opposite Venus	6:32 PM	9:32 PM	
Mercury trine Uranus	10:36 PM	1:36 AM	(November 16)
Mercury sextile Saturn begins (see November 16)			
Mercury square Neptune begins (see November 17)			

Mood Watch: The Gemini Moon morning brings curious and intellectually stimu-lating moods. As the Moon enters Cancer, it's a good time to refresh the home with flowers and therapeutic scents. Moon in Cancer emphasizes the need for a homey atmosphere and a safe and cozy realm to explore one's feelings. When in doubt, take a bath or pamper yourself with whatever works to create a calming and soothing affect. For those working people who don't have time for such luxuries, it may be best to acknowledge that moodiness and emotional traffic is a standard practice of the Cancer Moon influence.

Mercury trine Uranus (occurring Nov. 14 – 17) Mercury in Scorpio is trine to Uranus in Pisces. This combination stirs up an intelligent, compelling and awak-ening thought process, one that is usually well defined. This is a good time to record your thoughts and delight in brilliant thinking and information. Much of this brilliant thinking may seem like propaganda or information with a radical twist. Catch phrases, radical concept statements and ideas are often born under this aspect. Sensationalism or matters of censorship may be emphasized. Mercury in Scorpio dredges up important topics such as birth, sex, death, and the regenerative force realized through overcoming illness. Uranus is in the sign of Pisces, creating radical change in areas of addiction, the arts, music, psychology, and religion. This aspect last occurred July 21 – 23, reaching its peak on July 22, when Mercury was in Cancer.

November 16th Sunday

Moon in Cancer

	PST	EST
Mars enters Sagittarius	12:26 AM	3:26 AM
Mercury sextile Jupiter	8:00 AM	11:00 AM
Mercury sextile Saturn	4:27 PM	7:27 PM
Moon trine Uranus	6:25 PM	9:25 PM
Moon opposite Jupiter	7:39 PM	10:39 PM
Moon sextile Saturn	8:28 PM	11:28 PM
Moon trine Mercury	8:56 PM	11:56 PM

Mood Watch: It's a watery day with the Sun and Moon both in water signs. Another day of the waning Moon in Cancer reminds us it's times like these that allow us to share our emotions openly, and sort to through the ebb and flow of our ups and downs. The Moon reflects on our emotional cycles. The important thing to

205

remember always with the emotional realm is to keep the energy flowing.

Mars enters Sagittarius (Mars in Sagittarius: Nov. 16 – Dec. 26) While Mars travels through Sagittarius, Sagittarian people are likely to apply some extra energy to creative and outgoing projects – they will be feeling the heat of Mars activity in their lives. Mars is a fiery influence, and Sagittarius serves this energy very well as a mutable fire sign. Philosophers, athletes and travelers are particularly open to generating vast amounts of output and energy as the force of Mars activates the Sagittarian perspective. Since the turn of the century, Mars has been the feisty one in this particular sign. The last few times Mars has been in Sagittarius, there has been no lack of war related activity. When in Sagittarius, Mars has stirred up our viewpoints over areas where the god of war has stepped beyond the usual bounds. Mars forces us to take some course of action, even if the course of action is the *choice* of inaction, at which point new vistas of understanding will evolve, and the warrior within will begin to take shape. Mars, the king of action, does not have to apply war-like activity all the time, as it simply represents the energy and strength necessary to take action. Sagittarius says, *"I see."* Perhaps we can actively take hold of a vision, a picture or a philosophy that can be manifested through our actions towards a positive, more balanced approach to what we hope to create for ourselves in the future. Mars means business in Sagittarius, and this is not the time to actively close our eyes – this is the time to open our eyes to the activities taking place around us.

Mercury sextile Jupiter (occurring Nov. 14 – 17) Mercury in Scorpio is sextile Jupiter in Capricorn. Mercury influences news and talk, while Jupiter influences commerce, wealth, and prosperous advancement. This would be an excellent time to inquire about opportunities, to discuss potential work or career related advancements and to communicate visions and goals. This is also a good time to help people to improve their skills and apply them. Putting our minds to work on urgent, vital, and important information, particularly while Mercury is in Scorpio, is the sort of thing that gets noticed by employers and business partners. Opportunity is out there for both the employer and the employee. This is a good time to share information and promote your capabilities. Mercury sextile Jupiter brings joyful, philosophical, and mind expanding conversations. This aspect last occurred March 26 – 28, reaching its peak on March 27, when Mercury was in Pisces sextile Jupiter in Capricorn.

Mercury sextile Saturn (occurring Nov. 15 – 17) Mercury in Scorpio is sextile to Saturn in Virgo. Opportunities are now available to assist us in communicating vital information in a more organized and pragmatic fashion. This aspect gives people an opportunity to learn vital lessons concerning boundaries, limitations, responsibilities and timely completion. This is a favorable aspect to discuss where to set up boundaries and how to implement security systems, and to teach people about handling responsibilities and disciplines. This aspect last occurred July 12 – 15, reaching its peak on July 14, when Mercury was in Cancer sextile Saturn in Virgo.

November 17th Monday

Moon in Cancer / Leo

	PST	EST
Moon trine Sun goes v/c	5:42 AM	8:42 AM
Moon enters Leo	1:08 PM	4:08 PM
Moon trine Mars	3:04 PM	6:04 PM
Mercury square Neptune	3:30 PM	6:30 PM

♏

Mood Watch: A moody Monday greets us, especially with the waning Cancer Moon going void-of-course this morning and remaining void until afternoon. If you must work among a decidedly crabby crowd of moody folks, pace yourself and don't let the negative qualities of such moodiness get to you. There are likely to be traffic jams and delays. Those feeling particularly run down at this time could be highly susceptible to getting a cold or the flu. Rest and take vitamins if the signs of vulnerability are evident. Every once in awhile, a good Cancer Moon comes along and impresses us with the need to tend to the emotional side of our being. Nurture yourself and be sure to release those useless and pent-up emotions in a safe direction. This is the time to let moods flow, and it is important not to take other people's moodiness personally. Later in the day, Moon in Leo brings a sunny and warm disposition to the mood as it entices us to be playful.

Mercury square Neptune (occurring Nov. 15 – 19) This aspect often brings a struggle to communicate with regard to the spirit world and human spirituality. Efforts to explain our beliefs may be especially challenging. Neptune is in Aquarius, stirring up issues around human divinity and humanity's beliefs in this confusing and changing period of the dawning age. While Mercury in Scorpio is squaring Neptune, dramatic kinds of thought will be challenged, particularly with respect to issues that concern divine experience (birth, sex, death); relaying this information may seem all the more difficult with this aspect. Anticipate religion related arguments and disputes. Deep subjects must not be treated lightly while Mercury squares Neptune. This aspect last occurred April 27 – 30, reaching its peak on April 29, when Mercury was in Taurus square Neptune in Aquarius.

November 18th Tuesday

Moon in Leo

Mood Watch: There are no significant exact lunar aspects occurring today, and fortunately, the Moon isn't void-of-course either. This is not to say that today will be an uneventful Leo Moon day. Leo Moon energy always demands people's attention, as there is usually some element of entertainment or amusement at work. The waning Leo Moon often leads our attention to the self, particularly the internal process of the self. This is a good time to seek out a personal hobby or to interact with family members in a creative and enchanting sort of way. Leo Moon draws us to the power of the sun, and there may be some yearning for the sun, or a special celebration for its life giving force. Even in those places where the sun's warming effects are not prevalent, we are there to shine.

November 19th Wednesday
Moon in Leo / Virgo – LAST QUARTER MOON in LEO

	PST	EST	
	PST	EST	
Moon opposite Neptune	2:14 AM	5:14 AM	
Moon square Mercury	6:49 AM	9:49 AM	
Moon square Sun	1:31 PM	4:31 PM	
Moon trine Pluto goes v/c	4:48 PM	7:48 PM	
Moon enters Virgo	5:13 PM	8:13 PM	
Moon square Mars	10:14 PM	1:14 AM	(November 20)

Mood Watch: Today people will be inclined to be entertained and to get their minds on enjoying life. We now come to the **Last Quarter Moon in Leo** (Moon square Sun). When the Moon is waning in Leo it urges us to take special care of ourselves as well as the children in our life. Projects of interest are sometimes considered children as well. If there is a hobby of special interest to you, take the time to brighten and enliven this work which represents your own talent and self-reflection. Throughout the working (or playing) day, jokes will fly, toys of special interest will be admired and moods will reflect childlike frolic and revel. If you're serious about not being distracted by such playfulness perhaps a quiet workspace is the key. If you must work with others, allow the frivolity to flow; the work will get done but the child in everyone has to play now and then. Later today, the Moon goes void-of-course for a little while and it may be difficult to keep track of things. Tonight's Moon in Virgo brings health oriented moods.

November 20th Thursday
Moon in Virgo

	PST	EST
Moon trine Venus	10:46 AM	1:46 PM
Sun conjunct Mercury begins (see November 25)		

Mood Watch: This is a time to focus on health and a sense of well being. However mundane the task may seem, the need to maintain, clean, perfect, and upgrade our surroundings is ever present. Waning Virgo Moon is driving home the reality that we need to tend to and exercise those basic but important health practices. This is a good time to flush toxins, drop or decrease bad health habits, and clean up our surroundings. With the proper banishing of illness that has transpired and still lingers, the critical nature of our moods can subside. Healing and cleansing our surroundings helps to combat sluggish feelings.

SAGITTARIUS

Key Phrase: "I SEE" or
" I PERCEIVE "
Mutable Fire Sign
Symbol: The Centaur
November 21st through
December 21st

November 21st Friday

Moon in Virgo

	PST	EST	
Moon opposite Uranus	3:21 AM	6:21 AM	
Jupiter trine Saturn	4:12 AM	7:12 AM	
Moon conjunct Saturn	6:15 AM	9:15 AM	
Moon trine Jupiter	6:16 AM	9:16 AM	
Sun enters Sagittarius	3:44 PM	6:44 PM	
Moon sextile Mercury	9:06 PM	12:06 AM	(November 22)

Mood Watch: Prudent resourcefulness comes in handy during waning Virgo Moon. It's all a question of how to narrow down complex matters. Virgo asks many questions. As ever, caution and skepticism fill our moods.

Jupiter trine Saturn (occurring Aug. 20 – Dec. 11) For the third time this year, Jupiter trine Saturn reaches a peak, and this brings the most advantageous time to harvest the rewards of prosperous growth. It is also a time to give some guidelines and structure to our current economic growth. Here, we can take advantage of all kinds of gifts and opportunities, and this will come easily if we do it responsibly. Jupiter in Capricorn and Saturn in Virgo emphasize the need for prudent and safe investments. This favorable aspect first occurred January 9 – 31, and it reached its peak on January 21. Then on September 8, this aspect reached a second exact peak. For a recap on the story of this long winded harmonious aspect between the two most significant planets influencing the development of our economic structure and well being, see September 8 and January 21.

Sun enters Sagittarius (Sun in Sagittarius: Nov. 21 – Dec. 21) Sun in Sagittarius represents the final laps of autumn and the shortest days of the solar year. The Sagittarius expression, "I see," opens our eyes to some new discoveries during this time. This mutable fire sign achieves visionary awareness by reaching out into the world of possibilities, the stars, and beyond. The Sagittarius time of year – often thought of as being early winter – is actually still fall season, and sees to the closing

209

of autumn by putting to sleep the last of the restless foliage in preparation for the pending winter's great slumber. Sun in Sagittarius days bring a focus on prosperity. Jupiter is the ruling planet of Sagittarius and inspires Sagittarians to excel, expand, and prosper. As the holidays begin and the Christmas season unfurls, the pressure to consume elaborate foods and purchase gifts, while keeping the great economic wheel turning, can be monumental for absolutely everyone. We are often required to pull together an outstanding number of social events and personal expenditures. The concept of prosperity has been tested to the extremes each time this season unfolds; it is, therefore, very important to get back to the basics of what one identifies as prosperous. The true challenge for many of us will be met when we finally reach out towards the higher vision of what prosperity really means. Sun in Sagittarius serves as a good time to direct the forces of vision and inspiration towards attaining a sense of wealth and well being. Tiny Tim (of Charles Dickens fame) was a character who was not disappointed by the lack of food on his table Christmas day; he recognized the sacredness of sharing the company of his loved ones. Don't let the complications of the expectations of others spoil your own sense of attainment and satisfaction with life itself and with the people you have the privilege to share it with. Simple pleasures can bring prosperous joy. Sagittarius emphasizes travel, sports, and philosophy – all those things that require adaptable enthusiasm. There are many ways of seeing and many directions in which to look.

November 22nd Saturday

Moon in Virgo / Libra	PST	EST	
Moon square Pluto goes v/c	12:02 AM	3:02 AM	
Moon enters Libra	12:20 AM	3:20 AM	
Moon sextile Sun	1:10 AM	4:10 AM	
Moon sextile Mars	8:57 AM	11:57 AM	
Mercury enters Sagittarius	11:09 PM	2:09 AM	(November 23)

Mood Watch: The waning Libra Moon is a good time to teach tolerance. It is up to each of us individually to set a precedent or some plainly stated guidelines for what does and doesn't work in our relationships. A good working relationship usually undergoes a fairly regular readjustment process, and now is a good time for that.

Mercury enters Sagittarius (Mercury in Sagittarius: Nov. 22 – Dec. 12) Mercury, the planet of communication, information, and news is traveling through the sign of Sagittarius. New perspectives are bound to come up. News is always more philosophical and visionary when Mercury is in this sign. Word travels fast and further than expected. Sagittarius is the challenging "detrimental" place for Mercury, and this is a time when Mercury's greatest weapon – words – are best communicated with carefully considered diplomacy. People will be increasingly curious to know what is happening in the world, and to be more aware of global perspectives. Mercury in Sagittarius offers an opportunity to share your vision of a better world with others, and also brings adventure to the world of communications.

November 23rd Sunday

Moon in Libra

	PST	EST
Moon square Venus	12:36 AM	3:36 AM
Moon square Jupiter	4:01 PM	7:01 PM
Moon trine Neptune	5:35 PM	8:35 PM

Mood Watch: Despite a couple of lunar squares in today's aspects, the waning Libra Moon guides us towards the achievement of harmony. Today is the birthday of Harpo Marx (1888 - 1964); the mischievously sublime harpist, and the master of joy and bountiful humor, reminds his fellow kinsfolk to live life to the fullest – no spoken words necessary. Positive affirmations are the key to today's success, and they can be planted within. Teamwork, compromise, and cooperation will bring us closer to a sense of peace.

November 24th Monday

Moon in Libra / Scorpio

	PST	EST
Moon sextile Pluto goes v/c	9:45 AM	12:45 PM
Moon enters Scorpio	9:55 AM	12:55 PM

Mood Watch: The Libra Moon morning emphasizes the need to share our plans and aspirations with others. As the day progresses, the Moon goes void-of-course for ten short minutes and then swiftly enters Scorpio. There is beauty, sensation and an electrical field of awareness at work. The events of the day may seem laced with strong doses of emotion. A waning Moon in Scorpio calls to us to let go of strong destructive tendencies, and challenges us to cease hurting ourselves and others, and to transform our lower impulses into higher aspirations. Under the correct circumstances, this is a good time to let go of the pain you've been concealing.

November 25th Tuesday

Moon in Scorpio

	PST	EST	
Sun conjunct Mercury	8:52 AM	11:52 AM	
Moon sextile Venus	5:19 PM	8:19 PM	
Moon trine Uranus	10:47 PM	1:47 AM	(November 26)
Mercury conjunct Mars begins (see November 28)			
Sun conjunct Mars begins (see December 5)			

Mood Watch: A protected and safe environment may be essential to address and release the more intense emotions which tend to surface during the waning Scorpio Moon. This is a good time to face up to truth, and to be aware of the tendency towards lies and deception. Despite some emotional pitfalls, today's Scorpio Moon will be the best time to make progress in our work this week; tomorrow's tediously long void-of-course Moon will seem to slow all progress. However, progress isn't everything; from the place of true desire, Scorpio's lunar expression allows us to create new incentives to live every moment with the precious awareness that life is rich and death is certain.

Sun conjunct Mercury (occurring Nov. 20 – 30) This is the sixth and final time the Sun will be conjunct with Mercury this year. Today's conjunction will create a much more thoughtful, communicative, and expressive year ahead for those Scorpio and Sagittarius folks celebrating birthdays November 20 – 30. This is your time (birthday people) to record ideas, relay important messages, and pay close attention to your imaginative thoughts as they are touched by Mercury, creating the urge to speak and be heard. Your thoughts will reveal a great deal about who you are, now and in the year to come.

November 26ᵗʰ Wednesday

Moon in Scorpio / Sagittarius

	PST	EST	
Moon sextile Saturn	2:34 AM	5:34 AM	
Moon sextile Jupiter	3:50 AM	6:50 AM	
Moon square Neptune goes v/c	4:32 AM	7:32 AM	
PLUTO ENTERS CAPRICORN	5:02 PM	8:02 PM	
Moon enters Sagittarius	9:14 PM	12:14 AM	(November 27)
Venus sextile Uranus begins (see November 28)			

Mood Watch: Starting very early, the darkly waning Scorpio Moon will be void-of-course for nearly the entire day. It is as if the Moon positioned itself here on purpose to intensify our understanding of today's monumental shift of Pluto in Capricorn for the next fifteen years (see below). Scorpio takes our mood into deep places, and allows us to transform our spirits through life's milestones. Beware of all signs of danger and hang in there. Much later, the Sagittarius Moon takes us on a journey of the soul.

Pluto enters Capricorn (Pluto in Capricorn: Nov. 26, 2008 – March 23, 2023) Pluto initially entered Capricorn, for the first time this year on **January 25** and it remained there until June 13. Since June, Pluto has been traveling trough the late degrees of Sagittarius for the last time. Today, Pluto will bid farewell to Sagittarius for the last time in this lifetime – until the year 2242 – when Pluto will have traveled all around the zodiac, returning to Sagittarius again.

THE HISTORY OF PLUTO IN CAPRICORN:

Throughout our history, the phases of Pluto in Capricorn indicate a tendency to revolve around the themes of revolution and authoritarian influence. The last time Pluto was in Capricorn takes us to the revolutionary days of the late eighteenth century. Pluto traversed through Capricorn from January 1762, right up through the Spirit of 1776, finally exiting Capricorn in 1778. This was a time of war, revolution, turmoil, and victory in the annals of American history. Not only did the American Revolution spring up, but those who were born during this time brought about the French Revolution and the tenacious dictatorship of Napoleon.

One more round of history takes us back to a former Pluto in Capricorn phase – 1516 to 1532 – a time that ushered in the sixteenth century with a series of discoveries about nature and the cosmos. It was only just a couple of decades prior, when Christopher Columbus and Amerigo Vespucci had enlightened their countrymen with descriptions of the world's vast continents – with this they dispelled the myth of a flat world. This was a time of discovery just as much as it was a time of revolution, as the Renaissance was still in the process of great change. It was a time when Jewish and Moslem scholars peacefully defined new frontiers of knowledge in the field of Astronomy. Martin Luther (1483-1546) was in the throws of advancing his own revolutionary views while also opposing the Peasants' Revolt (1524 – 1525).

THE FUTURE OF PLUTO IN CAPRICORN:

What might we expect with a modern Pluto in Capricorn phase (2008 – 2023) just ahead of us? History indicates radical changes and transformation have been known to occur around leaders and revolutionaries. Classically, it is the planet Uranus that is known for stirring up chaos and revolution. If we look at the Pluto in Capricorn relationship to Uranus, we see that a major conflict will soon arrive. In late May 2010, Uranus will enter Aries, meaning it will be in the unfavorable *square* position to Pluto in Capricorn. The square of Pluto to Uranus (occurring May 2010 to April 2017) is likely to bring unprecedented styles of leadership and/or dictatorship. This may be particularly true while Uranus and Pluto are in the cardinal signs of Aries and Capricorn. Institutions will be expected to have a pioneering fervor to dominate the world stage with unwavering control. While the transformational qualities of Pluto are in conflict with the revolutionary chaos of Uranus, phenomenally large and disruptive changes will emerge on the planet.

Pluto in Capricorn is likely to bring revolution in leadership reflecting the power of institutions, particularly corporate establishments that will influence government and world trade. We have already seen many clues as to how this corporate power has taken over in the overall economic picture. Pluto represents transformation and a new generation of cultural thought and expression. Capricorn represents things such as establishment, large-scale business, engineering, agriculture, civil service, and bureaucracy. Pluto's power structures, influenced by the cardinal earth sign, Capricorn, will address important large-scale environmental concerns such as global warming. How these institutions will tackle the problems arising from these concerns has everything to do with economic feasibility and the adaptability of corporate structure.

Capricornian focuses relish corporate growth and the establishment of industry standards to ensure the wealth of corporate participants. Heavy industrial equipment and sophisticated types of environmental control will continue to bring an alarming chain of physical effects around us. Capricorn also represents the energy of its ruling planet, Saturn, which minds the physical world in a very conscientious fashion. The serious realms of Saturnian ruled Capricorn demand physical mastery, balance, control, and a sense of how to dependably master these boundaries through determination, discipline, and focus. This is a time when empires will be built, and at the same time, dysfunctional landscapes may be entirely lost or abandoned, whether due to human related consequences or natural disasters – or both.

Meanwhile, Pluto is known as the underworld god, the one who tests and evaluates the stability of all things, and discerns where there is weakness. Pluto removes or annihilates weakness with illness, famine, decay, and putrefaction. Pluto purifies or cleans away that which is dead and gone. Where Pluto traverses, permanent change will occur. Out of this transformation, an entirely different perspective will affect our understanding of how things work on the physical plane. This will be seen particularly in the eventual legacy of the generation that will be born during this time of Pluto in Capricorn. It is futile to take the doomsday approach to the consciousness that will be raised from these shifting earth changes through the year 2023.

Pluto in Capricorn makes it everyone's responsibility to pay more attention to the physical. It may not be all gruesome. Pluto's tests bring great rewards to humanity, and the mastery of the physical world is certainly the test that has had us on the run since the very beginning of time.

Over the course of the next quarter century, Pluto's influence will change things noticeably, permanently, and in no uncertain terms. While Pluto is in Capricorn, some things that we now know to be elements of our existence from the very beginning of time will be forever changed. Much of what we depended on in the past was a far cry from the things we depend on now. Take electrical power, for instance – we didn't have it for centuries, and now most of civilization depends on it. Back when Pluto traversed through Gemini, and also through Cancer (the opposite of Capricorn), end of the 19th and beginning of the 20th centuries produced such giants of electrical engineering as Nikola Tesla, Samuel Morse, Antonio Meucci, Thomas Edison, George Westinghouse, Werner von Siemens, Charles Steinmetz, and Alexander Graham Bell. These were just some of the masters whose influences gave way to the remarkable changes of the dawning 20th century. How about our heat sources and our methods of transportation? Things have definitely changed in those departments, and changed permanently. Will we ever go back to the ways we lived before? Not likely, but much of what we were capable of 100 or more years ago is not the sort of thing we are accustomed to now. Electricity, modern plumbing, computers, super highways, jet travel, all-night convenience stores, etc. are now considered necessities. This is an important time to record everything we know and love, and to recognize the impermanence of systems we have come to depend on. It is also a good time to understand emergency procedures, to examine alternative measures for handling power outages, natural disasters, and national emergencies. Pluto in Capricorn is poised to remind us the destruction of impractical or outmoded systems is imminent at this stage of our history. Have we not already seen the signs? The Pluto process takes a long time. If our systems shut down, how will we access the resources necessary to survive? Much like the past, our resources are the keys to the cultural and economic changes of the future.

This explanation has basically covered the history and future of Pluto in Capricorn. For more information on Pluto in Capricorn, as well as Pluto through the previous generations of the zodiac, *see January 25*, back when Pluto first entered Capricorn this millennium.

November 27th Thursday
Thanksgiving Day, USA

NEW MOON in SAGITTARIUS	PST	EST
Uranus goes direct	8:09 AM	11:09 AM
Moon conjunct Sun	8:54 AM	11:54 AM
Moon conjunct Mercury	11:31 AM	2:31 AM
Moon conjunct Mars	1:56 PM	4:56 PM
Venus conjunct Jupiter begins (see December 1)		

Mood Watch: The **New Moon in Sagittarius** (Moon conjunct Sun) inspires us to look at life in a whole new way. A hopeful outlook is felt strongly as the Moon reaches the new mark this morning. New Moon in Sagittarius encourages us to

214

start new exercise programs, look into new philosophies, and to explore new territory in our lives. Sagittarius says, "I see," so vision and insight are the primary incentives to explore new ground. Today is a good day to optimistically look ahead and get in touch with a new vision for the coming month.

Uranus goes direct (Uranus direct: Nov. 27, 2008 – July 3, 2009) Since June 26 Uranus, known for stirring up calamity, has been retrograde. Now the planet of chaos and rebellion moves steadily forward through the mid-course degrees of Pisces, awakening the spiritual needs of humanity, perhaps even inspiring breakthroughs in human rights, or promoting creativity in art and music. The work of radical and revolutionary forces resumes course as Uranus moves direct until early July, 2009. We all feel the need to break out of oppressing conditions of life. As Uranus moves forward, the volatile quality of its work demands the utmost intelligence and knowledge as each level of urgency is unveiled. Uranus is the ruler of Aquarius and teaches us to seek higher levels of intelligence through unusual, brilliant, and open minded measures. The next time the urge for unabashed rebellion makes you kick up your heels, remember to kindle the light of love for humankind's wisdom. This is, after all, the Age of Aquarius.

November 28th Friday

Moon in Sagittarius

	PST	EST
Venus sextile Uranus	1:20 AM	4:20 AM
Moon square Uranus	10:57 AM	1:57 PM
Moon square Saturn	3:07 PM	6:07 PM
Moon sextile Neptune goes v/c	4:53 PM	7:53 PM
Mercury conjunct Mars	7:39 PM	10:39 PM

Mood Watch: The youthfully waxing Sagittarius Moon directs us towards a congenial, cooperative and flexible expression of mood. There will be times when the squaring lunar aspects bring challenge, but this does not stop us from keeping an eye out for opportunity as our moods begin to brighten considerably after an emotionally challenging week of events. Tonight's void-of-course Moon may account for the feeling of being lost at times.

Venus sextile Uranus (occurring Nov. 26 – 29) Venus in Capricorn is sextile to Uranus in Pisces. This aspect occurred February 5 – 8, reaching its peak on February 6. When Venus was in Taurus, this aspect repeated May 16 – 19, reaching its peak on May 18. For more information on today's repeat aspect of Venus sextile Uranus, *see February 6*, when it first occurred.

Mercury conjunct Mars (occurring Nov. 25 – Dec. 2) Due to Mercury's retrograde pattern last month (Sept. 24 – Oct. 15), this aspect takes place for the third time this year. This is an excellent time to get others motivated through speech. This may also be a time of angry words being spoken. Heated discussions among friends and lovers are most likely to occur with this aspect, especially since these two planets are conjunct in the fiery sign of Sagittarius. If you're traveling, this is an especially important time to watch what you say in foreign territory. Some might say the best way to win an argument is to begin by being right; taking this approach during this aspect is likely to win you favors but not friendship. Take caution with your words; if they are intended to incite a battle, this would be a marvelous time to put that message out there! Mercury conjunct Mars also happened on September 8 and 23, when Mercury and Mars were in Libra.

November 29th Saturday

Moon in Sagittarius / Capricorn

	PST	EST
Moon enters Capricorn	9:48 AM	12:48 PM
Moon conjunct Pluto	9:59 AM	12:59 PM
Venus trine Saturn	8:36 PM	11:36 PM

Mood Watch: The void-of-course Sagittarius Moon brings spacey moods this morning. A little later, the Moon enters Capricorn and our moods may seem somewhat subdued emotionally. Capricorn is the achiever; hence, not only do we wish to get grounded and overcome emotional hurtles, but now we are aspiring to climb to some higher ground. Capricorn Moon brings focus and determination into the spirit of the day.

Venus trine Saturn (occurring Nov. 27 – Dec. 2) This aspect first occurred January 27 – February 1, reaching its exact aspect on January 29. It also occurred on April 29 – May 4, reaching its exact peak on May 1. For more information on Venus in Capricorn trine Saturn in Virgo, *see January 29.*

November 30th Sunday

Moon in Capricorn

	PST	EST	
Moon sextile Uranus	11:55 PM	2:55 AM	(December 1)

Mood Watch: Moon in Capricorn provides our moods with a steady persistence to meet important goals and make progress with our work. Let the progress of your work shine and take joy in your accomplishments. A very busy new month awaits us, and this is a good time to make some headway. Waxing Capricorn Moon is a great time to set goals and to assess personal progress and achievements.

December 1st Monday

Moon in Capricorn / Aquarius

	PST	EST	
Venus conjunct Jupiter	12:44 AM	3:44 AM	
Moon trine Saturn	4:22 AM	7:22 AM	
Moon conjunct Jupiter	7:08 AM	10:08 AM	
Moon conjunct Venus goes v/c	7:43 AM	10:43 AM	
Moon enters Aquarius	10:45 PM	1:45 AM	(December 2)

Mood Watch: This morning the Capricorn Moon goes void-of-course, and remains this way throughout the entire day and most of the evening. What starts out as industrious moods quickly fade into overly serious and ambitious moods that are likely to be disgruntled by a lack of adequate progress. Don't be deceived by high expectations.

Venus conjunct Jupiter (occurring Nov. 27 – Dec. 4) This is a time to enhance love relationships and realize the precious value of love in its most limitless sense, since the influence of Jupiter reminds us the resources of love in the universe are inexhaustible, and love's great bounty is designed to be shared. This conjunction first occurred January 29 – February 4, reaching its peak on February 1.

216

December 2nd Tuesday

Moon in Aquarius

	PST	EST	
Moon sextile Sun	9:44 PM	12:44 AM	(December 3)
Moon sextile Mars	11:21 PM	2:21 AM	(December 3)
Mercury square Uranus begins (see December 4)			

Mood Watch: Progressive, open-minded, and truthful attitudes will keep us inspired as the Moon waxes in Aquarius. There is a spark of political controversy in the air. Remember to enjoy the freedom we now have and hold precious. Protect and uphold your rights! The more our rights are exercised the stronger they become. The benefits of good deeds are said to increase one's good karma threefold.

December 3rd Wednesday

Moon in Aquarius

	PST	EST
Moon sextile Mercury	7:20 AM	10:20 AM
Moon conjunct Neptune goes v/c	6:14 PM	9:14 PM

Mood Watch: Aquarius Moon brings humanitarian openness, and people are likely to be inspired by knowledgeable and helpful acts of goodwill. Tonight's void-of-course Moon in Aquarius brings the potential for unusual circumstances to crop up unexpectedly. Late autumn storms are unpredictable and chaotic. Technical failures or power outages may occur under the void Aquarius Moon. Some patience may be required this evening and early tomorrow.

December 4th Thursday

Moon in Aquarius / Pisces

	PST	EST	
Moon enters Pisces	10:24 AM	1:24 PM	
Moon sextile Pluto	10:53 AM	1:53 PM	
Mercury square Uranus	9:52 PM	12:52 AM	(December 5)
Mercury square Saturn begins (see December 6)			

Mood Watch: Since last night, the void-of-course Moon in Aquarius has been testing our humanitarian senses, our endurance, and our tolerance. The morning will bring more of the same, but before too long, the Moon enters Pisces, and the colorful and serene quality of our moods adds a richly intuitive spirit to the atmosphere. Adaptable moods bring comfort where it is needed.

Mercury square Uranus (occurring Dec. 2 – 6) Mercury in Sagittarius is square to Uranus in Pisces. This creates explosive mental states and causes some people to speak abrasively or to promote overly radical ideas. Tact and diplomacy are likely to go right out the door when religion is discussed. Communications and philosophical debates may come up against unusual or explosive viewpoints. Spiritual harmony is always best achieved when we exercise discretion. This really is a time to watch what you say: communications have the potential to shake matters up considerably. This aspect first occurred May 18 – June 3, but due to the retrograde pattern of Mercury at that time, it never actually reached its peak. This aspect also occurred July 2 – 7, reaching its exact peak on July 5, when Mercury was in Gemini.

December 5th Friday
FIRST QUARTER MOON in PISCES

	PST	EST	
Moon square Sun	1:24 PM	4:24 PM	
Moon square Mars	1:25 PM	4:25 PM	
Sun conjunct Mars	2:03 PM	5:03 PM	
Moon conjunct Uranus	10:05 PM	1:05 AM	(December 6)

Mood Watch: The **First Quarter Moon in Pisces** (Moon square Sun) often brings our hearts and minds to a peaceful place, but today this may be challenged by the square dance of the Moon with Mars and the Sun, which are currently conjunct (see below). A spacey, dreamy sort of consciousness leads to strong psychic awareness which may be uncomfortably hot with fiery emotion in the afternoon. While the first quarter Moon is in Pisces, calming kinds of music, art, and poetry will fill us with inspiration, intuition, and hope. Unhappy people may turn to intoxicants to escape their troubles. Passive, cheerful, and kind sentiments will be greatly appreciated. Deep meditation and spiritual practices will empower the imagination.

Sun conjunct Mars (occurring Nov. 25 – Dec. 16) Sagittarius folks celebrating birthdays Nov. 25 – Dec. 16, are undergoing a Mars conjunction to their natal sun. Mars stirs up newness and extreme energy into the lives of these birthday people. If you were born during this time, obvious and genuine changes are occurring, and there is heat in most facets of your life. Positive Mars changes involve the breaking down of old structure and the creative reconstruction of one's personal desires and environment. Negative Mars changes often involve accidents, breakups, fevers and the collapse of overheated internal organs, as well as bouts of impatience and anger. Bursts of energy now fill your life, birthday Sagittarians. This may be the most energy and action you'll have to contend with all year. Use it wisely and creatively while you've got it, and allow the activities of your days to infuse you with rich enthusiastic vigor. Attempt as best you can to use the heat of anger to be constructive, as opposed to destructive. Also remember this will be your year to take action and accomplish much!

December 6th Saturday
Moon in Pisces / Aries

	PST	EST
Moon square Mercury	1:25 AM	4:25 AM
Moon opposite Saturn	2:34 AM	5:34 AM
Moon sextile Jupiter	6:23 AM	9:23 AM
Mercury square Saturn	11:13 AM	2:13 PM
Moon sextile Venus goes v/c	4:42 PM	7:42 PM
Moon enters Aries	6:45 PM	9:45 PM
Moon square Pluto	7:21 PM	10:21 PM
Mercury sextile Neptune	8:37 PM	11:37 PM

Mood Watch: Abstract concepts are everywhere. Mystery, fantasy, enchantment and make-believe are high on the Saturday matinee movie-goer's priority list. More tranquil practices might include a long meditative walk in pleasant places near water. Later today, the Moon goes void-of-course for a couple of hours; beware of holiday drunks, traffic delays, and emotionally taxing scenarios. This evening's

218

Aries Moon brings a warrior spirit. Drive and determination are evident in our moods.

Mercury square Saturn (occurring Dec. 4 – 8) It happens on the exact same day as last year – Mercury in Sagittarius is square Saturn in Virgo. This may be a difficult time to acquire or to communicate travel information accurately for timely efficiency during travels. It may be a challenging time to communicate instructions or to inform someone of the end of something. It may also be challenging to sell someone on a product, or to successfully request a raise or promotion. Whatever the desired effect may be, it is wise to use caution when attempting communications during Mercury square Saturn. Saturn is in Virgo, creating limitations and structural changes in matters of accounting and with regard to health related concerns. This aspect makes it difficult to put a message out there and be taken seriously. Some people may become very tongue tied and feel quite off track. Mercury square Saturn last occurred May 1 – 5, reaching its peak on May 3, when Mercury was in Gemini.

Mercury sextile Neptune (occurring Dec. 5 – 8) Mercury in Sagittarius sextile Neptune in Aquarius reassures us that communicating our philosophies and our beliefs also empowers our belief in humanity. This is an opportunistic time to cautiously attempt communication with regard to beliefs and spiritual matters. Mercury is in Sagittarius placing a philosophical emphasis of talk on such Neptune-related subjects as spiritual growth, guidance, and inspiration. Take this opportunity to transmute thoughts and beliefs into a workable understanding and to share it with others in a way that encourages them. Prayers, channeling, and spells are all very effective with Mercury sextile Neptune. This is the time to get the word out to Great Spirit, and to reinforce a sense of faith. This aspect last occurred April 13 – 15, reaching its peak on April 14.

December 7ᵗʰ Sunday

Moon in Aries	PST	EST	
Venus enters Aquarius	3:36 PM	6:36 PM	
Moon trine Mars	10:49 PM	1:49 AM	(December 8)
Sun square Uranus begins (see December 10)			
Mars square Uranus begins (see December 11)			

Mood Watch: Waxing Moon in Aries activates our moods with ambitious gusto, and always provides an incentive to initiate things, such as this year's holiday decorations and lighting scheme. The momentum and positive force of the energy around us picks up greatly as the late autumn days of Sagittarius occur. Sun in Sagittarius and Moon in Aries bring creative zeal and enthusiasm to the ways in which we express ourselves.

Venus enters Aquarius (Venus in Aquarius: Dec. 7, 2008 – Jan. 3, 2009) For the second time this year, Venus (the planet of love) enters the knowledgeable domains of Aquarius. For more information on Venus in Aquarius, *see February 17.*

December 8th Monday

Moon in Aries / Taurus	PST	EST	
Moon trine Sun	12:04 AM	3:04 AM	
Moon sextile Neptune	9:04 AM	12:04 PM	
Moon square Jupiter	12:23 PM	3:23 PM	
Moon trine Mercury goes v/c	1:33 PM	4:33 PM	
Moon enters Taurus	10:53 PM	1:53 AM	(December 9)
Moon trine Pluto	11:33 PM	2:33 AM	(December 9)

Mood Watch: This morning's waxing Moon in Aries brings a comfortably active working pace to kick off a new work week. The Sun and Moon are in fire signs inspiring us to keep warm and active. This will be the best time of day to make some progress. Later today, as the Moon in Aries goes void-of-course, people may seem impatient and short-tempered, and there may be a lot of attempts to try to rush through things that can't be rushed. Traffic problems and accidents are likely to be especially prevalent this evening. Much later, the Moon enters Taurus, and our moods will be brought to a much more practical and down-to-earth level of interplay.

December 9th Tuesday

Moon in Taurus	PST	EST
Moon square Venus	1:35 AM	4:35 AM
Sun square Saturn begins (see December 12)		

Mood Watch: Waxing Taurus Moon focuses our attention on the matter of what we do or don't have in order to get by. Of course, there is also the matter of what we *want* to have in order to make the pending holidays festive. Money management and money related issues are very strong this time of year, especially when the Moon is in Taurus. Sensible buyers do not waste their energy on overpriced gifts. Quality and value are important, but so are our imaginative capabilities – and our pocket-books. Simple and practical gifts are a time honored tradition. The strongly waxing Taurus Moon also sets the stage for a lot of concern with regard to the handling and movement of valuables and goods. Slowly and steadily, let the bull's consummate pace keep the labor from being overtaxing.

December 10th Wednesday

Moon in Taurus / Gemini	PST	EST	
Sun square Uranus	4:03 AM	7:03 AM	
Moon sextile Uranus	5:41 AM	8:41 AM	
Moon trine Saturn	9:46 AM	12:46 PM	
Moon square Neptune	10:36 AM	1:36 PM	
Moon trine Jupiter goes v/c	2:22 PM	5:22 PM	
Moon enters Gemini	11:34 PM	2:34 AM	(December 11)
Mercury conjunct Pluto begins (see December 12)			

Mood Watch: Throughout morning and afternoon, the waxing Taurus Moon focuses our moods on taking care of business. For many folks, the drive to shop and buy is overwhelming. The message is out there: shop till you drop – its Christmas time. Taurus Moon brings an earthy and stubborn determination to get things done right. Later this afternoon, the Taurus Moon goes void-of-course for the remainder of the evening. Traffic delays and time consuming physical jobs lead to tiredness and evening laziness. Comforting settings will ease the desire to drop after we shop.

Sun square Uranus (occurring Dec. 7 – 13) This occurrence of Sun square Uranus particularly affects Sagittarius people celebrating birthdays December 7 - 13. The square of Uranus (in Pisces) to these Sagittarius folks' natal Sun brings about challenging events and a strong dose of unrestrained chaos. This may be the year for you Sagittarius birthday folks to surrender to those aspects of life that are truly out of your control, and to concentrate more rationally on those facets of life over which you do have control. Sometimes the aftermath of Uranus influence is an improvement, but with the square aspect at work, it is likely these people will feel personally challenged. It is important to understand that some types of personal challenges are best left alone, while others must be confronted directly without causing destructive damage, particularly to the self. On the other hand, birthday Sagittarius folks, if your life has no foundation, there is no point in holding onto the illusion of stability at this juncture of your sojourn. This aspect will pass, and it is vital not to give this rapid change too much resistance, lest you be bound to the reversals of trying to fight chaos with logic at a time when resistance is futile. Matters will settle down in due time; try to be detached from chaotic events as they occur, and the outcome will seem less costly. If you need it, project the picture of peace and it will be there for you at the other end. This aspect last occurred June 9 – 16, reaching its peak on June 12, when the Sun was in Gemini square Uranus is Pisces.

December 11th Thursday
Moon in Gemini

	PST	EST	
Moon trine Venus	6:10 AM	9:10 AM	
Mars square Uranus	10:50 PM	1:50 AM	(December 12)
Sun sextile Neptune begins (see December 13)			
Mars square Saturn begins (see December 15)			

Mood Watch: The lunar energy level is pumped up to maximum capacity; in other words, it's the full Gemini Moon eve! This is a time to talk matters over. There will be lots of phone calls and communications at work. Gemini Moon shines brightly, reflecting full ideas and thoughts for our moods to toy with. This is a frivolous, fun, silly, and fickle time for some, and for others there is the tendency to be burned out by too much information. It will take some thought to figure out how to put all these puzzles and details of our lives into a workable order. Happy Full Mooning!

Mars square Uranus (occurring Dec. 7 – 16) Mars square Uranus is sometimes tyrannical, and is never an aspect to be underestimated. Masculine fortitude and the enigmatic force of chaos are in a volatile and difficult phase of expression when Mars is square to Uranus. This aspect was suspiciously present when the December 26, 2004 tsunami tidal wave disaster of the century swept the Indian Ocean. Today, Mars is in the sign of Sagittarius and, while it squares to Uranus, the resulting tensions may cause extensive damage in the forces of offensive and defensive action. While Uranus is in Pisces, chaos abounds in the sacred territory

221

of our beliefs. The events of Mars square Uranus do not always predictably yield natural disasters, but unfortunately they are often the catalyst for difficult human trials. This aspect is like a pressure cooker; it may seem dormant at first, but if not carefully handled, the aftermath can be a real mess! It is wise to completely avoid extremely risky undertakings that may rock the boat of fiery activity during Mars square Uranus. This is no time to step into the eye of the storm! Fortunately, this is the only time this aspect will occur this year.

December 12ᵗʰ Friday
Moon in Gemini / Cancer – FULL MOON in GEMINI

	PST	EST	
Mercury enters Capricorn	2:12 AM	5:12 AM	
Moon square Uranus	5:10 AM	8:10 AM	
Moon opposite Mars	5:29 AM	8:29 AM	
Moon opposite Sun	8:37 AM	11:37 AM	
Moon square Saturn	9:14 AM	12:14 PM	
Moon trine Neptune goes v/c	10:00 AM	1:00 PM	
Mercury conjunct Pluto	10:42 AM	1:42 PM	
Sun square Saturn	6:19 PM	9:19 PM	
Moon enters Cancer	10:40 PM	1:40 AM	(December 13)
Moon opposite Pluto	11:33 PM	2:33 AM	(December 13)

Mood Watch: The Moon is full this morning, and so are the overall lunar activities of this time. The **Full Moon in Gemini** (Moon opposite Sun) emphasizes conversations, talks, sales, discussions, secretarial deeds, and writing. This is a time of built up emotional energy, and there is a strong need to converse and be heard. The Moon has already reached its peak of fullness this morning, and it isn't long before it goes void-of-course for the rest of the evening. We persevere with acute awareness at this time on the focus of transforming personal vision. The full lunar expression of Gemini accentuates the reflective awareness that each of us has our own unique way of seeing things. Sagittarius Sun reminds us of our challenge to develop, as well as to examine our own individual philosophies. Mass consensus occurs in countless forms of media and often conflicts with personal philosophy. Gemini keeps us looking at the two sides of every coin or every philosophy. Gemini seeks all the possible details while Sagittarius strives for the bigger picture. Full Gemini Moon is classically a very busy and swiftly moving time. The Gemini persona keeps our feelings busy, and while the Moon is void-of-course, we are likely to be scattered or frazzled, and actively striving for answers only to find more questions. Investigate the imagination for further details. Record your thoughts and share them with others.

Mercury enters Capricorn (Mercury in Capricorn: Dec. 12, 2008 – Jan. 1, 2009) While Mercury travels through Capricorn, communications tend to be more serious and to the point, although not necessarily less complex. In negotiations, there is an emphasis on enterprise. While this versatile planet goes through Capricorn, our realms of communications have a determined and persistent quality of expression, like a demanding voice waiting to be heard and received with hospitality. This fits with the solar days of Capricorn, when the harsh realities of winter demand clarity of purpose in our communications. Communication is one of the tools of survival, and this is an important time to use those skills wisely and sensibly. Mercury in Capricorn also focuses talk on such issues as commercial and corporate progress, market control, the attainment of goods and resources, and the necessity for discipline.

Mercury conjunct Pluto (occurring Dec. 10 – 14) Mercury conjunct Pluto raises issues of power. The areas of our lives that have required challenge, struggle, sacrifice and transformation now bring us to a place where we can talk about them. With Mercury and Pluto newly in the sign of Capricorn, a very strong sense of duty is instilled in the delivery of messages. This is a time when people instinctively know their own fate, and the course they must travel in the year to come. Mercury conjunct Pluto in Capricorn allows us to voice our hardships, and to contemplate and deliberate over the powerful occurrences that challenge and change our lives. There will be a great deal of intensity in our conversations at this time, especially with regard to the fate of the world and our ongoing efforts to end hardship and suffering.

Sun square Saturn (occurring Dec. 9 – 15) This occurrence of Sun in Sagittarius square Saturn in Virgo especially affects Sagittarians who are celebrating birthdays December 9 – 15. These folks may experience personal challenges of impatience, loss of control, a poor sense of timing, or difficulty identifying with current obligations. The challenge is to overcome obstacles that intrude on one's discipline and accuracy. This may be a time of sacrifice, loss or compromise, and may also be a time of complexity and insecurity for these birthday folks. Saturn represents those things in life we are willing to work for and maintain. It also represents our sense of discipline and our application of effort and focus, and helps us learn about our limitations and where our strengths can be realized. This is a good time for Sagittarius birthday folks to conserve energies and take losses and difficulties in stride. Through the tests of this time, a stronger human being emerges to take on future tests with greater confidence and ability. Avoiding responsibilities or hardships now will only make life more difficult later. This aspect last occurred May 19 – 25, reaching its peak on May 22, affecting the Taurus/Gemini cusp born people.

December 13th Saturday

Moon in Cancer

	PST	EST
Moon opposite Mercury	12:59 AM	3:59 AM
Sun sextile Neptune	6:05 AM	9:05 AM
Mars sextile Neptune begins (see December 16)		

Mood Watch: The Cancer Moon, although extremely full, now wanes. This is a good time for us to take in and process our emotional patterns, to absorb our feelings, and to process them in a nurturing fashion. This is also a good time to choose nourishing and healthy foods, and to be aware of the tendency to overeat unhealthy types of victuals.

Sun sextile Neptune (occurring Dec. 11 – 15) This occurrence of Sun in Sagittarius sextile Neptune in Aquarius creates a very opportunistic time for Sagittarius people celebrating their birthdays December 11 – 15. These Sagittarius folks are experiencing an opportunity for an awakening in the realm of spirituality and creativity.

There is an awareness of the self that goes deep here, and these birthday people are likely to be spacey and difficult to reach while this phenomenon of great depth is occurring. It may be a time for these folks to get away from it all and find a sanctuary in which to meditate and open up to some valuable answers with regard to age old questions. These folks will have an opportunity to better understand the work of their path, but this is probably only true if they act on their own intuitive sensibilities without the influences of others. This will be your year (Sagittarius birthday people) to enhance and strengthen your intuition and primal instincts while they are easily available. This aspect last occurred April 10 – 15, reaching its peak on April 13, when the Sun was in Aries sextile Neptune in Aquarius.

December 14th Sunday

Moon in Cancer / Leo

	PST	EST	
Moon trine Uranus	4:27 AM	7:27 AM	
Moon sextile Saturn	8:40 AM	11:40 AM	
Moon opposite Jupiter goes v/c	2:27 PM	5:27 PM	
Moon enters Leo	10:23 PM	1:23 AM	(December 15)

Mood Watch: Today's Moon in Cancer leaves many folks feeling somewhat withdrawn, and they are likely to be absorbed in their feelings. Moods emphasize feelings, and mother moon now wanes as we seek refuge from the cold and harsh elements of the world. Nurturing care, restful spaces, and moments of peace are what people feel like pursuing today, and wherever there is internal upheaval, there is a need to vent strong feelings. Remember – feelings pass. Troubled feelings flow best when they are properly expressed and released, as opposed to retained and dwelled upon. This afternoon's void-of-course Cancer Moon shifts our senses into an especially temperamental state of being. Tonight it may be difficult to stop worrisome, redundant, or unproductive moodiness.

December 15th Monday

Moon in Leo

	PST	EST
Moon opposite Venus	1:22 PM	4:22 PM
Mars square Saturn	2:46 PM	5:46 PM

Mood Watch: The waning Leo Moon reminds us to tend to the needs of the self. In the spirit of giving, start with the self; be sure to make the effort to give yourself something you need today. Do this, and the energy and vitality you give yourself will shine through by example – it will be a gift of light for others to share. From a sense of satisfaction and assurance, the expression of affection brings peace and happiness.

Mars square Saturn (occurring Dec. 11 – 19) Mars is in Sagittarius and Saturn is in Virgo; competition is very stiff as independent companies take a beating in actively trading markets. This aspect is known for creating confrontations between offensive and defensive forces, and is usually not a good time to start a new enterprise. When deploying forces in battle, this aspect often brings fiery and sometimes tragic endings. It is wise to proceed with extra caution. This may be an especially difficult time to muster the strength to finish up projects, or to end affairs amicably.

Hang in there; it's less than a week until we kiss this cycle of Mars square Saturn good-bye. Fortunately, this is the only time that Mars will square Saturn this year.

December 16th Tuesday

Moon in Leo

	PST	EST
Mars sextile Neptune	6:15 AM	9:15 AM
Moon opposite Neptune	10:55 AM	1:55 PM
Moon trine Mars	11:11 AM	2:11 PM
Moon trine Sun goes v/c	4:46 PM	7:46 PM

Mood Watch: The Sun and Moon are both in fire signs; it may appear that someone has turned up the heat. Most of us are easily drawn towards the need to find warmth and affection, or just plain attention. While some are content to make this a thoroughly relaxing day of self indulgence, others are intent on sharing the Christmas spirit with full-blown theatrics and sheer animal magnetism. By evening, the void-of-course Leo Moon brings laziness and idleness; it's a good time to kick back and relax.

Mars sextile Neptune (occurring Dec. 13 – 19) Mars in Sagittarius is sextile to Neptune in Aquarius. Personal initiative – when taken – brings the potential for a spiritual awakening in humanity. Mars sextile Neptune is a splendid time to *act* on our *beliefs*. This aspect brings the vitality of Mars' energy into a favorable position with the spirit-awakening influence of Neptune. This is a place where we can safely dump our anger and can potentially make a connection with a spiritual healing process. Those who act on their visions and on the ceremonies of their particular belief systems will have an opportunity to connect with a very profound spiritual experience. This aspect makes the active work of artists, poets, and musicians into unique and very powerful statements about being in an endowed and sacred state of awareness. There is an irony at work with these two forces; Mars is active and masculine, while Neptune has a very nebulous and passive guise that affects our deeper inner sense of beliefs and spirit. When these two planets are placed in a favorable position to each other, personal spiritual breakthroughs can be made. This is the only time this aspect occurs this year.

December 17th Wednesday

Moon in Leo / Virgo

	PST	EST
Moon enters Virgo	12:36 AM	3:36 AM
Moon trine Pluto	1:52 AM	4:52 AM
Moon trine Mercury	3:50 PM	6:50 PM

Mood Watch: The waning Moon in Virgo brings out moods of frugal clarity. There is reluctance to spend money on commercial goods that have escalated in prices. Simple resourcefulness will go far. The positive aspect of Virgo calls for clarity, purity and healing. This is a time of placing importance on the logical and methodical application of reason. There is no reason in negative feedback; positive or constructive criticism is the kinder way to orchestrate a point. The Moon passes through the mutable earth of Virgo during this time of the mutable fire of the Sun. The way of peace and success comes through the release of stress, and the intake of inspired vision.

December 18th Thursday

Moon in Virgo

	PST	EST	
Moon opposite Uranus	10:07 AM	1:07 PM	
Moon conjunct Saturn	2:59 PM	5:59 PM	
Moon square Mars	7:08 PM	10:08 PM	
Moon trine Jupiter	10:06 PM	1:06 AM	(December 19)

Mood Watch: Sun in Sagittarius and Moon in Virgo is an excellent time to communicate, organize, and to make plans. It is also wise to bear in mind that with the waning Moon in Virgo, many folks may decide to withdraw into a much more analytical perspective on matters. Early in the day, Moon opposite Uranus implies the need to tear things apart, to create chaos in order to restructure the unconstructive patterns to which we have fallen pray. There will be a serious effort to create practical structure in our lives today.

December 19th Friday

Moon in Virgo / Libra – LAST QUARTER MOON in VIRGO

	PST	EST
Moon square Sun goes v/c	2:30 AM	5:30 AM
Moon enters Libra	6:23 AM	9:23 AM
Moon square Pluto	7:53 AM	10:53 AM
Sun conjunct Pluto begins (see December 22)		

Mood Watch: The **Last Quarter Moon in Virgo** (Moon square Sun) calls for the release of doubt. These are the final days of Sun in Sagittarius; applying the vision of how one wants to see their future-self is not an easy task, especially if poisonous and debilitating addictions are involved. However, the Sagittarian outlook often projects selfhood in an outward fashion in order to envision the demands of an expanding spirit. That same Sagittarian awareness is just as capable of traveling inward and perceiving the needs of the inner self. Let the doubts and fears of your life be flushed away at this time so, through clarity, you may achieve the benefits of your visionary picture of health, wealth, and well being. All of that said, most of today falls under the influence of the Libra Moon. Waning Libra Moon is an excellent time to call a truce with loved ones, and to focus on harmony.

December 20th Saturday

Moon in Libra

	PST	EST
Moon square Mercury	6:21 AM	9:21 AM
Moon trine Venus	10:02 AM	1:02 PM

Mood Watch: Today's waning Moon in Libra focuses our moods on the need for balance, and everyone is trying to create equilibrium, no matter what it takes. Those who are more acutely aware of the need for balance are steeped in a world of imbalance. Moon in Libra focuses our moods on the importance of teamwork, and the interaction of our friends and loved ones. Friendships and partners play big roles on days like today. Be careful not to get caught up in too many balancing acts in order to please everyone. Perhaps the most obvious way to create balance on the darkest days of the year is to infuse light and good cheer into the course of our affairs. ♑

CAPRICORN

Key Phrase: " I USE "
Cardinal Earth Sign
Symbol: The Goat
December 21st, 2008 through
January 19th, 2009

December 21st Sunday
Winter Solstice
Moon in Libra / Scorpio

	PST	EST
Moon trine Neptune	12:19 AM	3:19 AM
Sun enters Capricorn	4:03 AM	7:03 AM
Moon sextile Mars	7:21 AM	10:21 AM
Moon square Jupiter goes v/c	8:57 AM	11:57 AM
Moon enters Scorpio	3:37 PM	6:37 PM
Moon sextile Sun	4:39 PM	7:39 PM
Moon sextile Pluto	5:10 PM	8:10 PM

Mood Watch: A sense of balance affects our earliest morning moods, but ever so quickly, the waning void-of-course Libra Moon slips into the picture, causing us to feel disorientated and making it difficult for many folks to make clear decisions throughout the day. This is a good time to avoid complex procedures and risky interactions. Later today the Moon slips into Scorpio. The events of the day may seem laced with strong doses of emotion. A waning Moon in Scorpio calls to us to drop and let go of strong destructive tendencies, challenges us to cease hurting ourselves and others, and invites us to transform our lower impulses into higher aspirations.

Sun enters Capricorn (Sun in Capricorn: Dec. 21, 2008 – Jan. 19, 2009) Spark up the lights – it's **Winter Solstice!** Today the Sun King returns from the ashes of the longest night. This is the time of Saturn-ruled Capricorn. Sun in Capricorn is the time to step into success. Jack Frost is nipping at our heels, but the Sun King returns! The lengthening days of the Sun are finally here and a new season and cycle begins. The symbol of Capricorn is the mountain goat. The Capricorn goat consciousness is revealed to us through the high and lofty heights the goat commands. No mountain is too high for the true archetypal Capricorn, and the focus of this season is always placed on accomplishing the highest of goals and

227

achievements. The working pace for the New Year is established here. Capricorn energy emphasizes corporate growth, the creation and maintenance of institutions, construction and development, and the use and control of industrial services and equipment. Many outstanding Capricorns are devoted to their careers and lifestyles with unyielding tenacity. Capricorn days of the Sun are splendid times to focus on goals, and to discipline one's nature to make daily tasks add up to something worth accomplishing. Although tedious and often predictable, the Capricorn nature makes sure the job is done – and done well.

December 22nd Monday
Chanukah begins (ends December 29)

Moon in Scorpio	PST	EST
Sun conjunct Pluto	1:23 AM	4:23 AM

Mood Watch: The spirit of Scorpio Moon gives us the awareness of deeper, more subtle levels of emotional interplay. The Pluto ruled sign of Scorpio puts us in touch with transformation. Our emotional field is now undergoing a transformational process that allows us to work through the darkness of this time. Insights run strongly and very profoundly for some folks during this seemingly dark time of the soul.

Sun conjunct Pluto (occurring Dec. 19 – 25) The Sun is conjunct with Pluto in the sign of Capricorn. Pluto, a.k.a. God of the Underworld, has officially entered the Saturn ruled sign, Capricorn *(see Pluto enters Capricorn: Jan. 25 & Nov. 26).* Pluto represents transformation – in particular, those ways in which the generations of humankind affect change and make their mark. Pluto in Sagittarius (1995/96 – 2008) has been the eye opener of global awareness. This occurrence of Sun conjunct Pluto strongly affects Sagittarians and cusp born Capricorns – most specifically, those who are celebrating birthdays December 19 – 25. These Sagittarius/ Capricorn birthday folks will experience challenges of mind-altering proportions. Sun conjunct Pluto affects the core of the personality and diminishes those parts of the self which are weak and no longer viable. Pluto's energy melds with the personality to bring out the strongest points of one's character, the very best that one can muster. Pluto removes all impurities by transforming the old self through unpredictable trials. Take this opportunity to make some personal breakthroughs, birthday folks, and find your power! Learn to harness your power willingly and responsibly while great transformation is occurring in your life. Give in but don't give up.

December 23rd Tuesday

Moon in Scorpio	PST	EST	
Moon sextile Mercury	1:19 AM	4:19 AM	
Moon square Venus	2:39 AM	5:39 AM	
Moon trine Uranus	5:12 AM	8:12 AM	
Moon sextile Saturn	10:35 AM	1:35 PM	
Moon square Neptune	11:33 AM	2:33 PM	
Moon sextile Jupiter goes v/c	10:29 PM	1:29 AM	(December 24)
Mercury sextile Uranus begins (see December 24)			

228

Mood Watch: Today will have its share of ups and downs, as the strong influence of the Capricorn Sun will attest; perseverance is the key to this time. The waning Scorpio Moon puts us in touch with the intensity and suspense of the countdown to Christmas. Waning Scorpio Moon may be a very harsh time emotionally for some folks, and past memories may be haunting them. The magic of Scorpio Moon encourages bravery and brings warmth, acceptance, mental relaxation, positive goals, and a fair portion of physical exertion to help ease our hearts and satiate some of those aching desires.

December 24th Wednesday
Christmas Eve
Moon in Scorpio / Sagittarius

	PST	EST	
Moon enters Sagittarius	3:13 AM	6:13 AM	
Mercury sextile Uranus	8:33 AM	11:33 AM	
Mercury trine Saturn begins (see December 26)			
Venus conjunct Neptune begins (see December 27)			
Mars conjunct Pluto begins (see December 28)			

Mood Watch: Swiftly and early, the waning Moon enters Sagittarius, and this brings joy and wonder. The mutable fire sign Moon gives us the edge to adapt quickly to busy situations, and this is a great time to travel, despite the highly anticipated holiday traffic. As for Old Saint Nicholas, have no fear; the watch for Santa's sleigh on the radar screen begins tonight with joyous anticipation. Cheers!

Mercury sextile Uranus (occurring Dec. 23 – 25) Mercury in Capricorn is sextile to Uranus in Pisces. Serious investigations may lead to sensational conclusions. This is a good time to keep an open mind and to expect radical commentaries. This aspect last occurred April 26 – 28, reaching its peak on April 27. For more information on Mercury sextile Uranus, *see April 27*, when this aspect first occurred.

December 25th Thursday
Christmas
Moon in Sagittarius

	PST	EST	
Moon square Uranus	5:46 PM	8:46 PM	
Moon sextile Venus	9:22 PM	12:22 AM	(December 26)
Moon square Saturn	11:09 PM	2:09 AM	(December 26)

Mood Watch: This spirit of this waning Sagittarius Moon of Christmas brings insightful and adventurous moods. Philosophical perspectives bring entertaining insights to the day's events. Warm, fun-loving gestures bring resilient and hopeful moods. Although the square of the Moon to Uranus in the evening brings chaos and havoc, our ability to look at the bright side of life comes built-in with the Sagittarius Moon, which also brings prosperous and joyous moods. Peace and wellbeing to you and yours.

229

December 26th Friday

Boxing Day
Moon in Sagittarius / Capricorn

	PST	EST	
Moon sextile Neptune	12:14 AM	3:14 AM	
Mercury trine Saturn	3:38 AM	6:38 AM	
Moon conjunct Mars goes v/c	3:25 PM	6:25 PM	
Moon enters Capricorn	3:56 PM	6:56 PM	
Moon conjunct Pluto	6:07 PM	9:07 PM	
Mars enters Capricorn	11:30 PM	2:30 AM	(December 27)

Mood Watch: Darkly now, the Moon wanes in Sagittarius on this New Moon eve. It will reach the new mark in Capricorn tomorrow, but for now, deep, profound, and exhilarating visions may be found in the shadows of our moods. This is a good time to internalize personal visions and to picture the things that will bring joy and happiness to you. Later today the Moon goes void-of-course, then it quickly shifts into Capricorn. Although we have already reached the crossroad of winter Solstice, there are many aspects of our moods that are still releasing emotional turmoil and dark memories. Capricorn Moon allows us to do this swiftly, with a sense of relief and detachment.

Mercury trine Saturn (occurring Dec. 24 – 28) Mercury is in Capricorn where essential priorities and important goals are discussed and communicated. Mercury in Capricorn trine Saturn in Virgo brings practical and clear discussions with regard to where – and how – to draw the lines for ourselves. This is a good time to make an impression, to teach and to communicate to others those important matters requiring clarification. It's also a great time to study or practice memorization skills. Timely information and news bring gifts or blessings. News concerning the end of a long and arduous task brings relief. This aspect last occurred April 17 – 19, reaching its peak on April 18, when Mercury was in Taurus and Saturn was in Virgo.

Mars enters Capricorn (Mars in Capricorn: Dec. 26, 2008 – Feb. 4, 2009) Now the planet Mars, known to many as "the god of war," is in the sign of Capricorn. The main thrust of activities will be inspired by the industrious push of Capricornian persistence. Mars in Capricorn is the place where it's exalted. Activities will shift towards dynamic, ambitious and enterprising endeavors. With Mars in Capricorn a sense of duty is instilled. Activities, if successfully managed, will produce long lasting results. This is *not* a good time to create enemies; the inherent difficulties will also produce long lasting results, and long standing enemies are not a good thing to have when trying to create a sense of forward moving progress. The last time Mars was in Capricorn was January 16 – February 25, 2007, when US Democrats regained a legislative majority, but their initial attempts to pull troops out of Iraq failed. Before that, during February through March 2005, Mars in Capricorn also brought a difficult time for our ruthlessly warring planet, with exceptionally high casualty rates in Iraq. Before that, Mars entered Capricorn in March 2003, when the US war on Iraq began. Interestingly enough, the time Mars entered Capricorn before that was the week of September 11th, 2001. It appears that here in the beginning of the 21st century, the guns of war are activated in no uncertain terms when Mars is in Capricorn. Keep your eyes open!

December 27th Saturday

NEW MOON in CAPRICORN

	PST	EST
Moon conjunct Sun	4:22 AM	7:22 AM
Venus conjunct Neptune	4:28 AM	7:28 AM

♑

Mood Watch: We now awaken to the day of the **New Moon in Capricorn** (Moon conjunct Sun). Whew! It was dark there for awhile but the stiff upper lip is setting in, and we are ready to begin raising some light again. New Moon in Capricorn urges us to create new goals and set new heights for ourselves. In the marketplace, there is the classic busy shuffle and serious, determined moods abound. This is a grounding time for us, as much as it is uplifting and challenging at the same time. Let the blessings of your heart fill the gap when the sadness of missed loved ones creeps in. Strength of will is enhanced by the bounty of love in one's heart. New Moon brings new light – rejoice!

Venus conjunct Neptune (occurring Dec. 24 – 29) Venus conjunct Neptune, if utilized, will bring great wisdom. This conjunction last occurred March 4 – 9, reaching its peak on March 6. For a recap on Venus conjunct Neptune in Aquarius *see March 6.*

December 28th Sunday

Moon in Capricorn

	PST	EST
Moon sextile Uranus	6:46 AM	9:46 AM
Mars conjunct Pluto	12:01 PM	3:01 PM
Moon trine Saturn	12:03 PM	3:03 PM
Moon conjunct Mercury	7:52 PM	10:52 PM
Mercury conjunct Jupiter begins (see December 31)		

Mood Watch: The newly waxing Capricorn Moon affects our moods with the need to stay on track and take matters very seriously in a guarded fashion. Capricorn Moon allows us to better handle the strong and daunting astrological aspects of this time. It also allows us to be practical, constructive, and level headed.

Mars conjunct Pluto (occurring Dec. 24, 2008 – Jan. 2, 2009) For the first time in our lifetime, Mars and Pluto are conjunct in Capricorn. Powerful forces are likely to take some form of disruptive and very possibly destructive action. Over the course of the next quarter century, Mars will make this conjunction with Pluto every couple of years, and during these times, the exalted Mars in Capricorn will probably have a strong affect on the decisive blows of authorities in power. Major physical changes, which are likely to be offensive, are set to occur on the battlefields of planet Earth. This is an especially important time to take precautionary measures in dealing with authorities. Expect some definite social and political tension to escalate around this time. There is no use in worrying. It is wisest to be vigilant and clear about what is happening in our lives during abrupt challenges, and to use caution in all that we do. Like a catalyst, Mars conjunct Pluto is simply giving the fiery energy of unsettled warring countries an outlet for confrontation.

December 29th Monday

Moon in Capricorn / Aquarius

	PST	EST
Moon conjunct Jupiter goes v/c	1:19 AM	4:19 AM
Moon enters Aquarius	4:43 AM	7:43 AM

Mood Watch: The newly waxing Aquarius Moon brings brilliant, exciting, unusual, and joyous feelings. This is a time when we reach out to all the people we know and learn from them. It's also a great time for giving. Aquarius Moon brings out strong feelings for our fellow humans, and this is a great time to apply some love for humanity. Charitable events and humanitarian deeds are greatly emphasized. New technological toys will be a big hit today.

December 30th Tuesday

Moon in Aquarius

Mood Watch: Moon in Aquarius focuses our moods on the need to apply knowledge in order to cut corners through the congested systems of humanity. The newly waxing Moon in Aquarius focuses our moods on idealistic, inventive and humanitarian expression. Aquarius brings out the need to face ourselves and learn things about who we are.

December 31st Wednesday

New Year's Eve

Moon in Aquarius / Pisces

	PST	EST	
Moon conjunct Neptune	1:30 AM	4:30 AM	
Mercury conjunct Jupiter	3:41 AM	6:41 AM	
Saturn goes retrograde	10:08 AM	1:08 PM	
Moon conjunct Venus goes v/c	10:32 AM	1:32 PM	
Moon enters Pisces	4:28 PM	7:28 PM	
Moon sextile Pluto	6:54 PM	9:54 PM	
Moon sextile Mars	11:47 PM	2:47 AM	(January 1, 2009)

Mood Watch: This morning's youthfully waxing Aquarius Moon encourages us to act on our intelligent sensibilities and to seek knowledge where it is needed. As the Moon goes void-of-course, we may find our resources for knowledge and technical advice are limited. Humanitarian efforts may backfire at times as this busy final day of the year presses us onward to meet the challenge of New Year's Eve celebrations and congested social galas. By nightfall the Moon enters Pisces, and the celebration may turn tipsy and topsy-turvy. Waxing Pisces Moon on a holiday eve encourages drunkenness, psychic feelings, and colorful artistic endeavors. Tonight it may be best to plan out some sensible and practical guidelines and stick to them. *HAPPY NEW YEAR!*

Mercury conjunct Jupiter (occurring Dec. 28, 2008 – Jan. 3, 2009) Mercury and Jupiter are conjunct in Capricorn. News and discussions (Mercury) revolve around our joys, our prosperity, and our wealth (Jupiter) – particularly with regard to fulfilling our desires and abiding by our deep passions in life. This aspect creates expansive talk which spreads quickly with news about the economic state of affairs. Thoughts and information (Mercury) with regard to a prosperous and visionary breakthrough (Jupiter) will be highlighted. It's a great time to boost the moral of others by complimenting them on their skills. This could be a prosperous aspect for communicating the need for a job or financial loan. Early born Capricorns having birthdays at this time are about to be showered with a wealth of information and opportunities which are worthy of their time and effort.

Saturn goes retrograde (Saturn retrograde: Dec. 31, 2008 – May 19, 2009) Saturn represents discipline, responsibility, and the tenacity required to get the job done. Sacrifices may be necessary in order to complete important projects, and discipline and perseverance are essential. While Saturn is retrograde in Virgo, staying on top of health matters as well as accounting and bookkeeping will be big priorities. For some folks, this will be a time of completion, of ending the treadmill of old cycles, and of learning to let others take responsibility for themselves. During this time, there will be a lot of work to do, retracing steps in the areas of life that need restructuring. When Saturn is retrograde, it may be difficult, although not impossible, to begin new endeavors that require structure and the investment of time or commitment. We may be haunted by incomplete projects, and unsolved problems of the past could dominate the stage. Being careful of what we commit to at this time may prevent the need to drop other unfulfilled commitments midstream. If we haven't already dropped a few unnecessary responsibilities, we may have to do so soon. Learn how to delegate your tasks fairly to those who can handle them. Keep a steady check on quality control while Saturn is retrograde.

Ephemeris 2007 Noon GMT
Longitudes based on Greenwich Mean Time (GMT) at Noon

JANUARY 2008

Date	☉	☽	☿	♀	♂	♃	♄	♅	♆	♇
1	10♑26	23♎18	19♑06	02♐07	29♊43R	03♑08	08♍24R	15♓23	20♒17	29♐09
2	11 27	05♏10	20 43	03 20	29 22	03 22	08 22	15 25	20 19	29 11
3	12 29	17 01	22 21	04 33	29 02	03 35	08 21	15 27	20 21	29 14
4	13 30	28 54	23 59	05 46	28 41	03 49	08 19	15 29	20 22	29 16
5	14 31	10♐53	25 37	06 58	28 21	04 03	08 17	15 31	20 24	29 18
6	15 32	23 00	27 15	08 11	28 02	04 16	08 15	15 33	20 26	29 20
7	16 33	05♑17	28 52	09 24	27 42	04 30	08 13	15 35	20 28	29 22
8	17 34	17 46	00 30	10 38	27 24	04 44	08 11	15 37	20 30	29 24
9	18 36	00♒25	02 07	11 51	27 06	04 57	08 09	15 39	20 32	29 26
10	19 37	13 16	03 43	13 04	26 49	05 11	08 07	15 41	20 34	29 29
11	20 38	26 18	05 19	14 17	26 33	05 24	08 04	15 44	20 36	29 31
12	21 39	09♓33	06 54	15 30	26 19	05 38	08 02	15 46	20 38	29 33
13	22 40	22 59	08 28	16 44	26 05	05 51	07 59	15 48	20 40	29 35
14	23 41	06♈38	10 00	17 57	25 52	06 05	07 57	15 51	20 42	29 37
15	24 43	20 30	11 30	19 10	25 41	06 18	07 54	15 53	20 44	29 39
16	25 44	04♉36	12 58	20 24	25 29	06 32	07 51	15 56	20 47	29 41
17	26 45	18 53	14 23	21 37	25 19	06 45	07 48	15 58	20 49	29 43
18	27 46	03♊19	15 45	22 51	25 09	06 59	07 45	16 01	20 51	29 45
19	28 47	17 51	17 04	24 04	24 59	07 12	07 42	16 03	20 53	29 47
20	29 48	02♋22	18 17	25 18	24 50	07 25	07 39	16 06	20 55	29 49
21	00♒49	16 47	19 26	26 31	24 42	07 38	07 35	16 08	20 57	29 51
22	01 50	00♌59	20 28	27 45	24 34	07 52	07 32	16 11	20 59	29 53
23	02 51	14 53	21 24	28 58	24 27	08 05	07 29	16 14	21 02	29 55
24	03 52	28 26	22 12	00♑12	24 21	08 18	07 25	16 16	21 04	29 57
25	04 53	11♍38	22 52	01 26	24 17	08 31	07 21	16 19	21 06	29 59
26	05 54	24 27	23 22	02 40	24 13	08 44	07 18	16 22	21 08	00♑01
27	06 55	06♎57	23 42	03 53	24 10	08 57	07 14	16 25	21 10	00 03
28	07 56	19 11	23 52	05 07	24 08	09 10	07 10	16 28	21 13	00 04
29	08 57	01♏12	23♒50R	06 21	24 07	09 23	07 06	16 31	21 15	00 06
30	09 58	13 07	23 37	07 35	24 07	09 36	07 02	16 33	21 17	00 08
31	10 59	24 59	23 13	08 49	24♊08D	09 49	06 58	16 36	21 19	00 10

FEBRUARY 2008

Date	☉	☽	☿	♀	♂	♃	♄	♅	♆	♇
1	12♒00	06♐53	22♒38R	10♑03	24♊09	10♑01	06♍54R	16♓39	21♒22	00♑12
2	13 01	18 54	21 52	11 16	24 11	10 14	06 50	16 42	21 24	00 13
3	14 02	01♑06	20 58	12 30	24 13	10 27	06 46	16 45	21 26	00 15
4	15 03	13 30	19 57	13 44	24 16	10 39	06 42	16 48	21 28	00 17
5	16 03	26 10	18 49	14 58	24 19	10 52	06 37	16 51	21 31	00 18
6	17 04	09♒06	17 39	16 12	24 23	11 04	06 33	16 54	21 33	00 20
7	18 05	22 19	16 26	17 26	24 28	11 17	06 28	16 58	21 35	00 22
8	19 06	05♓46	15 14	18 40	24 33	11 29	06 24	17 01	21 38	00 23
9	20 07	19 27	14 05	19 54	24 39	11 41	06 20	17 04	21 40	00 25
10	21 07	03♈19	12 59	21 08	24 46	11 53	06 15	17 07	21 42	00 27
11	22 08	17 19	11 58	22 22	24 54	12 06	06 10	17 10	21 44	00 28
12	23 09	01♉26	11 04	23 36	25 03	12 18	06 06	17 13	21 47	00 30
13	24 10	15 37	10 18	24 50	25 12	12 30	06 01	17 17	21 49	00 31
14	25 10	29 49	09 38	26 05	25 22	12 42	05 56	17 20	21 51	00 33
15	26 11	14♊00	09 07	27 19	25 33	12 53	05 52	17 23	21 54	00 34
16	27 11	28 07	08 44	28 33	25 44	13 05	05 47	17 26	21 56	00 35
17	28 12	12♋10	08 28	29 47	25 55	13 17	05 42	17 30	21 58	00 37
18	29 13	26 04	08 20	01♒01	26 07	13 29	05 38	17 33	22 00	00 38
19	00♓13	09♌47	08♒19D	02 15	26 19	13 40	05 33	17 36	22 03	00 40
20	01 14	23 17	08 25	03 29	26 31	13 52	05 28	17 40	22 05	00 41
21	02 14	06♍32	08 38	04 43	26 44	14 03	05 23	17 43	22 07	00 42

FEBRUARY 2007 (Cont'd)

Date	☉	☽	☿	♀	♂	♃	♄	♅	♆	♇
22	03♓14	19♍31	08♒56	05♒57	26♊58	14♑14	05♍18R	17♓46	22♒09	00♑43
23	04 15	02♎14	09 20	07 11	27 12	14 25	05 13	17 50	22 12	00 45
24	05 15	14 42	09 49	08 26	27 27	14 37	05 09	17 53	22 14	00 46
25	06 16	26 56	10 23	09 40	27 42	14 48	05 04	17 56	22 16	00 47
26	07 16	08♏59	11 02	10 54	27 58	14 58	04 59	18 00	22 18	00 48
27	08 16	20 54	11 44	12 08	28 14	15 09	04 54	18 03	22 21	00 49
28	09 16	02♐47	12 30	13 22	28 32	15 20	04 49	18 06	22 23	00 50
29	10 17	14 41	13 20	14 36	28 49	15 31	04 45	18 10	22 25	00 51

MARCH 2008

Date	☉	☽	☿	♀	♂	♃	♄	♅	♆	♇
1	11♓17	26♐42	14♒13	15♒51	29♊07	15♑41	04♍40R	18♓13	22♒27	00♑52
2	12 17	08♑53	15 10	17 05	29 26	15 52	04 35	18 17	22 29	00 53
3	13 17	21 19	16 09	18 19	29 44	16 02	04 30	18 20	22 32	00 54
4	14 17	04♒04	17 10	19 33	00♋03	16 12	04 26	18 24	22 34	00 55
5	15 18	17 10	18 15	20 47	00 22	16 23	04 21	18 27	22 36	00 56
6	16 18	00♓38	19 21	22 02	00 41	16 33	04 16	18 30	22 38	00 57
7	17 18	14 27	20 30	23 16	01 01	16 43	04 12	18 34	22 40	00 58
8	18 18	28 35	21 40	24 30	01 21	16 52	04 07	18 37	22 42	00 59
9	19 18	12♈57	22 53	25 44	01 41	17 02	04 02	18 41	22 44	01 00
10	20 18	27 26	24 08	26 58	02 02	17 12	03 58	18 44	22 46	01 00
11	21 18	11♉59	25 24	28 13	02 23	17 21	03 53	18 48	22 48	01 01
12	22 18	26 27	26 42	29 27	02 45	17 31	03 49	18 51	22 50	01 02
13	23 17	10♊48	28 02	00♓41	03 07	17 40	03 45	18 54	22 53	01 02
14	24 17	24 58	29 23	01 55	03 30	17 49	03 40	18 58	22 55	01 03
15	25 17	08♋54	00♓46	03 09	03 53	17 58	03 36	19 01	22 57	01 04
16	26 17	22 38	02 10	04 23	04 16	18 07	03 32	19 05	22 59	01 04
17	27 16	06♌07	03 36	05 38	04 40	18 16	03 27	19 08	23 01	01 05
18	28 16	19 24	05 03	06 52	05 03	18 24	03 23	19 12	23 02	01 05
19	29 16	02♍29	06 32	08 06	05 27	18 33	03 19	19 15	23 04	01 06
20	00♈15	15 21	08 02	09 20	05 51	18 41	03 15	19 18	23 06	01 06
21	01 15	28 02	09 33	10 34	06 15	18 49	03 11	19 22	23 08	01 07
22	02 14	10♎32	11 06	11 48	06 39	18 57	03 07	19 25	23 10	01 07
23	03 14	22 51	12 40	13 03	07 04	19 05	03 03	19 28	23 12	01 07
24	04 13	05♏00	14 15	14 17	07 28	19 13	03 00	19 32	23 14	01 08
25	05 13	17 00	15 52	15 31	07 53	19 21	02 56	19 35	23 16	01 08
26	06 12	28 55	17 30	16 45	08 19	19 29	02 52	19 39	23 17	01 08
27	07 12	10♐47	19 09	17 59	08 45	19 36	02 49	19 42	23 19	01 08
28	08 11	22 40	20 50	19 13	09 11	19 43	02 45	19 45	23 21	01 08
29	09 10	04♑39	22 32	20 27	09 37	19 51	02 42	19 48	23 23	01 09
30	10 10	16 47	24 16	21 41	10 04	19 58	02 39	19 52	23 24	01 09
31	11 09	29 11	26 01	22 56	10 31	20 04	02 35	19 55	23 26	01 09

APRIL 2008

Date	☉	☽	☿	♀	♂	♃	♄	♅	♆	♇
1	12♈08	11♒54	27♓47	24♓10	10♋57	20♑11	02♍32R	19♓58	23♒28	01♑09
2	13 07	25 01	29 35	25 24	11 24	20 18	02 29	20 01	23 29	01♑09R
3	14 06	08♓34	01♈24	26 38	11 52	20 24	02 26	20 05	23 31	01 09
4	15 06	22 34	03 14	27 52	12 19	20 30	02 23	20 08	23 33	01 09
5	16 05	06♈59	05 06	29 06	12 46	20 36	02 20	20 11	23 34	01 09
6	17 04	21 43	06 59	00♈20	13 13	20 42	02 18	20 14	23 36	01 09
7	18 03	06♉39	08 54	01 34	13 41	20 48	02 15	20 17	23 37	01 08
8	19 02	21 39	10 50	02 48	14 08	20 54	02 12	20 21	23 39	01 08
9	20 01	06♊31	12 48	04 02	14 36	20 59	02 10	20 24	23 40	01 08
10	21 00	21 10	14 47	05 16	15 05	21 05	02 08	20 27	23 42	01 08
11	21 58	05♋30	16 47	06 30	15 33	21 10	02 05	20 30	23 43	01 07
12	22 57	19 29	18 48	07 44	16 02	21 15	02 03	20 33	23 44	01 07

APRIL 2008 (Cont'd)

Date	☉	☽	☿	♀	♂	♃	♄	♅	♆	♇
13	23♈56	03♌06	20♈51	08♈59	16♋31	21♑20	02♍01R	20♓36	23♒46	01♑07R
14	24 55	16 24	22 55	10 13	17 01	21 24	01 59	20 39	23 47	01 06
15	25 54	29 24	25 00	11 27	17 30	21 29	01 57	20 42	23 49	01 06
16	26 52	12♍10	27 06	12 40	18 00	21 33	01 56	20 45	23 50	01 06
17	27 51	24 44	29 12	13 54	18 29	21 37	01 54	20 48	23 51	01 05
18	28 50	07♎08	01♉20	15 08	18 59	21 41	01 52	20 50	23 52	01 05
19	29 48	19 23	03 27	16 22	19 29	21 45	01 51	20 53	23 53	01 04
20	00♉47	01♏31	05 34	17 36	19 58	21 48	01 49	20 56	23 55	01 04
21	01 45	13 32	07 42	18 50	20 28	21 52	01 48	20 59	23 56	01 03
22	02 44	25 29	09 49	20 04	20 58	21 55	01 47	21 02	23 57	01 02
23	03 42	07♐22	11 55	21 18	21 28	21 58	01 46	21 04	23 58	01 02
24	04 41	19 13	14 00	22 32	21 58	22 01	01 45	21 07	23 59	01 01
25	05 39	01♑06	16 04	23 46	22 29	22 04	01 44	21 10	24 00	01 01
26	06 37	13 04	18 06	25 00	23 00	22 06	01 43	21 13	24 01	01 00
27	07 36	25 10	20 05	26 14	23 31	22 09	01 43	21 15	24 02	00 59
28	08 34	07♒31	22 03	27 28	24 02	22 11	01 42	21 18	24 03	00 58
29	09 32	20 10	23 58	28 42	24 33	22 13	01 42	21 20	24 04	00 57
30	10 31	03♓12	25 50	29 56	25 04	22 15	01 41	21 23	24 05	00 57

MAY 2008

Date	☉	☽	☿	♀	♂	♃	♄	♅	♆	♇
1	11♉29	16♓42	27♉40	01♉09	25♋36	22♑16	01♍41R	21♓25	24♒05	00♑56R
2	12 27	00♈41	29 26	02 23	26 07	22 18	01 41	21 28	24 06	00 55
3	13 25	15 09	01♊08	03 37	26 38	22 19	01 41	21 30	24 07	00 54
4	14 24	00♉01	02 47	04 51	27 10	22 20	01♍41D	21 33	24 08	00 53
5	15 22	15 11	04 23	06 05	27 41	22 21	01 41	21 35	24 08	00 52
6	16 20	00♊27	05 55	07 19	28 12	22 21	01 42	21 37	24 09	00 51
7	17 18	15 39	07 22	08 33	28 44	22 22	01 42	21 40	24 10	00 50
8	18 16	00♋36	08 46	09 47	29 16	22 22	01 43	21 42	24 10	00 49
9	19 14	15 11	10 06	11 00	29 48	22♑22R	01 43	21 44	24 11	00 48
10	20 12	29 20	11 22	12 14	00♌20	22 22	01 44	21 46	24 12	00 47
11	21 10	13♌01	12 34	13 28	00 52	22 22	01 45	21 48	24 12	00 46
12	22 08	26 18	13 41	14 42	01 25	22 21	01 46	21 50	24 13	00 45
13	23 06	09♍13	14 45	15 56	01 57	22 21	01 47	21 53	24 13	00 44
14	24 04	21 50	15 43	17 09	02 30	22 20	01 48	21 55	24 13	00 43
15	25 02	04♎13	16 38	18 23	03 03	22 19	01 49	21 56	24 14	00 41
16	25 59	16 26	17 28	19 37	03 36	22 18	01 51	21 58	24 14	00 40
17	26 57	28 30	18 14	20 51	04 08	22 16	01 52	22 00	24 14	00 39
18	27 55	10♏29	18 54	22 04	04 41	22 15	01 54	22 02	24 15	00 38
19	28 53	22 25	19 31	23 18	05 14	22 13	01 55	22 04	24 15	00 37
20	29 50	04♐18	20 02	24 32	05 47	22 11	01 57	22 06	24 15	00 35
21	00♊48	16 10	20 29	25 46	06 20	22 09	01 59	22 07	24 15	00 34
22	01 46	28 03	20 51	27 00	06 53	22 06	02 01	22 09	24 16	00 33
23	02 43	09♑59	21 09	28 13	07 26	22 04	02 03	22 11	24 16	00 31
24	03 41	21 59	21 21	29 27	07 59	22 01	02 05	22 12	24 16	00 30
25	04 39	04♒08	21 29	00♊41	08 32	21 58	02 07	22 14	24 16	00 29
26	05 36	16 30	21 32	01 54	09 06	21 55	02 10	22 15	24 16	00 27
27	06 34	29 08	21♊30R	03 08	09 40	21 52	02 12	22 17	24 16	00 26
28	07 31	12♓06	21 24	04 22	10 13	21 49	02 15	22 18	24 16	00 25
29	08 29	25 30	21 14	05 36	10 47	21 45	02 17	22 20	24 16	00 23
30	09 27	09♈22	20 59	06 49	11 21	21 41	02 20	22 21	24♒16R	00 22
31	10 24	23 42	20 41	08 03	11 55	21 37	02 23	22 22	24 15	00 20

JUNE 2008

Date	☉	☽	☿	♀	♂	♃	♄	♅	♆	♇
1	11♊22	08♉29	20♊19R	09♊17	12♌29	21♑33R	02♍26	22♓24	24♒15R	00♑19R
2	12 19	23 35	19 54	10 31	13 03	21 29	02 29	22 25	24 15	00 17
3	13 17	08♊52	19 27	11 44	13 37	21 25	02 32	22 26	24 15	00 16

236

JUNE 2008 (Cont'd)

Date	☉	☽	☿	♀	♂	♃	♄	♅	♆	♇
4	14♊14	24♊09	18♊57R	12♊58	14♌11	21♑20R	02♍35	22♓27	24♒15R	00♑15R
5	15 11	09♋14	18 25	14 12	14 45	21 15	02 39	22 28	24 14	00 13
6	16 09	23 59	17 52	15 26	15 19	21 10	02 42	22 29	24 14	00 12
7	17 06	08♌18	17 19	16 39	15 53	21 05	02 46	22 30	24 14	00 10
8	18 04	22 08	16 45	17 53	16 27	21 00	02 49	22 31	24 13	00 09
9	19 01	05♍31	16 12	19 07	17 01	20 55	02 53	22 32	24 13	00 07
10	19 59	18 28	15 41	20 20	17 36	20 49	02 57	22 33	24 12	00 06
11	20 56	01♎05	15 10	21 34	18 11	20 44	03 00	22 33	24 12	00 04
12	21 53	13 25	14 42	22 48	18 45	20 38	03 04	22 34	24 11	00 02
13	22 51	25 33	14 17	24 02	19 20	20 32	03 08	22 35	24 11	00 01
14	23 48	07♏33	13 54	25 15	19 55	20 26	03 12	22 36	24 10	29♐59
15	24 45	19 27	13 35	26 29	20 30	20 20	03 17	22 36	24 10	29 58
16	25 42	01♐19	13 20	27 43	21 05	20 14	03 21	22 37	24 09	29 56
17	26 40	13 12	13 08	28 56	21 40	20 07	03 25	22 37	24 08	29 55
18	27 37	25 06	13 01	00♋10	22 15	20 01	03 30	22 38	24 08	29 53
19	28 34	07♑03	12 58	01 24	22 50	19 54	03 34	22 38	24 07	29 52
20	29 31	19 06	13♊00D	02 38	23 25	19 48	03 39	22 38	24 06	29 50
21	00♋29	01♒15	13 07	03 51	24 00	19 41	03 43	22 39	24 05	29 49
22	01 26	13 32	13 18	05 05	24 35	19 34	03 48	22 39	24 05	29 47
23	02 23	26 02	13 34	06 19	25 10	19 27	03 53	22 39	24 04	29 45
24	03 20	08♓46	13 54	07 32	25 45	19 20	03 58	22 39	24 03	29 44
25	04 18	21 47	14 20	08 46	26 20	19 13	04 03	22 39	24 02	29 42
26	05 15	05♈10	14 49	10 00	26 56	19 05	04 08	22 39	24 01	29 41
27	06 12	18 55	15 24	11 14	27 31	18 58	04 13	22 39	24 00	29 39
28	07 09	03♉05	16 03	12 27	28 07	18 51	04 18	22 39	23 59	29 38
29	08 06	17 37	16 47	13 41	28 43	18 43	04 23	22♓39R	23 58	29 36
30	09 04	02♊28	17 35	14 55	29 19	18 36	04 28	22 39	23 57	29 35

JULY 2008

Date	☉	☽	☿	♀	♂	♃	♄	♅	♆	♇
1	10♋01	17♊30	18♊27	16♋09	29♌54	18♑28R	04♍34	22♓39R	23♒56R	29♐33R
2	10 58	02♋35	19 24	17 22	00♍30	18 21	04 39	22 39	23 55	29 32
3	11 55	17 34	20 25	18 36	01 06	18 13	04 45	22 38	23 54	29 30
4	12 53	02♌16	21 31	19 50	01 41	18 06	04 50	22 38	23 53	29 29
5	13 50	16 37	22 40	21 04	02 17	17 58	04 56	22 38	23 52	29 27
6	14 47	00♍32	23 54	22 17	02 53	17 50	05 01	22 37	23 51	29 26
7	15 44	14 00	25 12	23 31	03 28	17 43	05 07	22 37	23 49	29 24
8	16 41	27 03	26 33	24 45	04 04	17 35	05 13	22 36	23 48	29 23
9	17 39	09♎44	27 59	25 59	04 40	17 27	05 19	22 36	23 47	29 21
10	18 36	22 06	29 28	27 12	05 17	17 19	05 25	22 35	23 46	29 20
11	19 33	04♏14	01♋02	28 26	05 53	17 12	05 31	22 34	23 44	29 18
12	20 30	16 13	02 39	29 40	06 29	17 04	05 37	22 34	23 43	29 17
13	21 27	28 06	04 19	00♌54	07 06	16 56	05 43	22 33	23 42	29 15
14	22 25	09♐58	06 03	02 07	07 42	16 49	05 49	22 32	23 40	29 14
15	23 22	21 52	07 51	03 21	08 18	16 41	05 55	22 31	23 39	29 13
16	24 19	03♑50	09 41	04 35	08 55	16 33	06 01	22 30	23 38	29 11
17	25 16	15 55	11 35	05 49	09 31	16 26	06 08	22 29	23 36	29 10
18	26 14	28 07	13 31	07 02	10 08	16 18	06 14	22 28	23 35	29 09
19	27 11	10♒30	15 29	08 16	10 44	16 11	06 21	22 27	23 34	29 07
20	28 08	23 03	17 30	09 30	11 20	16 03	06 27	22 26	23 32	29 06
21	29 05	05♓48	19 33	10 44	11 57	15 56	06 33	22 25	23 31	29 05
22	00♌03	18 47	21 37	11 57	12 33	15 49	06 40	22 24	23 29	29 03
23	01 00	02♈01	23 42	13 11	13 10	15 42	06 47	22 23	23 28	29 02
24	01 57	15 31	25 48	14 25	13 47	15 34	06 53	22 22	23 26	29 01
25	02 54	29 17	27 55	15 39	14 24	15 27	07 00	22 20	23 25	29 00
26	03 52	13♉20	00♌02	16 52	15 01	15 20	07 07	22 19	23 23	28 58
27	04 49	27 39	02 09	18 06	15 38	15 13	07 13	22 18	23 22	28 57

JULY 2008 (Cont'd)

Date	☉	☽	☿	♀	♂	♃	♄	♅	♆	♇
28	05♌47	12♊10	04♌15	19♌20	16♍15	15♑07R	07♍20	22♓16R	23♒20R	28♐56R
29	06 44	26 49	06 22	20 34	16 53	15 00	07 27	22 15	23 19	28 55
30	07 41	11♋31	08 27	21 48	17 30	14 53	07 34	22 13	23 17	28 54
31	08 39	26 09	10 32	23 01	18 07	14 47	07 41	22 12	23 16	28 53

AUGUST 2008

Date	☉	☽	☿	♀	♂	♃	♄	♅	♆	♇
1	09♌36	10♌36	12♌35	24♌15	18♍44	14♑40R	07♍48	22♓10R	23♒14R	28♐52R
2	10 34	24 47	14 37	25 29	19 22	14 34	07 55	22 09	23 12	28 50
3	11 31	08♍37	16 39	26 43	19 59	14 28	08 02	22 07	23 11	28 49
4	12 28	22 04	18 38	27 56	20 36	14 22	08 09	22 06	23 09	28 48
5	13 26	05♎09	20 37	29 10	21 13	14 16	08 16	22 04	23 08	28 47
6	14 23	17 52	22 33	00♍24	21 51	14 10	08 23	22 02	23 06	28 46
7	15 21	00♏17	24 29	01 38	22 28	14 05	08 30	22 00	23 04	28 45
8	16 18	12 27	26 23	02 51	23 06	13 59	08 37	21 59	23 03	28 45
9	17 16	24 27	28 15	04 05	23 43	13 54	08 44	21 57	23 01	28 44
10	18 14	06♐21	00♍06	05 19	24 21	13 49	08 52	21 55	23 00	28 43
11	19 11	18 14	01 55	06 33	24 59	13 44	08 59	21 53	22 58	28 42
12	20 09	00♑09	03 43	07 46	25 37	13 39	09 06	21 51	22 56	28 41
13	21 06	12 11	05 29	09 00	26 15	13 34	09 13	21 49	22 55	28 40
14	22 04	24 23	07 14	10 14	26 53	13 29	09 21	21 47	22 53	28 40
15	23 01	06♒47	08 57	11 28	27 31	13 25	09 28	21 45	22 51	28 39
16	23 59	19 25	10 39	12 41	28 09	13 21	09 35	21 43	22 50	28 38
17	24 57	02♓17	12 19	13 55	28 47	13 17	09 43	21 41	22 48	28 37
18	25 54	15 25	13 58	15 09	29 25	13 13	09 50	21 39	22 47	28 37
19	26 52	28 47	15 36	16 22	00♎03	13 09	09 58	21 37	22 45	28 36
20	27 50	12♈22	17 12	17 36	00 41	13 05	10 05	21 35	22 43	28 35
21	28 48	26 10	18 46	18 50	01 19	13 02	10 12	21 33	22 42	28 35
22	29 45	10♉07	20 20	20 03	01 57	12 59	10 20	21 31	22 40	28 34
23	00♍43	24 13	21 51	21 17	02 35	12 56	10 27	21 28	22 38	28 34
24	01 41	08♊25	23 22	22 30	03 14	12 53	10 35	21 26	22 37	28 33
25	02 39	22 40	24 51	23 44	03 52	12 50	10 42	21 24	22 35	28 33
26	03 37	06♋58	26 18	24 58	04 31	12 48	10 50	21 22	22 34	28 32
27	04 35	21 13	27 44	26 11	05 10	12 45	10 57	21 19	22 32	28 32
28	05 33	05♌24	29 09	27 25	05 49	12 43	11 05	21 17	22 30	28 32
29	06 31	19 26	00♎32	28 39	06 27	12 41	11 12	21 15	22 29	28 31
30	07 29	03 16	01 53	29 52	07 06	12 40	11 20	21 13	22 27	28 31
31	08 27	16♍51	03 13	01♎06	07 45	12 38	11 28	21 10	22 26	28 31

SEPTEMBER 2008

Date	☉	☽	☿	♀	♂	♃	♄	♅	♆	♇
1	09♍25	00♎09	04♎32	02♎19	08♎23	12♑37R	11♍35	21♓08R	22♒24R	28♐30R
2	10 23	13 08	05 49	03 33	09 02	12 35	11 43	21 06	22 23	28 30
3	11 21	25 49	07 04	04 47	09 41	12 34	11 50	21 03	22 21	28 30
4	12 19	08♏14	08 17	06 00	10 19	12 34	11 58	21 01	22 19	28 30
5	13 18	20 24	09 28	07 14	10 58	12 33	12 05	20 59	22 18	28 30
6	14 16	02♐24	10 38	08 27	11 37	12 33	12 13	20 56	22 16	28 30
7	15 14	14 18	11 45	09 41	12 16	12 32	12 20	20 54	22 15	28 30
8	16 12	26 10	12 50	10 54	12 55	12♑32D	12 28	20 51	22 14	28 30
9	17 11	08♑05	13 54	12 08	13 35	12 32	12 35	20 49	22 12	28♐30D
10	18 09	20 09	14 54	13 21	14 14	12 33	12 43	20 47	22 11	28 30
11	19 07	02♒24	15 52	14 34	14 54	12 33	12 51	20 44	22 09	28 30
12	20 06	14 56	16 48	15 48	15 33	12 34	12 58	20 42	22 08	28 30
13	21 04	27 47	17 40	17 01	16 13	12 35	13 06	20 39	22 06	28 30
14	22 02	10♓58	18 29	18 15	16 52	12 36	13 13	20 37	22 05	28 30
15	23 01	24 29	19 15	19 28	17 32	12 37	13 21	20 35	22 04	28 30
16	23 59	08♈18	19 58	20 41	18 11	12 39	13 28	20 32	22 02	28 30
17	24 58	22 21	20 36	21 55	18 51	12 41	13 35	20 30	22 01	28 31

SEPTEMBER 2008 (Cont'd)

Date	☉	☽	☿	♀	♂	♃	♄	♅	♆	♇
18	25♍56	06♉34	21♎11	23♎08	19♎30	12♑42	13♍43	20♓27R	22♒00R	28♐31
19	26 55	20 53	21 40	24 21	20 10	12 44	13 50	20 25	21 59	28 31
20	27 53	05♊12	22 05	25 35	20 49	12 47	13 58	20 23	21 57	28 32
21	28 52	19 28	22 25	26 48	21 29	12 49	14 05	20 20	21 56	28 32
22	29 51	03♋39	22 39	28 01	22 09	12 52	14 13	20 18	21 55	28 32
23	00♎50	17 42	22 48	29 15	22 49	12 55	14 20	20 16	21 54	28 33
24	01 48	01♌36	22♎50R	00♏28	23 29	12 58	14 27	20 13	21 52	28 33
25	02 47	15 21	22 45	01 41	24 09	13 01	14 35	20 11	21 51	28 34
26	03 46	28 57	22 33	02 54	24 49	13 04	14 42	20 09	21 50	28 34
27	04 45	12♍22	22 14	04 08	25 30	13 08	14 49	20 06	21 49	28 35
28	05 44	25 35	21 48	05 21	26 10	13 11	14 56	20 04	21 48	28 35
29	06 43	08♎36	21 13	06 34	26 50	13 15	15 04	20 02	21 47	28 36
30	07 42	21 23	20 32	07 47	27 31	13 19	15 11	19 59	21 46	28 37

OCTOBER 2008

Date	☉	☽	☿	♀	♂	♃	♄	♅	♆	♇
1	08♎41	03♏56	19♎43R	09♏00	28♎11	13♑24	15♍18	19♓57R	21♒45R	28♐37
2	09 40	16 15	18 48	10 13	28 51	13 28	15 25	19 55	21 44	28 38
3	10 39	28 23	17 47	11 26	29 31	13 33	15 32	19 53	21 43	28 39
4	11 38	10♐21	16 42	12 40	00♏12	13 37	15 39	19 51	21 42	28 40
5	12 37	22 12	15 34	13 53	00 52	13 42	15 46	19 48	21 41	28 40
6	13 36	04♑03	14 23	15 06	01 33	13 47	15 53	19 46	21 40	28 41
7	14 35	15 56	13 14	16 19	02 13	13 53	16 00	19 44	21 40	28 42
8	15 35	27 57	12 06	17 32	02 54	13 58	16 07	19 42	21 39	28 43
9	16 34	10♒12	11 03	18 45	03 35	14 04	16 14	19 40	21 38	28 44
10	17 33	22 46	10 05	19 58	04 16	14 10	16 21	19 38	21 37	28 45
11	18 33	05♓42	09 15	21 11	04 57	14 16	16 28	19 36	21 36	28 46
12	19 32	19 03	08 35	22 24	05 39	14 22	16 34	19 34	21 36	28 47
13	20 31	02♈50	08 04	23 36	06 20	14 28	16 41	19 32	21 35	28 48
14	21 31	17 01	07 43	24 49	07 01	14 34	16 48	19 30	21 34	28 49
15	22 30	01♉31	07 34	26 02	07 42	14 41	16 54	19 28	21 34	28 50
16	23 30	16 12	07♎36D	27 15	08 23	14 48	17 01	19 26	21 33	28 51
17	24 29	00♊58	07 49	28 28	09 04	14 55	17 08	19 25	21 33	28 53
18	25 29	15 40	08 12	29 40	09 45	15 02	17 14	19 23	21 32	28 54
19	26 28	00♋12	08 45	00♐53	10 27	15 09	17 20	19 21	21 32	28 55
20	27 28	14 29	09 26	02 06	11 08	15 16	17 27	19 19	21 31	28 56
21	28 28	28 30	10 17	03 19	11 49	15 24	17 33	19 18	21 31	28 57
22	29 27	12♌15	11 14	04 31	12 31	15 31	17 39	19 16	21 31	28 59
23	00♏27	25 44	12 18	05 44	13 12	15 39	17 46	19 14	21 30	29 00
24	01 27	09♍00	13 28	06 56	13 54	15 47	17 52	19 13	21 30	29 01
25	02 27	22 03	14 43	08 09	14 36	15 55	17 58	19 11	21 30	29 03
26	03 26	04♎55	16 02	09 22	15 18	16 03	18 04	19 10	21 29	29 04
27	04 26	17 36	17 25	10 34	16 00	16 11	18 10	19 08	21 29	29 06
28	05 26	00♏07	18 51	11 47	16 42	16 20	18 16	19 07	21 29	29 07
29	06 26	12 27	20 20	12 59	17 23	16 29	18 22	19 05	21 29	29 09
30	07 26	24 38	21 51	14 12	18 05	16 37	18 28	19 04	21 29	29 10
31	08 26	06♐39	23 23	15 24	18 47	16 46	18 34	19 03	21 29	29 12

NOVEMBER 2008

Date	☉	☽	☿	♀	♂	♃	♄	♅	♆	♇
1	09♏26	18♐34	24♎57	16♐36	19♏29	16♑55	18♍39	19♓01R	21♒29R	29♐13
2	10 26	00♑23	26 32	17 49	20 11	17 04	18 45	19 00	21 29	29 15
3	11 26	12 11	28 08	19 01	20 53	17 14	18 50	18 59	21 29	29 16
4	12 27	24 01	29 44	20 13	21 35	17 23	18 56	18 58	21 29	29 18
5	13 27	06♒00	01♏21	21 26	22 17	17 32	19 01	18 57	21 29	29 20
6	14 27	18 11	02 58	22 38	23 00	17 42	19 07	18 56	21♒29D	29 21
7	15 27	00♓41	04 36	23 50	23 42	17 52	19 12	18 54	21 29	29 23
8	16 27	13 34	06 13	25 02	24 25	18 02	19 17	18 54	21 29	29 25

NOVEMBER 2008 (Cont'd)

Date	☉	☽	☿	♀	♂	♃	♄	♅	♆	♇
9	17♏28	26♓55	07♏51	26♐14	25♏07	18♑12	19♍22	18♓53R	21♒29	29♐26
10	18 28	10♈45	09 29	27 26	25 50	18 22	19 27	18 52	21 30	29 28
11	19 28	25 04	11 06	28 38	26 33	18 32	19 32	18 51	21 30	29 30
12	20 29	09♉49	12 43	29 50	27 16	18 42	19 37	18 50	21 30	29 32
13	21 29	24 50	14 20	01♑02	27 59	18 53	19 42	18 49	21 31	29 34
14	22 29	09♊59	15 57	02 13	28 41	19 03	19 47	18 49	21 31	29 35
15	23 30	25 05	17 34	03 25	29 24	19 14	19 52	18 48	21 32	29 37
16	24 30	09♋59	19 10	04 37	00♐07	19 24	19 56	18 47	21 32	29 39
17	25 31	24 33	20 47	05 49	00 50	19 35	20 01	18 47	21 33	29 41
18	26 31	08♌45	22 23	07 00	01 32	19 46	20 05	18 46	21 33	29 43
19	27 32	22 34	23 59	08 12	02 15	19 57	20 09	18 46	21 34	29 45
20	28 32	06♍00	25 34	09 23	02 58	20 08	20 14	18 46	21 34	29 47
21	29 33	19 07	27 09	10 34	03 41	20 20	20 18	18 45	21 35	29 49
22	00♐34	01♎57	28 45	11 46	04 25	20 31	20 22	18 45	21 36	29 51
23	01 34	14 33	00♐20	12 57	05 08	20 42	20 26	18 45	21 36	29 53
24	02 35	26 58	01 54	14 08	05 51	20 54	20 30	18 45	21 37	29 55
25	03 36	09♏14	03 29	15 19	06 35	21 05	20 34	18 44	21 38	29 57
26	04 36	21 22	05 04	16 30	07 19	21 17	20 37	18 44	21 39	29 59
27	05 37	03♐23	06 38	17 41	08 02	21 29	20 41	18 44	21 39	00♑01
28	06 38	15 18	08 12	18 52	08 46	21 41	20 45	18 44	21 40	00 03
29	07 39	27 09	09 47	20 03	09 29	21 53	20 48	18 44	21 41	00 05
30	08 39	08 57	11 21	21 14	10 13	22 05	20 51	18 44D	21 42	00 07

DECEMBER 2008

Date	☉	☽	☿	♀	♂	♃	♄	♅	♆	♇
1	09♐40	20♑45	12♐55	22♑24	10♐56	22♑17	20♍55	18♓45	21♒43	00♑09
2	10 41	02♒36	14 29	23 35	11 40	22 29	20 58	18 45	21 44	00 11
3	11 42	14 34	16 02	24 45	12 23	22 41	21 01	18 45	21 45	00 13
4	12 43	26 43	17 36	25 56	13 07	22 53	21 04	18 45	21 46	00 15
5	13 44	09♓09	19 10	27 06	13 50	23 06	21 07	18 46	21 47	00 17
6	14 45	21 56	20 44	28 16	14 34	23 18	21 09	18 46	21 48	00 19
7	15 46	05♈10	22 18	29 26	15 18	23 31	21 12	18 47	21 50	00 22
8	16 47	18 52	23 52	00♒36	16 02	23 43	21 15	18 47	21 51	00 24
9	17 47	03♉05	25 26	01 46	16 47	23 56	21 17	18 48	21 52	00 26
10	18 48	17 45	27 00	02 56	17 31	24 09	21 19	18 49	21 53	00 28
11	19 49	02♊48	28 33	04 05	18 15	24 22	21 22	18 49	21 54	00 30
12	20 50	18 05	00♑07	05 15	19 00	24 34	21 24	18 50	21 56	00 32
13	21 51	03♋24	01 41	06 24	19 44	24 47	21 26	18 51	21 57	00 35
14	22 52	18 34	03 15	07 33	20 28	25 00	21 28	18 52	21 58	00 37
15	23 53	03♌27	04 49	08 42	21 13	25 13	21 30	18 52	22 00	00 39
16	24 54	17 56	06 23	09 51	21 57	25 27	21 31	18 53	22 01	00 41
17	25 55	01♍58	07 57	10 59	22 41	25 40	21 33	18 54	22 03	00 43
18	26 57	15 33	09 30	12 08	23 25	25 53	21 35	18 55	22 04	00 45
19	27 58	28 43	11 04	13 16	24 10	26 06	21 36	18 57	22 06	00 48
20	28 59	11♎31	12 37	14 24	24 54	26 19	21 37	18 58	22 07	00 50
21	00♑00	24 02	14 10	15 32	25 39	26 33	21 38	18 59	22 09	00 52
22	01 01	06♏19	15 43	16 40	26 24	26 46	21 40	19 00	22 10	00 54
23	02 02	18 25	17 15	17 48	27 09	27 00	21 40	19 01	22 12	00 56
24	03 03	00♐23	18 46	18 55	27 54	27 13	21 41	19 03	22 13	00 59
25	04 04	12 17	20 17	20 03	28 39	27 27	21 42	19 04	22 15	01 01
26	05 06	24 07	21 46	21 10	29 24	27 40	21 43	19 05	22 17	01 03
27	06 07	05♑57	23 14	22 17	00♑09	27 54	21 43	19 07	22 19	01 05
28	07 08	17 47	24 41	23 23	00 54	28 08	21 44	19 08	22 20	01 07
29	08 09	29 39	26 06	24 30	01 39	28 21	21 44	19 10	22 22	01 10
30	09 10	11♒36	27 29	25 36	02 24	28 35	21 44	19 12	22 24	01 12
31	10 11	23 40	28 50	26 42	03 09	28 49	21 44	19 13	22 26	01 14